A WORLDVIEW APPROACH TO

Ministry Among Muslim Women

A WORLDVIEW APPROACH TO

Ministry Among Muslim Women

Cynthia A. Strong and Meg Page
Editors

William Carey Library
Pasadena, CA

Cover design by Amanda Valloza, book design and layout by Karen Brightbill, with special thanks to Candace Dyar.

Published by William Carey Library
1605 E. Elizabeth Street
Pasadena, California 91104
www.WCLBooks.com

William Carey Library is a ministry of the U.S. Center for World Mission, Pasadena, California.

Printed in the United States of America

Library of Congress Cataloguing-in-Publication Data
A worldview approach to ministry among Muslim women/Cynthia A. Strong and Meg Page, editors. p. cm.
Includes bibliographical references, glossary and index.
ISBN 13: 978-0-87808-370-1
ISBN 10: 0-0989 9-370-7
1. Missions to Muslims. 2. Muslim women—Religious life. 3. Women missionaries—Islamic countries. 4. Christianity and other religions—Islam. 5. Islam—Relations—Christianity. 6. Islam. I. Strong, Cynthia A. II. Page, Meg.
BV2625.W67 2007
259.088'297–dc22

2006034439

*Dedicated to those
who have given their lives
in service to God
among Muslim women*

CONTENTS

PART III. Strategic Issues: Discipling Women in Muslim Contexts

PART IV. Case Studies: Worldview Transitions

AUTHOR PROFILES

Miriam Adeney has a Ph.D. in Anthropology and is Associate Professor of Global and Urban Ministries at Seattle Pacific University. She has also been a research professor at Regent College. Recently she coordinated a book writing program for Asia, Africa and Latin America.

Mary Bennett has lived and worked in a Southeast Asian city for the last fourteen years in neighborhood ministry to women and children.

Mary Ann Cate became interested in working among Muslim women while serving in the Peace Corps in 1965. Together with her husband, Pat, Mary Ann planted churches in Iran and Egypt and developed a Women's Ministry program at Christar providing support, encouragement and training for missionary women. Her passion is the mobilization and care of women who will reach Muslim women with the gospel.

Laurel Chadwick and her husband have lived and worked extensively among Muslims in East and North Africa.

Elizabeth Edwardson and her family have lived in Southeast Asia since 1992.

Annette Hall has served as a nurse in Jordan, the Gaza Strip, and in Paris, France, since 1973. She has used orality and chronological Bible storying for many years, teaching workshops in both French and in English for workers around Europe, North Africa, and the Middle East. As part of her work she has written a set of Bible studies for MBBs.

Farah Al Hasd has lived in the Middle East and worked among Muslim women since 1988.

Victoria Lindahl worked with an unreached Muslim people group in Northwest China. She later worked with a large Russian-speaking Church in Kazakhstan to establish a cultural church among the same people group. In the Fall of 2000, she began a missions training school to train nationals, many of whom now serve as cross-cultural missionaries throughout Central Asia. Currently she coordinates a prayer network for Central Asia.

Fran Love grew up as an MK in Southeast Asia, and later returned with her husband to work among Muslims in Asia. Fran has spent the last thirteen years in America and England helping Christian women to understand Muslim women.

Janelle Metzger and her family were members of a multi-agency team in the Arabian Gulf that became a model for partnerships in that region. They now work in North America, networking with local churches and ministries as well as with other agencies.

Sarah Mullin and her husband have ministered in North America and Africa among an unreached Muslim people group since 1992. Together with their team they have developed a discipleship approach that is reproducible in their host culture. Jennifer has a ministry of discipleship among women using a Chronological Bible Study approach.

Evelyne A. Reisacher has a Ph.D. in Intercultural Studies with an emphasis on Islam and serves as Assistant Professor of Islamic Studies at Fuller Theological Seminary. She has worked extensively among first and second generation Muslim immigrants in her native France.

Farida Saïdi is the founder and co-director of L'AMI, a Christian organization that serves the North African community in France and North Africa. She is an active member of numerous Christian organizations, and she lectures and leads workshops internationally on issues relating to North African Leaders for Mission. Farida is currently pursuing a doctorate in Islamic studies with an emphasis on Muslim-Christian relations.

Beth Stricker and her family have been workers in Africa for twenty years. In 1991 their work focused on a people group where persecution was the norm and severe. This experience led Beth and her husband to study persecution globally, developing discipleship material for environments where persecution, suffering and martyrdom are common experiences.

Cynthia A. Strong served with her husband, David, in Korea and the Philippines before becoming interested in ministry to Muslims. Today she has a Ph.D. in Intercultural Studies with an emphasis on Islam and teaches graduate and undergraduate courses on Islam.

LaNette Thompson has been working with Muslims in West Africa since 1986. She has done extensive work in Chronological Bible Storying and the learning needs of non-literate people.

Yvette Wray left nineteen years of teaching high school math and science to work in South Asia. For two years she taught English to Muslim women and girls in her home through a program called "Chat 'n Chai." She now works to motivate churches and other GCC organizations to share the good news of Jesus Christ with their Muslim neighbors.

FOREWORD

Whether or not Muslim women wear veils, there have been veils between their faces and those of Christians who long to lead them to Christ. From the inside the veils have blurred the Muslim's view of Jesus, and from the outside they have obscured the Christian's perception of the variety of faces behind them and the divergent ways they see the world. The present book gives clarity to the views in both directions.

Part I shows how Christian workers can begin to understand the perspective that Muslim women have, by living alongside them and seeing what they value and how they communicate. This will include the assumptions they have about the world, from formal and folk Islam to other cultural elements. Understanding these helps to show how Muslim women can see through the distortions of their veils to how Jesus fulfills their hope for a changed life, cleansing from shame, authority over dark powers, and healing of their hearts.

In Part II we see representative faces and the perspectives they bring from the major socio-economic groups (urban, rural, educated, and less-educated), religious styles (Islamist and mystical), and regions of the Muslim World (Middle and Far Eastern; Central, South, and Southeast Asian; and North and Sub-Saharan African). Each will follow a unique path to the narrow way.

The third part indicates some of the means God is using to change the world-views of Muslim women. Some have seen Christ more clearly through their tears while being persecuted. Others were led to the biblical Jesus from the introduction they had to him in the Qur'an. In some cases God used family life and inter-agency partnerships as signs of his transforming work. Effective discipling of new believers and leadership development require that workers integrate their lives with new believers, use teaching methods appropriate to their learning styles, and deal with issues from their culture that hinder their growth.

The final part gives case studies of the worldviews of Muslim women in transition as they follow Christ and grow in church fellowships. This continues the practice throughout the book of scholar-practitioners grounding their academics in experience. The appendices give resources for the reader to enter a new Muslim culture and look through the veil of Muslim women to see how they view their world and how they in turn can see Jesus as the one who fulfills their hopes. For another veil—the veil of the temple—has been rent, and they can see the glory of God in the face of Jesus Christ.

J . Dudley Woodberry, Pasadena, CA

PREFACE

In most countries, even those that are predominantly Muslim, the gospel has been present for hundreds of years through Bible translations and groups of gathered believers. Despite the presence of Word and witness, very few Muslims have believed in Christ. This can be understood, on the one hand, in terms of real and perceived differences in theology, beliefs and practices between Muslims and Christians. It is also true, on the other hand, that workers and local believers have tended to share a gospel that was irrelevant to the local worldview, using language and worship forms that were unclear, frequently misunderstood, and sometimes even offensive to Muslims.

This is changing. In many settings the gospel is being shared through understandable insider language and appropriate cultural forms such as storytelling and drama. Muslim-friendly translations of the New Testament, the Bible, the JESUS film and chronological Bible storying sets are important elements of this new approach. Glory be to God, Muslims are responding in unprecedented numbers. Sometimes entire extended families are coming to faith as new believers remain in their local communities and share their faith through transformed lives and contextualized oral witness.

Expressing the Christian faith in local language, thought forms and behaviors involves contextualization. Contextualization has been widely recognized as an important element of effective evangelization. Critical contextualization involves building a bridge between the worldview of the missionary and the worldviews of specific people groups to develop approaches and materials that make the gospel understandable and attractive in the target group. Since the goal of contextualization is to provide maximum relevance of the Word to culture, understanding worldview is essential to developing a relevant approach.

This sounds simple enough: understand the Muslim worldview, adapt materials and approaches to that worldview, widely sow this contextualized gospel, and Muslims will soon embrace the good news. However, the Muslim world is not monolithic. More than one-fifth of the world's population, or 1.4 billion people in over 2,000 distinct ethno-linguistic groups, are Muslim. They can be found in every region of the world and in most countries. Although Islam is an important element in the worldview of each of these people groups, other cultural, historical, and environmental factors also shape the distinct worldview of each group, resulting in various expressions of the faith.

To cite a few examples, workers in the Middle East have learned that Wahhabi women in Saudi Arabia consider informal and presumptuous talk about God disrespectful. In contrast, many Sufi women in India are drawn to the informal personal testimony of believers who know God and have personally experienced His power in their lives. Workers in West Africa assumed that the best way to reach Muslim women was through their believing husbands. Then a deeper investigation into the worldview of West African Muslim women revealed that their behavior and decisions were more significantly influenced by other relationships and needs. In each case, understanding the local worldview was the key step in determining the best way to communicate the gospel to distinct groups of Muslim women.

Our goal is to provide Christian workers, students, neighbors, friends and church groups with the basic perspectives and tools they need to understand and effectively share the good news of salvation with Muslim women. This book is divided into four sections. Each section presents helpful insights into different aspects of effective ministry. Part One provides a theological foundation for ministry, and introduces important anthropological tools that will enable the reader to study and understand the worldview of Muslim women.

The heart of the book, in Part Two, features original research from eight different Muslim worldview groups, along with samples of evangelistic strategies and materials currently in use in these areas. Part Three considers several strategic issues related to ministry among Muslim women, including the use of the Qur'an, the role of the missionary family, and leadership development in Muslim contexts. The book concludes with a series of case studies which enable the reader to walk alongside eight different women as they share the gospel with Muslim women.

Many women from around the world have contributed to the development of this book. We would like to thank each of the contributors, their agencies and supporters, along with many others whose prayers and encouragement made this book possible. It is our prayer that God will use this book to prepare His Church to effectively share God's truth and love with Muslim women so that they, too, will understand, believe and effectively share the gospel with others.

The Editors

Part I

FOUNDATIONAL ISSUES

Understanding Muslim Women

1

Christ, the Hope of Muslim Women

Fran Love

Hope for the complete salvation of Muslim women is based on the will of the Lord revealed in the Holy Bible. In this article, the author explains how the faithfulness of Christian workers and the mercy of God combine to enable Muslim women to experience all the riches and glory of Christ.

Close to 3000 years ago the Prophet Isaiah predicted something that might have set Jewish hearts racing with anticipated excitement: "In that day the Root of Jesse will stand as a banner for the peoples; the nations will rally to him," (Isa. 11:10, NIV) which Paul later interpreted, "One who will arise to rule over the nations" (Rom. 15:12, NIV). What Jew would not look forward to the day when, through the heir to David's throne, they would rule over the nations? But then Paul adds something that is not part of Isaiah's original prophecy, "the Gentiles will hope in him" (Rom. 15:12, NIV).

Why would the promised rule of a Jew over the nations be a point of hope for them? Isaiah explains, "He will reveal justice to the nations. He will be gentle —he will not shout or raise his voice in public. He will not crush those who are weak or quench the smallest hope. He will bring full justice to all who have been wronged. He will not stop until truth and righteousness prevail throughout the earth. Even distant lands beyond the sea will wait for his instruction" (Isa. 42:1-3, NLT). No wonder Matthew, one thousand years later, added the phrase that Paul would use as well, "and in his name the Gentiles will hope" (Matt. 12:21, NASB).

Yet did the Gentiles know about this promise, recorded as it was in the Jewish scriptures? Apparently not, and that is why the Lord had to work specifically with Peter and Paul to push them to the Gentiles. After blinding Paul on his way to seize disciples in Damascus, Jesus said, "he is my chosen instrument to take my message to the Gentiles" (Acts 9:15, NIV). And it was a destiny Paul exulted in, regardless of the suffering it caused him: "I am glad when I suffer for you in my body, for I am completing what remains of Christ's sufferings for his body, the church. God has given me the responsibility of serving his church by proclaiming his message in all its fullness to you Gentiles. This message was kept secret for centuries and generations past, but now it has been revealed to his holy people. For it has pleased God to tell his people that the riches and glory of Christ are for you Gentiles, too. For this is the secret: Christ lives in you, and this is your assurance [hope] that you will share in his glory" (Col. 1:24-27, NLT).

Muslims easily fall into the category of non-Jewish Gentiles. The truth of God's heart for Muslims hits us with force when we substitute the word "Muslims" for "Gentiles": "in him Muslims will hope." The truth that Christ will bring justice and therefore Muslims will hope in him should guide us as we proclaim and demonstrate the gospel to Muslims who have grown from bewilderment against the West's greed and military imperialism to an often terrifying resolve against it. But justice is not all that is promised them: "the riches and glory of Christ" are for Muslims, too. Note that Paul does not say "Western forms of Christianity are yours," but simply "Christ is yours".

In the verses from Colossians mentioned above, there is one phrase I would like us to dwell on: "for it has pleased God to tell his people that the riches and glory of Christ are for you [Muslims], too." Many of us need God to reveal to us again what he has in store for Muslims. The rise of terrorism from Muslim fundamentalists coupled with the difficulty of working among people who are not responding to the gospel as we desire, are making us weary and willing to settle for little crumbs of Christ rather than the riches and glory promised. Do we live every day with the expectation that our neighbor, our friend, the disciple who attends a fellowship will have all the riches and glory of Christ in him and her? Do we pray as though we believe this? Do we work as though we believe this? Do we encourage one another with this? Or have we lost hope, given up? Imagine with me what it would look like if a Muslim woman experienced all the riches and glory of Christ living in her!

CHRIST: A WOMAN S HOPE FOR A CHANGED LIFE

This same Good News that came to you is going out all over the world. It is changing lives everywhere, just as it changed yours that very first day you heard and understood the truth about God's great kindness to sinners. (Col. 1:6, NLT)

How does Christ change the lives of Muslim women? For those of us who come from Christian backgrounds and who live in countries where we are free to choose our own individual religion, this is a question we may not know how to answer, simply for the reason that often we cannot relate to the processes and the questions that bring a Muslim woman to commit her life to Christ. What are issues that concern her in the conversion process? What questions does she ask?

Fifteen Algerian Women
Fifteen Algerian women believers living in France were asked to comment on issues surrounding their conversion process. From their responses, the woman doing the interview deduced that the women were concerned more with the social relationships of their new community and less with the pillars or doctrines of faith. During the time they were becoming more attracted to Christ, the women were already addressing future concerns such as, "How is it going to be when I am a believer; what are the practicalities of Christian life for me as a former Muslim; what are the consequences of this choice; and am I going to be able to deal with it emotionally and relationally?" They were very concerned about being rejected by the family, especially by their mothers, at whose feet lies paradise according to Islam. Would they, by rejecting the faith of their mothers, be rejected from paradise?

Muslim women grow in their understanding of God by asking questions about their social identity and their roles and functions in it. They want answers to questions such as: "What if my husband divorces me?" "How can I do this to my mother?" "Can God give me a son?"

Western approaches to conversion stress an evangelism that packages the gospel into propositions that cover the first point, "I am a sinner," all the way to the last point, "I have accepted Jesus Christ as my personal lord and savior." What this interview shows us is that Muslim women's conversion is a process of discipleship in which their real-life questions are answered, not in a systematic way, but as they arise from the woman herself. Both Muslims and Christians learn about God as they encounter Christ in their context.

The interviewer challenged us to remember that non-Muslims need a paradigm shift if they are to understand the questions that Muslim women ask before conversion. They are often very practical rather than theological questions. Do we have answers for Muslim women's genuine questions? As non-Muslims can we even grasp the emotional resonance of these questions?

Ann's Story

Ann is an Arab woman who has had her life changed by Christ. But it was a road of coercion and betrayal that slowly moved her into Christ's arms. Jean is a Western woman who lives in Ann's country, and who shared with Ann, week after week, stories of Christ's love for her. Ann began to respond, reporting to Jean how she would take the small portions of scripture Jean would write out for her into the bathroom, the only place in the house where she could get some time to herself to read them. Jean was assured that Ann had felt the call of Christ on her life.

One day Ann confessed to Jean that she had been coerced by a fundamentalist relative to spy on her. The New Testament that Jean gave her went straight to them. Conversations between Ann and Jean were reported as well. Imagine Jean's sense of betrayal and the fear she might have felt knowing that a growing number of fundamentalists in the country had vowed to kill western infidels with their secularizing influence. Jean was perplexed as well. Why was Ann confessing this to her?

Ann poured out her heart to Jean, finally relieved at being able to speak truthfully to this woman whom she had grown to admire and love. During the month of Ramadan, Ann went through an intense spiritual battle, so intense she wanted to end her life. At the end of this time, Ann heard about the deaths of Christian aid workers in her country. She was outraged at the evil of the fundamentalists, not just those who would take the lives of good people, but who would also stoop to lie about how evil all the foreigners were. "Evil?" questioned Ann. "Jean is not evil. She is good and kind, like those who were killed."

Ann knew that Jean would respond in love to those who hated her. Jean attended a neighborhood women's party, at which two trained women Islamic preachers spoke for forty-five minutes. They asked her if she prayed. "Yes," replied Jean, "and I believe that God wants us to pray continually, not just five times a day." At this the two preachers moved to sit directly in front of her, in a move Jean wrote, "to convert the only heathen in the bunch." They proceeded to blast her with the typical arguments. When she responded with her belief in

Christ's crucifixion, they yelled that she needed to seek God's forgiveness for her blasphemy. Seeing it was going nowhere Jean finally smiled, touched them, and said they could talk for a solid year and never convince her. She had forgiveness, peace and knew where she would go when she died. Jean asked, "Do you know where you will go when you die?" They gave her a shocked, bewildered look, got up and sat in their places again. The other women who had been listening intently gave her a thumbs-up, because as Jean assumed, "I stood up to women that even they found obnoxious."

Ann has been changed by Christ's love, as has Ann's mother, and she is now praying for other family members to come to faith as well. She and her mother sing Christian songs they have learned, and when circumstances allow, they visit Jean to sing, pray and read the Word of God together. Ann's mother especially feels sad that she cannot freely share her faith with her husband, as it would likely mean divorce and complete separation from her children, if not death. Whenever possible she brings up the differences between Islam and Christianity and hopes that her comments will open the eyes of the family (Ann 2003, 2004).

CHRIST: HER HOPE TO CLEANSE HER SHAME

> Anyone who trusts in him will never be put to shame. (Romans 10:11, NIV)

According to Mosaic laws there are many things that defile women, among them menstrual blood, vaginal discharges, birth, using mediums or spiritists, leprosy and other skin diseases, contact with a dead person, and bestiality (Cf. Lev. 12:2-8; 15:19-25; 18:24; 19:31; Num. 5:3; 35:33-34). Certainly some of these are no fault of the woman. She is defiled not just by sin but by being a woman. For many women, the result of this kind of defilement is a brooding and ever-present sense of shame.

Islam, with similar attitudes to pollution as those found in the Old Testament, reinforces this shame by pressuring women to keep intact the honor of their families. By staying within the boundaries of harem and veil, women reduce chaos (*fitnah*) that might ensue from mingling with men, and they maintain the natural order of society's fundamental unit, the family. Thus, women become the barometers for pure Islam. Fatima Mernissi, a Moroccan author, asks why it is always Muslim women who pay the price for the honor of society: "Traditionally women were the designated victims of the rituals for reestablishing equilibrium. As soon as the city showed signs of disorder, the caliph ordered women to stay at home. Will it be we, the women living in the Muslim city, who will pay the price? Will we be sacrificed for community security in the coming rituals to be performed by all those who are afraid to raise the real problem—the problem of individualism and responsibility, both sexual and political?" (Thornton 2004).

Zhor Ounissi, an Algerian author, member of the Algerian parliament (1977-1982), and the newly independent country's first female minister, links women's invisibility with the sanctity and honor of men: "Whoever has a daughter has a time bomb and to prevent the bomb exploding, you must hasten to place it in a safe place. To hide it and reduce it minimizes risk and preserves honor until that daughter may become a wife. Thus have I seen some of them [men] linking their sanctity to their wives" (Ounissi 1998:153).

Hope's Story

Hope was born in a small South Asian country that proudly proclaims itself to be free of all infidel presence. The country's President has sworn that no religion outside of Islam shall be allowed, and urges citizens to be vigilant against foreign efforts to disintegrate the "unity, peace and tranquility" made possible by Islam.

Throughout childhood and into her early teens, Hope kept searching for that promised peace and tranquility. She wanted to be close to God, and was careful to do everything required of a good Muslim. Nevertheless, she was dissatisfied, searching for answers to questions troubling her young mind. Timidly she would ask them of her teachers and family, but realizing this behavior only got her into trouble, she soon stopped.

Religious duties that included praying and fasting were dominated by the most important obligation of Muslim girls—to bring honor to their families. Yet even this Hope found difficult, and at the age of sixteen she became pregnant. Her family, ashamed and heartbroken, endured the ridicule of neighbors who felt it was their duty to shame Hope. Shame, a powerful tool, can be cruelly used to put young girls like Hope in their place, a deterrent to avoid any future individual behavior that negatively affects the community.

The government put Hope under house arrest, and compounded by the guilt of bringing shame to her family Hope's health soon suffered; as a result she went into premature labor at seven months. All night Hope and her family waited for permission from the office of the Minister of Interior to be admitted to hospital. Finally at seven in the morning Hope was escorted to the hospital by police. Sadly, it was too late to prevent further labor and her daughter was born. The doctors warned Hope that her baby would probably die, but if she should live she would be brain damaged and live in a vegetative state all her life.

Islamic law demands that adulterers be punished by flogging. Hope was to receive the full penalty of 100 lashes. She says,

> They drew a square on the ground and I was supposed to stay in the square and bear out the lashes. The pain was so strong it felt like a million knives through my body. But what broke my heart was the humiliation. There were lots of people watching and some of them passed remarks as I screamed with pain. Nevertheless, I went through that as obediently as I could because I believed that the lashes were God's punishment for my sin, so that after going through them, he may forgive me.

Soon after her beating, Hope was exiled to a place far from the city in which she had grown up. This is the custom in her country. Dangerous criminals are incarcerated in prison, but other prisoners are exiled to distant towns to be carefully watched by neighbors and local authorities. Her family paid for her to stay in the home of another family, and continued to show their concern through regular contact and gifts. Again, Hope was made to feel the shame of what she had done through the vilifying humiliation heaped on her by neighbors who felt it was their religious duty to punish her. In their eyes they had a chance to remind her that she was a loose woman who was a sinner.

She worked hard to survive in the large extended family of the home to which she was exiled, completing chores from morning until night. Thoughts of her newborn, fighting for her life in an incubator at the city's hospital, far away from her, filled her mind. She was homesick, lonely and faced a future that was very uncertain and hopeless. Yet above all this she was haunted even more by a greater fear: "The hardest realization was that I knew, because of my sin, I would probably never make it to heaven."

An illness forced Hope to return to the hospital in which she had given birth, and there she saw for the second time her three-month old daughter. While recuperating at home, she met the family's new neighbor, a foreigner. Surprisingly, she felt at ease with him and soon poured out her heart about her exile. Later he sent her a letter and a Bible. Far from being happy or even curious, she was annoyed, "Why on earth is he sending me this? The last thing I need is to be messing up with such unbeliever things." Hope thought of burning the Bible later and so kept it in her possession.

Months passed and Hope forgot about the Bible, until one day, looking for something else she came across it. Her immediate reaction was to burn it right then, but something stopped her. "I should read this. Not everyone in my country gets an opportunity to read such books." The Holy Spirit directed Hope to the book of Psalms, and there she found beautiful things about God, a surprise to her since she believed as all Muslims do that the Bible had been changed by humans to fit their erroneous doctrines.

From then on Hope spent every moment of her free time reading the Bible. Its text was full of hope and promises, and it spoke to her of a God who became human in order to feel her pains and worries. God was slowly leading Hope to a passage of Scripture that he knew would be just the one that would envelop her heart with his love:

> If you confess with your mouth Jesus as Lord, and believe in your heart that God raised him from the dead, you will be saved. For it is with your heart that you believe and are justified, and it is with your mouth you confess and are saved. As the Scripture says, anyone who trusts in him will never be put to shame. (Rom. 10:9-11, NIV)

Hope recalls, "These words touched me very deeply because I had lost hope of being saved, and I had experienced a depth of shame beyond anything a girl of my age, still unprepared for life, could bear." In a dream shortly after reading these words in Romans, Hope was beckoned from a tunnel to a distant light which kept getting brighter the closer she walked to it. At the threshold of that light, Hope knew she had to make a choice to either move forward or stay where she was. She looked back and saw only darkness and gloom. Resolutely she stepped over the threshold into the light. Suddenly she felt a hand on her head and heard a voice saying, "From this day I will be with you and I will never leave you." Hope knew she was in the presence of God.

Hope has put her trust in a God who has felt her shame and who invites her to give her shame to him: "Let us keep our eyes on Jesus, on whom our faith depends from start to finish. He was willing to die a shameful death on the cross....Therefore, because we have a God who understands our weaknesses ... let us come boldly to him for help" (Heb. 12:2 and 4:15-16, NLT).

Jesus came not only to forgive Hope's sins and to give her eternal life, but also to cleanse her of the defilement that crushed her with shame. "For if the blood of goats and bulls and the ashes of a heifer sprinkling those who have been defiled, sanctify for the cleansing of the flesh, how much more will the blood of Christ ... cleanse your conscience from dead works to serve the living God?" (Heb. 9:13-14, NASB). Satan will use shame to hurt people. He uses what they do to accuse them before God. Christ came to destroy that evil work. To replace shame, he bestows honor: "If anyone serves me, the Father will honor him" (John 12:26, NASB; Cf. Rev. 12:10; 1 John 3:8, Heb. 2:14-15, Acts 10:38 and Luke 4:18).

Oh, and about that man who gave her the Bible? He is now her husband. And her daughter? "Today she is a very bright, healthy and beautiful teenager. She loves music and is a gifted violinist."

CHRIST: HER HOPE OF RESCUE FROM THE AUTHORITY OF DARKNESS

He has rescued us from the domain of darkness, and transferred us to the kingdom of his beloved Son. (Col. 1:13, NASB)

"Witchcraft Rules for Women in Islamic Morocco" proclaimed the Reuters headline (Vrban 2004). Sorcery and magic are cultural phenomena among Morocco's 30 million people. They are a part of everyday life. Although Islamic leaders preach against magic in mosques, in reality they turn a blind eye to these practices, choosing instead to fight for more political agendas or to argue for doctrinal purity. For physical illnesses people get medical attention, but for emotional, social and psychological problems they turn to the clairvoyants. The problems that compel most women to go to these sorcerers, despite the severe financial strain it causes, revolve around family issues, particularly marital ones. "If your husband leaves you and you don't look for help to get him back, people think badly of you as a wife and a mother," explains one Moroccan woman. A woman working in the Gulf describes a recent experience:

Lydia's sister-in-law was over the other day and we got into a discussion about evil spirits. Lydia leaned over and whispered to me, "She has an evil spirit in her!" So we spent the next hour talking about our experiences with evil and I just kept telling stories from my life and scripture about how Jesus has the power to set us free.

At one point the sister-in-law said, "Yeah, my friend told me that Jesus' power is better." She listened intently and then poured out her story about her husband who left her and how she wants more power to bring him back. My heart broke for her and I tried to listen and encourage her in this difficult situation. (Lydia 2004)

What is magic and why do Muslim women, the majority of Muslims who practice it, get involved in it? Magic refers to the manipulation of supernatural powers for one's own good. While the precise rituals and forms vary from culture to culture, what remains uniform is the underlying belief in spirits and the conviction that they can be harnessed and controlled. Prayers, spells, incantations, curses, amulets and charms are all used to gain power and to ward off evil.

A helpful way to look at the practice of magic is to examine it from six categories: powers (beings, such as demons or *jinn*; or forces such as *mana*); power people (such as *imams* and *shamans*); power objects (such as charms and amulets); power places (such as Mecca, saints' tombs); power times (such as Muhammad's birthday, the night of power during Ramadan, the pilgrimage); and power rituals (such as prayers and incantations often using portions of the Qur'an).

Perhaps in your neighborhood there is a woman known for her special powers. You may have seen little children wearing beads against the evil eye, or strings tied around their necks or wrists. Are there places where people fear to walk unless they have first asked permission from the ruling spirits of that location? Is there a woman who is afflicted with severe itching every Thursday night, right before the break of the Friday holy day? Perhaps you have heard whispers that a curse has been cast against a friend.

Muslim Women and Magic

Why do Muslim women practice magic? What are they looking for? First, they look for blessing: "I want prosperity, fertility and success." Second, they seek protection against supernatural powers against which they believe themselves to be helpless: "Will a jealous woman's curse work against me?" Third, they want to know the future:"Will my child be able to get into a good school?" "What will happen to me if I get involved in this business?" And last, they want justice or revenge:"My family has cheated me of money. What can I do to get it back? What can I do to get even?"

When we look at their motivations, we realize that we are similarly wired. We want blessing, protection, guidance and justice. Even a part of us wants revenge. That is why God warns us to leave it alone, trusting him to work out a just resolution to our predicaments. The Bible is full of promises and prayers for all these things. At the visible level all we see are the hurtful occult practices of Muslim women. But when we look below, at the motives of their hearts, we see ourselves. Then compassion begins to germinate in us, eventually enabling us to pass from judge and juror to friend and helper.

If we prohibit this behavior among Muslim-background believers (MBBs) without looking into the heart motives—all their longings, their fears, their concerns—we will never see true transformation. Yes, they may stop the external practices, but their hearts will be restless, looking for answers to their hearts' needs. Often an MBB needs to go through a deliverance from the powers of the occult, yet once she has we must continue to disciple her in scriptural principles concerning how believers obtain blessing, protection, guidance, and justice.

Far deeper than her motives, lurking as a sinister shadow is the Deceiver who whispers to her, "No one really cares for you. If they do, they cannot help you. Even God cannot help you. You are all alone. It is up to you to take control of your own life." (Cf. Rom. 1:25 and 2 Cor. 4:3). All women want to know that their home is in a safe place with people they trust, and ultimately we know that only God can meet that deepest longing of all. We must disciple MBBs, asking the Lord to reveal to them the extent of the lies they have believed. Often it happens that it is only when the lie has been exposed, and the MBB receives the truth of Christ through his Holy Spirit, that she will be truly free. For, it is the truth that sets her free.

What can we do then to help Muslim women understand this? First, we can invite them to participate in community; we can invite them to belong. Perhaps we need to show them community, before we can show them Christ. Perhaps we need to let them know they belong, before we press them to believe. Community and then Christ? Belonging and then belief? Can this be the order in which we proclaim and demonstrate the good news? Proclamation reaches the Muslim woman's head. It gives her knowledge. Demonstration reaches the Muslim woman's heart, and she is invited to experience what the proclaimer and demonstrator are saying and doing.

What can they belong to and whose community will they experience? Perhaps it is a women's gathering in your home. Several friends of mine who host such gatherings are amazed at how the woman who professes "I am NOT a believer" nevertheless prays for the other women, injects her comments about the Scriptures being studied, and brings her share of food and drink to the gathering. For others, you may simply be inviting them to belong to you and to your family. You don't stop visiting them if they don't visit you, you don't drop them if their behavior seems inappropriate to you. You do what you can to make them feel welcome and to know that they are your friend.

Second, we can communicate with Muslim women in multi-sensory ways. We don't talk to Muslim women, we talk with them. We don't simply want to change them, we want to connect with them. We reach out to women who suffer from rejection and shame with a smile, a touch, a warm meal in our homes, a soft voice, and a genuine laugh of good humor. While not the message itself, these things trigger in them an understanding of the message. One easy thing we can do is evaluate the way we use body-space: are we keeping ourselves physically distant from people who are accustomed to repetitive body contact?

Third, we can bless Muslim women. We can always look for opportunities to bless. Is she sick? We can pray for her and bring her something to cheer her up. Is she traveling? We can write down verses from Psalms asking for God's protection, and slip them to her as a gift before she departs. Is she broken hearted by the mistreatment of a neglectful or even cruel husband? We can hug her. We can cry with her, and assure her that we are praying for her. Is her child sick? We can quickly visit her, pray with her over the child, and then leave her with medicine. Is she lonely? We invite her to go with us on a shopping excursion into town. Remember, we proclaim and we demonstrate the good news of Jesus Christ. We continually invite her to understand who Jesus is and to experience his touch for herself.

Julia's Story

Julia is a beautiful forty year old American who has chosen to live in Asia, along with her husband and three children. When she first arrived in her new country, she held herself aloof from her Muslim friends and neighbors. She was generous with her time, she learned their language, she smiled a lot, and made many friends. But in her heart, she was different than them. They were Muslims, after all, and she was a Christian. Why wouldn't they choose to change? Why were they always poor? Couldn't they be more industrious and less deceitful with financial transactions? Why were they so weak and constantly afflicted with one ailment or another?

Then Julia met Beloved (Colgate 2002:171-183), At first, her reactions to Beloved were typical, "I was troubled by her continual struggle. Her pain triggered something in me that made me feel awkward and helpless somehow. And so, by the time I had concluded that this girl was a total mess, I had also set myself up to remain fairly detached from her."

But her conscience wouldn't let her rest. She knew that as long as she stood apart from Beloved, Beloved would fall deeper into darkness. One day Beloved came to her, suffering with another one of her frequent migraines, and asked if she and Julia could talk about a problem that was burdening her. Julia agreed, but asked for time alone first, so that she could pray. She needed more than cultural insight; she needed the power of the Holy Spirit.

During prayer the Lord did something that Julia says, "would forever change the way I see people like Beloved and the way I see myself." It wasn't power that Jesus gave her, but compassion. Julia saw how her heart had the same needs as Beloved; that although their external behavior may have looked different, they had been traveling on similar parallel paths.

But how was Julia going to move from her path onto Beloved's? Where was the point of intersection where she would be able not only to identify with Beloved, but also bring Jesus' healing touch to her? Could Julia be like Jesus, who was numbered with the transgressors, and yet interceded for them (Cf. Isa. 53:12)? Through the loving counsel of trusted friends, Julia came to realize that she had been as deceived as Beloved, and this surprised her: "I don't have a history of occult practice like Beloved. So why, Jesus, are your powerful interventions so necessary for me?" She confronted the lies she had believed and that had led her to erect her own coping mechanisms, no, not the occult practices of Beloved, but patterns of withdrawal, self-condemnation, and anger. As Jesus was rescuing Julia, so now Julia was rescuing Beloved, talking to her about her pains and the lies that Satan had been feeding Beloved all her life.

Julia progressed from being separate from Muslim women to realizing she was on parallel paths, to the final step of intersection—the place where she could invite Muslim women to experience Jesus along with her. Perhaps some of us may find ourselves at one point or another. Are we separating ourselves from Muslims, trying to ignore, probably not successfully, the nagging niggles of resentments, judgments and condemnation? Or are we in despair over our sameness—we've lost hope that Jesus can change them when we look at the mess of our own lives? Let us not lose heart. Jesus is still inviting us to walk with him, and he wants you to invite Muslim women on that journey so that in some way they experience Jesus with you.

Julia continues to give generously, even at cost to her own comfort and rest. Recently, while on a much-needed holiday, she was asked by two other workers if she wouldn't mind going with them to pray for a sick fourteen year old girl in a nearby village. "But Lord," she cried, "I was feeling so restful. Must I involve myself in spiritual warfare here on my vacation?" Her friends did not relent, instead they told her why they thought she should go with them (Julia 2004).

When Julia entered the home of the sick girl, she found an emaciated girl lying on the floor. Her body was twisted and her movements contorted. They greeted her in the name of Jesus, searching her eyes for a welcome. Yes, they were welcome, the girl communicated without words. She had a very beautiful face that shone with hope that Julia and her friends might be able to help her.

Julia began to ask questions, "Why do you think this happened? What do people say?" The older women replied, "This girl has been ill for a whole year now. But her condition came upon her in one day. She had gone to draw water from a well in a house that has not been inhabited for a long time. Of course, there were spirits in the house. Something happened at the well to startle her. The next day she was as she appears today, unable to talk, walk, or care for herself. The medical doctors and even the shamans can offer no hope."

Before they prayed for her healing, Julia explained the good news fully, with great joy, speaking straight into the eyes of this beautiful, broken girl, in the hearing of many others. The girl clearly responded to their love, and Julia saw that truth was gaining entrance. They then told the older women in the room that they would like to pray for the girl's healing now in the name of Jesus and hoped that they would give their blessing to this. "Yes, of course. Please!" exclaimed the women. They spent a good amount of time praying, noticing that the girl became agitated and frightened when they addressed the issue of what might have happened at the well.

After the "amen" was said, Julia asked to speak privately with the girl's mother, who at first expressed bitterness that this calamity had happened to her daughter despite all her efforts to provide a good Muslim upbringing. Julia casually asked, "By the way, do you have magical powers?" "Yes, I do," the mother smiled proudly. "The powers help me in my business." They continued to discuss the family customs, and Julia applied the truth of Scripture. Suddenly the woman looked distracted. Her eyes and mouth softened. "I have just realized that I have hurt my daughter's heart on many occasions by ignoring her. I don't know if there is any connection to her physical condition, but I need to repent of this. I will ask my daughter to forgive me."

We know it was the Spirit of God that had revealed this to the woman. Julia knew from her own experience how Christ brings truth and how he rescues all of us from evil powers and from evil lies. Out of this experience she was able to invite this woman into a conversation about truth through which this woman experienced for herself a revelation from God.

Two months went by before Julia had her first update on the girl. One of the women who had gone to pray with Julia was back in the same area, and happened to see the girl's mother. She exclaimed, "She's healed! She's restored! She walks and talks and she is asking where are the three women who came to pray!"

CHRIST: HER HOPE FOR HEALING THE DEEPEST PARTS OF HER HEART

> He felt great pity for the crowds that came, because their problems were so great and they didn't know where to go for help. (Matt. 9:36, NLT)

When Jesus interacted with women he did a lot more than heal them physically. His words, his look, his touch assured them that he was seeing them and that he was responding to whatever it was that brought them, often desperate, to him. Sometimes the women could not even articulate what it was they wanted. Mary sat at his feet and listened, and Jesus spoke the words that strengthened her, "Mary, you have discovered the one thing really worth being concerned about. I won't take that away from you." Simon raised his Pharisee's eyebrow and sneered at the woman sobbing at Jesus' feet, but Jesus told Simon to look at her, not as he had because, of course, he had seen her, but to see inside her the way Jesus was seeing.

To the woman Jesus said, "Your faith has saved you. Be at peace" (Luke 10: 38-42). Confronted by a room of men angry at a woman's display of devotion to him, Jesus said, "Leave her alone." And rather than speaking to her directly, he continued to address the men, "She has done a beautiful thing to me and wherever the Good News is spoken throughout the world, her deed will be talked about in her memory" (Matt. 26:6-13). Jesus knew this woman needed him to be her advocate against those who would hinder her. She needed his affirmation of her actions as well as his defense against those who would disallow her piety.

I quoted from Matthew, Chapter 9 in the verse opening this section. Right after Matthew makes his observation about Jesus' concern for people, he records his first commissioning of the disciples to preach the gospel, heal the sick and cast out demons. People are desperately looking for someone to help with their problems. There aren't enough people out there to help them. So Jesus asks his disciples to pray for helpers; then in a move calculated to speed along the answer to their own prayers, Jesus sends them out.

Our service to Christ is to bring Muslim women to him, not after they have already become "saved" but as they are, with their heartaches, their brokenness, their questions, and their joys. Only Christ can speak the words "you are saved" to a Muslim woman. Every time she thinks about him or is asked to consider his words or prays to him or allows another to pray to him on her behalf, she is turning to him. This process of turning to him draws her closer to the center, and Lord willing, there will be that day when she hears him say, "Daughter, your faith has saved you."

Fareeda's Story

Fareeda is an Arab. She has had numerous encounters with Jesus. Her story is told by her American friend.

Our Muslim friends have never turned down an opportunity for prayer. Muslims value prayer, they believe in it, and they even sometimes seek us out, as Christians, to pray for them. If someone is going through a difficult circumstance or is suffering from an illness, we offer to pray for them and never has the answer been, "No." A perfect example of this is a woman, whom we will call Fareeda. When we first met Fareeda, she and her husband had been struggling with infertility for seven years. I prayed for her, and within a few weeks she became pregnant. She continued to bring us her prayer needs, and it was miraculous, almost humorous, the way each of these prayers was immediately answered. As is often the case, praying for her led to many opportunities to demonstrate and explain the gospel.

For many years we have become increasingly interested in healing prayer. More and more we have begun seeking out prayer not just for sickness, but also for deeper emotional wounds. If God is willing to heal a broken foot, how much more would He be willing to heal a broken heart? We have seen this sort of deep healing prayer change the lives of new Christians in this country, we have seen it change the lives of the urban poor with whom we worked in Pittsburgh, and we have experienced it profoundly in our own lives. We began to ask the question, "If Muslims are so willing to be prayed for when they are sick, why not begin to offer to them the power of deep healing prayer for wounds of the heart?"

We told Fareeda that, just as we prayed for her baby to be returned after her husband kidnapped it, so we can ask God to heal the things that make us sad or torment us. She responded by saying, "Can that happen to me?" So I sat her down and prayed for her. We have prayed for Fareeda many times, but this time it was different somehow. During this prayer Fareeda dared to go back to her most painful memory. She asked *Isa Al Masi* (Jesus the Messiah) to show her where he was during this painful time. Then she said, as if shocked that it actually worked, I see Jesus right there with me when I try to remember the event. He is holding me tight like he is my father and he is saying, *"labis."*

The word *"labis"* means "alright" or "not bad" or "everything is OK." It is used all the time in our dialect, and it is the most colloquial and idiomatic word we have. At first it seemed strange that Jesus would say something so informal, but then we realized, "Jesus speaks the dialect." He comes to all of us in a way that is familiar, and meets us where we are. At that particular moment Fareeda needed to hear, *"labis."* For several minutes after that Fareeda simply sat in silence, her teary eyes closed, and a large grin on her lips, enjoying the embrace of the Lord. When I asked her if she wanted Jesus to be a permanent part of her life she answered, "Yes," without equivocation. Fareeda has since said that she "feels like a princess" and "for the first time in her life she feels close to God." She has also begun to have compassion for others who are suffering from their own "heart wounds." She wants to offer them the same healing that she has experienced.

What God is doing with Fareeda represents the very first fruits of our ministry in this place. We have begun the incredibly difficult task of teaching, modeling, and guiding her as she works out what it means to follow the ways of Jesus. We are confident that there are many others like Fareeda who long to be closer to God, desire a touch of his healing power, and don't want to change cultures. God knows who they are. He is at work drawing them to himself, calling them to a life long journey of healing and wholeness. We praise God that Fareeda has joined us on this journey and we know that many more will follow. They will follow because the God who loves them heals them, and the God who heals them speaks their dialect.

Jesus touched Fareeda at her deepest heart wound. As a result she is finding it a joy to keep turning to him. Yet from experience we know that there might be other things in Fareeda's heart that she will need to offer to Jesus for healing.

Constance works with a church in Turkey. She discovered that MBBs readily renounce any occult practice when they finally shift their allegiance to Christ. Yet this is only the beginning of the road of discipleship. If these new believers will not deal with the deeper issues of their heart, they will not grow spiritually.

Constance has identified anger and lack of forgiveness as the number one problem among MBBs. Other problems include unhealthy ties between mother and sons; children's dishonor of their parents; painful memories due to childhood abuse or trauma; and vows and judgments that have the same effect as curses against those who have injured them. At times, when she has been counseling MBBs, they will remind Constance that they have a right to their anger due to the severity of the sin committed against them. She doesn't argue, but gently points out that their anger is hurting only them. She also reminds them that Jesus cares and will heal their anger and bring his justice to the situation if they will allow him. Sometimes they simply cannot give it up, and they end up leaving the church and walking away from her. It's too hard to forgive because forgiveness means that they must first confess any sinful reactions, then they must pray for the offender, blessing him/her, and then finally they must wish them well and do them good (Cf. Luke 6:27-37).

Others have experienced the same things that Constance is encountering. A professor in Indonesia writes, "In our experience, the need for deliverance from occult bondage was obvious from the start. We have watched with joy as new believers destroy occult objects, renounce occult abilities, and receive deliverance from demons. However, we were puzzled by an ongoing lack of joy in their walk with the Lord, especially in regards to relationships with others. Misunderstandings and hurt feelings between believers and others caused some to fall away from the faith" (Travis). Indonesians have a word for this condition, *sakit hati*, literally a sick heart or in other words, a heart that has been wounded and continues to be wounded at both small slights and large injustices.

Believers are encouraged to pour out their heart pain to the Lord, instead of attempting to forget and deny it. Then they are asked to hear what Jesus is saying to them. It is in these moments when Jesus is speaking, that the lies of Satan are exposed. They were hurt by a trusted relative, and Satan told them, "You will be shamed in the community until you do something to vindicate your honor." They suffered a trauma in childhood, and Satan suggested, "You are powerless against evil. You must seek my power to defend yourself." They were rejected by a father, a mother, a lover, and Satan said, "Nobody loves you. You must do something to make yourself alluring."

This healing prayer, combined with Scripture and the regular discipline of fellowship and worship, helps new disciples become grounded in the love of Christ. This enables them to close their ears to Satan's lies, and to both survive in their Muslim community and thrive in their walk with Christ and with other believers.

OUR MINISTRY: AN ACCEPTABLE OFFERING

For I am, by God's grace, a special messenger from Christ Jesus to you
Gentiles. I bring you the Good News and offer you up as a fragrant
sacrifice to God so that you might be pure and pleasing to him by the
Holy Spirit. So it is right for me to be enthusiastic about all Christ Jesus
has done through me in my service to go. (Rom. 15:15c-17, NLT)

We have seen how Christ is the hope of Muslim women. All of his riches and
his glory can be experienced by them. He changed Ann's life from an informant
to the fundamentalists to a witness to her family. He healed Hope of her shame
of her pregnancy and the words inflicted on her by neighbors bent on fulfilling
their religious duties to shame her into good behavior. He rescued Julia from
her struggles with the powers of darkness, resulting in a freedom that gave
Julia the compassion to invite Beloved and a young crippled girl to experience
Jesus' power. He healed Fareeda in the deepest part of her hurting heart. Is it
any wonder then that the Bible promises that in Christ the Muslims will hope?
Look at all the amazing things he is doing for them.

Isn't it glorious that we get to be a part of this? Should we not be enthusiastic
about it? We serve Christ, knowing that it is acceptable to him, a fragrant sacrifice.
Substitute your name every time Paul says "I" in the verses quoted above,
Romans 15:16-17. Can you sense him inviting you to experience his hope, his
riches and his glory? Now think of a Muslim woman or an MBB you know. Can
you substitute her name for every pronoun "you" that Paul uses? Can you make
this your prayer and his promise?

R E F E R E N C E S

Ann. 2002. Newsletter from Ann to the author.

Colgate, Julia. 2002. *Jesus' victory in spiritual warfare: Far as the curse is found.* In *From
fear to faith: Muslim and Christian women,* eds. Mary Ann Cate and Karol Downey,
171-83. Pasadena, CA: William Carey Library.

Julia. 2004. Newsletter from Julia to Fran Love, May 2004.

Lydia. Email correspondence from Lydia to Fran Love, 6 July, 2004.

Ounissi, Zhor. 1998. *Birth of a writer. In the house of silence,* autobiographical essays by
Arab women writers, ed. Fadia Faqir, U.K., England: Garnet Publishing Ltd.

Vrban, Diana. 2004. *Witchcraft rules for women in Islamic Morocco.* Available online from
Reuters_News-@reuters.com.; accessed 20 April, 2004.

Thornton, Ted. 2004. *Review of Islam and democracy: Fear of the modern world*, by
    Fatima Mernissi. Northfield, MA: Northfield Mount Hermon School. Available
    online from http://www.nmhschool.org/tthornton/mehistorydatabase/
    fatima_mernissi.htm; accessed July, 2004; Internet.
Travis, John. 1998. The C-1 to C-6 spectrum. *Evangelical Missions Quarterly* 34(4):407-408.

2

How to Study Women in Their Cultural Contexts

Miriam Adeney

Communicating the gospel in relevant cultural terms is every missionary's goal, but not every missionary is an anthropologist. In this article, Miriam Adeney summarizes a simple anthropological approach that can uncover domains of culture and lead to relevant communication.

THE WORD ...

*R*esearch includes deciding the categories or questions on which you want information, procuring information and filing information for retrieval later. Information can be procured from data bases, libraries, archives, background interviews, interviews (including life stories), and observations, as well as through other sources or techniques such as maps, kinship charts, censuses, focus groups and game exercises.

A culture is a system. To get a balanced understanding of your friends' lives, you need to investigate all the major parts of the system. The Cultural Research Questions at the end of this paper list six parts: Family, Social Structure, Communication Patterns, Economy, Religion, and Values. If you prefer a simpler approach, you can condense these categories into three: Economy, Social Structure, and Values. These will focus on your friends' material realities, their social relationships and their worldview. But culture systems are messy. According to the philosopher Kierkegaard, "every man is an exception." For women, this may be even more true. Given all these "exceptions," a culture system will display variation and sometimes contradiction and conflict between the components.

In a single culture, Muslim women will differ, depending on their education, wealth, religious training and commitment, political passion, family traditions, tribe or subgroup, and other factors. They will differ according to their role in the life cycle, whether single, married with children, divorced or widowed, or grandmother. They will differ because of their unique life experiences or their personalities. When we select women for interviews, we have to think about these factors.

We must also ask questions that extend *beyond* the balanced culture system. For example, what multinational forces are influencing these people? These could be business companies, migrant labor, political movements, consumer advertising, world soccer, or Christian evangelism. What changes in this society might we anticipate in the next twenty years? What are the structures of domination and oppression, from within or from outside the society?

The Cultural Research Questions can be applied both to your reading and to participant observation. On the field, you can read through the questions once a week, and choose a new question to guide your observations. At the end of the week, review what you have seen. Then choose another question from another category. At the end of six weeks, you will have begun to learn in all of the categories, with minimal effort.

There are other good sets of cultural categories/questions. The HRAF questions, available in college libraries, are much more comprehensive. Regional branches of the Summer Institute of Linguistics sometimes have extensive sets of questions. One benefit of our set is that it is relatively short. You can use it as a platform on which to develop your own questions, tailored to your setting and your interests. My book, *Daughters of Islam,* has chapters on economics, family patterns, Muslim beliefs, and contextualized learning styles, as well as stories of Muslim women who have come to Jesus. The Cultural Research Questions were essential for developing these chapters.

You also must read a textbook on cultural anthropology (not general anthropology). This will help you know what you are looking for. Consider Paul Hiebert's *Cultural Anthropology* or Hiebert's and Eloise Meneses' *Incarnational Ministry: Planting Churches in Band, Tribal, Peasant, and Urban Societies.* Browsing through journals like "Missiology" and "Human Organization: Journal of the Society of Applied Anthropology" will introduce you to cultural questions and models of research.

... BECAME FLESH ...

If people were only objects, studying them through the grid of cultural questions would be enough. But people also are subjects. To know them, we must live alongside them, laugh with them, cry with them, and plod through boring days with them. This will take us beyond words to know them as we ourselves want to be known. This will cultivate empathy.

When Elizabeth Fernea was a new bride, she went with her anthropologist husband to rural Iraq. There she spent her days with the women in the harem of the local shaykh. Today, many years later, she is the renowned author of books and producer of films about Muslim women. But it is her first book, *Guests of the Sheikh*, that is a gem of culture research. Elizabeth spent time among the women, sharing their lives. Then she went home—or they went home—and she wrote down what she had seen and heard. Long ago, the apostle John was told, "Write what you see" (Revelation 1:11). John testified, "That which we have heard, which we have seen with our eyes, and our hands have handled... that which we have seen and heard we declare" (1 John 1:1-3). Elizabeth Fernea did this, too. She wrote what she saw and heard.

Her recall of details at a social event is remarkable. After a visit, she would describe for several pages the carpets, furniture and myriad specific knick-knacks, the food, the gardens, the people, the conversation, and the music. In situations where it is inappropriate to take notes, some researchers will excuse themselves frequently to go the bathroom in order to write their observations before they forget them. Elizabeth retained enough in her memory to wait until she got home to write in her journal. In any case, it is vital to look through your notes immediately after an event. Then you can clarify your handwriting and fill in details. You may want to find a quiet spot to work on these even before you get home.

Developing the Survey

What does the observer observe? Often she will begin with a *survey* question, followed by *parts* questions and *function* questions. A *survey* question might be: "Can you show me around your kitchen?" Or "Can you tell me about weddings?" A *parts* question might be: "What are all the spices you use?" Or "Who are the people that constitute the wedding party?" A *function* question might be: "How do you prepare couscous?" Or, "How is the bride prepared for her groom at the wedding?"

Ultimately, the researcher is looking for *patterns*. A single event is not enough.

The researcher seeks behaviors or beliefs or material objects that recur again and again. These elements make up the patterns of the culture.

Next, she looks for *variations* within the pattern. How much flexibility does this behavior pattern exhibit? Do these variations correlate with other variations, like gender, age, ethnicity, class, or profession? Too much random variation suggests that this is not a well-defined pattern. The researcher will have to look further. Participant observation is a bedrock research method for anthropologists. Interestingly, Jesus modeled participation. In contrast to the gods of many religions—who are believed to observe human dilemmas and occasionally send visions or prophets or scriptures—God in Jesus came to live alongside us. He shared people's tears and parties and dusty feet.

To research Muslim women, we must study them systematically, using some tool like the Cultural Research Questions. We must relate to them empathetically, participating in their lives, their work, their relaxation, their griefs and their jokes. But there is more. We must also know ourselves, and the biases we bring to our research.

Some American values may make it harder for us to understand Muslim women. Our *individualism* keeps us isolated. We often do not know our friends' parents or children. Self-reliant, we relate to people as though they were isolated in a social vacuum. But in the beginning God said it was not good for man to be alone (Gen. 2:18). We were created to live in communities of meaning. Muslims do this. Matheny comments, "We usually stress the benefits of salvation for the individual, but Muslims may be more aware of the needs of society." Goldsmith tells of a Muslim convert who became convicted of the truth of the claims of Christ not because of personal need but because he was deeply conscious of the needs of his people. Might it therefore be right to start our Christian witness in such societies with a message of what Christ can do for a whole society rather than just for the individual believer?

The American concept that *change means progress* may also create difficulties. Muslims value their heritage. When Muslim civilization first spread from the Arab world to Persia to West Africa to India to Indonesia, it brought monotheism, literacy, and ethics rooted in scripture. Muslims pioneered medical, mathematical, scientific, architectural and engineering breakthroughs as demonstrated in the Taj Mahal. Muslim peoples enjoy sophisticated philosophical, theological, and literary heritages. During Europe's Dark Ages, Muslims kept the wisdom of Greece and Rome alive. Finally, through their ordinary family structures, Muslims help bring order to God's world. Parents and children, brothers and sisters and extended relatives often enjoy strong ties. Frequently they will sacrifice for one another. Instead of rushing to a changing future, Muslims are often seeking to return to the glories of the past.

The American belief that *persuasion happens through well-reasoned arguments* can lead us to communicate in ineffective ways. Jesus taught through stories. God often chose to communicate that way, too. Much of Scripture is story. In nearly every culture stories command attention. They touch us rationally, aesthetically, emotionally, spiritually, and physically, as we laugh, shiver, or cry. They draw us into active learning as they whet our curiosity. Analysis and logic—the inheritance of the Greeks—are necessary tools for communication. But logic is like a narrow blanket on a cold night with three people in the bed. It is not big enough. It doesn't cover the subject. To persuade Muslims, we also need songs, dramas, liturgies, object lessons, action projects, memorization— symbolic, imaginative styles of communication.

"Depiction is power. The representation of others is not easily separable from the manipulation of them," says anthropologist Clifford Geertz. "What gives US the right to study THEM?" To minimize manipulation in our descriptions, we must know our own biases.

Meeting Muslim Women

How can we meet Muslim women? Go where the women are. In rural Morocco, spend time at the seamstress's shop, at the women's bath, or at any place where women make things. In North America, go to a Middle Eastern restaurant. Tell the manager you enjoyed the food. Ask him if he can recommend a woman who could teach you how to cook in this style, either in her home or yours. Or see if there are Muslim children in the local school. Get to know the mothers. Talk about the difficulty of raising godly children in our society. As you become friends, wish them a happy holiday when a Muslim festival approaches. Maybe they will invite you to a celebration. In return, you can invite them to a Christmas or Easter event. You also can ask for a tour of the mosque, and in return offer a tour of your church, or find a Muslim manicurist. In North America, this profession is popular among Muslims. If you live in a Muslim country, you might open a beauty salon yourself!

Five weeks ago, I was in Costa Rica. My host's sister-in-law, Rosa, was studying for a beautician's license. She liked to come over and practice on us. I received the best pedicures of my life—exfoliated up to the knee! Rosa is a lovely Christian woman. As she rubbed the pumice stone gently over my calluses, she murmured, "Feet are the foundation of everything that we do. So it's important to take care of our feet." While Latin music played in the background, the breeze of a fan wafted over us, and the aroma of olla de carne drifted in from the kitchen, she continued, "Jesus didn't wash feet using plastic gloves. He touched people." Then she told about clients who asked her spiritual questions. And I saw how women like Rosa could have an excellent entrée into the world of Muslim women.

... AND LIVED AMONG US ...

What are the practical strategies for basic grassroots research? Here are four areas to consider. One, select your human sources. Sociologists do surveys. Anthropologists do observations and interviews. Since I'm an anthropologist, I have a bias toward those methods. Of course we need the broad sweep of information that a survey gathers. But the information won't mean much unless it's understood in context. Observations and interviews help us to dig deeper into a specific context.

Selecting Key Informants

How do you select your key human resources—the people you'll observe, or those you'll interview, or those who will be your assistants? For a source person, choose someone who is: in the main stream of the group; articulate; overflowing with particular details rather than abstractions, trusted and trusting. Your source does not need to be a leader. In fact, that could be a disadvantage. Leaders have agendas, and things to hide. But no source represents everybody. Inevitably, your source will typify some sections of the community more than others. To bring this to light, ask yourself questions like these: Was she physically close to what she is describing? Does she speak the language and know the culture well? What social class or group (or denomination) does she represent? How might this limit what she sees? What is her primary vocation—homemaking, business, mission? How might this limit what she sees? Finally, given the above, what is likely to be underrepresented in her account? Who might express a different view?

Consider then how you will compensate for your source's bias. Will you interview others from other groups? Or will you simply point out the bias in your report? The human source you work with over a period of time will influence your life profoundly. Her worldview, her laugh, the way she walks, what she likes to eat, will become part of your life story too. What you know about being human will be shaped partly by her. Choose her prayerfully.

Conducting an Interview

When I began interviewing Muslim-background women for the case studies in *Daughters of Islam*, I worked hard to develop a set of interview questions. These ranged over several areas that I thought were important for Muslim women, and for ministry among them, including how a woman was attracted to the gospel; what helped her grow; her family context and cultural heritage; her economic situation and political involvements; her possibilities for fellowship and service; for marriage, motherhood, and singleness. Although the set of questions only covered a page and a half, it was detailed. But, in the end, I did not use the questions as I had planned. The women were overwhelmed by the questions. The categories intimidated them. They quickly became tongue-tied.

Then I stumbled on a better approach. I simply asked a woman, "Tell me— were you raised in a religious family?" In every case when I began with that question, the interviewee's face would light up and she would begin to talk and would keep on talking. Her story would flow. Meanwhile, I would glance occasionally at the questionnaire discretely positioned on my lap. As the woman told her story, I would note the questions she addressed. When she ran out of steam, I would introduce a question almost casually. At the end, I might take her back to a couple of subjects she had touched on lightly, in order to get a fuller picture. So, in the end, most of my questions were covered. But they were approached in a roundabout way, led by the woman herself.

Getting the facts right is our duty, but it is never achieved completely. Life stories always are changing. "What is truth in reporting?" I ask in the preface to *Daughters of Islam*. I describe the variety and types of women interviewed, and the steps taken to ensure accuracy. Then I continue:

> Do these women remember their stories accurately? Do they uncon-
> sciously overemphasize certain elements in such a way that historical
> reality is distorted? At best, our tellings are incomplete. Whether on
> the woman's part, or on the author's part, misrepresentations occa-
> sionally will occur…What I can assert is that no woman was a new con-
> vert. Each had been seriously committed to the Lord Jesus Christ for
> more than a year, in many cases for more than a decade. And each
> had a good reputation with several other mature Christians. This 'cloud
> of witnesses' testified to each woman's authenticity… Since the inter-
> views, spanning seven years, a couple of women have gone through
> dark nights of the soul, according to word-of-mouth reports. Others

have blazed gloriously through stark problems. In other words, these women are as complex and as common as the rest of us: treasure in jars of clay....The mind boggles at the awesome complexity of the gospel, the Church, cultures and human beings, as well as the darkness of our own history and hidden motives. Still, to say we see through a glass darkly is not to say that we do not see. (Adeney, 2004: 7-8)

The "life story" is a particular kind of interview. You can procure some life stories in an hour. Others take years, like the research leading to *Babo of Kano: A Woman of Nigeria*. Although I take notes by hand rather than by tape recorder, I always write down a few phrases in a woman's exact words. This gives each story an authentic, original flavor. Conferences are excellent places to conduct interviews. Here people are gathered together. You can make appointments with several of them. Some years ago, a friend and I went to the annual conference of Iranian Christians International. There we procured the life stories of nine Muslim-background women.

Coding the Data

A mass of data is not research. It is simply overwhelming, maybe even depressing! You need data stored in categories so that you can retrieve what you need when you need it. Even before you begin research, you must develop some guiding questions/categories. Inevitably these will change as you proceed. Some categories will become irrelevant. Instead, new categories or new combinations will be needed. Still, you need the initial questions to give you direction.

The Cultural Research Questions provide one set of categories. Alternatively, there are categories provided by computer assisted qualitative data analysis software. For example:

Sage Publications and Scolari Software http://www.sagepub.com
- Qualitative Solutions and Research
- Qualitative Research Web Sites http://www.nova.edu/ssss/QR/web.html#q
Using these categories, you can combine and reconfigure data in a variety of ways, to see if new patterns emerge.

Writing the Report

How do you present your findings? Books based on cultural research are woven together by the threads of structure, statistics, stories and symbols. Whatever your basic organizing matrix, make your writing interesting. The elements of action, people, dialogue, sensory details, strong verbs, questions and local phrases and issues will help. Participant observation should yield sensory details. "When I barely open my notebooks, I still smell the creosote with which, before setting off on an expedition, I used to saturate my canteens to protect them from termites and mildew. Almost undetectable after more than half a century, this trace instantly brings back to me the savannas and forests of Central Brazil, inseparably bound with other smells—human, animal, and vegetable—as well as with sounds and colors. For as faint as it now is, this odor—which for me is a perfume—is the thing itself, still a real part of what I have experienced." Those are the words of anthropologist Claude Levi-Strauss.

Stories enliven our reports, and stories are everywhere. Rick Bragg, former bureau chief for the New York Times, says, "To say I searched for stories would be a lie. I did not have to search. (Life) hurled stories at you like Nolan Ryan throws fast-balls. All you had to do was catch them." We live in the middle of stories. All we have to do is catch them.

One more topic writers must consider is this: What is safe writing? Christians who write about Muslim-background believers need to take precautions. I used aliases for most of my sources. We must also ask: Will my sources read what I write? Will it help or hurt? Laila Abu-Lughod dedicated her *Writing Women's Worlds* with these words: "For Fajriyya, whose daughters may one day read this." Even though I used aliases, I omitted a few raw episodes from my cases. The sources didn't ask me to do this. They hadn't thought about what print publicity would mean. But I had. So I chose to omit some episodes that might have stained them deeply if anyone recognized their story, notwithstanding their alias.

... AND WE SAW THE GLORY OF GOD ...

To be born a woman is a wonderful thing. To work and relax among women in another culture adds richness. To live alongside Muslim women, to learn from them, to share your story and God's, is a privilege. Muslim women are not victims. We don't go to them because we have so much and they have so little. We are all gifted women and hurting women. The only difference is that we have been blessed with the good news of the gospel and commissioned to share it. The world of women is yours. To appreciate it to the hilt, ask God to give you the gift of curiosity. Then use it. "The Word was made flesh, and lived among us, and we saw his glory" (John 1:14).

REFERENCES

Abu-Lughod, Laila. 1993. *Writing women's worlds: Bedouin stories*. Berkeley: University of California Press.

Adeney, Miriam. 2002. *Daughters of Islam*. Downers Grove, IL.: InterVarsity Press.

Hiebert, Paul. 1994. *Anthropological reflections on missiological issues*. Grand Rapids: Baker Books.

Hiebert, Paul and Eloise Meneses. 1995. *Incarnational ministry: Planting churches in band, tribal, peasant, and urban societies*. Grand Rapids: Baker Books.

Fernea, Elizabeth. 1995. *Guests of the shaykh: An ethnography of an Iraqi village*. New York: Anchor Books.

3

Deep Knowledge:
Understanding a Popular Muslim Worldview

Cynthia A. Strong

Missiologists combine field experience with academic research to uncover world-view assumptions outside the range of Western experience. Drawing on research from her dissertation, Cynthia Strong details several important worldview assumptions from a Southeast Asian Muslim worldview and then suggests how Christian truths can be explained to Muslim women in light of their central beliefs.

One of the greatest challenges we face is making Christianity relevant and meaningful to people whose worldviews differ from our own. Nowhere is this more evident than when we attempt to work with people who practice what Westerners call "popular" or "folk" Islam. Not only are we confused by the seemingly illogical ideas behind these beliefs and practices, but we are amazed at how casually they are juxtaposed with more "orthodox" traditions in day to day life. A woman, for example, may place a bolo knife or other metal object next to her baby to protect it from evil spirits while she leaves the room for prayers. A man may use a simple divining method to determine which path to take from his house to the mosque. At the mosque, women in modest *hijab* may collect spittle from men exiting the mosque to treat their sick, believing it to be empowered with *barakah* or blessing from their recitation of the Arabic Qur'an. How are we to understand these beliefs? Are they examples of formal and informal religion or do they represent different cognitive abilities—the educated knowing the meaning of the religion while the uneducated are preoccupied with superstitions and myths? Do they imply the failure of religious specialists—the *imams* or prayer leaders and the *ulamas* or judges—to clearly define and enforce theological truth? Or are Muslim assumptions about the world and how it interrelates simply different from Western assumptions? Most importantly, if the reality assumed by so many Muslims is different from our own, how do we address the problem?

In this article, I will share several insights into popular Islam from my study of Yakan Filipinos, a Muslim tribal group in the southern Philippines. In particular, I will discuss the concept of coherentism—how people justify their beliefs by means of coherence—and how it may affect our presentation of the gospel. Simply put, coherentism refers to the way that beliefs are linked together within a worldview. The most important beliefs, Robert Audi says, do not stand alone but are "woven into the whole fabric" of a society (1988:158). They make sense because they fit or "cohere" with many other aspects of the culture. To have a relevant witness, then, coherentism suggests a Christian must explore the local worldview and present the gospel with as much reference to the entire belief system as possible in order for it to be understood and accepted.

Most Christian workers, admittedly, are already aware they need a relevant message; missionaries have been discussing relevance in terms of contextualization and felt needs for decades. What we may not realize is the degree to which we still continue to present Christ in our own worldview terms and the limitless ways the gospel can cohere with beliefs in other worldviews that we have yet to consider.

THE YAKAN FILIPINO WORLDVIEW

To illustrate, let us consider some aspects of Yakan Filipino worldview. Between 1990 and 1994, I conducted intermittent ethnographic research among Yakan Muslim women on Basilan Island. My fieldwork was only a few days old when I discovered that Yakan women do not personally understand many aspects of their own religion. Repeatedly, when I asked them how they would treat disease, deal with specific problems or interpret spiritual phenomenon, they simply replied, "you go to the one who knows." A personal knowledge of these things, indeed, would imply that the person was a bona fide religious practitioner—an *imam* (prayer leader), *tabib* (herbal doctor and spirit specialist) or *lendungan* (shaman) with expert knowledge, often as a result of their personal relationship with spirits.

After obtaining several life history studies from local Yakan women, I began to search for clues to Yakan religious knowledge through a study of their rituals, sacred stories and collective behaviors. Studies in the *Shari'ah* law and *Shafi'i* jurisprudence, along with Malay beliefs and rituals, rounded out my study.

I discovered that the Islam brought to Southeast Asia by Sufi traders and mystics in the thirteenth and fourteenth centuries had a remarkable coherence with the Yakan's indigenous Malay beliefs. The Islam of many Middle Eastern Muslims, in contrast, especially those who follow a more legalistic form of the faith, does not have the same coherence. Succinctly said, law-based Middle-Eastern Islam lacks the coherence that medieval Sufi Islam had with many Southeast Asian beliefs. When Southeast Asian Sufi Muslims encountered fundamentalist Muslims in Indonesia in the 1960s, many of them turned to Christ, preferring the Christianity being presented with power by Dutch missionaries to the letter of the *Shari'ah* law. If the gospel can be presented to the Filipino Muslim and other Southeast Asian Muslims in terms of a coherent Christian worldview, might such a turning to Christ occur in other places as well?

Cosmic Alignment

To begin, we must ask what worldview assumptions are central in the Southeast Asian worldview? One of the most important is the need for cosmic alignment. The cultural and racial roots of the Yakan, as I have indicated, are in Malaysia (cf. Sherfan 1976:11, Marohomsalic 1995:5). During the thirteenth and fourteenth centuries when Muslim traders from Arabia, Gujarat and Persia brought Sufism into Southeast Asia, they encountered a civilization already permeated with Hindu beliefs. One of these was a belief in cosmic order. To avoid chaos, Hindus believed it was important to be properly aligned with the cosmos, symbolized by the orderly progression of planets and stars. Cambodians demonstrated this belief by building temples such as Angkor Wat in the exact form of constellations above. In other parts of Southeast Asia, cosmic orientation was linked with the formidable *naga* serpent, on whose back the world was believed to rest (McCoy 1982:144-145). Since alignment with the serpent was critical to avoiding disaster, its movements were charted in almanacs or calendars similar to those used by many Filipinos today (Benjamin 1979). The use of omens and divination to determine the right path, to know when the rice will sell and the most propitious day to take a trip is also indicative of this need for cosmic alignment. Since the cosmos was well ordered, people believed that by ordering their lives according to its rhythm and pattern of the stars and forces they could ensure order and avoid chaos on earth as well.

During the thirteenth century, Sumatran shaykhs brought an Islamic cosmology into the Southeast Asian context that cohered with these beliefs (Bousfield 1985:207). The *Ka'bah* in Mecca, which is only one of several sites in Arabia featuring pre-Islamic astronomical orientations, replaced Angkor Wat as the new center of cosmic alignment; "a physical pointer to the presence of God" (King 1993:XIII:306, 1993:I:254; 1993:X:24). Instead of orienting themselves physically with the *naga* serpent, Muslim Malays used the *qibla* to turn toward Mecca and what they felt was a more powerful cosmic center in Islam. The Muslim calendar with its auspicious and inauspicious days, furthermore, met the need served formerly by *naga* serpent calendars to determine right times and places (cf. Musk 1989) while the explicit laws of the Qur'an and Hadith met their need to know how to behave to avert cosmic disorder. For many Southeast Asian Muslims, thus, the *Ka'bah* is revered not only because of its association with Abraham and Ishmael but also because it fulfills implicit needs for cosmic alignment.

Spirit Beliefs

Islamic teaching about the *jinn* also resonated with Malay and Filipino beliefs. Pre-Islamic Malay-Filipinos believed in spirits that were both benevolent and dangerous. The former could be asked to help with crops, health and good fortune, while the latter were appeased and controlled with rituals and offerings (Scott 1994:78). "People not like us," another category of spirits, had their own animals and farmlands. Seen only by trained specialists, these spirits were believed to cause illness or misfortune if they were insulted or harmed.

Islam provided new categories for these spirits and sanctioned their relationship with humans. According to the Qur'an, *jinn* are spirits made from smokeless fire (Q 55:15). Often invisible (Q 7:27), Muslims believe they are intelligent and have tremendous physical powers. Contrary to biblical teaching, Muslims believe Muhammad, was sent to both humankind and the *jinn* (Q 46:29-32). In the Qur'an, when a group of *jinn* responded to Muhammad's preaching they became submitters and were given hope of Paradise (Q 72:1-2). *Jinn* may not be killed, therefore, even if they change into snakes or possess a person; they must be addressed as fellow Muslims and reminded of the laws of Allah (Dawood 1996:5236).

Islam also recognizes the vengefulness of the spirits. When humans accidentally urinate on them, pour hot water on them, or kill them, *jinn* may lawfully punish humans, according to Islam (Philips 1989:32-33). While not approved by Muslim jurists, thus, offerings of placation are common in Muslim societies. Since Southeast Asians experienced spirits in similar ways and recognized their potential benefits as well as danger, Islamic teaching gained credibility among the people.

Some Qur'anic parallels with Malay-Filipino beliefs were even more remarkable. According to the Qur'an, each human has a twin spirit or *qarina*—a devil or *jinn* of the opposite sex who accompanies the person and can be jealous of a spouse (Q 43:36). Muhammad had such a partner in Muslim belief, although he was aided by Allah and could order his *qarina* to do good (al-Ashqar 1998: 90-91). When Spaniards came to the Philippines in the sixteenth century, they found that Filipinos believed in twin spirits, as well. Called *umalagad*, or spirit ancestors, they were considered personal guardians and companions (Scott 1994: 80-81). The coherence of these beliefs speeded Filipino acceptance of Islam.

Islam not only provided a sacred history for local spirits, it also provided the knowledge to deal with them through Islamic rituals and the Qur'an. The call to prayer, for instance, is used all over the Muslim world for keeping evil *jinn* and other spirits at bay. Qur'anic prayers, words and phrases are used to scold, threaten and curse the *jinn*, thereby controlling them (Philips 1989:63). Most importantly, the Yakan know they can take refuge in God by reciting the last two chapters of the Qur'an, Surahs 113 and 114 along with the Verse of the Throne (Q 2:255)—a verse considered particularly powerful in warding off devils and breaking their spells (Philips 1989:72-76). Thus Islam provided Muslim Filipinos with a coherent explanation of indigenous spirits in Qur'anic stories, a rationale for their behaviors, and a means of controlling them through Qur'anic words and phrases. Believing Islam offered greater power over the spirits, the Yakan saw the relevance of Islam to their assumptions and needs and accepted it as their faith.

Incantations and Power Words

Among the more interesting Muslim beliefs are those concerned with divination, incantations and metaphysical power. This knowledge links the Yakan not only with the Qur'an but with the science of ancient Greeks, translated into Arabic during the ninth through eleventh centuries. While Westerners simply label these practices "magic," or "superstition," they have numerous referents in Muslim eyes. "White magic," for instance, describes something that appears to be real but is a falsification. This is known as *sihr*, and is reprehensible in Muslim law.

"Black magic" or sorcery is forbidden in Islam as well, especially if it is gained through the assistance of evil *jinn* or transmitted by fallen angels (Bosworth 1997:567, 569).

During the medieval period, however, definitions of magic were broader. When Muslim armies advanced into Persia, Syria and Egypt, they added Hellenistic philosophy to basic Muslim beliefs. During Filipino Islamization, Sufi mystics combined Neoplatonic teachings on astrological science with Muslim beliefs in the power of the Qur'an to tap into the spirituality of the planets or manipulate the secret properties of numbers and magic squares. Classified by Muslim scholars as "occult" or hidden sciences *(khafiyyah)* in contrast to the open sciences *(jaliyyah)* such as mathematics, they were none the less plausible. Hadidji Khalifa, for instance, drawing on Ibn Khaldun, understood *sihr* to refer to the *physical sciences* of the time. Using Greek categorization as his guide, he considered divination; natural magic; the powers of the Most Beautiful Names of God; numbers; sympathetic magic; demonic conjuration; incantations; the invocation of the spirits of plants; instantaneous disappearance from sight; spells and the use of medicinal plants all part of the natural universe (Bosworth 1997 :568). As sciences, these domains were also the most sophisticated knowledge of the time.

Today's acceptance of these practices is, thus, logical for many Muslims, given their assumptions. The use of incantations and charms, for instance, was permitted by the Prophet Muhammad as long as Muslims avoided *shirk* or associating anything with God—a common practice among Jews as well (Mishkat, Book XXI, Chapter I). Many such objects were made from the words of the Qur'an, the names of important Muslims, including Muhammad, and most of all, from the ninety-nine names of God.

Southeast Asians had believed in the benefits of occult power for hundreds of years before Islam came. Hindu Malays had introduced Filipinos to Sanskrit words and charms for power, including *mantra*, which were used in farming, fighting, curing sickness, treating snakebites, countering vampires, at birth and at teeth filing. They were also used to enhance a person's beauty, to weaken a rival or to divert a bullet (Winstedt 1925:52-53). When Islamic mystics arrived, Malay specialists studied Islamic books of divination and borrowed their Qur'anic amulets. Into their old incantations they placed the more efficacious names of Allah and Muhammad, although oftentimes in impious contexts (Winstedt 1925:46-47).

Today, many such books on divination and spells, called *kitabs*, teach the

numerical value of the letters of the Arabic alphabet and are used for divination
(Nasr 1976:206-207). Even more commonly known is the Da'wah Table, a system of incantations to establish friendship or hatred, to cause and cure sickness and death, and to achieve one's wishes using the twelve signs of the zodiac,
the seven planets and the four elements. Although much of the lore is based
on Hindu customs and Neoplatonic ideas from Persian Sufism, it built on
assumptions that were considered scientific at the time (Hughes 1895:72-73).
Many Muslims understand Qur'anic charms and incantations to be gifts of
mercy sent down by God. Thus, it is no wonder Southeast Asians and Filipinos
celebrated this new form of knowledge (Skeat 1967:465). Ricklefs, for instance,
refers to a nineteenth century version of the *Babad Tanah Jawi* which says, "At
that time many Javanese wished to be taught the religion of the Prophet and to
learn supernatural powers and invincibility" (1985:40).

A CHRISTIAN RESPONSE
When I asked Yakan women about their religious knowledge, they referred
obliquely to these things as "deep knowledge." One said she had been given a
wedding invitation by a *jinn*. Another said she needed to have a "strong power"
to prevent her husband from being interested in another woman. A third
recalled a time when Yakan women knew *tawal* or incantations that could
enhance their beauty. All were sensitive to cosmic alignment, whether in the
construction of their house, their position in prayer or their placement in the
grave. None of these women had the personal knowledge to deal with the situations themselves; in each case it was necessary that they consult a specialist
to have the benefit of specialized metaphysical knowledge. This dependence
on specialists contrasts sharply with the personal knowledge that all Christians
have with respect to God's will and power. When I asked a woman who had
attended the Yakan Christian school to recall her strangest experience there,
she replied, "They expected me to pray!" "Why was that strange?" I asked.
"Because I don't know the language of the spirits!" she replied.

Huge epistemological shifts are taking place in the Islamic world that affect
the women we desire to reach. Caught between the assumptions of medieval
Islam with its potions, incantations and powers and the law of revivalist Muslims
who reject these rituals as *bid'ah* or innovation, many women do not know
what they believe. They vary in their familiarity with the older worldview, in
their personal experience with spirits and powers, and in the trust they place
in indigenous religious specialists vis á vie *Shari'ah*-trained imams. Older

women and women in the interior will likely value Islam for the way it meets the old worldview—its preoccupation with cosmic order, *jinn* and powerful words. Younger women, however, taught in modern schools, will likely be ignorant of this worldview and more open to a modern interpretation of Islam. An effective presentation of the gospel, thus, must be adjusted to address both views.

A Response to Religious Specialists

Most importantly, we must show the coherence of the Christian faith to world-view needs in areas outside our own. Several suggestions can be made towards a coherent apologetic. First, Muslims must know that Christians can have spiritual knowledge themselves, independent of religious specialists, because we are individually born of God (John 3:16). In their terms, all Christians are specialists—we know the language of God and are thus able to speak with God through the Holy Spirit (Shaw 1981). Even the most uneducated Christian woman, thus, can know the mysteries of the universe because she is indwelt by the Holy Spirit and through His illumination can understand the Word of God. It is necessary to stress, however, that this is personal knowledge—each Christian must believe and be "in Christ" herself to grow in godliness. Depending on the missionary for prayers, rituals and spiritual advice, thus, may be in line with cultural patterns but it may also indicate a failure of discipleship.

A Response to Cosmic Alignment

The need for alignment, secondly, may also be addressed from the Bible. A natural cycle of time, based on God's divine plan, is described in Ecclesiastes 3. Jesus also spoke of a cosmic time that was based on the wisdom of God; in perfect alignment with His Father, Jesus knew when "his time" had come (John 17:1). He urged his followers to be alert for hidden times and seasons discernable only through His Spirit (Mark 13:33). The basis of Christian alignment, thus, is not through astrology, divination or the use of science but through Christ. Indeed, the Bible teaches it is not for human beings to know God's sacred times (Acts 1:7) but to walk in trust, depending on Him at all times (Ps. 62:8). While the Muslim convert may long and ask for "Christian" ways to divine the future or make practical decisions, they must be led to trust in God and imitate Abraham's walk of faith. Ultimately, well being in the New Testament is not through imitating a cosmic pattern or praying in a certain direction but being aligned with God through Jesus Christ.

Even holy sites are unnecessary in Christian belief; when God takes up residence in the believer through faith in Christ, there is no longer a need for a spatial center like Mecca "where God is;" God already lives in His new temple, the Christian believer. Thus, for women who long to know which path to take or the correct direction and time for prayer, the good news is that they can be born again of God into true freedom. As God's spirit mercifully flows through them, He will direct their paths (Prov. 3:5-6) and work *all* things for their good and God's glory (Rom. 8:28). They will then also be able to glorify God in all things, even eating and drinking, rather than through only religious rituals (1 Cor. 10:31).

A Response to Spirits

Many Christians, thirdly, must understand the complexity of Muslim interactions with spirits in order to provide a relevant discipleship. As we have seen, Islam leaves Muslims vulnerable to spirits by its teaching that *jinn* can also accept Muhammad's teachings and become Muslims. When women have relationships with spirits in the Zar cult or contract spirit marriages and barter with spirits for what they need, they may not feel they are contradicting the Qur'an. Only when women realize the selfish nature and evil intent of all demonic spirits will they see their true plight.

More importantly, Muslim women must learn to fear God more than they fear the spirits. Early Christians recognized God's sovereignty over illness, trials and death (1 Cor. 11:30; Matt. 10:28). They were unafraid of spirits because Christ overcame all evil powers in His resurrection (Eph. 2:1-10). Although Muslims believe only Solomon had power over the *jinn*—through his magic ring (Philips 2000)—Christians know that even the lowliest Christian can rebuke these evil spirits (James 4:7; Luke 10:17). A Christian's primary concern, therefore, is not learning prayers to defeat Satan or learning about the demonic world but avoiding sin. Sin alone can cause the Christian to grieve the Spirit of God and separate her from God's power and purposes (Eph. 4:30). Understanding and addressing all the ways Muslims interact with the *jinn* will help to assure them of the truth of the Word and the sufficiency of Christ.

A Response to Powerful Words

Finally, for many Muslims a primary relevance of Islam is in the practical use of Qur'anic words as spells. Spoken at the right time and the right way, these Arabic words are believed to shield babies from danger, recall children from the possession of spirits, protect women's chastity and provide inner cleansing. Undoubtedly, these spells "work" in a magical way but because they are associated with the *barakah* of Qur'anic words and are performed for good purposes, they are not synonymous with "magic" in Muslim thinking.

Too often we have tried to replace the belief in spells and divination with education or modern science. These are, however, secular explanations that disassociate God from the world and ignore the reality of the powers themselves. Muslims must understand that the powers behind occult sciences do not come from God or glorify Him; while they may actually manipulate objects and control people's behaviors for a time they will not result in a lasting moral transformation. Only those who are born again into the life of Christ have the spiritual power to avoid adultery, cease thieving and love others as they live out Christ's life in the Holy Spirit. We must teach the superiority of spiritual gifts and the day-to-day transforming power of the Holy Spirit as a response to Qur'anic powers (1 Cor. 12; Matt. 22:29; Luke 1:35; Acts 1:8; Rom. 15:19; 2 Cor. 4:7).

Conclusion

"Alternative realities" are possible because "reasonable individuals deduce the workings of their universe from a variety of different assumptions" (Hexham and Poewe 1986:16). As Hexham and Poewe remark, "anyone who wants to communicate effectively with members of new religions must enter their thought world … by recognizing the logic of their beliefs" (1986:14). By and large, Western Christians are products of the Enlightenment and a modern worldview. In our personal and conceptual experience, we are on the other side of the Copernican revolution from many of our Muslim neighbors and may need to think in more biblical terms to understand them. What seems logical to many Muslims is foreign to us, not because we are more rational or better educated, but because our assumptions and epistemologies differ. As a result, we fail to see the significance of these concepts for the people we serve and the way they cohere to make Islamic teachings plausible.

Unintentionally, our presentation of Christ is likely to be more relevant to a modern or postmodern time and context than to the worldview of many our Muslim neighbors still in a premodern framework. In the power and illumination of the Holy Spirit, let us work for coherence, striving to apply the gospel to all their concepts in order that they may know God's deep knowledge—that in Jesus Christ, men and women can know and be known by God.

REFERENCES

Ashqar, Umar Sulaiman al-. 1998. *The world of the jinn and devils*. Jamaal al-Din M. Zarabozo, trans. Boulder, CO: Al-Basheer.

Audi, Robert. 1988. *Belief, justification and knowledge. An introduction to epistemology*. Belmont, CA: Wadsworth Publishing.

Benjamin, Geoffrey. 1979. Indigenous religious systems of the Malay peninsula. In *The imagination of reality: Essays in Southeast Asian coherence systems*, ed. A. L. Becker and Aram A. Yengoyan, 9-27. Norwood, NJ: Ablex Publishing.

Bousfield, John. 1985. Good, evil and spiritual power: Reflections on Sufi teachings. In *The Anthropology of evil*, ed. David Parkin, 194-208. New York: Basil Blackwell.

Dawood, Abu. 1996. Sunan of Abu-Dawood (Abridged). Alim. Version 4.5. [CD-ROM] (ISL Software Corporation).

Hexham, Irving, and Karla Poewe. 1986. *Understanding cults and new religions*. Grand Rapids, MI: Eerdmans.

Hughes, Thomas Patrick. 1895. *A Dictionary of Islam*. London: W. H. Allen and Company.

King, David A. 1993. *Astronomy in the service of Islam*. Norfolk, UK: Variorum.

Marohomsalic, Nasser A. 1995. *Aristocrats of the Malay race. A history of the Bangsa Moro in the Philippines*. Quezon City: Graphic Arts Inc.

McCoy, Alfred W. 1982. Baylan: Animist religion and Philippine peasant ideology. *Philippine Quarterly of Culture and Society* 10:141-194.

Musk, Bill A. 1989. *The unseen face of Islam*. Eastbourne, Sussex, UK: MARC.

Nasr, Seyyed Hossein. 1976. *Islamic science: An illustrated study*. Westerham, Kent, UK: World of Islam Festival Publishing Company.

Philips, Abu Ameenah Bilal. 1989 *Ibn Taymeeyah's essay on the jinn (demons)*. 4th ed. Riyadh, Saudi Arabia: International Islamic Publishing House.

_____. 2000. "Islam and fortunetelling." Available online from http://www.islamweb.net/english/aqeeda/basic-aqu/basic-30.html; accessed 22 January, 2002.

Scott, William Henry. 1994. *Barangay. Sixteenth century Philippine culture and society*. Manila: Ateneo de Manila University Press.

Shaw, R. Daniel. 1981. Every person a shaman: The use of supernatural power among the Samo of Papua New Guinea. *Missiology* 9:359-365.

Sherfan, Andrew D. 1976. *The Yakans of Basilan Island: Another unknown and exotic tribe of the Philippines*. Cebu City, Philippines: Fotomatic (Phils.) Inc.

Skeat, Walter William. 1967. *Malay magic: Being an introduction to the folklore and popular religion of the Malay Peninsula*. New York: Dover. (Original: Macmillan and Co., 1900).

Smith, Ebbie C. 1970. *God's miracles: Indonesian church growth.* South Pasadena, CA: William Carey Library.

Winstedt, Richard Olaf. 1925. *Shaman, saiva and Sufi. A study of the evolution of Malay magic.* London: Constable and Co., Ltd.

4

Honor and Shame in Muslim Contexts

Laurel Chadwick

In this study of honor and shame Laurel Chadwick draws on worldview studies by Roland Muller to explore the importance of honor and shame for Muslim women and its implications for understanding and reaching Muslim women.

For many years I have lived and worked among Muslim women, studying their religion and languages, customs and habits. I have worn their clothing, cooked their food, and lived in their homes. I have held cooking classes and as well as aerobic and craft classes, given driving and English lessons and consumed gallons of coffee and tea. I have taken whatever opportunities were in my path to establish and cultivate relationships and to share the hope of the gospel of Jesus Christ. But much of it, as far as I know now, has born few eternal results.

A few years ago several women in my city began meeting together to discuss, among other things, the reasons why we have seen so little response to the gospel among the women in our country. At one of those meetings someone introduced us to a chapter in Roland Muller's book, *Honor and Shame*, which I found intriguing. His premise was quite simple; Muslims think differently than we do in the West—not that I did not already know that. It does not take long living among a people of a different culture and religion to figure out that they think differently. But his book told me why they think differently. Almost twenty years ago when I was first trained in Muslim evangelism, one of my professors who had worked among Iranians for many years told us that we could think of our minds as running clockwise and the Muslim mind as running counter-clockwise. Although I understood what he said, I never really knew what it meant until I understood why this was so. I began to do further study on the subject. In my research I came across a surprising lack of information and articles. It is obvious that further research is needed and I will only be scratching the surface. I hope however to help the reader understand that there are differing worldviews, investigate the implications of thinking with an honor and shame worldview, see how this worldview is lived out in the lives of the women we live among, and look for and use this worldview's applications from God's Word in presenting the gospel to women from an honor and shame culture.

THREE DIFFERENT WORLDVIEWS

Let's begin at the beginning, in Genesis, where the first worldview was developed. Adam and Eve, according to Genesis 3, lived in the Garden of Eden and fellowshipped with God until, tempted by Satan through the serpent, they made a decision to disobey God's command and eat the fruit of the tree of the knowledge of good and evil. Thus they fell out of relationship with God. According to Muller, the three emotional responses to this fall became the bases for the three worldviews in existence today: guilt/righteousness, honor/shame, and power/fear (Muller 2000, 21).

According to Genesis 3:7 when Adam and Eve fell from relationship with God, their eyes were opened and they realized they were naked. As a result, they covered themselves. This emotional response, says Muller, displays the feeling of guilt. They had broken God's command and they felt guilty. Continuing with the text in verse eight, when Adam and Eve heard God walking in the garden they hid from Him. Why? They hid because they felt shame. Their relationship with God was now broken. When God asked them where they were in verse ten, Adam told God that they were hiding because they were afraid. Trust in God had now been broken as well. Thus, guilt, shame, and fear were all experienced as a result of the Fall when Adam and Eve's relationship with God was broken (Ibid., 17-19).

Bruce Thomas, in his article, "The Gospel for Shame Cultures," takes a different but closely related position when viewing this event. He points out that Adam and Eve first felt shame, not guilt. Before the Fall, Adam and Eve were naked (*arowm* in Hebrew) but felt no shame. After the Fall their eyes were opened and they knew they were naked (*eyrom* in Hebrew) so they made coverings for themselves. But even after they made coverings for themselves they hid themselves from God when He came into the garden. This is because they knew they were still naked and they felt ashamed. Thomas makes the point that using a different Hebrew word in the second instance indicates Adam and Eve knew they were unable to cover their own nakedness. Interestingly and perhaps symbolically, he says, God ended up providing the needed coverings for Adam and Eve by killing and skinning an animal (Thomas 1984, 286). Whichever view you take, the point is still the same; among other responses, Adam and Eve felt shame in the garden after the Fall and needed to restore their relationship with God.

The Guilt/Righteousness Worldview

Over these many years the three emotional responses, guilt/righteousness, honor/shame, and power/fear, have formed three distinct worldviews. According to Muller, the guilt/righteousness worldview has its roots in Europe and was heavily influenced by the Roman Empire. Roman law judged everything on the basis of right and wrong. The early Christian church was heavily influenced by this worldview, as is evident in much of its theology. Tertullian, for instance, a lawyer trained in Roman law, was the first to make a case for systematic theology (Muller 2000, 29). His work became the basis for the Western theological approach. As products of our environment, we who are from the West also live under the guilt/righteousness framework. We judge everything on the basis of whether it is right or wrong, good or bad. In our theology we assume that everyone is guilty and needs to be saved (made righteous). In our cultural stories our heroes wear white hats and our villains wear black hats and the good guys always win. In our worldview perceptions, additionally, we are right while the rest of the world is wrong.

This is particularly true today on the international political scene. Kenneth Betts of MEABT (Canada) in his article, "Escalating Cultural Conflict," envisions a scenario where Country A is a law abiding, right vs. wrong society that is proud of its fight for justice both nationally and internationally. Its residents like to watch movies that show the hero adapting to whatever social role he must take as he struggles in his search for justice. Country B, in contrast, honors its historical figures and is proud of its contributions to the world in the areas of thought and philosophy. The residents of this country enjoy movies where the hero must be clever and not necessarily orthodox as he struggles to find the honorable solution. Hypothetically, the two countries interact and Country B breaks the laws of Country A. In their pursuit of justice, the residents of country

A publicly dishonor some important residents of Country B. Country B is now insulted and one of its citizens retaliates, becoming a local hero. This retaliation again breaks the laws of Country A and the whole country joins together in an outcry to the highest diplomatic channels demanding compensation for the crime. Country B's leaders and residents are shocked that their entire country is being blamed for this incident and feel this attack on their honor cannot be ignored. Diplomatic actions are put in operation in order to avoid armed conflict. Country A is consumed with its quest for justice while Country B is outraged by the attack on its honor. Country A declares a just war against Country B and Country B declares a moral war against Country A. In this interchange it is obvious that both parties are thinking through an entirely different grid (Betts 2004).

This conflict can be replicated on a personal level. Muller, in his chapter on shame-based cultures, tells of storytellers who sit in the coffeehouses in the Middle East and tell stories about heroes and rulers who are wise in dealing with shame and restoring honor. King Solomon in the Bible is an example of this type of wisdom as he settled the question of what to do with the baby claimed by two mothers; his clever solution restored honor to the situation. Muller comments that this is very different from the entertainment in a guilt/ righteousness culture where the hero's responsibility is to find the guilty party and punish him. In this case, only after justice is achieved can righteousness and goodness be restored and everyone live happily ever after (Muller 2000, 51). People in the honor/shame culture, however, view the world as shame filled and alienated and believe that maintaining honor is the only solution to living peacefully.

When we who are from a guilt/righteousness worldview share the gospel with others we start from our perspective of good vs. bad, right vs. wrong, guilt vs. righteousness. We lean heavily on logical arguments found in the Roman Road or the Four Spiritual Laws and their emphases on guilt: we are guilty; we are sinners in need of a Savior, Christ died for our sins and when we accept Him as our Savior we are made righteous. And this is true: we are guilty. We have broken God's Law. But, according to Muller, Genesis 3 does not relate all the truth.

The Power/Fear Worldview

Because the power/fear worldview is not within the scope of this paper we will look only briefly at its characteristics. This is important not only for the purpose

of comparison and contrast but also to counter the thinking that each culture
has only one worldview; every culture has a mixture of all three worldviews, to
a greater or lesser extent. Succinctly, power/fear-based cultures are preoccupied
with appeasing the spirits and gaining supernatural power. Much effort, therefore, is put into determining what the spirits want and then appeasing them so
that the people will have the necessary power to sustain their lives. This worldview is lived out through sacrifices, voodoo, amulets, and mantras, among other
things. Much of Sub-Saharan Africa, India, South America, as well as many
Aborigines, and Native American Indians live under this system. Muslim cultures with a fair amount of Folk Islam (which are numerous) are operating with
a mixture of both power/fear and honor/shame worldviews. This should be
kept in mind when approaching them to share the gospel message. The
power/fear grid may be just as applicable as the honor/shame worldview in
many cases.

The Honor/Shame Worldview
In the honor/shame worldview, people worry about becoming defiled and
restoring lost honor. Defilement is as serious to people in this group as sin is to
the guilt-based culture. Among the things that defile are eating pork, not keeping the fast, drinking alcohol and ritual uncleanness. In an excellent example
of how ritual defilement overshadows "sinful" behavior in the honor/shame
perspective, Thomas tells how the daughter of a divorced woman would feel
her mother's hair every morning when she awoke. If her hair was wet she would
know that her mother had been having sexual relations with a man the night
before (Thomas 1984, 284). Why, we ask ourselves, would this woman "incrimi-
nate" herself by washing her hair so her daughter would find out she had committed adultery? She washed her hair because the thought of ritual uncleanness
after sexual intercourse was for her and her culture a much greater offense
before God than committing adultery. Remaining ceremonially unclean would
be unthinkable. Even the ground on which this woman walked would have
been considered cursed if she remained defiled.

According to Muller, guilt does not have the same power or influence in an
honor/shame culture as it does in a guilt/righteousness culture. Take, for example, being stopped by a policeman while driving your car. The first response of
someone from a guilt/righteousness background is that they must have done
something wrong. They feel guilty. Once, driving a car in a country where
honor/shame is the norm, we were stopped by the police. When my husband

rolled down the window he greeted the policeman and was told that he was speeding. My husband then stated, "I'm sorry officer. I did not see you," to which the policeman responded, "Okay, just go." There was no sense of guilt at all. Because the policeman was more focused on the shame of being caught rather than the righteousness of violating the law, my husband's guilt was not even an issue.

The Guilt/Righteousness Worldview

People who live with a guilt/righteousness perspective try to act rightly in social situations. Westerners, for instance, are taught as children what is right and what is wrong according to the law. When we do something that is socially incorrect we may be embarrassed but we only embarrass ourselves. In an honor/shame world children are taught to act honorably and not shamefully. When a child acts shamefully he not only embarrasses himself, he also embarrasses his family and his clan. He does not respond to the embarrassment with feelings of guilt, he responds with feeling shame. During a seminar I attended on honor and shame, the leader, who is married to a person from an honor/shame culture, made the observation that if a person does something wrong and no one finds out, it's okay. If someone finds out then the person is ashamed because everyone knows. They feel dirty in front of the group. According to Muller, shameful deeds are covered up. If they cannot be covered up then they must be avenged (2000, 48). This is the philosophy behind honor killings. If a person disgraces their family or tribe they must be killed in order for honor to be restored.

THE IMPORTANCE OF HONOR

One day I asked a Muslim friend of mine for her definition of honor. She said that honor is the most important thing in her culture. You never touch a person's honor. Honor is their very being, their core. When you want to show a person that he or she is highly esteemed you throw a big party or do something extravagant that will publicly display your feelings for them. This brings them honor. To touch a person's honor by embarrassing them or slighting them will result in disgrace. Once this happens it is difficult, if not impossible, to restore their honor and right the situation.

As a teacher in an honor/shame culture, I have observed among young people that shame is used as a form of punishment when a student misbehaves. The pupil is sent to a person in authority who determines the offense and berates the child. It is announced to anyone within earshot that the child is not a good student and refuses to work well. The authority figure may even show an inordinate amount of anger toward the child. Then, another teacher or significant person will step in on behalf of the child and "apologize" for him or her thus appeasing the (feigned) anger of the authority figure. At this point the child, crying remorsefully is showing the proper amount of "shame," whether heart-felt or not. When the child is brought back into the classroom by the authority figure, it is announced before the whole class that this child must now behave in the classroom. The crying plus this "public" announcement of shame is often enough to curtail further infractions. One child, threatened with being removed from the class and taken to the principal, physically held on to the corner of the classroom wall so as not to be put through the process of public exposure.

The Problem of Lying

One issue of great difficulty for people coming from the guilt/righteousness worldview is the problem of lying. For people from a guilt/righteousness worldview, telling the truth is always right and lying is always wrong. The issue for people from an honor/shame worldview, however, is determining whether what is being said is for an honorable reason or not. If a person lies to protect the honor of another person or family, for example, then the lie is viewed as good. If the person lies to protect himself, however, or for another selfish motive, then it is bad (Muller 2000, 51). Once, while coming through customs in the United States, I was in line behind an older Muslim couple laden down with suitcases, obviously bringing gifts for their relatives who were living there. The customs inspector asked the couple if they had any food with them to which they replied, naturally, "No, no food," accompanied by their right hand slightly beating their chest in a typical gesture that means, "Forgive me." Standing there and observing, I could see what was happening and knew there was little I could do to intervene. Had the couple understood that their food items were inconsequential and that by telling the truth they could have passed through customs without a hitch, perhaps they would have admitted that they had it. On the other hand, they might have thought, what customs agent would ask such a stupid question? Of course they had food. What self respecting Muslim would have showed up at a relative's house without olives, figs, dates, cookies, and other desirables? That would have been unthinkable! Not wanting to be deterred, the customs agent asked them to put one of their suitcases on the counter. When it was opened the food was discovered. The agent, who was obviously not having a good day, went ballistic. All their suitcases were opened and they all contained food. Finally, a customs agent named Ahmed came to the rescue. Peace was restored and the couple was allowed to leave with their possessions intact. The last comment I heard the first customs agent make when Ahmed approached was, "But they LIED to me."

Honor and Shame in the Qur'an

Viewing the honor/shame worldview from a Muslim perspective, it might be helpful to look at the creation story in the Qu'ran. In Surah 7 verses 19-27, Adam and Eve were told by God to live in the garden but not to go near the tree. In my Turkish edition, the commentator states that the Lord gave Adam and Eve "a limited faculty of choice" and that at this point the tree was the "only forbidden thing in the Divine Law." The passage continues, "But Satan whispered to them that he might manifest to them that which was hidden from them *in their shame*" (emphasis mine). Satan, according to the Qur'an, told Adam and Eve they would become angels or gain immortality if they ate the fruit. When they did eat it, however, they only felt shame and hid themselves from God. When God approached them, Adam and Eve said they had wronged themselves and if God did not forgive them they were lost. In the next verse, the children of Adam are reminded that they have been shown the "raiment to conceal your shame . . . but the raiment of piety, that is best." This raiment of piety is described by the commentator as a sense of shame or good deeds (Ozek 1994, 152). Verse 27 again tells Adam's children not to let Satan fool them like he fooled their parents when he removed their "robe (of innocence)" from them and showed them their *shame* (emphasis mine). This passage illustrates the Muslim attitude toward sin. According to Faruqi, "In the Islamic view, human beings are no more 'fallen' than they are 'saved.' Because they are not 'fallen' they have no need of a savior. But because they are not 'saved' either, they need to do good works—and do them ethically which alone will earn them the desired 'salvation'" (Faruqi quoted by Geisler and Saleeb 2002, 45).

Shame, as we have seen, is greatly emphasized in the Qur'anic creation story. If it plays such an important part there, should it not also play a significant part in our presentation of the Fall—our need to cover our shame as well as find forgiveness for sin?

Other biblical passages also express the importance of removing our shame and being restored to a position of honor before God. They may not use the theological terms we are used to using but include terms such as "cleansed," "fulfilled," "satisfied" and "blessed." In her book, *Daughters of Islam*, for instance, Miriam Adeney tells of an innovative American pastor who explains the communion table in terms of wholeness. "This table is for people who want to be healed," the pastor says. "Jesus came for the healing of the brokenhearted. He died for the healing of the nations. He burst out of the category of death, rising to life again, in order to bring us to health. Our wholeness is in him" (2002, 100). A similar shift in emphasis from sin and forgiveness to shame and honor may give our gospel presentation greater meaning for Muslim women.

Honor and Shame in the Lives of Biblical Women

As women reaching women, we are particularly sympathetic to the predicament of Muslim women who want to stand honorably before God and yet are considered polluted. Because of sexual intercourse, menstruation and routine care for their children, Muslim women are always in contact with things that make them unclean and therefore in a shameful position before God. Adeney describes the Islamic view of women as both "polluted and polluting ... Women are always 'behind' spiritually." Because they cannot pray when they are menstruating or fast when they are pregnant or nursing they are constantly behind and never really able to make up what God requires (2002, 116). I believe the interest of Muslim women will be piqued if we tell them about other women who struggled with shame and despair and yet found restoration in the God of the Bible.

While I have presented the following principles in a didactic format, they need not be mentioned by the storyteller when she is telling the story. In eastern storytelling formats, the point is generally understood within the context of the story and no further explanation is needed. Most often we just need to tell them the story without the "three points" of teaching which so often accompanies it in the West. Even the titles of these stories—"From Barren to Blessed," "From Death to Life," "From Unclean to Clean," and "From Thirst to Satisfaction"— underscore the idea that the gospel can be expressed in other than Western terms. Although the following stories relate the gospel using non-western concepts, they express women's universal needs and show the fulfillment that all women can only find in Jesus Christ.

From Barren to Blessed

"From Barren to Blessed" describes the story of Jacob and his wives found in Genesis 29–30. In the story, Jacob meets Rachel, falls in love and wants to marry her. Rachel's crafty father switches the bride and Jacob ends up with both Rachel and her sister, Leah, plus two concubines, giving fourteen plus years of his life in service to his father-in-law. As the story of these women unfolds, God sees that Leah is not loved by her husband and so he brings her honor by giving her many children. In the end she honors God through her worship. Rachel, being barren, first seeks to remove her shame through her maid and then finally through the blessing of God she bears two sons herself.

These women cried out to God in their barren state for a restoration of honor and God heard their cry. He removed their shame and disgrace and he filled them with honor. Just as God took those women from barrenness to joy, from emptiness to fulfillment, he can do the same for us, whatever our need. God delights in giving us joy and fulfillment and blessing.

From Death to Life

The second story, "From Death to Life," in 1 Kings 17:7-24, tells the story of Elijah's interaction with a widow and her son. When a drought caused a lack of food, God sent Elijah to be cared for by this widow. Even though she lacked food for herself and her son, she trusted the word given by the man of God and fed him first, consequently providing food enough for all of them throughout the drought. Sometime after this, the woman's son became very ill and died. Taking him to Elijah, she questioned why this should happen to her. Elijah cried out to God asking him why he had brought this tragedy on this woman and God heard Elijah's cry, returning the boy to him. With his resurrection, the woman believed that Elijah came from God and also that the words he spoke truly came from God.

God through Elijah assured the woman that if she listened and did what God had told her to do during the drought He would bless her and take care of her. Later God asked the woman to trust Him further for the life of her son. Through this incident God reminded the woman of her broken trust relationship because of her sin and taught her that He was the God who restores trust and gives life. She believed His word. We, too, can believe that God will give us life. Like the widow from Zarepheth, we can have this life when we trust God for it.

From Unclean to Clean

The story "From Unclean to Clean" in Leviticus 15: 19-30, Matthew 9:20-22 and Luke 8:42b-48 relates Jesus' encounter with a woman who had been ill for twelve years. According to her religious law, a woman was unclean during her regular monthly flow of blood. Any encounter with her would cause others to be unclean, as well. Only through a prescribed sacrifice could her unclean-ness could be removed. But this poor woman could never stop bleeding long enough to make the sacrifice. When she saw Jesus and remembered that he had healed others she thought that perhaps if she just reached out and touched him no one would see that she was transferring her uncleanness to him. She knew it was a shameful thing to do but in desperation she stretched out her hand and touched the edge of his cloak. Immediately her bleeding stopped. When Jesus asked who had touched him she knew she would have to admit her shameful act. Instead of giving her a rebuke, however, Jesus told her that her faith had healed her; she was clean. She could go in peace. Who is this man, our listeners will wonder? What kind of power is this? If he did this for that woman, who could never get caught up with the religious duties she must perform to be cleansed, can he do this for others too? Could he do it for me?

From Thirst to Satisfaction

Our final story, "From Thirst to Satisfaction" is for women who may be a bit far-ther down the road in their understanding of God. Found in John 4:4-26, this is the story of Jesus and the woman at the well. This story can be used to intro-duce Jesus as the thirst quencher. Even though it was culturally inappropriate for Jesus to even talk with this woman, during the surprising conversation Jesus offered her eternal water so she would never thirst again. He was the one with the living water to quench her eternal thirst. Here was a woman who had a multitude of sins in her past and was presently living in sin. The same Jesus who answered the woman's greatest need—the need for eternal satisfaction—in spite of the many sins that she needed to be forgiven, promises to do the same thing for us today.

Conclusion

As members of an honor/shame worldview, Muslim women are concerned about shame and being defiled. They long to restore their lost honor. Under-standing how important this is for them and the resources that are in Christ, let us adjust our presentation of the gospel to meet their need.

REFERENCES

Adeney, Miriam. 2002. *Daughters of Islam.* Downers Grove, IL.: InterVarsity Press.

Betts, Kenneth. 2003. *Escalating cultural conflict.* Available online from http://meabt.com/conflict.htm; accessed 28 January, 2004.

Faruqi, Isma'il R. 1994. *Islam.* 3d. Edition. Amana Publications.

Geisler, Norman L. and Abdul Saleeb. 2002. *Answering Islam: The crescent in light of the cross.* 2d ed. Baker Books.

Muller, Roland. 2002. *Honor and shame.* Xlibris Corporation.

Ozek, Ali, Nureddin Uzunoglu, Tevfik Rustu Topuzoglu, and Mehmet Maksutoglu. 1994. *The Holy Qur'an with English translation.* Istanbul, Turkey: Acar Matbaacilikyayincilik Hizmetleri Press.

Thomas, Bruce. 1994. The gospel for shame cultures. *Evangelical Missions Quarterly* 3 (June 30): 284-290.

5

Muslim Family Law and Its Implications for Christian Ministry

Evelyne A. Reisacher

Muslim Family Law is a key component for understanding and working with Muslim women. In this article, Evelyne Reisacher explores the relationship of Muslim family law to the Shari'ah or Islamic law, describes its impact on Muslim women and suggests how an understanding of the law can aid workers in their ministry to Muslim women.

When I asked Hayat, a young Christian and former Muslim from North Africa, what her favorite book of the Bible was, she answered: "The book of Leviticus, because it gives me clear guidelines on how a godly woman should act and behave." On another occasion a Pakistani mother of five children explained to me why she did not want to become a Christian: "I love the words of Jesus in the gospel, but if I decide to follow him, what will my daily life look like? What will I do with the laws my family follows? How will Christianity work for me on a practical and legal level?"

These conversations and many more like them made me ponder how family laws in Islam affect ministry and outreach to Muslim women. How, for instance, do Christians take into account the legal aspect of Islam when they share their faith in Jesus? What responses can they offer to women's questions about the law? In this article, I will examine the influence of family law on ministry to Muslim women. After a brief overview of Islamic law, I will explore Muslim family law, highlighting those areas that Christians who reach out to Muslims will need to take into account.

ISLAMIC LAW: SOME DEFINITIONS

It is not my intention to present here an in depth study of the concept of law in Islam. There are many works on this topic in English available to the interested reader (Schacht 1964; Esposito 2001; Goldziher 1981). However, in order to reflect on the role of family law in ministry to Muslim women, it is important to first offer a brief introduction to the concept of Islamic law since family law is one of its branches.

Religious law is a familiar concept in Islam, commonly referred to by its Arabic term, *Shari'ah*. Joseph Schacht (1964:1) wrote, "Islamic law is the epitome of Islamic thought, the most typical manifestation of the Islamic way of life, the core and kernel of Islam itself." By following *Shari'ah* Muslims express their obedience to God and strive to build families and societies that honor him. Christians are not unfamiliar with this worldview. Jesus said:"Whoever obeys the law and teaches other people to obey the law will be great in the kingdom of heaven" (John 5:19).

The shaping of the *Shari'ah* law has been gradual in the history of Islam. Some texts and decisions were developed during the first century of Islam and others followed later. Rules of law continue to be defined as the Muslim community encounters new situations for which no legal decision exists.

Traditionally, Muslims consider the law to be revealed in the Qur'an. According to Muhammad Al-'Ashmawi (1998:51), 200 of around 6,000 Qur'anic verses have a legal aspect. The Hadith also contains numerous passages where the Prophet Muhammad answers legal issues concerning the life of the Muslim community. When Muslims would come to him and ask questions such as, "How should Muslims act in such and such a situation?" his answers became rules to follow, some taking the form of legal texts.

In Islam, *Shari'ah* is considered in its broad meaning, the guideline from God on how Muslims should conduct their lives and relate to each other in society. As N. Coulson (1964:1) stated, "Law, in classical Islamic theory, is the revealed will of God, a divinely ordained system preceding and not preceded by the Muslim state, controlling and not controlled by Muslim society."

A significant number of Muslims hold that *Shari'ah* has a divine character, given by God for the well-being of their community. Muslims may differ greatly on the interpretation of legal texts and their application; nevertheless they will agree that God intended believers to have good laws. Non-Muslims sometimes equate or restrict the concept of *Shari'ah* to practices such as stoning for adultery or wearing the *burqa*. For Muslims, the concept of *Shari'ah* is broader than a few rules and regulations; it is God's way of life that believers must follow.

Religious Law and Secular Law

There are regular debates within Islam about the place and role of Shari'ah in society: should it be the constitution of the state, or should it be an ethical rule limited to the private sphere of individuals? Can Muslims live under secular laws while following religious laws privately? There are also those who argue for an adaptation of religious laws to fit the current context.

Today the terms of equation between Islam and the State are different in different countries. Virtually all states in the Muslim world have legislation that derives from non-Muslim sources. However some states integrate *Shari'ah* in their constitution. Others find a balance between secular laws and religious laws. There are also Muslims who believe that *Shari'ah* should be limited to the ethical realm. Muhammad Sa'id Al-'Ashmawi, a Muslim judge from Egypt, for instance, believes that the importance of the *Shari'ah* lies not in the legal but in the moral aspects of Islam. The Qur'an "is concerned to inscribe the fault in the soul of the believer, to elevate his conscience and morality in order that it might be its own proper *Shari'ah* in the sense of the way leading to God" (Al-'Ashmawi 1998:51). Therefore, no generalization should be made across countries, since *Shari'ah* comes in different forms.

What about Christianity and the Law?

How can Christians understand the role that religious law plays in Islam? To some extent they can draw analogies from their own experience. For example, Christians also have to define the relationship between biblical laws and those of the society they live in. Most Christians today accept that biblical laws are limited to the private sphere, but others will take action to fight the laws of their country that go against biblical values. Some will even argue that laws of the country must be inspired by the Bible. This is a form of accommodation of biblical laws to civil jurisprudence. Christianity has in its history also witnessed at times this tension between secular and religious aspects of law.

FAMILY LAW

In this section, I will show the role of Family Law in *Shari'ah*. I will also explain in greater detail how laws move from sacred texts to their implementation in daily life.

Family law is one branch of *Shari'ah* alongside international law, commercial law, penal law and financial law. Family law protects the family which is the core of Muslim society and thus, receives a special treatment in Islam. Muslim family law includes regulations about marriage contracts, provision for dower, grounds for divorce, maintenance of the wife, rights of children and relatives, paternity, child custody, inheritance, family finances and other matters. Its value should not be underestimated; one minister from the Arab Gulf, answering a question by an American reporter said, "We are willing to change and reform many things in our societies, but do not touch our family system." Christians often do not realize how much Muslims can perceive Christian teaching as a threat when the latter see it as profoundly altering their family and societal structures.

Family law includes regulations for both males and females. Females, however, often feel more directly affected by its regulations. This is because first, when a family law is passed it can either drastically reform the lifestyle of women or introduce a conservative regulation that puts women's status at odds with the rest of the world. For example, the family code defined by the Taliban in Afghanistan reintroduced seclusion for women whereas it did not restrict men's movements. Second, females are more affected because legal discourse is overwhelmingly dominated by male voices, because women cannot traditionally become religious jurists and lawmakers. Third, family law defines gender roles that affect core issues for women, much more than commercial, penal or international laws do. One example is the reform of Algerian law passed in early 2005 which maintains the role of the *wali* (guardian) for females when they marry. For all these reasons, women may feel the brunt of family law more than men.

The Stronghold of Shari'ah

Family law also touches on intimate interpersonal relationships and deep moral values (Quraishi and Syeed-Miller 2004:30). As the most protected part of *Shari'ah*, it is the one branch of law that Muslims will advocate for first when there is no religious law in a region. In Canada, for example, some Muslims have recently requested the creation of *Shari'ah* courts for Muslim marriages. A number of Muslim couples in that country consider their religious identities important enough not to sacrifice at a secular altar.

Andrew Rippin (1993:20) wrote:"While matters such as politics and taxation remained only theoretically under the guidance of the religious code in medieval Islam, areas of personal law—marriage, divorce, inheritance—were the stronghold of religion." Other authors say that in the most reformed legislations of the Muslim world, there have been only slight changes made to the Family Code. For example, Graham-Brown (2001:28) writes that after the Independence of Algeria in 1961, "The Algerian constitution gave equal rights to all citizens, but until 1984 no changes were made in personal status codes."

In areas where there has been a progressive limitation of the scope of the *Shari'ah*, courts are often left to deal with family matters such as marriage, divorce, custody of children, relatives and inheritance. However, Rippin adds, "It is however, precisely in many of those areas that the contemporary world has effected a great deal of change and where the pressures, especially of nineteenth-century European values, have been felt the most."

Jurisprudence

The application of *Shari'ah* is called *fiqh* which means "jurisprudence." It is the science of law or the legal activity of humans (Chapman 2003:110). Jurisprudence is an important practice in Islam and many of its religious leaders deal with it, for example the *faqih, mufti, ulema,* and *qadi.* The four major schools of Sunni jurisprudence developed in the second and third centuries of the Islamic calendar. They are the Hanafite school which is the oldest, the Malikite, Shafi'ite, and Hanbalite. Traditionally, these schools of law were limited to specific regions of the world. Today one country may harbor all four. *Shii* Islam has also developed several schools of law such as the Ja'farites, Zaydites or Ibadites. It is important to know there are different schools of laws because they sometimes differ in the way they define and apply laws. In Islam, rules were given by God to protect the family and society. Some of these laws are included in the Qur'an such as laws concerning marriage (Q 4:23-28), divorce (Q 2:226-231), inheritance (Q 4:8-18), motherhood (Q 2:233), or widowhood (Q 2:234-236). When Muslim legislators find no legal evidence in the Qur'an, they refer to what the Prophet Muhammad did, said or tacitly approved in the Hadith, which is considered the second source of authority for jurisprudence. The most authoritative Hadith compilations were collected and recorded during the second and third centuries after the death of the Prophet Muhammad.

When the Qur'an and the Hadith do not suffice to define legal matters, the third source of jurisprudence is the consensus of the community or *ijma'*. It consists essentially of the decisions of *ulemas*, theologians and lawyers. *Ijma'* is based on a hadith of the Prophet Muhammad who said that the community cannot agree on an error. Eventually, if there is no example of regulation in the Qur'an and Hadith and the consensus of the legal scholars do not provide enough information to deal with a legal case, *Shari'ah* resorts to a fourth source which is called *qiyas* or analogic reasoning (Dwyer 1990:2). Analogy allows scholars to apply to a novel case a ruling made to fit analogous cases.

The practice of analogical reasoning allows the scholars of the law, *ulemas* or *muftis*, to issue individual legal religious opinions. For example, if a Muslim woman wants to know whether God allows dating through Internet, religious leaders may issue a *fatawa* after consulting the Qur'an, the Hadith and *ijmas*. New *fatwas* or legal pronouncements may be published in local newspapers or announced during Friday sermons at the mosque. There are some *fatwas* that apply to a single neighborhood whereas others apply to an entire country. Their number is infinite. In addition, one *fatawa* can be overruled by another one. In Sunni Islam, *fatawas* are issued after analogical reasoning. These do not result in drastic innovations because the process of independent reasoning, or *ijtihad*, was considered closed early in Muslim history. Today, a number of Muslim scholars advocate reopening the door of *ijtihad* but this is debated within the Muslim community.

It is not recommended that laypeople issue *fatwas* or legal decisions; this is a very complicated process undertaken by religious leaders only. In fact, going through the religious literature is no small task. According to Fatima Mernissi, "One is overwhelmed by the number of volumes, and one immediately understands why the average Muslim can never know as much as an imam" (Mernissi 1998:113). By browsing the Hadith without serious textual analysis, furthermore, one may find references that seem to contradict each other. I once attended two conferences on women's issues in the same week where speakers in the one only quoted *ahadith* reflecting a positive view of women and speakers in the other quoted only the negative ones without ever comparing the two.

Laws Are Not Static

Importantly, family law has different facets in the Muslim world. The *burqa*, for example, a garment concealing a woman from head to toe, was imposed by law under the Taliban regime in Afghanistan but not in other countries of the Muslim world. The Turkish government prohibits veiling at school, unlike Saudi Arabia where it is proscribed. In some Muslim countries polygamy is allowed, while in others it is tolerated but not encouraged, and in still others, such as Tunisia, it is forbidden. In some Muslim countries women are protected in case of divorce and in others they are not. Canonical law is given a place that varies in each country and is sometimes transformed by its contact with secular laws.

Shari'ah also can be modified by customary practices. In Bangladesh, for example, the bride's family must give bridal wealth to the husband's family. According to Qur'anic teaching, however, the opposite should occur: the bridegroom should give the dower to the bride. In the realm of family law there is diversity within unity; all these differences make it difficult to draw generalizations. Therefore it is important to approach legal discussions by first conducting a serious study of each situation and context.

In addition to written law, there are also unwritten laws. Believers do not always have access to legal texts when they need them to find God's will for an unusual situation. At one funeral I attended, the corpse of the deceased person was taken inside the house for a few hours. The women who were present raised a number of legal questions and demonstrated a great concern to do things right, asking among themselves, "What shall be done with the carpet on which the corpse was laid? How should we behave inside the house? Is it legal to wail? Should the room be ritually cleansed after the corpse leaves?" Since there was no imam present at the time the women began to suggest all kinds of interpretations. In a religious system where every act is codified as approved by God or not, debates can occur at any moment and "self-made" legal experts can rule over neighborhoods and households. These laws are sometimes more difficult to reform than the written laws themselves.

MINISTRY TO MUSLIM WOMEN

After examining *Shari'ah* and the family law, I will now underscore their implications for relations between Christians and Muslims. I will also explore a number of issues affecting communication and ministry to Muslim women.

Muslims and Christians are both concerned with obeying the divine plan for family and society. When the people of Israel entered the country of Canaan, for instance, God said, "Do not follow their customs. You must obey my rules and follow them. I am the Lord your God" (Lev.18:3-4). Like Muhammad's companions who wondered what they should do with a man and a woman caught in adultery, the Jewish teachers of the Law and the Pharisees also came to Jesus one day and asked: "Teacher, this woman was caught having sexual relations with a man who is not her husband. The Law of Moses commands that we kill with stones every woman who does this. What do you say we should do?" (John 8:4; Lev. 20:10). The Pharisees, in another case, asked Jesus:"Is it right for a man to divorce his wife for any reason he chooses?" (Matt. 19:3) while in Islam, believers also discuss on what grounds a believer can divorce his wife (Q 65:1-3; Sonbol 1996). Like the *Shari'ah*, the New Testament epistles contain many discussions on family regulations. Paul especially defines how men and women should relate in Christ (Eph. 5:25-6:1-9; Col. 3:18-25). This similarity of concerns between Muslims and Christians provides a rich platform for sharing and interacting.

Another commonality is the fact that both religious family systems have been given to communities who functioned initially essentially under patriarchal rules. Scholars regularly discuss how this patriarchal context has impacted Muslim and Christian jurisprudence (Barlas 2003). Rippin, for instance, (1993:116) wrote: "Islamic law, with its enunciated roots firmly in the Qur'an, has instituted a social system based upon the presumption of an extended family grouping within a patriarchal system." Christians deal with a similar issue of how the patriarchal system prevalent in the Old and New Testament contexts impacted the religious teaching on family and society. This provides another interface for discussion between the two faiths.

The Importance of Old Testament Laws

I have underscored the fact that Muslims and Christians share common concerns in regards to law. However, there are also a number of differences. Christians do not conceive of religious laws the same way Muslims do. Colin Chapman (2003:109) wrote, "Christians will no doubt find it hard to understand why we need to give attention to law, since the concept of law seems foreign to Christians who are taught that salvation is by faith, not by works."

Since the New Testament stresses grace over law, those who share the gospel sometimes forget that someone who does not know the Old Testament legal system may find it difficult to fully understand the meaning of grace. Muslim women have no difficulty understanding a religious system that integrates divine laws. A comparison between Old Testament Jewish law and Islamic law shows similarities and contrasts but a common worldview: in both communities law is the basis for social welfare (Neusner, Sonn and Brockopp 2000). Therefore I suggest that Muslim women will better relate with what is said in the New Testament if they know about the legal teaching of the Old Testament.

There are numerous examples of laws in the Old Testament that resonate with Muslim laws and I will only quote a few examples here. First, there are regulations for sexual relations: men should not have sexual relations with their wife during her monthly period (Lev. 18:19; Q 2:222) and they need to bathe after sexual relations (Lev. 15:16-18; Q 4:43). Adultery, second, is strongly forbidden in both the Old Testament and the Qur'an (Exod. 20:14; Deut. 22:22; Q 24:2), and finally, the Qur'an and the Old Testament both forbid marriage to close relatives (Lev. 18:1-18; 20:10-21; Q 4:22-23). I discussed male guardianship earlier in this article. In Numbers 30:5, the rules about special promises show that when a father does not agree with the pledge his daughter has made, "the promise or pledge does not have to be kept. Her father would not allow them. So the Lord will free her from her promise" (Num. 30:5). Therefore we see there was some type of guardianship in the Old Testament as well. Muslim women will not feel at odds with these Old Testament laws when reading Leviticus, Numbers and Deuteronomy.

Jesus Came to Fulfill the Law
Muslim women can also easily understand the reactions of the New Testament women when they listened to Jesus. He often referred to Old Testament laws when he discussed religious issues with people such as, for example, the adulterous woman, the Pharisees or the leaders of the Sanhedrin, the highest Jewish court of his time (John 8:1-11; Mark 2:23-27).

Jesus knew how to speak to the heart of people concerned by legal issues. In Matthew 5, for example, he discusses the Law of Moses, sexual sin, and divorce. One of my students once wanted to write a paper on spirituality and women in Southeast Asia. She had developed a questionnaire with questions such as "Do you have the assurance of salvation?" and "How do you picture paradise?" A few weeks into her research she realized that rural women were not interested in such questions. What they really cared about, as one woman expressed, "What will happen to me if my husband repudiates me?" These women were more concerned about legal questions than metaphysical questions.

Although there are many similarities between biblical and Qur'anic legal issues, there are also differences that need to be taken into account. One major difference is that the entire sacrificial framework central to the Old and New Testament does not exist in the Qur'an. Furthermore, when laws are compared in detail, there are significant distinctions. Some of these distinctions point to a difference in the ultimate goal of the rule of law. In another example, instead of simply discarding the Old Testament laws, Jesus said he came to accomplish the law. He therefore gave practical steps for people to meet God's standards. In one example he said, "Anyone who divorces his wife is causing her to be guilty of adultery" (Matt. 5:31). He also helped people look at the legal issues from a new perspective when he said, "I tell you that if anyone looks at a woman and wants to sin sexually with her, then he has already done that sin with the woman in his mind" (Matt. 5:27-28).

Significantly, according to the New Testament, the laws were given not only to lead people to obey God, but also to reveal that they are sinners. Sin was in the world before the law and "The Law shows us our sin" (Rom. 3:20). Does this mean that every law of the Old Testament must be applied literally today or that we need to reinstitute law courts to make sure all believers abide by the religious laws? Very few churches today have religious courts that judge every person's actions. Legal discussions have instead turned to ethical discussions that set moral standards. Stoning the man and woman who commit adultery as recommended in the Old Testament is not practiced in Christian circles (Lev. 20:10). Having two wives in the practice described in Deuteronomy 21 verses 15-17 has been overruled in most contexts by the passage of 1 Timothy 3:2. Still, a number of Old Testament passages will inspire Christian thinking about the importance of laws such as the verse: "Remember to obey all my commands. Then you will be God's holy people" (Num. 15:40).

Jesus in the Qur'an is depicted as declaring what was licit and illicit (Q 3:50). Somehow Jesus is portrayed as performing jurisprudence or *fiqh*. I encourage Christians to model this practice and show a greater interest in the legal concerns of Muslim women in order to understand their worldview and concerns. Too often Muslim women who turn to Jesus are left in a legal vacuum. They do not know how the law and faith relate. That is why Hayat continues to cling to the book of Leviticus and why my Pakistani friend did not want to become a Christian; she did not know what the family system would look like for her. Family issues need to be discussed with women who are exploring Christianity. I do not believe that we have yet investigated all the facets of this problem. I am not saying that we need to put Muslim women under a new legal system, but we need to recognize that it is not easy for them to understand the Christian worldview. How can they be expected to know what their life will be like when they hear comments such as, "In Christ, you are free from the law"? What can this mean since laws continue to exist and are necessary for a well functioning society? How, they may wonder, does Christianity regulate family relations? In Islam, those who transgress the laws of Allah are called unjust (Q 2:229). One can easily understand that Muslim women may ask, "What kind of family laws exist in Christianity?"

Should Christians Oppose Muslim Laws?

Another issue that needs to be discussed in this context is whether Christians should oppose Islamic family laws that appear to them repressive or unjust. Christian writers in the past have considered it important to speak against practices that according to them disfavored to women. Samuel Zwemer (1926), for example, discouraged child marriage as he saw it practiced in certain Muslim countries during his lifetime.

As Christians, should we fight for women's rights in the Muslim world and support family law reforms? Let us look at some examples. Safia K. Mohsen (1990:20), reporting on a case of adultery in Egypt, argues that the criminal law discriminates against women because the "penalty for a guilty husband is a maximum sentence of six months but for a women it is two years." She continues, "Despite legal and law enforcement attitudes that favor the rape victim, rape remains one of the most under-reported crimes in Egypt" (Mohsen 1990:22). In Pakistan, similarly, the details of the 1979 Hudud Ordinance and the Law of Evidence "blurred the line between *zena* and rape, making it difficult to establish the guilt of a rapist and putting women in a difficult situation" (Mogheissi 1999:29).

While there are many ways that Christians can respond to these and similar reports, let me suggest a few responses. First, looking at the example of Jesus is important. His support and concern for women's issues is obvious as we read the gospels. Christians can show similar concern for women in general. Second, Christians must realize that Muslims are also concerned about women's issues. Islam has its feminists, modernists, postmodernists, conservatives and fundamentalists who debate women's issues from different perspectives. On the issue of wearing the veil for example, there are women who are against wearing it and those who marched in the streets of Istanbul in April 2002 because they sought the freedom to wear it in schools. One needs to listen to the arguments of Muslim feminists, and also those of female fundamentalists and Muslim women who describe themselves as postmodern. Third, Christians who criticize Muslim regulations on family issues should be willing to discover how Muslims perceive family structures which are foreign to their context. Many Muslims may be attracted by secular laws, and others may feel threatened by what they feel is the disintegration of the traditional family system in the part of the world

impacted by Christianity. Fourth, as Christians we should not look at family
issues in Islam with condescension, thinking we have all the answers. Throughout history, churches have evolved in their understanding of the issues related
to family and gender. In the West, people have been debating the relationship
of church and state for centuries. Some laws were considered non-negotiable,
and others not. Christians have constantly engaged in hermeneutical reasoning
on family issues. Even today, Christians are trying to reflect on the relationship
between the biblical view on family and the non-biblical view. Finally, it is
important to evaluate the positive and negative elements of every family law
and suggest ways of better defending the rights of every member of the family
as well as the family itself.

Conclusion

Family law is an important issue for Muslim women which must be taken into
account in ministry. Therefore Christian women must give concerted reflection
to how the gospel relates to this law. In many places, Muslim women are far
more concerned with the implementation of their religion as a vital part of their
lives than they are with the theoretical understanding of the underpinnings of
their faith. They are concerned not just with the spiritual aspect of their religion,
but also the legal aspect. One way for Christians to understand this is to look at
the Old Testament and see how family laws were given to both the people of
Israel and to Christians in the New Testament.

Christians are not unfamiliar with religious laws affecting women since the
Old and New Testaments refer to legal family issues. They can take advantage
of these concerns and worldviews to better understand Muslim women. They
can, for example, imagine how hard it is for a Muslim to question God about
his decrees and commands, even though the way these commands are applied
is subject to discussion in the Muslim world. Muslim women who investigate Christianity may be surprised that the Bible talks a great deal about the family and
that the church has also dealt with a number of these issues in its own context.

Christians, like Muslims, are concerned with how they can honor God in
their family life. When they live in a secular context, Christians look at their
scriptures to see whether their family life is in tune with God's commandments.
There are, however, differences of approach in Christianity and Islam that will
need to be underlined and contrasts that must be taken into account; the way
the laws are defined and applied in the two religions is not the same. In addition,
while most Christians do not advocate a literal application of Old Testament

jurisprudence, the laws of many countries affected by Christianity have been influenced by a biblical model.

Christians have been able to live under secular family laws although they find it hard to live under the family laws of other religions. When they are under secular family laws they usually follow biblical laws through ethical and moral channels. Christians need to reflect more deeply on how to communicate with Muslims on family issues and must be sure they have answers to the questions Muslim women ask in the area of family life.

Since family law is not monolithic in Islam, I suggest that each context must be studied specifically. Family laws evolve differently and changes occur on a regular basis in the Muslim world. Christians involved in ministry may have to refer to legal experts to be able to understand certain situations. I do not believe that Christians must agree with the *Shari'ah*, but they must understand how Muslim believers apprehend God's laws and what an absence or alterations of these laws would entail.

Christians who do not live in a context where divine laws are enforced by *qadis* and courts may find it difficult to understand women who live in countries bound by *Shari'ah*. They may not understand the threat a religious legal vacuum will create for some women. Furthermore, not all Muslim countries abide by family laws, and in many contexts Muslims live under secular laws. In this case, devout Muslims will try to honor God by defining Muslim ethics and moral standards.

In those areas where Christians feel they need to suggest reform of Muslim family laws they will have to act with sensitivity, wisdom, understanding that they are dealing with the most protected part of Muslim law. They must also understand that Muslims who advocate a greater application of *Shari'ah* believe it is for the good of society and will bring the world under the rule of God. They should understand that other Muslims, by contrast, will say that some laws are outdated and need to be reformed. It is also important that Muslims become more familiar with the Christian perspectives of divine family laws. Many Muslims have as much difficulty understanding the Christian definition of family as Christians have understanding the Muslim definition.

Finally, Jesus' view of the family and his interpretation of the Old Testament Jewish family law provide a model for Christian ministry to Muslim women. Jesus presented a very unique way of dealing with family law, teaching his followers why these laws were given and the place they had in Christian practice. Where the Old Testament said, "The Lord God commands you this day to follow these decrees and laws: carefully observe them with all your heart and with all your soul (Deut. 26:16)," Jesus said, "You are my friends if you do what I command you" (John 15:14). These reflections may open new avenues for ministry to Muslim women. Christians can join Muslims in their reflection on how to deal with family issues and present their own understanding on how God envisions family relationships from a biblical perspective.

REFERENCES

Anderson, J. N. D. 1959. *Islamic law in the modern world.* NY:New York University Press.

'Ashmawi, Muhammad Sa'id al-. 1998. Shari'a: The codification of Islamic law. In *Liberal Islam: A sourcebook*, ed. Charles Kurzman, 49-58. Oxford, UK:Oxford University Press.

Barlas, Asma. 2003. Believing women. In I*slam: Unreading patriarchal interpretations of the Qur'an.* Austin, TX: University of Texas.

Chapman, Colin. 2003. *Cross and crescent: Responding to the challenge of Islam.* Downers Grove, IL: InterVarsity Press.

Coulson, N. J. 1964. *A history of Islamic law.* Edinburgh, UK: Edinburgh University Press.

Dwyer, Daisy Hilse. 1990. Law and Islam in the Middle East: An introduction. In *Law and Islam in the Middle East*, ed. Daisy Hilse Dwyer, 1-14. New York: Bergin and Garvey.

Esposito, John L., with Natana J. DeLong-Bas. 2001. *Women in Muslim family law.* 2d ed. Syracuse, NY: Syracuse University Press.

Gleave, Robert, and Eugenia Kermeli, eds. 1997. *Islamic law: Theory and practice.* London: I.B. Tauris Publishers.

Goldziher, Ignaz. 1981. *Introduction to Islamic theology and law.* Translated by Andras and Rugh Hamori. Princeton, NJ: Princeton University Press.

Graham-Brown, Sarah. 2001. Women's activism in the Middle East: A historical perspective. In *Women and power in the Middle East*, eds. Suad Joseph and Susan Slyomovics,. Philadelphia, PE: University of Pennsylvania Press.

Khadduri, Majid, and Herbert J. Liebesny, eds. 1955. *Law in the Middle East: Origin and development of Islamic law.* Vol. 1. Washington, D.C.: The Middle East Institute.

Masud, Muhammad Khalid, Brinkley Messick, and David S. Powers. 1996. Muftis, fatwas, and Islamic legal interpretation. In *Islamic legal interpretation: Muftis and their fatwas*, eds. Muhammad Khalid Masud, Brinkley Messick and David S. Powers, 3-32. Cambridge, MA: Harvard University Press.

Mernissi, Fatima. 1998. A feminist interpretation of women's rights in Islam. In *Liberal Islam: A sourcebook*, ed. Charles Kurzman, 112-126. Oxford, UK: Oxford University Press.

Mohsen, Safia K. 1990. Women and criminal justice in Egypt. In *Law and Islam in the Middle East*, ed. Daisy Hilse Dwyer, 15-34. New York: Bergin and Garvey.

Neusner, Jacob, Tamara Sonn, and Jonathan E. Brockopp. 2000. *Judaism and Islam in practice: A sourcebook*. New York: Routledge.

Poya, Maryam. 1999. *Women, work and Islamism*. London: Zed Books.

Quraishi, Asifa, and Najeeba Syeed-Miller. 2004. *No altars: A survey of Islamic family law in the United States*. Atlanta: Emory University; available online http://www.emory.edu.

Rippin, Andrew. 1993. *Muslims: Their religious beliefs and practices*. Vol 2: *The contemporary period*. London: Routledge.

Schacht, Joseph. 1964. *An introduction to Islamic law*. Oxford, UK: Oxford University Press.

Sonbol, Amira El Azhary, ed. 1996. *Women, the family, and divorce laws in Islamic history*. Syracuse, NY: Syracuse University Press.

Zwemer, Samuel Marinus. 1926. *Moslem women*. West Medford, MA: The Central Committee on the United Study of Foreign Missions.

Part II

Understanding Muslim Worldviews

6

Faith on Camelback: Reaching non Arabic-Speaking Urban, Less-Educated Muslim Women

Sarah Mullin

Ministry effectiveness can be greatly increased by identifying the worldview of the host culture. In this article Sarah Mullin describes her team's efforts to get close to people in their host culture, understand their worldview and identify the bridges that would make them more effective in evangelism and discipleship. The instruments detailed in this article for identifying a people's worldview are available in Appendix II and III.

*A*s a new missionary I was fortunate enough to join a team of missionaries who had worked with our host culture for a number of years and were diligent students of the culture. They didn't just speak the language fluently; they had adapted even their gestures, facial expressions, and body language to match that of their hosts. In an effort to be an incarnate witness, they lived like members of our host culture in both rural and urban centers, reading the literature, engaging in thoughtful discussions, and understanding the political and social structures of the country. They were also committed to helping new missionaries understand the culture through language courses and discussions on worldview.

In the mid-1990s our team began to document our culture's worldview in a similar vein. We used an instrument entitled "A Cultural-Social-Religious Profile of a Target People: A Development Process and Instrument" (Slack 1994). This instrument is a guide for conducting ethnographic interviews within the target population in order to understand its worldview. Divided into family, social, religious, economic and national political categories, it provides questions to guide the researcher in exploring each of these areas. For this study I have followed the outline of the worldview instrument our team used to focus on the issues most relevant to women, including family, social and religious structures. I will demonstrate how it was used to identify barriers and bridges for our culture, in the hope that this will help others think about their own host cultures. Finally, I will describe the approach we chose for evangelism and discipleship and why I believe it to be the most effective approach based on what we have learned about their worldview.

Our host culture is an unreached Islamic people group with folk Islamic practices. They are historically pastoralists, but can be found today in large urban centers as well as rural communities. The Bible has been translated into their language but the literacy rate is only twenty-four percent and in decline (Johnstone 2001). Literacy among women is much lower than men. In reality, the women are oral communicators. There are few missionaries among this group and Christian radio is the main avenue of evangelism.

The women in my host culture are survivalists who bring beauty, life and joy into relationships. The men provide the organization, but the women are the backbones of the families. They network well and support each other. Many have suffered greatly and live in poverty but are surprisingly resilient. They look for opportunities to learn and are quick to learn how to thrive in the situations they face. These are beautiful women who proudly adorn themselves with bright colors, gold jewelry and perfume. They love celebrations and are good cooks. They are hospitable and give generously to their friends. At the same time, they have an uncanny ability to analyze others and can use this to outsmart others to get what they want.

One of my friends is a good example. When I first met her she was living with her four children and pregnant with a fifth. Each of her children had different fathers from several marriages and divorces and she was divorced again, living in a small single room in a crowded urban center. She was tall, slender and beautiful, carrying herself with elegance and wearing colorful clothes and gold jewelry. She was desperate for work and applied to a women's sewing business, agreeing to come back for a skills test later. A week or so later she returned for the skills test—and more; it seems she had waited to return until she was in active labor! She managed to conceal her labor during the test until the point where organizational administrators were forced to help her.

Similar to her expectations, they rushed her to the hospital and helped pay for the delivery of her son, born just a few hours later. In gratitude, she named him after the organization and began working there following his birth, leaving her children with a friend. She could only work sporadically, however, because her children were frequently sick. After her landlord locked her out for failing to pay rent, she found a missionary who was able to provide money for her and she stopped working for a few months. She frequently was the center of disagreements due to her appetite for gossip and although she tried to attend Bible study she was sporadic in her attendance and concentration because of fatigue and stress. Even when she was tired and worn out she could still flash that beautiful smile and charm us with her wit.

CREATING AN ENVIRONMENT FOR LEARNING WORLDVIEW

Knowing how to reach women like this is dependent on worldview studies, however creating an environment for worldview studies takes work. We need to approach our host culture as learners. Then, through observations, we can make suggestions that help us understand the way they look at life. One of our teammates, for instance, went to the field as a single man and lived in a local hotel for a number of months as he learned the language. The rooms in these hotels have multiple beds so his roommates changed from day to day, but together they provided him with an inside view into our host culture. As a result, he became an expert in the language and culture and has been in this ministry for almost twenty years. His insights have been instrumental in helping the rest of us understand our host culture.

Learning the worldview well also requires knowing the language. Many of the men in our host culture have learned English, but fewer women have had this opportunity. It is critical, thus, that the women on our team speak the language fluently to be effective. Language learning may need to be adapted to the missionary's situation. When we first went to the field our children were toddlers and it was difficult for me to visit local homes to learn language. Instead, I invited ladies into our home for private language lessons several times a week. I also reviewed lessons from formal language classes and worked through a modified LAMP approach to language learning (Brewster 1976). Thus, I was able to learn the language at a slow steady pace that accommodated my family responsibilities.

Fluency in the language gives us tools to read the literature of our host culture and to understand their folk stories. In language class with other Westerners and language helpers, we read a story about a man who cleverly escaped death by deceiving another man who died in his place. Our language helpers, members of the host culture, laughed with delight and praised the deceiver for his success while we sat with our mouths open, criticizing the deceiver and sympathizing with the deceived man. I learned quickly that members of my host culture have a different view of deceit.

Lifestyle issues are also critical to learning worldview. In our host culture, for instance, women's legs are as sensual as breasts in American culture. When we considered the importance of modesty to the members of our host culture, it was easy to adopt a culturally sensitive style of dressing. Similarly, we realized we had problems when we wore our host culture's traditional clothes. We were in a large, multiethnic city where Western women had lived for decades without adopting traditional clothes. When we wore traditional clothes, therefore, we aroused suspicion and had to answer many questions about our motives. Therefore, we decided to wear nontraditional clothes that would be seen as modest by members of our host culture.

Even home furnishings are important to creating a learning environment. People with extravagant furnishings are perceived as being rich while Western furnishings are perceived as foreign. Since many Muslims consider carvings or drawings of animals and people as "graven images," it is recommended that Arabic Bible verses, tapestries, flowers or pictures of scenery be used as culturally sensitive decorations instead. We also adopted local forms of hospitality. Our guests feel welcomed when they receive genuine greetings, hugs, kisses or handshakes and are escorted in after they leave their shoes at the door. To avoid appearing stingy we must offer tea early in the visit, sweetened and accompanied with a generous serving of food that does not hold back on meat or oil. Since it is rude for people to serve themselves, we learned to forgo buffet style service and prepare their plates for them. Other rules, typical to all Muslim cultures, require the use of the right hand for eating and serving, avoiding pork and alcohol—even vanilla extract—and separating men and women so that the guest feels comfortable.

UNDERSTANDING THE WORLDVIEW
OF OUR HOST CULTURE

Analyzing our observations to formulate a worldview can be a daunting task. Using a worldview instrument enabled us to organize our observations and provided questions for further study. In the following section I will discuss what we learned about the family, social, and religious structures in our culture using Dr. Slack's instrument and how these structures impact the overall worldview.

The Influence of Family Structure on Worldview

To begin, family structure plays a significant role in the development of women's worldview. Polygamy, arranged marriages, high divorce rates, male absences, and household responsibilities all shape women's views of reality in a unique way. In our host culture, men practice polygamy and divorce is common and easy to obtain. Arranged marriages, polygamy and high divorce rates give the woman little control over her marriage. Their practice of female genital mutilation, furthermore, reduces the woman's pleasure on the wedding night so that the joy that should be there is often overshadowed with fear and pain. Women, thus, frequently associate marriage with disappointment and heartache.

As a young woman approaches the age of marriage—an important step in becoming an adult—she may fear that she will be the second, third or fourth wife of an old man. Or, if she is lucky enough to be the first wife, she must be clever enough to keep her husband from divorcing her or wanting a second wife. The jealousy created by the addition of a new wife and her future children generally sends shock waves through the original family. With the addition of another wife, the husband's time and money are divided and co-wives and their children often compare the way they are treated. Polygamy and divorce, thus, can lead to jealousy, deceitfulness, insecurity and fear. I have heard many women in my host culture confess to admiring American men who only take one wife. Surely, God's design of marriage as laid out in the Bible can be a bridge that appeals to them. While the Christian design of marriage can be a bridge into their culture, the responsibilities of marriage and motherhood can be a barrier to the gospel. Mothers are often preoccupied with their household duties. The husband's control over his wife, furthermore, can hinder her opportunity to explore Christianity. Young women between the ages of eighteen and twenty-four who have not yet married, I believe, are the best candidates for discipleship as they have the greatest independence from male authority and household responsibilities.

Although family structures in our culture are officially patriarchal with lines of authority and decision-making belonging to the father, uncles, and elder brothers, men are frequently absent. Women, therefore, have an unusually high level of power and can be courageously independent and even deceitful. During a time of conflict in my host culture, for instance, a fellow missionary observed that women encouraged their men to continue fighting by running a "war campaign" at home. Other women may temporarily leave their husbands in search of better opportunities for themselves and their children. One of my friends left her husband and four children in Africa for a job in Europe without any advance warning. She sent money for them to join her although it took several years and much grief before they were reunited. Another woman, a divorced mother of three, secretly arranged for her uncle to remove her children from her husband's family. Her husband and his new wife were planning to move with the children to another country, so she devised a plan to sneak the children away before he could take them. Without a doubt, this kind of independence is unique in a Muslim culture. Although I do not support dishonesty or deceit, I can understand how women in this culture may value courage in testing out ideas and plans that may meet with their husband's or father's disapproval. This unusual trait may also give them the courage they need to investigate Christianity.

Families in my host culture may also struggle to support themselves financially. Traditionally the people earned wealth through livestock or businesses. They tended their animals in difficult environments where they had to outwit predators and enemies, where they were at the mercy of droughts and famines. As a result, cleverness and deceit are highly esteemed character traits in my host culture, even among those who are urban dwellers and businessmen.

Frequently there may be too few breadwinners to support the entire family. In these cases, the needs almost always exceed the resources. Requests for financial assistance are common, and there is a perception that wealthy Westerners, both missionaries and aid agencies, will meet their needs. Opportunities to show Christ's love through medical, agricultural, veterinary, and educational ministries can meet human need and provide us the opportunity to build relationships, but we need to be careful that our ministries point to God as their ultimate provider.

Women's roles in the family lie in managing the home and children. Girls are expected to cook, care for their siblings and help with cleaning before their teen years and are usually competent in managing the home by the time they are married. My host culture values large families with boys favored over girls and young children over older children. Mothers control their children by promising rewards for good behavior or by threatening bad consequences for misbehaving. I have heard many women warn that a dog or cat is just behind the door and will bite the children if they don't obey her. Sadly, just as there is no dog or cat behind the door, there is also seldom a reward for good behavior.

Despite the lack of trust that can develop from this type of parenting, the mother's ties with her children run very deep. In times of family conflict, children are often more fearful of their father's anger than their mother's. In these instances a mother can act as a mediator between the father and the children. In fact, I know of three mothers who protected or forgave their adult children for becoming Christians, though not without conflict and until considerable time had passed. The children's awareness of favoritism and the mother's role as manipulator and mediator undoubtedly send mixed signals to the children. Growing up in an environment of unfulfilled promises and ulterior motives can hinder the child's ability to establish trusting relationships. When training new Christians it is important for them to see Christ's pure motives as our mediator between God and man in contrast to what they have experienced in their homes.

Influences of Religious Structure on Worldview

Islam, clan structure, and traditional customs give my host culture its bases for values, cohesion and security. While their culture is ostensibly based on Islam, most women in my host culture do not understand the teachings of Islam well even though they are Muslims. Their religious understanding is rather based on the example of their authorities, their fathers, husbands, uncles, and elder brothers, as well as on externals such as fasting, prayers, rites of passage, dietary and dress restrictions.

Additionally, while Muslim *imams* may be called upon to recite portions of the Qur'an over a sick family member or employed to curse a person's enemies, I have been told that women may be more involved in the spirit world than the officials. They can also seek relief or "guidance" from dubious practitioners whose main clientele are superstitious or otherwise afflicted people. Looking at the culture, thus, we could say that religious power and authority resides both with the Muslim *imams* and with the women.

While the power and authority of the Muslim *imam* is community-based and exercised through established authority in the mosque, women will engage in rituals and superstitious practices quietly within the family context. I remember being surprised to see a large knife in an infant's crib intended to ward off evil spirits and a new baby's face smeared with charcoal to hide its beauty from evil spirits. It is also common to see women place amulets around the wrists or ankles of small children for their protection.

Women's needs in the society are accommodated in religious rites and events. In a pre-birth ceremony, for example, a family might engage the *imam* to bless the delivery by pouring oil on the expectant mother's head. Another ceremony, occurring forty days after the baby's birth, is believed to instill the child with good morals. On the first day the child and mother can leave the house the baby will be carried by someone the parents admire and would like their baby to resemble in adulthood. The person carrying the baby will chant, "Walk as I walk, do as I do, be as I am" so the child will develop his habits. I have heard that children do tend to grow up like the individual who carried them out of the house.

Because they participate more frequently in mosque events where religious ideas are discussed, men may have more developed ideas about major world-view and religious concepts than women. They may be more able than women to answer questions on basic beliefs, their view of God, good and evil, the source of life and creation, and death. They may also be more familiar with religious perspectives on mankind, spirits, right and wrong, eternity, and securing con-verts or adherents than their wives. They may even be able to articulate the way that Islam views women better than the women. Women tend to agree. At the onset of a Bible study, two women told me that they wanted to study the Bible and Islam together so they could make an informed decision between the two.

This lack of understanding may be advantageous; when a Bible study begins in Genesis, I have found that women are pleasantly surprised at the similarities between the Old Testament stories and their understanding of Islam. Yet, some of the doctrinal issues that we gain from these stories will be new to them. While they agree that God is the all-powerful creator who has mercy on Adam and Eve, for instance, they do not know him as a personal God, nor do they realize the impact of their sin on their relationship with him. They may grasp the concept that God punishes sin but they do not recognize God's active role in drawing people to repentance and restoration (Miller 1992). Forgiveness for them is "dependent upon what man does rather than what God does, and man's deeds determine his destiny" (Ibid). Thus, they emphasize praying, fasting, giving to the poor, and other good deeds as a way to earn God's favor.

Women, like men, perceive God as the ultimate source of causation; they believe everything, both good and bad, comes from him (Ibid). This, however, creates a fatalistic attitude. I have heard women say they should not cry when grieving because that would imply disagreement with God's will. To them, God is a distant creator who keeps track of sins, punishes disobedience, and who *may* forgive when one repents. In their view, human beings were created weak, with little or no ability to overcome the desire to sin, and therefore with little responsibility for their sin (Miller 2001). This is especially significant in the story of Adam and Eve. As women study, they need to reconcile their Islamic beliefs that they were predestined to sin with the Christian belief that they are responsible for sin.

Along with other Muslims, women in our host culture view Christians as infidels who corrupted the *injil* and that people who deviate from Islam should be punished. This is certainly a barrier to the gospel. In Islam there is little opportunity for personal choice. This means, according to Miller, that Muslim women will need to break through psychological, social and theological barriers before they can accept the Bible as truth (Ibid). Psychologically, they will need to overcome the distaste of studying a religion that they consider inferior to Islam. They may also have to face social isolation and persecution if they believe it. Theologically, they must decide if they believe Jesus is a savior or a prophet; if he is God's Son or if God had no children; if forgiveness is obtained through faith or by works; if God is the Father, Son and Holy Spirit or if this is polytheism, and if Jesus had to die or if God could not have been defeated in death. When they do come to the point where they are willing to study the Bible, the familiarity of Old Testament stories can become a bridge, as I will explain later.

Influences of Social Structure on Worldview

In my host culture, an individual's place in the village society or community is important. Clan association and family heritage are traced through the father's lines; people are often able to recite their family genealogy over twenty-five generations. Within the clan, people are organized into clans, sub-clans, and families with most decisions being made by consensus. A study conducted by a sociology student in 1988 gives interesting insights into the value my host culture places on their clan. In this study, five graduate research assistants from five different clans asked individuals from their own clans a number of questions such as, "Which clans, do you think, are the most powerful clans?" "Which is the most numerous clan in relation to other clans?" and, "If you were the president, how would you distribute government posts among the clans?" The answers to these questions indicated clan ethnocentrism: 85 percent of the subjects said that their own clan was the most powerful and the most under-rated clan while 93 percent of the respondents indicated that their own clan was the most numerous. Ninety percent of the respondents, furthermore, indicated that they would give the 'lion's share' of the posts to their own clan or in-group. The author of this study, himself a member of the culture, says, "An important factor that appeared from the data is the defense of the kinsmen which means that (they) tend to give an unconditional support to their kinsmen without looking into the nature of the issue" (Ahmed 1988). This is one of the many manifestations of pride, a major characteristic of my host culture. Such clan loyalty could make it hard to accept members of another clan, particularly in a church context. This is an issue they really struggle with; I have heard accusations of tribalism launched against mature Christians in this regard.

The social structure will also impact how communication is facilitated within the group. My host culture is well known for its effective communication system. Historically nomadic, they developed an oral communication exchanging news between groups while watering their animals. Today, news is also passed quickly through radio programs, announcements in the mosque, internet, email, cell phones, and word of mouth. As one missionary said, "What is whispered in private tonight will be spread through the market tomorrow." Exploring the communication system will reveal that there are few secrets in this culture.

An ability to pass news rapidly can be both a barrier and a bridge for the gospel. Certainly, fear of being disclosed as a Christian creates an enormous barrier. It is said that there are three levels of persecution in the culture: persecution that originates from the government, from the local community, and persecution from the family. Governmental persecution, such as that found in China, can be averted by family or community protection and the underground church can still flourish. Persecution from members of the community, however, can be more difficult to avoid, especially in a culture where news travels widely in vast social networks. But the third level of persecution—that from the family—is the most difficult of all. Hindering seekers from even investigating Christianity, this concern for family honor, loyalty to Islam and fear of community criticism can stifle church growth. Because it is rare for individuals of my host culture to live alone, it is easy for family members to detect evidence of a Christian's faith. Fear of being discovered with a Bible is enough to keep some seekers or young Christians from even having one.

But just as their extensive communication system can hinder the gospel it can also provide a bridge. The people's ability to communicate orally facilitates the sharing of Bible stories even where Bibles are not available. Their interest in news motivates them to listen to the radio and Christian programs in their language. Even gossip can be a vehicle for evangelism. One woman wanted to study the Bible for five years but did not know who could help her. However, hearing gossip about a man who had become a Christian, she was able to find him as well as a woman to aid her in her study of the Bible.

The Influence of Worldview on Evangelism

Finally, the study of our culture's worldview, also made us more effective in evangelism and discipleship. First, our team concluded that evangelism is a process in our host culture. As Westerners we are used to a straightforward conversion experience, generally the result of a clear presentation of the gospel concluded with a prayer. This is possible within a culture where the gospel is acceptable and freely propagated. According to the Engel Scale, however, the people we work with have some understanding of cultural Christianity but no recognition of a personal need. As a consequence, they generally do not come to us ready to acknowledge their need for Jesus (Dayton 1981, 591). In fact, they believe that we are deceived pagans. Traditional gospel presentations, thus, have rarely produced fruit, perhaps because traditional presentations do not adequately help them to understand the gospel and its implications.

Muslim background believers from our host culture, in contrast, have understood their conversion as a process, one that begins with a willingness to question their Islamic beliefs and an openness to study Christianity. This is followed by the conviction that Christianity is true. Somewhere in this process there is a personal commitment to Christ. The testimony of one of our friends illustrates this process.

As a young man, our friend studied the Bible with a missionary and befriended his son. A frequent guest in their home and in another missionary's home, he was able to see authentic Christianity lived out before him. Unexpectedly, after ten years of contact with Christians, our friend became a Muslim fundamentalist. Since he could not reconcile the inconsistencies he saw in Islam with its ideals, he later concluded that Christianity was true. He joined a Christian fellowship, attended a local church, worked in a Christian mission office, and was a frequent guest in missionary homes. He considered himself to be a Christian. One day, however, when he was alone in his room he realized that although he believed Christianity was true, he had never confessed his sin and personally accepted Christ as his savior. That day he prayed "the sinner's prayer."

Others feel they became Christians at the start of their journey, when they first began their investigation of Christianity. One woman was in the midst of legal problems when she prayed, "Jesus, I don't know if you are real but if you are, please help me." From that humble beginning, she began reading a Bible and openly shared Bible stories with other women. Later she met a missionary who was able to disciple her and help her establish a firm basis for her faith using the chronological Bible study approach, but she maintained that she became a Christian when she first asked for help.

A third friend accepted a Christian invitation for prayer at a medical clinic. During that prayer time, a clear gospel presentation was given and she prayed to receive Christ. However, when she later met with a missionary for Bible study, she said that she wanted to study Christianity and Islam and make a decision between the two within a year. She may be "in process" but it is equally possible that the gospel presentation may not have adequately helped her understand the gospel and its implications for her life.

Knowing the worldview helps us know we need to come alongside these women as friends, living the Christian life before them while we adopt as much of their culture as possible. It will mean we want to make sure that our lives accurately portray of the Christian life, living out our faith even as we adopt local forms for prayer posture, hospitality, time orientation, relationships, and demonstrating compassion for others.

The Influence of Worldview on Discipleship

The goal of worldview understanding is to plant healthy, reproducing bodies of believers, or churches through effective evangelism and discipleship. Missionaries often describe this as presenting a gospel "that can be carried on the back of a camel." A number of years ago our team was rethinking our strategy for discipling Christians, looking for the most effective approach in light of their worldview. At the time we had some thirty-five people attending our fellowship group. The characteristic of the group, however, was in-fighting, suspicion, frequent requests for financial assistance and fear of persecution. The group had grown quickly, but we were not sure if all who attended were sincere in their faith. Few had been individually discipled.

As we considered the problems in our fellowship, it seemed that involving inquirers in individual discipleship and cell groups before they entered the large fellowship would provide both a means to screen out insincere people and an environment that would be more conducive for developing trusting relationships. This has been a model I have worked on with varying levels of success. Although I have discipled ladies, it is my goal that I will work myself out of a job as the women I disciple put their faith "on the back of a camel" and disciple others.

Individual discipleship is the starting point. It is not uncommon for a woman to request a Bible study when she is somewhere in between evangelism and discipleship or to come with ulterior motives. She may be trying to spy out our ministry or looking for monetary assistance. With these scenarios in mind, I meet each new lady as a "seeker" but hope she will actually be a disciple. Our first meeting takes place without any other national Christians present. This provides an opportunity for her to share her story, express interest in further spiritual growth, and for us to get to know each other. I have arranged these meetings in my home or in a neutral location such as an international school or a private restaurant where other members of her community will not see us. For security reasons, I don't share any information about other Christians or ministry activities at this time.

The objectives of this first meeting are to identify her genuine interest in Christianity, to explain the plan for Bible study, to assure her of confidentially and to begin to establish a relationship. I recommend that she does not tell others about her involvement in Bible study at this time. This is not to encourage secret believers or to encourage a woman to deny her faith but merely to encourage her to wait until she is able to explain what she is learning. Following the example of veteran missionaries in our ministry, I may also ask difficult questions such as, "How will your life change if you believe Christianity is true?" "How will a decision to be a Christian affect your relationship with your family, friends, and community?" and, "If your family rejects you, how will you provide for your financial needs?"

My attitudes definitely shape the discipleship relationship. If the woman is a sincere seeker, she will likely grow to be a member of my spiritual family. I will therefore need the same commitment that a mother must have to help her children. Since the believer will experience many ups and downs as she grows in Christ, furthermore, I need to be available to her, to listen and care for her and provide honest guidance and protection. I need to love her "like a mother" as in I Thessalonians, chapter two. As the relationship develops, I will encourage her to share personal issues by creating an atmosphere where she has the freedom to talk about her life. Thus, there are two aspects to my discipleship approach: consistent chronological Bible study and attention to personal issues. In her struggles with financial problems, grief over broken family relationships, fears from threats by Muslims (both real or anticipated), questions about the validity of Christianity, marital problems and other issues, I seek to be available to help her resolve these issues.

This does not mean that I will provide the solution to every problem, but I will be emotionally invested, sincerely praying, and encouraging her to seek God's answers for these issues. Even as I want her to turn to the Lord for help in times of need and recognize how the Lord provides for her, I expect to see her make mistakes and ask forgiveness, continuing to grow in Christ's likeness. I want her to see that the Christian life is a lifelong process filled with joys, victories, defeats and difficulties and I will try to always remember that she will learn this best by my example as we walk through experiences together.

If such a woman is interested in continued Bible study, my objective will be to establish a firm foundation for her faith. I will want her to personally understand the Bible chronologically, learning about God, sin, man, and redemption; experience a change of heart with a subsequent change in lifestyle; have an assurance of salvation; experience forgiveness, victory, answered prayer and spiritual fruit; become accountable to another Christian; realize she is a member of the body of Christ and value fellowship; cut her ties to folk practices; maintain relationships with her family and community; share her testimony and disciple others. I also hope she will understand God's attributes of holiness and love, our sinful human state and other crucial teachings based on biblical truth.

Around the time our team was writing up the worldview of our host culture, we saw the video, *Ee-Taow! The Mouk Story*, a New Tribes Mission presentation explaining the chronological approach that is used in the book "Building on Firm Foundations" (McIllwain 1999). One of our missionaries had been using the chronological approach for over twenty-five years and we felt this was the best approach we could use with members of our host culture (Zook 1989). The chronological method is culturally relevant because he begins on common ground with familiar people and stories, as is evident in another excellent video, "The Emmaus Road Connection" (Rodda 1993). By beginning on common ground where the lessons, principles, and individuals are similar to those in Islam, we can help build a bridge from Islam to Christianity, just as Jesus built a bridge for the disciples between Old Testament and New Testament concepts on the Emmaus Road.

In my use of the *Building on Firm Foundations* material I have adapted it slightly but basically I wait to introduce Christ until he is mentioned in Scripture. If someone asks questions about him, I tell her we will learn about him in later lessons, keeping in pace with the progressive revelation of the gospel message and allowing her to have a foundation with which to understand Christ's ministry. Knowing the worldview she comes from, I'm especially sensitive to stories about women who have been treated unjustly (Hagar), redeemed from brokenness (Rahab), grieved (Eve), and barren (Sarah). I know that Christ's words, "no one who has left home or brothers or sisters or mothers or fathers ...will fail to receive a hundred times as much in this present age ...and with them persecutions ...and in the age to come, eternal life" (Mark 10:29) will be especially powerful to her. Some lessons require a stronger emphasis on issues relevant to Muslim Background Believers such as the apparent plurality of God that is raised in the creation story, the story of the virgin birth, and the blessing falling in the line of Isaac. A discussion about Satan and the demonic is also important because of her culture's folk Islamic practices.

I try to create an atmosphere that will not intimidate her and keep her from feeling confident that she can disciple others in the same approach. Therefore I do not use Bible study books or handouts. However, I have typed up notes from the book for my own reference. When they have finished the study, the ladies are given a list of scripture references for each lesson so they can use them with other women. Because they are far less dependent on written notes that I am, I think this is sufficient but on a few occasions we have reviewed the lessons the women will teach others. We read the scripture in its entirety to keep a story format appropriate for oral learners, then discuss highlights and ask questions after the story is well established.

Initial discipleship begins with a one-on-one relationship. Bible studies must thus be more than a weekly meeting that takes place on the sofa. Ideally I will set aside three times a week with part of the time devoted to Bible study and several more hours for mentoring as we cook together, play with children and shop for groceries. As she sees me in my natural environment, I trust she will see the Christian life in practice even as I fulfill my responsibilities to my own family.

Although we start with a one-on-one relationship, my goal is always to get these seeking women into a cell group and eventually into a fellowship setting. Remembering her worldview, it is easy to see why power struggles, lack of trust, fear of persecution and limited exposure to healthy churches severely cripple a woman's ability to connect easily with other believers. Although it has not occurred often in my ministry, I have tried to follow a cell group or house church approach (Evan 1997). Cell groups can be reproduced locally, can be underground, do not require large buildings or programs, and are personal, developing as individuals are discipled one on one (Scoggins 1997). After believers have learned how to function as a cell group, cell disciples can be introduced to the larger fellowship. Although this is a labor-intensive model that requires a significant investment of time and emotional energy, it seems to work well with their worldview. With diligence and prayer, the gospel can be "placed on the back of a camel" and carried deep into their country where missionaries are not able to go.

Identifying the worldview of our host culture is intensive and time consuming but it can greatly increase our effectiveness in ministry. By creating an environment that enables us to get close to our host culture, we can identify the impact of family, social, religious, economic and national political structures on Muslim women. Instruments are available to guide us as we interview members of our host culture and to help us organize what we observe. As we understand their worldview, we can learn what bridges can help us be more effective in evangelism and discipleship and we can disciple them in a way they can use to disciple others. May God enable us to put this good news on the back of a camel!

REFERENCES

Ahmed, Mohamed Hussein. 1988. A study of inter-clan relations. M.A. thesis, Mogadishu.

Brewster, Thomas, and Elizabeth S. Brewster. 1976. *Language acquisition made practical: Field methods for language learners*. Lingua House.

Dayton, Edward R. 1981. To reach the unreached. In *Perspectives on the world Christian movement*, ed. Ralph D. Winter and Steven C. Hawthorne. Pasadena: William Carey Library.

Evans, W. 1997. Advantages of house churches. *Seedbed* 7: 4.

Johnstone, Patrick, and Mandryk, Jason. 2001. *Operation world*. Waynesboro, GA: Paternoster.

McIllwain, Trevor. 1999. *Building on firm foundations*. Sanford, FL: New Tribes Mission.

Miller, John G. 1992. Analysis of the ***** worldview. Unpublished manuscript for DMS 880: Worldview Change, Trinity Evangelical Divinity School.

_____. 2001. The preparation of a manual to train others in Muslim evangelism. Ph.D. diss., Trinity International University.

Rodda, David. 1993. *The Emmaus road connection*. Produced and directed by New
    Tribes Mission. 55 min. Videocassette.
Scoggins, Dick. 1997. House churches in the Muslim world. *Seedbed* 7:4.
Slack, Jim. 1994. Constructing a worldview: A cultural-social-religious profile of target
    people, a development process and instrument. Richmond, VA: Foreign Mission
    Board, Southern Baptist Convention.
Zook, Mark, and Gloria Zook. 1989. *Ee-Taow*. Produced and directed by New Tribes
    Mission. 60 min. Videocassette

7

Offering Bread Not Stones: Reaching Educated Arabic-Speaking Women

Farah Al Hasd

The educated, Arabic-speaking woman is intelligent, resourceful and often well-versed in the Qur'an. At the same time, she may trust in folk healers and be concerned with the evil eye. In this article, Farah Al Hasd uses familiar Arab worldview categories to compare and contrast aspects of the educated Middle Eastern woman's worldview with the worldview of an educated Western woman, providing insights into how these women can be reached for Christ.

"Which of you, if his son asks for bread, will give him a stone?" (Matt. 7:9 NIV)

Joumana's Story

Joumana ran into her youngest son's bedroom in answer to his screams. Another nightmare! She attempted to calm him down, to soothe his fears and eventually Ahmed fell into a troubled sleep that was still marked by desperate tossing and turning.

She sighed. How many times had Ahmed had these nightmares? She had lost count. He was such a little boy—barely a year old. She and Lou'ay had tried all the remedies that both their families had suggested, and not one of them had really worked. Some had brought temporary relief; others only seemed to make Ahmed's sleep worse. Joumana was at her wit's end. Suddenly she straightened up—she had made a decision. They would go visit that 'man of God.' It was said that he was very powerful and whatever he suggested worked. She had resisted this decision, knowing or perhaps fearing the cost, the demands it might make on their lives. Yet, the more Joumana thought about it, the stronger her determination grew. So, the day came. Lou'ay and Joumana both took Ahmed to see 'the man of God'. He lived in their city, but traced his roots to Morocco. The process took a while, but not as long as both had anticipated. The 'man of God' asked them a lot of questions about their family names and zodiac signs and then worked out some calculations. The results were very negative. The solution he suggested was to change Ahmed's name. At first Lou'ay and Joumana resisted, but the 'man of God' insisted it was the only way. He even suggested that they name their son, Ayman, after his son. They agreed.

That same night, they put their little boy to bed. "Ayman, go to sleep. Everything will be all right now." They tiptoed out hardly daring to believe he would sleep peacefully through night. They prayed for some time and then waited anxiously. After a while they tiptoed in quietly, but Ayman was sleeping, his breathing soft and even. One hour went by, two hours, three—still nothing, no anguished cries or sounds came from Ayman's room. Ayman experienced the same quiet peaceful sleep night after night. Now he is four and a half years old and has never had any reoccurrences with disrupted sleep. What a miracle! What relief!

Living in the midst of an urban teeming sea of Muslim women, I look into the faces of each one and one question after another runs through my mind. Where do I start? How do I begin to know them? What is their culture like? How do they perceive reality? What is the connection between belief, faith and practice in their daily lives? How do they cope when problems arise? How can I best communicate the good news of Jesus Christ?

IDENTIFYING WORLDVIEW

We who work among Arabic-speaking Muslim women need to equip ourselves to best translate the message of the gospel to the women we are reaching. We need to know not only how to identify a Muslim woman's worldview, but also to understand the influence of folk beliefs. Having discovered her view of reality, we must also know the barriers that will prevent her from understanding the gospel. Then, with the knowledge that we have gained of worldview and stumbling blocks, we must determine the bridges that will enable our Muslim friend to come to an understanding of the gospel and the offer of life that is found in Jesus Christ. The following categories will help us as we compare and contrast aspects of the educated Middle Eastern Muslim woman's worldview with the worldview of an educated Western woman.

Time

A central aspect of worldview is time. Western people have a fundamentally different concept of time than people from the Middle East. Take the simple example of a dinner invitation. When my mother in the United States invites friends for dinner, she has learned to expect them at the appointed time, at 5:30 p.m. for example. If they come a few minutes late, she is not worried. After ten minutes, however, her anxiety level will start to rise and will increase with each passing minute that the guests do not arrive.

Easterners, on the other hand, are much more relaxed about time. They do not feel the same sense of pressure to mark time or assess how fast it passes. They are often prepared to wait long hours, whether it is at the airport seeing someone off or going from one office to another to get an official's signature. According to Bill Musk, this is because our values for time are different. For the Middle Easterner, being on time or in a hurry communicates a lack of self-esteem. Punctuality is for those who serve others; servants have less dignity because they are fulfilling the commands of a higher authority. Anyone with self-respect does not accept being controlled by others and so learns a different orientation to time (Musk 1995, 112).

Since time is not 'of the essence' in Middle Eastern society, interruptions are not frowned upon or seen as sources of frustration. Rather, they are enjoyed and thought of as the highlights of the day. When we as Westerners go shopping or visit government offices, we are often dismayed at the "time we waste" if an official is absent or when we have to interrupt our schedule to greet people, drink tea, and tell a few jokes because our sense of order is disrupted (Musk 1995, 113).

How can this clash of cultures help us? First, simply acknowledging and understanding the differences in our worldviews can help us be more accepting and patient when we experience cultural conflict. Thus, my mother's guests should find out what her expectations are for her guests and act accordingly even as we should explore the expectations that our hosts have for their guests in the Middle East. Secondly, we must remember that we come as learners to our host country. We are not there to change the way their society is run. Instead we must learn to adapt to their ways of thinking and behaving so that we can better gain their trust and respect. Thirdly, we can explore the beliefs of our friends by asking questions —lots of them! Our friends will feel honored at our interest and will give us a better hearing when they do not feel threatened by our supposedly superior Western ways.

Recently, for instance, I made a four-hour visit to an Arab friend's house with two of my friends. By the end of the visit, I felt quite tired for several reasons— I made the visit after working, it was hot, and everything was conducted in Arabic, with some translation. I was ready to go home and relax! In my point of view, I felt that a four-hour visit was long enough. However, to the family I visited, it seemed like we had just arrived. In their eyes it was not right for us to leave so soon. They had not had their "fill of us," whereas we were ready to call it a day and leave. Identifying and understanding the value of time in Arab culture, will help us go that second and third mile if that is what Jesus requires of us. Jesus came unto his own as one who served his people and poured out his life for them. We must do likewise in giving of ourselves and our time to those women that we serve.

Relationships

Another area of difference between the East and West is in the area of relationships, particularly as they relate to hospitality. In the West we consider our homes a place of retreat. "A man's home is his castle," we say. Therefore, we usually do not drop in on each other uninvited for fear of imposing or interrupting the host. If someone does drop in on us and we want to discourage them from staying long, we might not even offer them a cup of coffee or tea.

To Arabs and other Middle Easterners, however, generous hospitality is a matter of pride and honor. "*Baytna, baytik*," our home is your home, they say. It is not unknown for them to go into debt to give the best that they can to their guests. A Muslim woman is taught the importance of hospitality from childhood. Even children delight to help serve. If you drop in on a friend, you will be ushered to the visitor's room, if there is one, and within a very short time served something to drink. If you come in the late afternoon and have not eaten, then what was set aside for tomorrow's meal may be cooked and served to you because it is a shame to offer a guest just leftovers. If you do not eat enough, their feelings will be hurt and they will tell you that you do not love them. They delight to serve and want to be sure that their guests are happy and comfortable. These are great lessons in generosity for us as Westerners to learn from our Muslim sisters!

Space

Another important value relates to the use of personal space. In Middle Eastern society, "'space' is not a very important commodity"(Musk 1995, 125). Many homes do not have a lot of space to spare as most families live in crowded towns and cities. For a family of five, therefore, there may only be one bedroom, which is generally reserved for the parents. The children will sleep in the living or family room. 'Home' is more about family and family interaction than about space and personal possessions. It is people, not things or space, which make up a 'home' (Musk 1995, 125-126).

Our "arms' length" policy in the West is also greatly challenged when we travel to the East. According to Edward Hall, a Westerner typically stands about four or five feet away during casual conversations or talks that include politics, local matters, recent vacations, the weather—public conversations that anyone can join. This area is called the Social Distance. If we want to speak on a more intimate basis, however, we will lower our voices and move closer together into a Personal Distance, somewhere from one to three feet away (Hall 1982, 119-123).

These differences in personal space may help explain why a Westerner feels more uncomfortable the more he gets to know an Arab. According to Musk, Arabs like to talk loudly and face to face with little space between them. They are uncomfortable with our Western attempts to keep them at arms' length and so will try to get closer to us. In turn, we feel uncomfortable being so close to a person that we can actually smell their breath. Living in an Arab society, we become quickly aware of the physical contact Arabs have with one another. We see men holding hands or linking arms with other men while women hold hands with other women. For Arabs this intimacy is an important affirmation of who he or she is as a human being, while for Westerners it is too close for comfort (Musk 1995, 127). While it may take some time to get used to this degree of physical contact, we must be careful not to be repulsed and draw away. Rather, we must learn to appreciate it as a demonstration of their regard for us as persons they care about.

Purity

One of the most important assumptions of the Middle Eastern worldview is that I must interact with God and with others in terms of purity. Because God demands purity, for instance, Muslims must be as clean as possible before they can perform the ritual *salat* (prayer). They must repeat the same ritual ablutions, washing the hands, wrists, the nose, face, ears, head, ankles and feet, every time they pray (Chapman 1995, 64). I have observed that Muslim women usually pray at home or at work rather than at the mosque, but during their menstrual period—they are not permitted to pray or even touch the Qur'an because of their impurity—they believe that God refuses to hear them. Every time they miss prayer and fasting, however, it adds to their spiritual obligations. This means that women are always spiritually "in arrears," trying to catch up on their lost days of prayer and fasting but always falling short of what God requires (Cate 2002, 145). One of my friends said this was such an issue she was even angry with God for imposing such a law.

Chastity or the preservation of a girl's virginity is also a matter of purity in a Muslim woman's world. Some countries still practice female circumcision as a means to ensure a girl's virginity until she gets married. Other places have much less stringent rules, but a woman's purity is evidence of the concern and length that her male relatives have gone to in order to protect their investment in her (Musk 1995, 28). This is such an important issue that in at least one country I know, a girl may decide to have an operation to repair her hymen before she gets married so that she can still appear to be a virgin on her wedding night.

Even after marriage, a woman has a huge responsibility to remain sexually faithful as a means of maintaining her husband's honor. A man is vulnerable to losing his honor and depends upon his women to protect it through their purity. Thus, a wife must be free from any hint of unfaithfulness throughout her married life. Since men who are not within the woman's circle of *mahram* relationships, i.e., those men with whom sexual relationships would be considered incestuous are potential sexual threats. Access to them must be carefully controlled because of the fear of the threat becoming a reality. Depending on the man, the response to any whisper of a woman family member being involved in extra-marital relationships can be very exacting. The community may often overlook such hardness (Musk 1995, 29-32). Even local sitcoms deal with this issue. In one episode, a married woman (with her husband's knowledge) contributed to the household expenses by dancing for mixed group parties. The brother of this married woman found out and severely beat her and her husband. Even honor killings are not unheard of today.

Folk Beliefs

Finally, folk beliefs are also an important aspect of worldview. Depending on the area, Muslim women may or may not know the basic foundational truths and practices of Islam. As children, for instance, they may have attended Islamic classes in public school, memorizing many verses of the Qur'an, Hadith and proverbs. They may have memorized the common objections to the Trinity, to Jesus as the Son of God and his crucifixion, to the corruption and mistakes in the Scriptures, the failure to recognize Muhammad as a prophet and his foretelling in the Bible. Some Muslim women will quote verses memorized from the Qur'an in their discussions with workers. Despite this knowledge of orthodoxy, however, educated Muslim women may still turn in moments of crisis to beliefs and practices that Westerners would consider "folk beliefs."

Many of us have prepared ourselves in various ways to deal with the reality of Islam which as a major religion has its own answers to the questions of what ultimate truth is and how it provides meaning in life. However, we are somehow astonished at the degree that folk religious practices such as magic, astrology, witchcraft and spirit worship influence Arabic-speaking Muslim women in their attempts to deal with the problems of everyday life. Omens, oracles, men of God, and prophets provide guidance to people facing uncertain futures. Rituals and medicines are used to counterbalance such catastrophes such as droughts, earthquakes, floods, and plagues as well to ensure successful marriages, child conception, and a prosperous business (Hiebert 1985, 222).

The "evil eye" is a common phenomenon in the Muslim world. This ornamental jewelry can be seen in many places—in homes, as necklaces, and often in the inside of taxis and buses swinging from the rear view mirror. When a baby is born, a turquoise stone set in gold is attached to the baby's clothes to protect its health and keep it from evil spirits. The educated younger generation may not place great faith in its protective powers and regard it simply as decoration, but it is still done because the older generation puts on the pressure to stick to traditional ways. Still others do so with a "just in case this really does work" attitude.

There is a varied depth of interest in astrology or divination based on the supposed influence of the stars on human events. Women when getting to know one another will quickly ask each other what zodiac sign they were born under. They say it is "just for fun and entertainment," but an underlying seriousness in the subject can often be detected. They will attempt to know what the future holds through reading coffee cups or tea leaves and palm reading. "I am just curious to know what my future holds," is a common comment. "I don't really believe in it," they may say, "it is harmless entertainment," but the desire to know is there.

In some homes "a cup of terror," a metal cup made of silver or brass, can be found. While some have a Qur'anic verse engraved on the outside, others have pictures of flowers and usually a mosque. Anyone in the home might drink from it, especially if they are anxious about some issue, they have had a nightmare, or they have a test. Drinking from this cup is meant to alleviate their fears and anxiety. Writing Qur'anic verses is also a common practice:

> In some areas when a person is sick, a verse will be written in ink or sandalwood paste on a plate or on the inside of a basin. The container will then be filled with water, which dissolves the writing. The water is poured into a glass and given to the patient to drink. Another method is to write the words of the Qur'an on a piece of paper and wash them off into a glass of water. Or, even more simply, an imam recites from the Qur'an and then breathes over a container of water which is then given to the sick person to drink. (Cooper 1985, 154)

Qur'anic verses may also be found in a man's jacket. If the wife wants to protect her husband from evil and wish him prosperity in business, she will write out a Qur'anic verse and sew it into his jacket. These verses can also be used as curses or charms. I once heard the story of a woman who noticed that her husband's behavior had changed toward her. After puzzling over it, she called in an *imam* to search her house. He found a charm with a Qur'anic verse on it. An acquaintance, jealous of this woman's wonderful relationship with her own husband, had put a curse on their relationship. The imam made a counter charm, and the relationship returned to normal.

IDENTIFYING BARRIERS

Sounding the depths of a Muslim woman's worldview requires time, energy, and prayerful discernment. But the knowledge and understanding we gain will help us uncover the issues that are preventing her from hearing, understanding and responding to the love of God in Jesus Christ. These issues or barriers are not the same for every Muslim woman. As we prayerfully get to know each woman individually, we will begin to recognize the barriers that are keeping her from faith. We must examine each of these barriers in the light of God's Word so that we will know and stand in the truth. Then we must ask God for wisdom and discernment to understand the best ways to break down the barriers in our friend's life. Some common barriers among Arabic-speaking Muslim women include the following.

Folk Beliefs

Folk beliefs prevent women from understanding and responding to the truth. While some are interested in hearing what we have to say, others are very adamant that their worldview is correct. In fact, one worker has observed that a major barrier is the way in which Muslim women tend to reinforce the beliefs and practices of Islam. This could be due partly to the fact that women as mothers have a strongly defined role in the home and partly because we all tend to fall back on what we have been taught. When discussing male and female roles, Bill Musk makes some interesting observations. He comments on our amazement when we see it is women, not men, who fight for a return to the more traditional ways as has been evidenced in Iran, Egypt or Pakistan. For example, a lot of Muslim women choose to wear the veil because of the honor it gives them in public settings (Musk 1995, 27).

Denial of Sin

At first glance, because both Christians and Muslims are aware of sin and its effects, it may seem that the concept of sin is not a problem. On the contrary, the denial of original sin in Islam is a major barrier to understanding of the gospel. A Muslim woman must realize the bad news about herself before the good news can be truly meaningful. Phil Parshall tells us that Muslims do not see sin as being inherited. Because Adam and Eve were free to choose, they could either walk in God's ways or succumb to the voice of Satan. A Muslim refuses the idea that the choice that Adam and Eve made affects him now. If he sins, it is his own individual choice (Parshall 1989, 120). In talking with Muslim women, it is easy to get frustrated at their apparent blindness and refusal to acknowledge that our sin nature was passed on down to us from Adam. "We have white hearts," they tell us. "How you can possibly say that my child is a sinner? He is innocent." Even mature women affirm that they have not done anything wrong in their lives. Their sense of self-righteousness and seeming pride in their goodness and ability to do good works makes us shudder for them on the Day of Judgment.

Fear of Divorce and Gossip

Another important stumbling block for women in the Muslim world is fear that manifests itself in many forms. Because they live in a patriarchal society that is run by men, Muslim women are subject to their fathers, uncles, brothers and husbands. They often must do what they are told or there are consequences to pay. Many don't want to "rock the boat." When they do, they can be ostracized. Thus, fear can keep a woman so locked up within her own system of belief that she is incapable of responding to the gospel unless those chains are broken.

What is a Muslim woman afraid of? The fear of gossip is strong. Appearances are of paramount importance. Not only is outward beauty extolled, but one's reputation and honor are to be guarded as well. One woman I know was afraid of a colleague at work who had taken her picture with a man. She was afraid that this would somehow get back to her father and then there would be "hell to pay." This fear of others talking about them behind their back fosters an attitude and spirit of distrust and lying. Even if a woman is spiritually open, the fear of others gossiping about her can keep her from taking positive steps to read or study the Bible. Many are afraid of the future, whether it is in school, at work, or regarding marriage. Women are very concerned about either getting married to the right man or once married, about divorce and especially about losing their children. In his chapter on women, Phil Parshall states that there is a strong fear of divorce. It is the husband who most often will tell the woman that he is divorcing her. As a result, a woman suffers from disgrace and a sense of failure for the society regards her as having displeased her husband in some way. Because of this fear, women put up with a lot of abuse and unkind treatment in order to stay married (Parshall 1994, 170). I can testify that divorce is a reality that women must consider. Quite a few of my friends have been divorced; one after only a month. Another was married and moved to the United States, only to have a bad car accident that disfigured her face. Her husband convinced her to return to her home country with its Muslim divorce laws and the very next day he divorced her.

Language Differences

Language can also prevent us from understanding one another. If I, as a worker living overseas, do not attempt to learn the language of the women I am trying to reach, then my attempts to minister will not be as effective. When we do learn our host culture's language, the appreciation we get is enormous. "We are honored that you want to speak how we speak, so we must help you as much as we can," was the comment my friend made. She did me the honor of being patient with me and speaking in Arabic even though she was anxious to learn and improve her English as well. Another factor to consider is not just learning the language, but knowing it from the inside. Many times we may know the literal meanings of words, but often we miss the deeper meanings and nuances that are present in their language, idioms, puns, proverbs and jokes. We must also not forget that the words said might not be received in the same way that they are intended, that is, we must be careful to be receptor oriented. For example, the most common meaning of the word "ma'lesh" that I learned was "Never mind; it's okay." However, when it was said about a woman worker who was in the process of losing her baby, it caused major misunderstandings as it sounded so uncaring! Finally, and perhaps most importantly, the use and understanding of religious language can be a major barrier that prevents a Muslim woman from understanding and responding to the gospel. Because it is easy to talk to Muslims about God and we use a lot of the same kinds of words, we can get caught into the trap of thinking that we are communicating well. We use 'God,' 'sin,' 'heaven,' 'hell,' 'creation,' 'grace,' 'mercy,' 'justice' and other terms. Superficially, it may seem like we are getting across to our friends, but we must be careful to ascertain what they believe about these concepts.

We will encounter many different kinds of barriers with each Muslim woman that we befriend. Each one will have her own special set of difficulties to overcome. But, however many barriers we encounter in a Muslim woman's life, we can claim the truths of God's Word. God promises that His Word is useful for teaching, rebuking, correcting and training in righteousness. As we wield the Sword of the Spirit against every hindrance and wrong belief that sets itself up against the knowledge of God, God Himself can help us overcome barriers and find those bridges of understanding that will bring our Muslim woman friends closer to Himself and into the kingdom of God.

IDENTIFYING BRIDGES

In our everyday world we construct bridges to get ourselves across a gap, a river, or a ravine. So, too, in our understanding of a Muslim woman's worldview, we must search for and build bridges. These will enable us to cross the barriers that we have learned about in each woman's life.

The first and foremost bridge that we need to build and keep building is love. God so loved Muslim women that He sent Jesus to become flesh and dwell among them. Jesus is our prime example of what it means to die to self in order for fruit to spring forth and to cross barriers and create bridges to reach into their hearts. We are to follow Jesus' footsteps in incarnating the gospel. He calls us to go beyond our comfort zones. Living with a local family or in the university residences is a "fishbowl" experience in which all that we say and do is commented upon, analyzed and criticized. Yet, if we want to show and offer these women a "new and living way" (Hebrews 10:20), we must submit ourselves to such intense scrutiny while allowing Jesus to live out His life through us.

Second, implicit in love is kindness, which is not only a fruit of the Holy Spirit but also a tangible way for us to bridge the gap enabling a woman to understand and respond to the gospel. A friend of mine was in a fair bit of pain from her swollen feet as she was in her last month of pregnancy. My praying for her when she was visiting me at home brought tears to her eyes. Later, I visited her with another worker who gave her a foot massage. Her appreciation was overwhelming and she remarked, "You are better than my sister. Doing such a thing would not have occurred to her."

Muslims, and Arabs in particular, are very sensitive souls. Relationships mean the world to them. Thus, if they accept me as their friend, then certain expectations are placed upon me. Woe to me if I am found lacking. Just the simple act of remembering their birthdays is a big deal for it lets our Muslim friends know that we care about them as people. In fact, any occasion which concerns them, such as looking for and getting a job, school marks, graduation, breaks in family and friend relationships, or a death, is worth our time and attention.

A third bridge would be relationships. The more time we spend with our Muslim women friends, the better we will understand their worldview, and the better we will be able to reach them at their point of need and correct their beliefs about God, the world and themselves. Since time is not "money" in their culture but is all about being in relationship, we must pour ourselves out for their sakes. It is important to listen to God and learn from Him which women He wants us to spend our time with. Jesus often spent all day—sometimes going without food—to minister to the needs around Him.

Naturally, as we take part in the lives of our Muslim friends, we can use religious occasions as a fourth way to build bridges. We can inform them as soon as possible about our own belief in God and our daily relationship to Him. We need to exalt Jesus Christ and lift Him up as often as we can. The other day I was visiting a friend who is not that open to the gospel. When I mentioned what I had read about The Sermon on the Mount and Jesus' standard about our thought life, this woman acknowledged how difficult it was to keep God's standard. This in turn, launched a short discussion about the heart. Their festivals and ceremonies, Ramadan, the Eid al Fitr and Eid al Adhan are always great occasions to ask questions and share the biblical perspective.

A fifth bridge is telling stories. In recent years much has been said and taught about storying and Chronological Bible Storying. I endorse it as an effective bridge-builder. At the start of our language learning we can begin to learn Bible stories in the native language. That way we'll be ready to tell them as the occasion demands. God promises that His Word will not return void, but it will accomplish His purposes of salvation. Some time ago, I visited a friend at her office. We were talking about improving ourselves in general and learning Spanish in particular. This prompted me to tell her Jesus' parable about the talents, which suitably impressed her. It is also helpful to tell the Genesis account of creation and the Fall since it leads to good discussions through which you will quickly discover your friend's point of view. One day, telling this story to a man and his wife with another worker, we ran into opposition from the wife. She did not want to believe that Eve was the first to disobey.

Another crucial aspect of bridge building is contextualization. When God crossed the barrier from heaven to earth, He came as the Word who dwelt among us. Although there is a lot of debate concerning contextualization, to me Jesus was and remains the greatest example of contextualization that has ever been achieved. Contextualization "includes the total matrix of society which embraces the social patterns of a people, their economic policies, politics, and a host of other integrative areas" (Cooper 1985, 186). Paul is another great model on which we can base our attempts to cross cultural, religious, and theological barriers in order to win Muslim women to Christ.

Christine Mallouhi, in her book, *Mini-skirts, Mothers, and Muslims*, gives very helpful advice on ways to be contextual, especially with regard to male and female role-models. She illustrates how Christians who live in Muslim contexts can model spiritual (biblical) values. Mallouhi deals with issues like how does a female dress and behave in public? Why does Christian 'fellowship' need to have precedence over 'teaching'? Her insights challenge us to demonstrate biblical values in ways that a Muslim can best understand.

Barriers cannot be crossed without the construction of bridges. As servants of the living God, we must extend the love and understanding that will draw Muslim women to a personal knowledge of God through Jesus Christ. We need to constantly be on the alert as to how God would have us combat the various hindrances that keep our Muslim friends in bondage and build bridges that would enable them to embrace the good news that awaits them.

EFFECTIVE STRATEGIES, MODELS, METHODS AND RESOURCES

In conclusion, I would like to summarize a number of resources that will help us develop effective strategies in our work with Muslim women. First, there are numerous resources that deal with building relationships with women. Books such as Cate and Downey's, *From Fear to Faith* have many good articles on how to start building relationships with women. Moreover, God has blessed us with gifts, talents and interests, however great or small, that we are to use in our ministry. God does not despise the day of small beginnings, nor will He refuse to use whatever we have to offer. In fact, He warns us not to bury our talent in the ground, even if we only have one. God expects some interest back! God has used my talents in numerous ways. I am not talented musically, for instance, but I love listening to music. I have found sharing music to be a great way to learn about my Muslim friends as is listening to their music and learning to dance with them. These activities give them pleasure and communicate that we care about them in ways they understand. I have also developed a reputation for cooking and baking. I once made a carrot cake for a friend who asked for the recipe. Now she makes it for her circle of friends who in turn have asked her for it. She has made the recipe her own by creatively adapting it to her own taste. What does this have to do with sharing the gospel? Jesus says that if we even give a glass of water in His name, He takes note of it and blesses us. We are to share and give freely of whatever we have been given. I have also taken my cross-stitch projects with me to my friends' homes to work on during visits. This has stimulated them to want to learn how to do it for themselves. During our visits, thus, they have also made something useful and pretty for their homes.

Second, we must communicate truth to our Muslim friends in understandable ways. None of us can communicate the love of God through the face of Jesus Christ without the help of the Holy Spirit. Thank God that when we ask Him for bread, He does not give us a stone! Instead when we ask for wisdom, He gives it to us generously. I believe it is important that we know where our Muslim woman friend is coming from. Within Islam there are many ways of looking at and interpreting beliefs. A basic example is the question of the *hijab* or head covering; Muslim women have different convictions about whether it should be worn or not. What is essential is how we use this religious outward form to talk about spiritual issues. We may ask her why she covers her head, but also push her further to wonder about her heart and how even her thoughts are exposed before God.

I always try to start with women where they are and lead them further into truth. This is why I believe in chronological storying and telling stories in general. Finding out what they believe about creation and Adam and Eve, for instance, is important for then I can tell the same story but from the biblical point of view. It seems that most women have a scant knowledge of what the Bible actually says. Above all, we must do everything in love, not having an argumentative spirit, but instead being a good, gentle and patient listener.

Third, we must seek to enable their response to Christ and to start viable, self-multiplying groups. Only the Holy Spirit can bring a woman from darkness into light; there must be conviction of sin in order for a person to see their need of a Saviour. But, we need to remember that we are introducing the message of Jesus into a culture that is not our own. We must learn from the mistakes of the past when Western workers tried to impose their Western culture, customs, and therefore, their particular brand of Western Christianity on a culture and people whose worldview was different. God has allowed many different cultures to develop and He wants to redeem those elements of each culture that do not measure up to His standards of righteousness. Jesus says we are to be the "salt of the earth" and the "light of the world." As Muslim women come to Christ and mature in Him, their respective cultures will inevitably change.

Our task is to take the gospel and make it as clear and understandable as we possibly can within each Muslim woman's context and worldview. We need to offer the gospel as a better and more excellent way than the one that a Muslim woman currently follows. We must demonstrate how the gospel will meet her needs in permanent life-changing ways. Since we desire men and women to come to Christ, we need to be willing to change our lifestyles, cultural practices and even our corporate worship to communicate these truths (Cooper 1985, 187-188). We must be sure that our behavior and external ways of doing things are not so offensive that the people we are ministering to are turned off and cannot hear the good news we profess to have. When a Muslim woman does come to Christ, we need to provide an environment of love and acceptance. We must not neglect to disciple her but must enable her to become a strong mature believer who will not turn back no matter how strong the winds of persecution and hostility blow. We need to stand with her no matter what the cost to us.

Finally, we can strive to use resources, methods and materials more effectively. As workers, we are grateful for the numerous resources that have been developed and are now available on reaching Muslims for Christ. Annette Hall's development of "Chronological Bible Stories," for instance, is extremely helpful and useful. The book, *All That the Prophets Have Spoken*, is a good tool for women interested in an historical and biblical idea of the gospel. *A Pictorial Panorama of the Bible* is also of benefit in discussions and *The Discovery Series Bible Studies* can be used with women who are open and hungry. Finally, *A Sufi Reading of Genesis*, as well as copies of the Gospels of John and Luke are wonderful gifts to give to families.

Studying worldviews is crucial to understanding Muslim women and providing an appropriate response. As we identify the barriers that hinder the gospel's presentation and trust in God for His guidance, we will discover the bridges that will enable us to satisfy Muslim women with the Bread of Life.

REFERENCES

Bennett, Shane, and Kim Felder, with Steve Hawthorne. 1995. *Exploring the land: Discovering ways for unreached people to follow Christ.* Littleton, CO: Caleb Project.

Cate, Mary Ann, and Karol Downey. 2002. *From fear to faith: Muslim and Christian women.* Pasadena: William Carey Library.

Chapman, Colin. 1995. *Cross and crescent: Responding to the challenge of Islam.* London: InterVarsity Press.

Cooper, Anne. 1985. *Ishmael my brother: A biblical course on Islam.* Monrovia: MARC.

Eade, Alfred Thompson. 1961. *The expanded panorama Bible study course.* Grand Rapids, MI: Revell.

Hall, Edward T. 1982. *The hidden dimension.* New York: Anchor Books.

_____. 1985. *Anthropological insights for missionaries.* Grand Rapids: Baker Book House.

Kraft, Charles H. 1979. *Christianity in culture.* Maryknoll: Orbis Books.

Mallahouli, Christine. 1994. *Mini-skirts, mothers and Muslims.* Carlisle, U.K.: OM Publishing.

Musk, Bill A. 1995. *Touching the soul of Islam: Sharing the gospel in Muslim cultures.* Crowborough, UK: MARC

Parshall, Phil. 1988. *The cross and the crescent: Understanding the Muslim mind and heart.* Amersham-on-the-Hill, UK: Scripture Press.

_____. 1994. *Inside the community: Understanding Muslims through their traditions.* Grand Rapids: Baker Books.

Sa'a, Yehia. 2001. *All that the prophets have spoken.* Hayden, ID: GoodSeed International.

8

How Will They Hear?
Reaching the Muslim Women of Sub-Saharan Africa

LaNette W. Thompson

Ministry strategies in Sub-Saharan Africa have often focused on Muslim men, assuming that women would be reached through the significant men in their lives. This has not happened. LaNette Thompson examines the identities of Sub-Saharan West African Muslim women and finds that their security and significance is bound by complex societal relationships. She identifies multiple barriers that prevent these women from understanding the gospel message and suggests ways to make the gospel relevant.

I will never forget the tears flowing down the old man's cheeks at the funeral of his first wife. A well-to-do man and a Muslim elder in his neighborhood, he had become a believer several years previously after being miraculously healed from a debilitating ear infection. We began a church in his courtyard. His teenage daughters and the youngest of his twenty-one children were eager to listen. But the elder sons were sullen and angry. His first wife was a powerful member of her Islamic women's association. She was respected by her peers until her husband's perfidious act of rejecting Islam stole her status and her identity.

"I talked to her about Jesus many times," he said through the tears, "but she said she couldn't follow Him. She said she couldn't betray her parents and friends." One time when he had insisted she attend a women's conference at church, she arrived in the flowing garments of a rich man's wife, expecting a social evening of gossip and dancing. She found instead a group of modestly dressed women with their Bibles opened on their laps. Their sincere welcome did nothing to dispel her unease. She soon made an excuse and hurried away. "I could have forced her," he said, "but I wanted her to believe on her own. Now it's too late."

Our organization, with limited personnel and in partnership with national partners, has focused on mass evangelism and reaching men, believing that the women would follow the men. But in West Africa, Muslim-background believer (MBB) churches are mostly made up of men. Muslim women have not automatically followed their MBB husband's faith. Recent research on the persecuted church also indicates that reaching Muslim men will not ensure that women are reached (cf. Beth Stricker's article "Hope that Perseveres" in this book).

Some female believers are building relationships with Muslim women and are engaging in small-group evangelism. Through these efforts, individual women are coming to Christ. But, for the most part, Muslim women in Sub-Saharan Africa remain untouched. What is this powerful societal hold that keeps African Muslim women from responding to the gospel, even when their husbands become believers? What barriers keep them from Christ? We have assumed that the most influential people in their lives were their husbands, but is this really true? Are they not more influenced by their fathers, their culture, and a society of women who regulate behavior through associations and commerce?

UNDERSTANDING WEST AFRICAN MUSLIM WOMEN

Selwyn Hughes in his book *Christ Empowered Living* states that our personal identity depends on security, self-worth, and significance. He defines these as a sense that one is unconditionally loved, valued as a person, and has a sense of meaning and purpose (Hughes 2003, 39). "The self is a series of reflected appraisals. We come to think about ourselves in the way we think others think of us. We value ourselves as we think we are valued" (Ibid., 40).

What does an African baby girl, born into a Muslim family, learn about herself from those around her? Where do African Muslim women find security, self-worth, and significance? Since these needs are not being met by a personal relationship with God, it is logical to assume a Muslim woman's identity and sense of self have been constructed by her society. This very identity is a barrier that prevents her from understanding the gospel message. To understand the way African women see themselves, we must examine the worldview into which they are born. There are vast differences between African family groupings. The following describes the worldview of a typical Sub-Saharan West African Muslim woman.

The World of West African Women

An African baby girl is born into a world of chaos and uncertainty. Historically, Sub-Saharan Africa has experienced continual hardships: slave raiding, wars, colonial conquest, droughts, famines, diseases, and shortages of marriage partners for women. Today this area continues to be threatened by political strife, droughts, famines and especially the destructiveness of AIDS. Dependence on family, building broad relationships, and the sharing of food and other goods are strategies African women developed over centuries to ensure survival (Maranz 2001, 2).

Historically, African women were valued and accumulated as wealth because survival and status depended upon large families. Their value was not in who they were as individuals but in what they could produce. In a typical African community, a male nucleus maintained its unity and authority over land and cattle through females. Daughters were married to other villagers, providing labor and children for their husbands, and guaranteeing a reciprocal arrangement as her kin received marriage partners from the daughter's new family. Women had many responsibilities and few rights. Older men controlled sisters and nieces. Even the young men were controlled as the older men regulated their prospects for wives (July 1992, 546). Stories abound in West Africa of men who, like Jacob, worked for years for their future fathers-in-law, only to be tricked at the last minute.

Although Africans are group-oriented and seek solace and support through their network of relatives and relationships, women often feel alone and solely responsible for their own welfare and that of their children. In most African societies, children legally belong to the father and his clan. If a woman offends her husband or his family or if she becomes sick or is otherwise unable to care for her children, they will be taken from her. This fear and the general lack of trust between the sexes cause women to seek financial independence. When health or relationship problems occur that are beyond their means or the means of their network, African women seek solutions in the spirit world.

Beliefs about Spirit Beings

African women believe life is pervaded by spiritual power, either personal spirit beings who guide their lives such as ancestors, gods, ghosts, and spirits, or impersonal spirits which can still be used to bless or curse (Van Rheenen 1996, 124). The earth is multidimensional, though most dimensions are invisible to the masses. A vital force often called "dynamism" is one dimension not visible to the ordinary person. This neutral power can be used for good or evil and is accessible to occult practitioners. It is believed to guide healers to the right herbs to cure illnesses and to give witches special powers.

Spirits and ghosts inhabit yet another dimension. They can also be manipulated by occult practitioners but are not all-powerful. Healers offer charms, amulets, and fetishes (at the right price) to manipulate dynamism and protect people from these spirits and ghosts (Imasogie 1986, 55). *Jinni* are considered to be the invisible neighbors of humans with similar characteristics and social structures. Specialists, possessed by *jinni,* give the message to others. Women are said to be more sensitive to possession. Pregnant women especially fear *jinni* because they believe their unborn babies will be taken by them. Often when a baby dies at birth, the *jinn* are blamed. To protect themselves, pregnant women may burn incense, wear charms, or observe taboos such as staying in their rooms when it is dark or only bathing in daylight (Brand 2001, 166-167).

Women also protect themselves through secret speech, chants and secret formulas. Two forms of speech that are particularly powerful are blessings and curses. The blessing or curse of a mother toward her son or a sister toward her brother is considered very powerful. A mother's blessing is seen as a necessity for a son's successful life (Brand 2001, 150).

Speech is believed to contain dynamism that is released when pronounced. Such speech is used while making amulets and to guide women through safe labor and delivery. Not all women know this secret speech. Knowledge ranges from some who know a few formulas to senior women who specialize in secret speech along with the knowledge of herbal medicine. This secret knowledge is generally passed on from mother to daughter after the daughter has proven worthy through a period of apprenticeship. It is passed down to only one person because it is thought to lose its power when dispersed. Female witchcraft is thought to not only be more powerful than that of men but to be a key to the success of a group's male heroes (Brand 2001, 149). The desire for protection from female witchcraft may be the source of male secret societies in some ethnic groups (Zobel 1996, 639-640).

When my neighbor Fatou was a teenager, her mother was approached by an aunt, a witch, who wanted her to become a witch, as well. Her mother refused. Not long after, she died. After Fatou married, she was asked to join the occult by the same aunt. Fatou refused. Later, this aunt was present at the birth of Fatou's first child, a baby boy. It soon became evident that the baby was lame. Her aunt told her she must be initiated into witchcraft or something would happen to each of her succeeding children. Feeling trapped, Fatou agreed, but only to use witchcraft for good and not for evil.

Few African Muslim women know much about formal Islam, but they are well-versed in folk Islam. Folk Islam answers the questions of the here and now and solves the problems of everyday life (Hiebert 1989, 49). Believing they cannot control the future, African women strive to control the here and now. *Maraboutage* is the Folk Islamic specialty concerned with manipulating spiritual power. *Marabouts* are primarily male, so a shift has occurred away from the traditional emphasis on female witches. Because of their association with Islam, these male practitioners are often highly valued members of society and this gives a certain divine legitimacy to their practices (Brand 2001, 151).

In our village, it was not unusual to see a Mercedes Benz parked in front of a marabout's mud house while the driver, who drove ten hours from the capital city, explained his problem and sought relief. Because the Qur'an is believed to be the living word of God, *marabouts* harness this power by knowing which Qur'anic verses to use for which need.

Women consult *marabouts* when they have problems in love, marriage, fertility, pregnancy, or child rearing. A woman may seek a *marabout's* help to gain power over female rivals or to gain personal power (Brand 2001, 152). A woman may also consult a *marabout* in order to keep the attention of her future husband or to keep her lover from straying. Women fear being left destitute or having to live with relatives who do not want them, so they do everything in their power to secure an income for themselves and their children.

An African Muslim woman may also ask a diviner to help her determine God's will. Historically, a diviner, a person with extra sensitivity to spiritual reality, endured years of training to learn the secrets of deciphering the past, present, and future, and to discover the answers to life's questions. Sacrifices to show gratitude for blessings as well as to seek forgiveness for sins were involved in every divination consultation (Imasogie 1986, 60-61).

With the coming of Islam, diviners reinterpreted their use of spiritual power as a way to determine God's will. The sacrificial system also took on an interesting twist. I once witnessed a female diviner as she threw cowry shells on the floor (for a fee) to determine whether it was safe for an African friend to travel. After much gazing and shaking her head and a few well-placed breaths on the shells, she concluded that God would give my friend a safe journey if she first gave a package of powdered milk to some children. This popular practice of helping others as a way of seeking favor from God is called in *Mande* languages *saraka*, meaning sacrifice. It comes from the Islamic concept of *sadaqa* or acts of charity (Jalloh 1997, 80).

Women are not averse to using everything at their disposal simultaneously. In times of sickness, they may ask a Christian neighbor as well as an *imam* for prayer, a *marabout* for an amulet, and a doctor for a prescription. When someone falls sick the question women ask is not "what caused the illness," but "who caused the illness."

Taking her Place in the Family

Another dimension of a West African woman's universe is inhabited by the ancestors. Such spirits are believed to be actively concerned with the family and are asked to provide protection and advice. Besides concern with the spirit realm and the use and abuse of power, the other major influence on an African Muslim woman is her family. In many ethnic groups, the preferred marriage arrangement is cross-cousins as this tends to consolidate family ties (Brand 2001, 69). Women live in extended families in which the father's brothers are also called "fathers." "Mothers" will include the co-wives of one's father (Van Rheenen 1996, 125). Cousins are all considered brothers and sisters. In fact, in many African languages there is no word for "cousin," just as often there is no word for "woman" apart from the word "wife."

In African thinking, people are always humans but must achieve personhood. The first step is to have a name. By having a name, a child receives a place among the living relatives, the ancestors, and those yet to be born. One must then be circumcised, get married, and have children and grandchildren in order to achieve personhood. Being married is much more important to women than to men, for without marriage they are always considered young girls. The nursing mother is perhaps the most profound symbol of personhood. Many ethnic groups believe that a child receives his mother's blood through the breast milk and that drinking this breast milk as transformed blood is a fundamental requirement for the child to become a person.

The final qualification for personhood is to display proper behavior as

dictated by society. Unlike formal education, traditional education is about
learning one's place in society (Brand 2001, 17-18). What is considered proper
behavior differs from ethnic group to ethnic group and within an ethnic group
by class hierarchy. In the Mande peoples, one of the largest people groupings
in West Africa, people are divided into three classes: the nobles, the specialists
such as iron and leather workers and bards, and the slaves. Correct behavior
for a noble is tied to the idea of shame and self-control whereas correct behavior
for the slave class is tied to bawdiness and lack of control. Mystery surrounds
the specialist class, and it is here we find the manipulators of the spirit realm
described earlier.

One aspect of correct behavior is to understand and appreciate the accepted
cultural classifications of knowledge. For example, most pregnant women do
not know what is happening to their bodies and are unprepared for labor and
delivery. Even educated women say they only know that childbirth will be
painful. They are not enlightened at the maternity clinics, but told only to
endure the pain. Once the baby is born, an elderly woman will spend time
with a new mother teaching her how to care for her baby. This seems strange,
since young girls from the age of four or five care for babies. One author suggests "knowledge is classified and the use of it limited to particular groups of
people; those who are not supposed to know explicitly affirm their ignorance"
(Brand 2001, 172-178). Africans readily share space and their belongings, but
are hesitant to share personal thoughts and knowledge. This is the reverse for
Westerners who readily share knowledge and personal thoughts but are often
reluctant to share space or belongings (Maranz 2001, 30-32).

As she grows, an African girl learns to properly relate to others. She learns
who must be treated with honor and respect. Respect implies expressing correct
greetings, holding one's tongue when appropriate, controlling one's emotions,
accepting authority, and not contradicting a respected person publicly. One
may have affection for the person one respects, but this affection is rarely
expressed. Typical relationships requiring respect are between father and child,
parents-in-law and daughters- or sons-in-law, and with the older brothers and
sisters of one's spouse. The mother-child bond is sacrosanct in that there is no
relationship worthy of more respect.

A Muslim girl also learns how to relate to those with whom she has a joking
relationship. Joking relationships exist between grandparents and grandchildren,
with one's mother's brothers, with younger brothers and sisters of one's spouse,
and in some cases with friends of the same age and between members of

certain families (Brand 2001, 18-19). Joking relationships exist between certain clans and between certain ethnic groups because at some point in the past, one group was particularly helpful to another and they entered into a joking relationship.

Women depend on their husbands to achieve full personhood after marriage. The marriage ritual emphasizes the bride's identity as an outsider in her husband's household. As such, she has little status. It is only as she consistently and respectfully obeys her mother-in-law or an older co-wife that her role will be redefined as an insider in her husband's lineage.

A woman is chosen as a marriage partner based upon her qualifications for being a good mother, meaning one who can link her child to a set of relationships and who, through her own adherence to cultural expectations, gives her child a sense of social connectedness (Riesman 1992, 10). In some ethnic groups, it is the husband's mother who decides when her daughter-in-law and son can move to their own hut. This happens after the mother has observed the girl long enough to determine whether she is worthy of her son. The marriage is not to be consummated until the mother gives her approval. In urban areas especially, men and women are choosing their own marriage partners and may set up their own households, but it is still a prerequisite that relatives from both sides of the union agree to the marriage and follow cultural practices (Brand 2001, 69).

A man inherits his patrilineal affiliation and ascribed status from his father, but his destiny comes from his mother. A man's destiny is said to be determined by his mother's own successful socio-moral career. Thus, the image of the mother as a *muso nyuman*, the morally good woman, symbolizes her son's access to the means to achieve, to gain reputation, and to succeed (Arnoldi 1995, 173).

For the mother and child, peace and well-being take root in their mutual physical contact. Evil is associated with separation and solitude is considered an expression of unhappiness. A woman does her work surrounded by her children. From the age of four or five, little girls try to help their mothers. The children's care is almost exclusively the responsibility of the mother. She must feed on demand and is severely criticized if she allows her baby to cry. For the first two years of its life, she cannot leave her baby for more than one or two hours at a time (Riesman 1998, 66). Women retain membership in their own kin group after marriage. A woman can be removed from her husband if she acts unworthily. An African man once told me that he had sent his daughter-in-law back to her family. As she was the mother of two children, one of which was a new baby, I asked about the children. "I sent the baby back with her," he said. "She will bring it to us when it is weaned." "What does your son say?" I asked. His son was an educated man, a nurse who worked in a hospital. The father was a non-literate housekeeper for an American family. "There was nothing he could say," the man replied. "I am the head of the household, and his wife was not showing me adequate respect." After a month of orchestrated negotiations, the daughter-in-law was restored to her father-in-law's courtyard and to her husband after having been suitably shamed for her bad behavior.

Activities are divided between what is suitable for women and what is suitable for men (Arnoldi 1995, 172). A man cannot ask a woman to do man's work and vice versa. Farming is under men's control and men make all the decisions from planting to the distribution of grain. Women have no control over their husband's or even their own clan's agricultural products. Only from small gardening projects can they make personal earnings.

A man may express unhappiness with his wife's cooking, housekeeping, or child-rearing, but he does not have the power to make her change because that would be interfering in the feminine world. A woman's submission is more a submission to what is expected of her by the culture rather than submission to her husband as an individual. A woman does not fulfill her role as an act of obedience to a man's orders but as an expression of her feminine nature.

Although the husband may not have the power to make his wife change, he can control her behavior by threatening to send her back to her family or by taking another wife. In Mali, when a couple takes out a marriage license, the groom chooses between a polygamous (up to four wives) and a monogamous marriage plan. If he decides on a monogamous marriage, he can change that only if his wife gives permission (Brand 2001, 81). Even men who intend to remain monogamous will often choose polygamous plans to keep their wives under control. Men suspect their wives' intentions and fear being at their emotional and sexual mercy. A man who seems to be too closely involved with his wife may be mocked or pressured to decrease intimacy. If a man's parents or siblings fear he is being controlled by his wife, they will often encourage him to seek a second wife or will attempt to break up the marriage to ensure they are getting their share of his income (Ibid., 156, 145).

Relationships in the Community

Because Africans are group-oriented, they do not usually think of themselves as individuals but as part of a larger whole in connection with others. Even the pursuit of women's rights is for the purpose of benefiting the group rather than the individual (Ibid., 4). A person finds meaning in life from relationships, not accomplishments. Someone without relatives or friends is a nonentity. People with many relatives, friends, and children will be remembered and honored long after their death.

Relationships define society's perception of beauty and wisdom as well as good and evil. Beautiful people are generous people who show hospitality and share their goods with others. Wise people are those who know how to untangle relational difficulties and negotiate peace for the community. "Good" people live in peace and harmony for the greatest good. People's greatest fear is to be alienated and alone.

African friendships involve concepts of solidarity, hospitality, obligatory interaction and community living. A fundamental component of African friendship is mutual dependence for material resources. Friendship and financial help go together. It does not matter how well one knows or even likes another, in a kin relationship a certain amount of material giving is obligatory. People are judged by how much and how freely they give to others. Even if a woman exudes friendliness and warmth, if she does not help the other financially, she is not a true friend. Because material wealth is viewed as limited, relationships can be highly competitive. "A network of friends is a network of resources (Maranz 2001, 64-65)."

African women often form associations for entertainment, status, and mutual aid (Strobel 1976, 191). Most women belong to a financial association formed to cover marriage or childbirth costs. In these associations, the major saving opportunity for women, members meet at regularly scheduled times to contribute a given amount to the group. Financial associations are usually headed by old and respected members of an important family who can keep track of contributions. Women can belong to several associations at a time. For an African Muslim woman, membership in such associations is evidence of her economic success and extensive social network. The height of financial and social success comes with membership in associations funding pilgrimages to Mecca (Lewis 1976, 147-149).

The fundamental economic consideration in African society is the survival of family and relatives. But hoarding goods is undesirable and the mark of a selfish person. In many rural communities, people are afraid to accumulate more goods or property than their relatives or neighbors for fear of being targeted for occult practices (Maranz 2001, 111). There are so many leveling agents at work in the culture—fatalism, reciprocal obligations, social obligations, jealousy, fear of the occult, public and family opinion–that it is difficult for a family to "get ahead" financially (Ibid., 148-151). Nearly every woman at some point in her life is involved in some type of income-producing activity, be it simply selling water or a few items at the market, spinning cotton, or making pottery. Apart from this trading, in many ethnic groups, it is not uncommon for women to engage in pre- or extra-marital sexual relations with men who provide them with gifts and money (Brand 2001, 135). Women who do not have another source of income will sometimes sell their bodies to provide food for their families. This is considered shameful and is usually hidden.

We were warned in our village that respectable people never ventured from their courtyards after dark. Those who were looking for sexual favors and those who wanted to sell their bodies would meet at night on the main street in front of the mosque. In our village, girls as young as twelve engaged in prostitution. When I expressed concern to my neighbor, she said, "There are two kinds of women . . . those who will and those who won't. Women have other options, but it means a lot of hard work."

Women keep their incomes separate from their husband's income. He usually does not even know how much she makes. An MBB couple I know went through a difficult time in their marriage when they decided to buy a house. He was a business owner and she a schoolteacher. It took her husband months of persuasion before she finally agreed to declare her income for a loan application. It was a turning point in their marriage and was an act of trust on her part, a trust that is lacking in most marriages. Experience has shown that it is best to keep one's financial situation private, especially from family members. Even adult sisters who share the same household keep their finances separate, each contributing to household expenses as needed.

In summary, an African Muslim woman is bound by her society. From birth her society constructs her identity. Her only options for security, self-worth, and satisfaction are in her family and in her ability to manipulate the spirit world. She may receive unconditional love from her children but not from her husband. She is valued only when she achieves personhood by becoming a mother and following the dictates of proper behavior. Her meaning and sense of purpose come from her place in society as well as in the money she manages to hide away. Traditionally, religious knowledge is reserved for men. Islam does nothing to dispel this belief. Statements such as my neighbor made, "I am just a woman. I cannot know God," express a core belief. Women, concerned for the here-and-now, do not see the importance of a religion that focuses on the eternal.

Individual action is valued only as it benefits society. Success means serving a purpose in society. If success harms the group, one has failed (Brand 2001, 157). Saskia Brand in her book *Mediating Means and Fate*, says: "It is difficult for men to (temporarily) break free from the group, for women it is twice as hard. As 'eternal minors' their deeds always reflect upon their father's or their husband's group as if they were carried out under their authority. The group will therefore see to it that public individual actions by women are discouraged as much as possible . . . women represent the stability of the community . . . and should not endanger the collectivity by extraordinary behavior" (Ibid., 157).

If an African Muslim woman accepts Christ and her husband is not a believer, she faces not only the possible loss of her children and material goods, but also her very identity as constructed by society. Her enemies may harness the spirit world to attack her as well. She has been taught to distrust her husband, so even if her husband becomes a believer and encourages her to do so, she is still vulnerable. No matter how old she is, without the approval of her own father and community, she risks upsetting the cultural balance. If her social network is made up of Muslim women on whom she relies socially and economically, the barriers increase. She not only lets down her family, she lets down her society and her future children.

To put this in terms of an American woman, if a she becomes a Christian, she will be forced not only to give up all of the money she has in her checking and savings accounts, she must also cancel all of her health and life insurance policies and give up her American citizenship. How many American women would become believers, if that were the price they had to pay?

REACHING WEST AFRICAN MUSLIM WOMEN

When confronted with the innumerable worldview barriers outlined above, it is easy to be discouraged. I have struggled with the question of "Where do we begin?" What is the role of Western missionaries who come from a worldview based on order, individuality and independence?

First, wearing the whole armor of God, especially the belt of truth, we must commit to informed prayer. Putting on the armor means knowing, believing, and living God's Word every day (Franklin and Lawless 2001, 106-108). We must seek our own security, self-worth, and significance in the person of Jesus Christ. We must live the truth that God is all-powerful, and has already won the battle. We must also become serious in prayer for Muslim women who are trapped by the occult and the spirit realm, realizing that God fights spiritual battles for us. We can do nothing in our own strength.

We must also come out of our prayer closets to change the impression African Muslim women have that Christian women pray only once a week when they go into a particular building. We should never visit a Muslim friend without praying for her and her family. We should pray for the sick, for concerns, for praise items. In the face of joys and difficulties, ours and theirs, African Muslim women must see us turn to God in conversational prayer. As we model our relationship with God through prayer, they will begin to grasp the concept of a personal God who loves us.

Second, there needs to be an emphasis in African Christian churches on the biblical teaching that husbands love their wives, for when Muslim women see no difference in the way their Christian friends are treated by their husbands, they are biased against the gospel. After reading about the practice of making fun of a couple if they appeared to be in love, I asked African Christian church leaders from various denominations if that practice occurred in their churches. "Oh, yes!" they all replied. "Even in the church the couple is mocked if they want to sit together or be together too much. People will make fun of the man especially, warning him that his wife will have too much control over him if he loves her too much."

One African couple who leads marriage seminars told me that their first assignment is for husbands and wives to sit beside each other. It usually takes about two hours before everyone will agree. This couple believes God guided them into family ministry—specifically doing marriage seminars in African churches—because this is the secret to seeing more people come to Christ. We need African couples such as this one doing marriage seminars, not Western missionaries. We can, however, sound the trumpet.

When a group of denominational leaders in our West African countries were told that one of the biggest hindrances to Muslim women coming to Christ was the failure of African Christian men to love their wives and provide for them, the Holy Spirit convicted many of the men present. We need to encourage men to use Chronological Bible Storying with their sisters and mothers, where relationships are strong. We need to challenge them to teach their wives and treat them with love and respect. MBB husbands in our churches must also be held accountable for this teaching.

Third, we must provide focused leadership training for our Christian sisters in Africa to enable them to effectively reach Muslim women. In our focus on the unreached, African Christian women must be the ones to take the message to their Muslim neighbors for only they have personal testimonies of how God is working within their worldview. We need to encourage African Christian women to relate to the wives of new converts and to believers' wives who are not yet interested in the gospel.

Research shows that a new convert bonds with the one who leads her to Christ. While we need to sow seeds among our relationships, we may need to forego the profound joy of leading a friend to Christ. Instead, we should introduce her to an African Christian woman who can not only lead her to Christ but disciple her and be part of her social network. If there are no African Christian women available, we must pray for a Dorcas, a Lydia, or a Priscilla who will lead a transformed life that will amaze their Muslim neighbors. We must train them to be leaders of a future movement, by moving into the role of "shadow" leader as quickly as possible.

We must include women in our training opportunities. Excluding them or not providing specific training for them reinforces their worldview concerning limited access to knowledge and that religious knowledge is only for men. Christian women need training in Chronological Bible Storying and Church Planting Movement principles.

Among most African Christian women, the need for a large social network has been met in the church. Therefore they often make the mistake in their witness to Muslim women of pressuring them to become active in the church, but the Muslim woman is usually not prepared to turn her back on her own social network. The Christian women interpret this hesitancy to come to church as a rejection of Christ. It is not. We need to help Christian women realize that MBBs may never be comfortable in our traditional churches. We must cast the vision to our African Christian women of working with their husbands to start house churches for MBBs. Often, their husbands may be involved in a house church, but they are so tied to the social network of women in their church, they do not want to leave it. Many times, African Christian husbands and wives are even members of different churches.

We need to encourage women to form associations like the Christian women's associations among the Creole in Sierra Leone in which members visit hospitals, orphanages, and homes for the handicapped at Christmas to sing carols and to present gifts. These associations not only provide avenues for Christian charity but also meet the worldview need for a large social network (Steady 1976, 226). We need to encourage our sisters to find culturally appropriate ways to include their Muslim neighbors in their celebrations, such as in Senegal where Sereer Christians take a local delicacy of a thick drink made from pounded millet, peanuts, and sugar to their Muslim neighbors at Easter (Maranz 2001, 73-74).

We need to help our African denominational missionary sending agencies to consider including as missionaries the wives of the men they send out, and encourage them to also provide relevant training for them. One pastor asked for my advice when God called him to be a home missionary to a Muslim village but his wife did not want to leave the church where she was a women's leader. I encouraged him to pray that God would convict his wife. I told him to discuss with his wife the fact that God might have a call on her life as well. This was a novel idea for him. I talked to him about his wife's fear of being alone and suggested ways in which he could encourage the women of his home church to support her. He told me that few West African denominational sending organizations consider the wives as missionaries and often will not even interview them before appointing their husbands.

We have some wonderful examples of African Christian couples giving of themselves sacrificially to work as missionaries. We need to publish booklets highlighting stories of these African missionaries to stretch the thinking of African children and teenagers, helping them to see the possibility that God might call them. We should also encourage our African churches to "adopt" an African missionary couple by praying for them, visiting them, and supporting them financially.

Fourth, we must give African Muslim women access to God's Word in ways they can understand. There is rarely a situation in which we cannot engage an African woman in a spiritual conversation. Africans are surrounded by the spirit world and continually seek to manipulate it. We must clearly and effectively bear witness to the Spirit of Truth. This usually means laying a foundation of truth by telling the stories of the Old Testament first.

African Muslim women live in an oral culture so we must use oral communication methods to reach them. We should use media to make Chronological Bible Storying tracks pertinent to women available on cassettes and in radio programs in local languages. We need to record testimonies of female MBBs and of effective Bible studies led by women for women. We should distribute these abundantly with plans in place for follow-up and gathering listeners into groups.

In one Muslim area of West Africa, God told an African woman in a dream to follow Him and to testify boldly in the marketplace about the true way of salvation. She obeyed. Our personnel heard of her and offered to put her testimony on cassette. They now distribute this cassette and have found a positive response from men as well as women listening to the tape.

We need to use more volunteers. Often they have access and can "get by" with things others cannot. After a college-age volunteer group taught AIDS awareness stressing abstinence and a moral lifestyle, a group of elderly African women walked a long distance to express their concern for the young people of their village and to thank the group for their teaching,

Often, the only Westerners Africans see are young people and families. In order to minister to a culture where age is respected, we need to motivate senior adults to be involved in volunteer work. Senior women volunteers from the United States could visit with elderly African Muslim women, to give testimony of their faith through translators and to introduce the African women to a personal Christ.

Yes, we must build relationships with Muslim women and become worthy to share our beliefs, but we must also be bold in our personal witness. Too often, we introduce Muslim women to a church or a religion instead of the person of Christ. The church and the religion will fail them. Christ will not. If they love him, they will suffer and we are reluctant to do anything that will cause them to suffer. We must remember that the New Testament witnesses told those in the new church to expect to suffer for their faith. We must trust God, believe the Bible, and move beyond our fear. We must not be ashamed of the gospel.

In focusing on Christ and the truth we will be taking our eyes off of the periphery and focusing on the core. We are often tempted to change society before God has changed hearts. Charles Kraft in his book, *Christianity in Culture*, discusses principles for transforming culture with God. He warns against seeking peripheral changes first, not because the changes are undesirable but because changes "forced at the periphery of culture cause 'ripples' of influence in toward the worldview core of the culture" (Kraft 1995, 362).

His example is the church's insistence on a new believer accepting monogamy in a polygamous society before he can be accepted into the Christian faith. Such insistence can cause strange things to happen to the unbelievers' concept of God. According to Kraft, with the insistence on monogamy as part of the gospel package, God is seen as turning against traditional leaders because they have more than one wife, as well as favoring familial irresponsibility because they must cast out their extra wives and children. God no longer wants to protect widows or is concerned that women be socially secure. God does not want men to attain wealth but to be dominated by their wives because they no longer fear their husbands will take another wife.

The God who once was conceived of as supporting them is now seen either as having unreasonably turned against them in favor of the white people and their customs or as having been defeated and displaced by another God—the God of the whites. In either case this single peripheral change in the family structure results in such a high degree of confusion and disequilibrium in the conceptual core (worldview) of the culture that there is little chance for the gospel message concerning salvation through a faith relationship with God to be heard clearly (Kraft 1995, 362-363).

I will never forget the tearful prayer request of the new believer, "Pray for me," she said. "I have been convicted because I do not love my co-wife and often fight with her. She is not a believer. Pray that I will be the example God wants me to be." Perhaps we need to encourage our female MBBs in polygamous marriages to see their situations as opportunities to witness instead of focusing on the institution that causes so much suffering. In the same way we need to encourage them to love their mothers-in-law as Ruth loved Naomi, even if she is an embittered old woman as Naomi was.

Fifth, focus on children's ministries and intentionally use those ministries to reach large groups of mothers and the community. "Teach our children," Muslim elders advised in one West African village. "The children will believe, and the women will follow. The men will follow the women." One missionary woman opened a preschool in a Muslim community using Christian teachers who visit the mothers and provide a Christian witness. This established a foundation for a group because the mothers have something in common—their children attend the same preschool.

We need to teach the Bible to children and hold them accountable to memorize large passages of Scripture, perhaps in music or chants. In our village, twice a week, Muslim boys go from home to home throughout the village chanting the Qur'anic verses they have learned. If they do a good job, they receive a few coins as an incentive for further study. We must encourage our Christian children to memorize and repeat scripture publicly in a similar way. In this way many would be exposed to God's Word.

We never know how God will use our efforts. Several years ago, an old Muslim woman accepted Christ after I shared with her using Chronological Bible Storying. A few days later as a means of reinforcing her decision, I asked her to tell me when she had accepted Jesus, "Oh," she said, "it was when I was a young girl, the first time I heard his name." As a young girl she had attended a Catholic church for a few months until her father found out about it, beat her, and refused to allow her to attend. Throughout her life she had never heard more of the message than Jesus' name and had been greatly influenced by her marabout father. It took Chronological Bible Storying to clarify the message, but God allowed her to live until she could hear the whole story!

Above all, we need to remember whom we serve. We need to confess our sin of believing the task is too big and our resources too small. He is the God of the universe, and the victory has already been won.

R E F E R E N C E S

Arnoldi, Mary Jo. 1995. *Playing with time: Art and performance in central Mali. Traditional arts of Africa.* Bloomington: Indiana University Press.

Brand, Saskia. 2001. Mediating means and fate: A socio-political analysis of fertility and demographic change in Bamako, Mali. *African Social Studies Series.* Boston: Brill.

Franklin, John, and Chuck Lawless. 2001. *Spiritual warfare: biblical truth for victory.* Nashville: LifeWay Press.

Hiebert, Paul. 1989. Power encounter and folk Islam. In *Muslims and Christians on the Emmaus road*, ed. J. Dudley Woodberry, 45-61. Monrovia, CA: MARC Publications.

———— 1994. *Anthropological reflections on missiological issues.* Grand Rapids: Baker Books.

Hiebert, Paul, and Eloise Hiebert Meneses. 1995. *Incarnational ministry: Planting churches in band, tribal, peasant, and urban societies.* Grand Rapids: Baker Books.

Hughes, Selwyn. 2003. *Christ empowered living: Reflecting God's design.* Nashville: LifeWay Press.

Imasogie, Osadolor. 1986. *Guidelines for Christian theology in Africa.* Ibadan, Nigeria: University Press Limited.

Jalloh, Alusine. 1997. Alhaji Momodu Allie: Muslim Fula entrepreneur in colonial Sierra Leone. In *Islam and Trade in Sierra Leone*, eds. Alusine Jalloh and David E. Skinner, 65-81. Trenton: Africa World Press.

July, Robert W. 1992. *A history of the African people.* 4th ed. Prospect Heights, IL: Waveland Press.

Kraft, Charles H. 1995. *Christianity in culture: A study in dynamic biblical theologizing in cross-cultural perspective.* Maryknoll, NY: Orbis Books.

Lewis, Barbara C. 1976. The limitations of group action among entrepreneurs: The market women of Abidjan, Ivory Coast. In *Women in Africa: Studies in social and economic change*, eds. Nancy J. Hafkin and Edna G. Bay, 135-156. Stanford: Stanford University Press.

Maranz, David. 2001. *African friends and money matters*. Dallas: SIL International and International Museum of Cultures Publications in Ethnography.

Niemeyer, Larry. 1993. The unmet challenge of mission to the matrilineal peoples of Africa. *Evangelical Missions Quarterly* 29:26-31.

Ojukutu-Macauley, Sylvia. 1997. Religion, gender, and education in Northern Sierra Leone, 1896-1992. In *Islam and trade in Sierra Leone*, eds. Alusine Jalloh and David E. Skinner, 87-117. Trenton: Africa World Press.

Riesman, Paul. 1992. *First find your child a good mother: The construction of self in two African communities*. New Brunswick, NJ: Rutgers University Press.

_____. 1998. *Freedom in Fulani social life*. Chicago: The University of Chicago Press.

Steady, Filomina Chioma. 1976. Protestant women's associations in Freetown, Sierra Leone. In *Women in Africa: Studies in social and economic change*, eds. Nancy J. Hafkin and Edna G. Bay, 213-237. Stanford: Stanford University Press.

Strobel, Margaret. 1976. From Lelemama to lobbying: Women's associations in Mombasa, Kenya. n *Women in Africa: Studies in social and economic change*, eds. Nancy J. Hafkin and Edna G. Bay, 183-211. Stanford: Stanford University Press.

Van Rheenen, Gailyn. 1996. *Missions: biblical foundations and contemporary strategies*. Grand Rapids: Zondervan Publishing House.

Zobel Jan Jansen, and Clemens Zobel. 1995. The younger brother in Mande: Kinship and politics in West Africa. Selected papers from the *Third International Conference on Mande Studies*, Leiden, March 20-24, 1995. Leiden: Research School CNWS.

Zobel, Clemens. 1996. The noble Griot: the construction of Mande Jeliw-identities and political leadership as interplay of alternate values, pp. 35-47. In *The younger brother in Mande: kinship and politics in West Africa*. Selected papers from the *Third International Conference on Mande Studies*, Leiden, March 20-24, 1995. Leiden: Research School CNWS

9

Stories Along the Silk Road:
Reaching Muslim Women in Central Asia, Russia and China

Victoria Lindhal

A number of the most unreached Muslim people groups are in areas formerly under Soviet control. Using original research and numerous worker interviews, Victoria Lindahl describes many of the common beliefs and self-understandings of Central Asian, Russian and Chinese Muslim women and suggests several current methods for evangelism and discipleship.

The Muslim people groups living in Central Asia, Russia and China are considered some of the least evangelized peoples of the world, long under the sway of both Islam and Communism. For most of the past century, this part of the world has been closed to foreign missionaries. Over the past fifteen years, however, with the fall of Communism in the Soviet Union, new doors have opened throughout Russia and the former Soviet Republics for the spread of the gospel. Expatriate workers have been permitted to obtain business or education visas and are now able to take up residence in these countries. Disillusionment among the people has also led to a greater hunger for the truth. Many former Muslims have become believers, churches have been planted and national leaders have been trained to take leadership.

In China as well, there has been a new openness for the Good News. English teachers and foreign language students have been permitted to live and work in the country. In Northwest China, where most of the Muslim population is located, many local students, teachers and even whole families have come to accept Isa, the Muslim name for Jesus, and His teachings. We are living in a strategic moment in time, making history for Christ along the Silk Road!

This part of the world is home to a large number of Muslim people groups. There are twelve million Muslims living in Russia alone, representing approximately forty different people groups (MIR 2004). Over twenty-five million Muslims live in China, primarily in the northwest provinces of Xinjiang and Ningxia. People groups there include the Uighur, Hui, Kyrgyz, Kazakh, Dongxiang and several other minority groups. The ethnic groups of the former USSR are represented throughout the Central Asian countries of Kazakhstan, Kyrgyzstan, Uzbekistan, Tajikistan and Turkmenistan. Many of these ethnic people groups are also Muslim. In Kazakhstan, 60.5 percent of the population is Muslim, which is the lowest percentage in this area, compared to Turkmenistan where 91.84 percent of the population is Muslim (Johnstone, 2001, 377).

As there are numerous unreached Muslim people groups spread across this region, it would be difficult to give detailed information on them all. Therefore, we will concentrate on the major people groups which include the Kazakhs, Kyrgyz, Uzbek, Tajik, Turkmen, Tatars of Russia and Uighurs of China. In 1990, there were only 1661 believers among the Muslims of Central Asia. By the year 1999, there were reportedly 43,109 (AD 2000 and beyond). Today there are estimated to be over 50,000! In 1990 there were less than 100 Kazakh believers. Today the count has risen to over 13,000! In 1990, there were only a handful of Uighur believers. Today there are estimated to be at least 2000. In fact, more Muslims have come to Christ in Central Asia over the past ten years than at any other time in history (Garrison 2004, 110).

Despite the phenomenal growth in Christianity in this part of the world, the need is still great! In fact, when considering the millions still unreached, we have barely scratched the surface in our efforts to evangelize and see church planting movements spread across this region. In this article we will explore what have we learned from our past efforts, where we have we been successful and where we have made mistakes. We will also investigate the barriers that prevent women in these countries from understanding and responding to the gospel and the bridges that enable understanding and response. Our goal is to see God's light shine on this strategic area of the world causing millions of

Muslim people to come to know Jesus as their Savior and whole people groups to be transformed for the glory of God.

EXPLORING THE CENTRAL ASIAN WORLDVIEW

The first step in reaching our goal is to have a clear understanding of the worldview of our target people groups. The Muslim people groups that are represented in Central Asia, Russia and China are diverse and therefore there are some differences in their respective worldviews, especially between the peoples living in the former Soviet Countries and those in China. There are also differences between city dwellers and women from the country or villages. However, there are also many similarities.

One common thread that is woven throughout the mindsets of all of these people groups is the cultural identity they find in Islam. In other words, to be a Muslim is not so much an expression of a religious identity as a cultural identity. Sometimes it is expressed as "To be a Kazakh, Uighur, Turkmen is to be a Muslim." Despite the fact that Islam is so strongly engrained, most Muslim women living in this part of the world have in fact a very limited understanding of the Qur'an and Islamic teaching. They are, on the other hand, very influenced by folk Islam. Miriam, a foreign worker, who along with her husband, has lived in Central Asia for over fifteen years, says that folk Islam is very prevalent and strongly influences Central Asian Muslims. They follow many occult practices like sorcery and witchcraft, wearing talismans, appeasing spirits of the dead, putting curses on one another, and using sorcery to attract a future wife or husband along with other occultist healing practices. Fatalism and folk Islam go hand in hand because people feel that due to the prevalence of evil spirits and their activity much of life is actually out of their control and under the control of demons and the world of darkness. As Miriam Douglas explains, "These women are shaped by a fatalistic worldview, in which the 'En shallah attitude', that 'whatever God wills will be' dictates their daily lives" (2004).

Another aspect of worldview is the family structure. Family and community are of utmost importance to the women in this region of the world. Bakhtigul, a Uighur woman in her late forties who was raised in a rural area in Kazakhstan, shares that marriage, a good family, a husband who respects and protects his wife and a good job are all important values in this society (Supasheva, 2004). Hospitality is also one of the trademarks of these Central Asian people groups. Guests are always invited into the home and served tea and a meal. Many families are very poor but they will serve the last of their food to guests and later go hungry themselves, if necessary. There is also great pressure to bring honor to families, extended families and their communities.

Hopelessness is also prevalent across this part of the world. Ruth and her husband have lived in a Central Asian country for twelve years, successfully planting a national church in their target people group. When questioned about the worldview of these women, Ruth shared that fear, hopelessness and shame affects everything they do, coloring their view of the world and spiritual things. The influence of seventy years of Communism, she said, has precipitated this hopelessness and quenched dreams for the future. Indeed, most people over the age of twenty-five have lost all hope for the future (Barton, 2004).

BARRIERS TO EVANGELISM

While despair can open a door to hearing the gospel, notable barriers prevent Central Asian women from understanding and responding to it. The greatest barrier is the mindset that Islam is essential to their national identity. In the former Soviet block countries the thinking is, "We are Muslim, rather than Russian, which is Christian." This includes the assumption that Jesus is a Russian God. The use of non-contextualized Russian to share the gospel with Russian-speaking Central Asians can put up a wall to prevent them from hearing the truth of the gospel. Using Russian words for "Jesus Christ," "Bible," and "Church," for instance, immediately paints a picture in Muslim minds of the Russian Orthodox religion. For them, becoming a Christian means that they must deny their cultural identity and risk being alienated from their families and communities. In China, as well, being a Uighur and thus Muslim gives these people an identity that separates them from the Han Chinese and atheism. There is also fear of government intervention if they convert, including the possibility of persecution or the likelihood that they will lose their jobs. The cost of becoming a believer is, thus, very high and this cost must be weighed carefully before a decision is made to accept Christ.

Another barrier is the common misconceptions within Islam regarding Christianity. These include the belief that Mary had sex with God the Father in order to conceive Jesus and therefore He is not God, that Christians worship three gods (i.e. the Trinity) and that the Bible is corrupted. Leila, an Azeri believer, who leads three home groups, feels that the cross and water baptism are also huge barriers to Muslims becoming Christians as the symbol of the cross and the tradition of baptism are perceived as being Russian Orthodox (Surkhaeva, 2004).

Geographical access and the lack of vernacular Bibles are other major

barriers to evangelism. Missionary efforts are still restricted in China and many
Central Asian countries. According to Miriam, "… another barrier is the lack
of scripture in their heart language and where there is scripture available, its
distribution is a formidable problem due to political restrictions. Communism
and Islam are individually huge strongholds over the minds of Central Asians
and ethnic hatred between people groups is particularly strong and creates a
barrier for the spread of the gospel" (Douglas, 2004).

One final barrier for women that must be mentioned is the pressure of
marriage. If a woman is married, she is often hindered by her husband from
accepting the truth. Many women are afraid to open themselves up to the Bible
for fear of what their husbands will do if they find out. In other cases, the husbands forbid their wives to associate with believers or attend home fellowship
meetings. If a young woman is not yet married, but of marriageable age, there
is much family and community pressure to be married. I have seen many girls
accept Christ but later fall away because they were pressured into marrying a
Muslim man.

BRIDGES FOR THE GOSPEL

While the barriers are many and great, they are not impossible to overcome.
Let us look at some of the creative ways that expatriate workers and local believers are successfully sharing their faith with their Muslim friends.

The most important bridge is good relationships. Lil, a single woman who has
lived in a restricted access country for many years, says, "Relationship building
with a believer is essential. It is even better if that believer is from their own people
group so that the 'seeker' can see that the truths of the gospel are not a foreign
thing" (Young, 2004). Natasha, a Russian girl who has worked cross-culturally
with Muslims in her own country as well as a neighboring country, stresses that
learning the heart language of the people is very important. She says that building
relationships and finding commonalities in spite of cultural differences are keys
to sharing the gospel. She has also observed that when a local Muslim woman
becomes a believer and her family and friends see the great change in her life
this builds a bridge to share Jesus with them (Klimenko, 2004).

Ainur, a single Kazakh woman who successfully planted a church and pas-
tored it for many years shares that family ties create a bridge. If one person in
the family believes, then the entire family or clan can be reached with the
gospel. She has seen this happen on several occasions. In one instance, a woman
came to the Lord, followed by her husband and family members from both of

their extended families! Approximately thirty people were saved through the testimony of this one woman and today both her husband and his brother are pastors of large Kazakh churches (Danieva, 2004).

Another bridge that can open the hearts of Muslim women is to find meaningful aspects of the culture and redeem them for the gospel. The Korban Festival, for example, is a celebration that remembers Abraham's willingness to sacrifice his son (Ishmael in their view). This can be a good redemptive analogy of the sacrifice of Jesus for our sins. Music also plays an important role in Central Asian culture. Worship songs written in the heart language of the people and played on their indigenous instruments have been a great key to opening the hearts of the people. Cultural dances can also be used in worship to bring them into the presence of the Lord.

Many teams of workers across Central Asia are building bridges through teaching English, health care programs and business and agricultural projects. Sabrina, who has worked specifically with women in Central Asia for many years, says, "Targeting individuals can be a barrier so targeting a community may be better. Ask 'how can we bring change to this community?' We need to consider health, education and employment needs as well as spiritual needs" (Towns, 2004). Karen and her husband, for instance, have established a successful agricultural project in a village in Kazakhstan. Karen shares, "Bridges are built in the context of working together in agriculture. All women who have become believers are wives of hired workers or workers themselves. The project is totally legitimate in the community, with government appointed leaders" (Taylor, 2004).

Personally, in my work in both China and Kazakhstan over the past sixteen years, I have found another key to be supernatural power encounters with the Living God. There are many examples of miracles, healings, dreams and visions that have been catalysts to women experiencing salvation. A few years ago, a man of peace in a Uighur village had gathered neighbors and friends in his home where a foreigner was present, to receive copies of the newly published "Holy Book" or portion of scripture in the Uighur language. As the foreigner stood up to distribute the books, a woman rushed forward and grabbed one out of his hand, excitedly sharing that a few nights before, she had seen this man in a dream and he had given her a book that explained the Truth! In another example, a thirteen year old girl was dying of a kidney disease. When local believers visited her in the hospital, they were shocked to see that her stomach was so swollen; she looked like she was nine months pregnant! The family members, who had originally strongly opposed Christians in their community, now were very happy to receive prayer in the name of Jesus and the girl was totally healed! Through this miracle, the girl's parents, brothers and sisters, uncles, aunts and cousins believed and about thirty people were drawn to salvation because they saw the power of God in action.

Muslim women in Central Asia also have many felt needs. When believing women, whether foreign or local, build relationships with these women and begin to care about them and their needs, they open up and respond to these believers and to prayer. They are very open to prayer in the name of Jesus and when answers to their prayers are evident, they often want to know more about the One who answered these prayers.

EVANGELISM AND DISCIPLESHIP METHODS

With the help of these various bridges, we can make inroads for sharing the truth of the gospel. Bible stories are helpful in communicating the truth to women with Muslim backgrounds, especially stories of Bible characters that are also mentioned in the Qur'an. Leila begins with Adam and Eve and how sin entered the world. She then goes to the story of Abraham, Isaac and the sacrifice lamb, which leads to Jesus, who gave His life as the sacrifice to take away the sins of the world. Ruth likes to focus on stories of women in the Bible. She looks for felt needs and applies the truth of the gospel to every situation. Holly, who has worked with Uighur women in China for many years, says "I would say that my focus has been to point Uighurs to the gospel so that they are confronted with their sin. Until they see their total helplessness, they will not grasp their need for a Savior. I also believe we need to be very careful that we don't rush them through the repentance stage. They need to be very aware of all the sin they have committed including any beliefs they had in Islam or superstitions and be willing to lay all of this at the cross. Otherwise in accepting Christ as their Savior, they will simply be adding Him to their other beliefs as a type of safety net rather than putting themselves completely in Christ's hands" (Baker, 2004).

When individual women make a commitment to Christ and are discipled, we are making steps towards our goal. However, our desire is to see viable self-multiplying groups of believers formed. We ultimately want to see national cultural churches planted and church planting movements across this region of the world. How will this happen? Almost everyone will agree that the house church model is a key to working in Central Asian cultures. In the countries that have more freedom for evangelism and registered churches, such as

Kazakhstan and Kyrgyzstan, so far most fellowships have been based on a more traditional, institutional, church setting model. However, many of these fellowships are now moving towards the cell church or house church models. Miriam says, "House fellowships are key because they are formed along family and social networks and can multiply and spread rapidly given the proper leadership and training. Home groups have the greatest potential to grow and multiply because the majority of Central Asians are village-based and in countries such as China, Uzbekistan and Turkmenistan the only option for fellowship is low-profile, small home meetings" (Douglas, 2004).

Natasha, the Russian girl previously mentioned, encourages a small beginning with just a few women who know each other, perhaps two minutes of prayer, five minutes of reading the Word and spending the rest of the time in fellowship. As time progresses and these women become more familiar with their relationship with God and each other, more time can be spent in prayer and in the Word. Leila, also previously mentioned, who leads three home groups with Azeri and Turkish women in Kazakhstan says that these groups were formed by first visiting and phoning individuals, relationship building by drinking lots of tea and then women in the group sharing with family and friends. Bakhtigul, who is also the leader of a growing home group, shares the keys to her success as follows: "At first I visited everyone individually, then I gathered them together. Prayer, tea, telephone calls and love and care all played a vital role." She says that it takes one or two years to start a group from scratch (Supasheva, 2004).

As we have seen, the needs of the Muslim women in Central Asia, Russia and China are great and the barriers to women responding to the gospel are many. However, we have also seen that there are many ways to build bridges and effectively share the gospel with these precious women. We have explored strategies and models that are effectively being used to build relationships with women, draw them to salvation and see them planted in Christian fellowships. We have seen that God is doing an incredible work in these previously unreached people groups.

I believe that Central Asia is on God's map and on His calendar! We are living in a "kairos" moment of time in this part of the world. "The harvest is truly plentiful, but the laborers are few. Therefore pray the Lord of the harvest to send out laborers into His harvest" (Matthew 9:37-38 NKJV). God is calling us to play a part in His great harvest of Muslims along the Silk Road. It is my prayer that what has been written in these pages will motivate and equip us for the task at hand. In the days and years to come, we will move forward to realize our goal of seeing the Muslim people groups of Central Asia, Russia and China transformed for the glory of God!

Resources Presently Being Used Effectively in Central Asia
- Scripture portions in the heart language of the target people group
- Worship cassettes in the heart language of the target people group
- Radio broadcasts
- The *JESUS* film in all languages
- The *Passion of the Christ* movie in Russian and Chinese
- Christian books in Russian and Chinese
- *I Married You* by Walter Trobish translated into Arabic Uighur
- Various tracts in Kazakh and Uighur
- *Firm Foundations* by New Tribes
- *More Than a Carpenter* by Josh McDowell
- *Healing of the Soul* by Paula Shields translated into Russian, Chinese and Uighur
- *Discipleship Deliverance Workbook* by Sylvie MacFarland translated into Russian and Uighur

REFERENCES

AD 2000 and Beyond Movement. 2000. *The 35/45 Turkic window: A gateway to the Muslim world.*

Barton, Ruth. 2004. Interview by author, 4 June.

Danieva, Ainur. 2004. Interview by author, 7 June.

Douglas, Miriam. 2004. Interview by author, 9 June.

Garrison, David. 2004. *Church planting movements.*WIGtake Resources.

Johnstone, Patrick. 2001 *Operation world* [CD-ROM]. Waynesborough, GA: Paternoster Lifestyle.

Klimenko, Natasha. 2004 Interview by author, 7 June.

MIR, *Muslims in Russia*; available online http://www.mirfocus.com/pages/who.html; accessed 3 June 2004.

Sarkhaeva, Leila. 2004. Interview by author, 7 June.

Supasheva, Bakhtigul. 2004. Interview by author, 7 June.

Taylor, Karen. 2004. Interview by author, 3 June.

Towns, Sabrina. 2004. Interview by author, 31 May.

Young, Lil. 2004. Interview by author, 12 June.

10

A Life of Ironies:
Reaching South Asian Educated Urban Muslim Women

Yvette Wray

*Yvette Wray explores the world of urban, educated South Asian women and dis-
covers that their higher levels of education and the greater social and cultural
freedoms of their urban environment have not significantly changed their view of
the world. However, these factors can make it easier for workers to reach them
with the gospel.*

According to Islamic tradition, Muhammad said, "The seeking of knowledge is obligatory for every Muslim" (Durrany 1993, 77). Unfortunately,
Islamic tradition also maintains that "a woman is short of intelligence" (Durrany
1993, 84). Despite a woman's right to education according to Islam, she has
long remained uneducated, and excuses abound for denying her right:"Education of girls ... 'makes them argumentative and they become unmarriageable'"
(Goodwin 1994, 5). It is "better to keep women illiterate than to give them
more freedom in sexual relationships" (Durrany 1993, 80). The great disparity
between a woman's right to education and its reality is clearly seen throughout
South Asia. Fortunately, however, the number of girls educated within the past
generation has significantly increased. Abdul Waheed, a lecturer in the depart-
ment of Sociology and Social Work at Aligarh Muslim University, did a field
study on Muslims in a specific town. "In each and every educational institution

there, you will find Muslim girls," he reported. "…education for women is now highly valued, something that was just not the case 20 years ago" (Philipose 2000). Within this same time, another significant change has occurred. Many women have moved from villages to cities. The shift from rural to urban living, as well as the increase in education, has greatly impacted women's daily lives.

As ambassadors of the gospel of Jesus Christ, we must consider how these trends have influenced the Muslim woman. Is the worldview of the South Asian educated urban Muslim woman different from that of the uneducated woman in the village? Does her educated urban status affect the presentation of the gospel message?

SOUTH ASIAN

There is not equality among men and women in Islam. A woman is given half the inheritance that a man receives. Testimony of two women in court is required to equal the testimony of one man. Men may have up to four wives, while a woman is only allowed one husband. One reason given for polygamy has long been the greater population of women. This is not the case in South Asia, where women are considered inferior to men. The birth of a girl baby is considered a curse, while the birth of a boy baby is considered a blessing. Worldwide, there are 101 females for every 100 males. In South Asia, there are approximately 94 females for every 100 males, with Sri Lanka the lowest at 93 and Bhutan the highest at 98 (Varisco 2003).

Muslim women in South Asia are as diverse as the countries in which they live. Pakistan, Bangladesh, and the Maldives are Muslim nations. India is a secular nation, but predominately Hindu. Nepal is a Hindu nation; Bhutan is Buddhist. Sri Lanka is a democratic socialist nation with a Buddhist majority. The wearing of *burqas* (long loose-fitting cloak used to hide a woman's body) reflects this diversity. In Pakistan, almost all women will wear a *burqa* when they go out. Although Bangladesh is also a Muslim nation, few women wear *burqas*. In India, many women wear *burqas* as a means of identifying themselves with the Muslim community, especially in middle class society (Dass 2004).

In South Asia, Hinduism has strongly influenced the practice of Islam. It is a common saying in Bangladesh, that "if you scratch a Muslim hard enough, you'll find a Hindu underneath." The stigma attached to widows, and the practice of Muslims offering food and flowers at *darghas* (tombs of Muslim saints) are two examples. The custom of giving dowry is not sanctioned by Islam. It is a very great reality, however, in South Asia, and required in most marriages. It, too, seems to be borrowed from the Hindu culture (Khan 1995, 125). Payment of dowry has become more widespread as a symbol of status, and is paid by most families, even those who cannot afford it.

EDUCATED

The following snippets from *The Times of India* classified ads, dated 30 May 2004, reflect the trend toward education:

Qualifications being sought:

...looking for convent educated fair girl...

...requires MBBS/BDS/Prof...girl...

...English speaking qualified professionals doctors, engineers...

...The girl should be M.D. in Pediatric or Medicine...

...pref S/W engineers...

...Conv Grd... (Convent graduate)

...high edu girl...

Qualifications offered:

...Engr. Govt. Ser...

...M.D.-Gynaec...

...BFA Com Art PGArt Edu...

... Convent B.A....

...final year Law student of leading Law School of Kolkata...

...convent ed...M.A. B.Ed...

...Graduate in Travel & Tourism...

...Conv. Educ. B.Sc./IATA...

...BPharm PG Pharma Mgmt...

...Post Grad...

...Master in Social work...

These qualifications clearly reflect the higher education level of the South Asian Muslim girl. These classifieds, however, are not ads by employers seeking employees; nor are they ads placed by those seeking employment. Instead, these snippets are from the "Matrimonials" section, "Muslims" subsection, where parents have placed an ad, and listed qualifications for the bride they are seeking for their son; and where the girl's parents have placed an ad that lists their daughter's qualifications. The parents often educate their daughter to improve her chances of a good marriage. According to the "Muslim Women's Survey"

(MWS) conducted in 2000-2001 by Zoya Hasan and Ritu Menon, "There seems to be a negative correlation between education and employment among Muslims" (Hasan 2002). In a study by *Siasat Daily* in Hyderabad, India, the newspaper determined that of the girls surveyed, only 21.95 percent who have completed their education are employed (Hussain 1995, 81).

The fact that the girl is well educated does not diminish the expectation of dowry. Because of her education, the girl does receive marriage proposals from more highly educated boys. The request for dowry, however, still comes with the proposal. And because the boy is highly educated, the demands are often greater. The girl's education increases her chances for a "good marriage", but in the end, it does nothing to increase her value in the eyes of the culture. One such example is Sumayia's daughter Mariyam (I will use pseudonyms). Mariyam has her degree in *Unani* (Greek) medicine, and is currently working as a doctor in a clinic. Last year, her parents received a proposal from a reputable family on behalf of their son, who is also a doctor. With the proposal, however, came the demand for an automobile and a specified amount of gold, as well as the typical household items that are part of the girl's dowry. They made another demand: they would not allow Mariyam to work after marriage. Ironically, although her qualifications attracted the boy's family, she would not be given the opportunity to use those qualifications.

URBAN

The shift from rural to urban areas seems to have had a positive impact on the life of the South Asian Muslim woman. There is greater opportunity in urban areas for female education. There also seems to be a greater respect or value given to women in urban areas than women experience in rural areas. The MWS determined that an urban woman in India has greater status and greater decision-making ability, is more likely to be included in the discussion of the number of children she will bear, and is less likely to face spousal/family abuse than women in rural areas. Overall, the urban woman seems to have more freedom, although she still requires a man's permission to go out (Hasan 2002). She also has a greater chance of working alongside men in salaried jobs (*Women of South Asia* 2002). In the parks in my city, a Muslim woman walking alone in the mornings is a very common sight. After her walk, she will gather with other women and talk. She is also seen in internet cafes. Nadine, who works in an urban center of more than 14 million, comments, "They are also more aware of the limitations their culture puts on them, compared to other places around the world where women have more freedoms" (Treadwell 2004).

Wafia is very aware of the limitations her culture has placed on her. She is the youngest of six children, with four older brothers, who dictate what she can and cannot do. Although Wafia only completed a seventh standard education, she has taken every opportunity to improve herself. She learned both traditional and modern skills; having received training in tailoring and knitting, she also learned to type, to speak English and to use email and the internet. She dreams of designing clothing and living independently from her family. Her family refuses to let her work outside the home, and regularly speaks of finding a husband for her. At twenty years of age, the only reason she has not yet married is because her family is financially unable to arrange it.

The situation is difficult to comprehend. Her family struggles to make ends meet. Her brothers do not shoulder the responsibility placed on them by Islam to provide for the family. Neither do they allow her to go out to work, which she desires and which would lessen the financial burden. Despite the constraints placed on her, Wafia shows great determination to do all she can. She tailors clothing in her home, and has also learned to calculate material and labor costs as she contracts work through local shops.

MUSLIM

In some ways, education and urbanization have influenced the spiritual life of the South Asian Muslim woman; in other ways, they have not. An educated woman more often reads the Qur'an in a translation she can understand; therefore, she is more familiar with what is true to her religion and what has been added by religious teachers or culture (Treadwell 2004). This urban, educated Muslim woman expresses less confidence in folk Islamic practices, such as protection against the evil eye, visiting *darghas* during times of trouble, and using charms containing Qur'anic verses, which supposedly have power over illness. Although she says she does not believe in these things, oddly enough, she still practices them! Helen, a long-time worker among Muslim women in South Asia says, "If she cannot become pregnant, she will have her mother-in-law or other family members go to a *pir* (spiritual leader), which can be done online now, to seek advice or guidance. She may go to a fertility doctor and use modern medicine, but she will not abandon the traditional practices. A single woman will still consult a *pir* about her exams" (Solis 2004). A mother still applies kohl to her children's faces to divert the evil eye. My friend's daughter, who has a bachelor's degree and works for an international firm, wears a *burqa* only when she dresses up in order not to attract the evil eye.

Sometimes the woman continues the traditional practices by choice; other times they are imposed on her. Syeeda grew up in Bombay and has a bachelor's degree in Hindi, and now lives in a city in South India. Syeeda did not use kohl on her children's faces. According to her, "No, no, because I'm from Bombay, we don't believe that." After fifteen years of marriage, her husband became ill; initially, they sought only medical help. As his health deteriorated, and medical intervention had less effect, however, they sought help from additional sources. They placed charms in each corner of their house, and sought the prayers of Christians, recognizing the power of prayer in Jesus' name.

Since her husband's recent death, Syeeda's life has changed in many ways. Some of the changes are universal; others are unique to her as a Muslim woman in South Asia. To retain her honor, she must remain in isolation for four months and ten days, the time necessary to determine whether she is pregnant so there will be no question about who fathered the child. The issue of paternity is important both for the sake of the family's honor and because of inheritance. Because of her financial responsibilities, this extended period of isolation was not practical. She returned to work after forty days, the official mourning period. Next, she faced the dilemma of what to wear. Neither her father nor husband had required her to wear a *burqa*. Her sisters and closest friends, however, now urged her to begin wearing one. No longer having a male in authority over her (her father is also dead, and her eldest son is not old enough to be considered the man of the family), she acknowledged that men could easily have the wrong impression of her if she did not wear a *burqa*. She knew, however, that if she began to wear it, she would have to wear it for the rest of her life, which she did not want to do. She has chosen to go out without a *burqa*, and to dress as before.

As a widow, some traditional practices, which she recognizes as superstitions adopted from the Hindu culture, will be imposed on her for the remainder of her life. She is no longer allowed to wear glass bangles or flowers, two very common accessories for women in India. A day or two before marriage, the bride and groom go through a cleansing ritual with turmeric. The *huldi* rite is a great social occasion for the close relatives, in which each family member smears turmeric paste onto the face of the bride. Syeeda can never again apply *huldi* to the bride's face because it could be an omen of the bride becoming a widow at an early age. Single, separated and divorced women can all participate, but not widows. As she told me this, with sadness, I expressed the absurdity of the practice, with which she agreed. Then I questioned, "What about when

[your daughter] gets married?" "No, not even then. What can I do?" she replied
with even greater sadness.

WOMAN

As I polled women working among Muslims, I consistently heard that education
and urbanization have little effect on the role of the woman in South Asian
Muslim culture. Her life is still dictated by men. She is still expected to marry,
obey her husband and mother-in-law, and give birth to sons, although the
MWS reported that more education leads to later marriages (Hasan 2002). In
producing sons, her status in the family increases (*Women of South Asia* 2002).
If she is unable to produce sons, she brings shame upon her family, which
increases the chance of her husband taking another wife. She remains responsible for maintaining the family's honor by what she does. She is still required
to perform the same household duties. In summary, she still has little control
over her life. The MWS found that education positively influences marital
communication. It states, however, "Seventy per cent of women, Hindu and
Muslim, all-India, across classes, reported that they needed permission to go
to work. A staggering eighty-six percent said they needed permission from their
husbands for all activities." And even though it was stated earlier that an urban
educated woman has greater decision-making ability, and is consulted more
often, the survey concludes, "it does not necessarily follow that women are
equal partners in decision-making or that they have any real choice in the
matter" (Muslim Women's Survey 2002).

Fatima's parents arranged her marriage at the age of fourteen. She had a
daughter soon after, and was divorced by the time she was eighteen. Fortunately,
her family took her back, and even paid for Fatima to complete her education.
Fatima became a buyer for a garment factory; she had a good income, and
traveled extensively. At one point, she became romantically attached to a *goonda*,
a man involved in the underworld. Finally she recognized her foolishness, and
left the man. One day, Fatima excitedly told Leah that she and her daughter
were moving to England to live! A very short time later, however, Leah again
saw Fatima in Dhaka. She discovered that Fatima had returned because the
goonda had threatened to kill Fatima's parents if she would not return to Dhaka
and marry him. Having no choice, Fatima became his second wife. After that,
she lost her business and her freedom. The last report Leah had about Fatima
came in 2002, when Fatima was in the hospital. She had been shot four times
by her husband. Because of her serious condition, she had not yet been

informed that her husband had also killed her sixteen year old daughter. Despite her education and her status, she had no control over her life (Pogue 2004).

IMPLICATIONS AND APPLICATIONS

The irony is evident: the changes that have occurred in the educated, urban South Asian Muslim woman's life have brought about no real change at all. She is still considered to have less value than her male counterpart, both in her culture and in her religion. After considering the impact of education and urban living on the Muslim woman, it can be concluded that her worldview itself is not so different from the more traditional Muslim woman described by J.O. Terry: she still lives in a world of relationships; her orientation is still on people; her identity is still defined by her male protector; she is still spiritually sensitive; she is still seeking to change her circumstances in order to satisfy her personal needs; and her hope still lies in the fulfillment of promises (Terry 1998, v-vii).

As an outsider (foreigner or non-Muslim), gaining access to the Muslim woman has always been a barrier to overcome. "Muslim women are the largest unreached people group in the world. They are the hardest to reach" (Solis 2004). A worker in Bangladesh describes the situation: "We knew that if Muslim women would become believers, then the entire family would follow. Gaining access to Muslim women in order to share the gospel had been an impossible task up until that point" (Greeson 2004:36). Reaching them, however, is vital, for they are the ones who train up the next generation in their faith (Treadwell 2004). Abdul, a former Muslim now involved in reaching other Muslims for Christ in South Asia, commented that the Muslim woman must be reached with the gospel if Christianity is to be passed on to the next generation. If only the husband is a believer, the family usually returns to Islam after his death (Abdul 2003).

So what is the significance of her educated urban status for us as we seek to bring the gospel to her—the good news that provides Jesus' sacrifice as the means of restoring her broken relationship with her creator God, the only one powerful enough to change her circumstances and to fulfill his eternal promise? The significance is not worldview, then, but access. There seem to be more opportunities for reaching her, both during her education and after. She is more open to others' beliefs (Treadwell 2004) and in a better position to learn about beliefs different from her own. "Educated women who are members of middle or upper-class urban families often live with far fewer of the restrictions borne by women of those classes who live in rural, traditional homes" (*Women of South Asia* 2002).

Christian schools have a reputation of providing excellent educations, as is evidenced in the matrimonial ads. In attending a Christian school, the Muslim woman is exposed to the gospel, both through curriculum and relationships. During her time at university, she lives in a less restricted environment which provides a greater chance to share the gospel. She is also often seeking ways to alleviate the stress she faces, which is greater than normal because of the obstacles she must overcome in order to continue her education (Hasan 2002).

With fewer restrictions, there are more points of access to the educated Muslim woman, but relationship remains the key (Solis 2004). Repeated contact is usually necessary before she will trust the outsider enough to seek a relationship. Relationship building can happen in the course of her daily routine, as she walks in the park, or stands at the bus stop with her child. Former Muslim women in one South Asian urban center share the gospel with their neighbors as they gather at the local water pump to wash dishes. Through this very natural opportunity, more than 3,500 Muslims—mostly women—have received salvation through Jesus Christ (MBB Women 2003).

Providing enrichment seminars remains a great way of gathering women. Gathering women is natural in the culture, but the groups have an added benefit. As they come to faith, there is a support group already in place (Solis 2004). The possibilities range from topics of general interest, such as parenting and health, to topics that are more specific, such as conversational English, basic computer skills, Western cooking, and business. The Daudi Bhora community is very business oriented, with even women managing their own businesses. Providing a business seminar, which teaches godly business principles, is a very specific means of gaining access to these women (Kaser 2004).

Because of her urban educated status, new media for sharing the gospel are available. With basic computer skills, the Muslim woman can access the entire world through the internet. Numerous websites use this medium to bring the gospel to Muslims. One website actually provides a list of links to Christian web sites seeking to reach Muslims with the message of Christ (Varisco 2000). She is also more likely to watch issue- and woman-oriented programs (Hasan 2002). Another medium now available to her is women's publications. The percentage of women wearing *burqas* in Kerala, a state in south India, marked a tenfold increase in a ten year period, providing solid evidence that such publications have great influence on Muslim women. *Burqa* manufacturers and salesmen recognized that advertising in women's magazines was the only way to reach women with their products. Where readership was highest, the increase in the women wearing *burqas* was also greatest (Basheer 2003). The influence that publications have on the lives of women is too great to discount. We must find a way of employing this medium in spreading the gospel.

We can conclude that there are now more ways of reaching out to the educated urban Muslim woman. We must use both the traditional and the new ways that are available. We must continue to gather her with other women and establish relationships. We must also provide opportunities for her to hear the gospel via the internet, woman-oriented television programs, and women's publications. She has been neglected for too long, and we must use every opportunity to share the great love God has for her. Every aspect of life for the South Asian educated urban Muslim woman is filled with ironies. The greatest irony of all, however, remains: she diligently works to earn what God desires to freely give her.

R E F E R E N C E S

Abdul. 2003. Interview by Yvette Wray, 9 July.

Basheer, M.P. 2003. *Behind the veil*. Available online http://www.sabrang.com-/cc/archive/2003/jan03/investi.html; accessed 1 May 2004.

Treadwell, Nadine. 2004. Interview by Yvette Wray, 8 June.

Durrany, K.S. 1993. *The impact of Islamic fundamentalism*. Delhi, India: Indian Society for Promoting Christian Knowledge.

Glaser, Ida and Napoleon John. 1998. *Partners or prisoners? Christians thinking about women and Islam*. Carlisle, UK: Solway.

Goodwin, Jan. 1994. *Price of honor: Muslim women lift the veil of silence on the Islamic world*. New York: Plume.

Gopalakrishnan, Amulya. 2003. Gender issues: Dispelling myths. *Frontline*. Available online http://www.flonnet.com/fl2001/stories/20030117002408700.htm; accessed 7 Jun 2004.

Hussain, Syed Mehdi. 1995. Muslim women and higher education: A case study of Hyderabad. In *Problems of Muslim women in India*, 72-88, ed. Asghara Ali Engineer. Bombay: Orient Longman.

Kasar, Suzi. 2004. Interview by Yvette Wray, 27 April.

Khan, Maulana Wahiduddin. 1995. *Woman in Islamic Shari'ah*. New Delhi: Goodword Books.

MBB Women. 2003. Interview by Yvette Wray, 9 July.

Philipose, Pamela. 2000. *Change in the air*. Available online http://www.islamfortoday.com/ womeninindia.html; Internet; accessed 18 May 2004.

Pogue, Leah. 2004. Interview by Yvette Wray, 2 June.

Solis, Helen. 2004. Interview by Yvette Wray, 4 May.

_____. 2004. Interview by Yvette Wray, 8 June.

Syeeda. 2004. Interview by Yvette Wray, 10 June.

Terry, J.O. 1998. *God and woman: A chronological Bible storying model for storying the Good News to a primarily oral culture Muslim and Hindu women's worldview*. Singapore.

Varisco, Daniel Martin. 2000. *Slamming Islam: Participant webservation with a web of meanings to boot*. Available online http://www.aaanet.org/mes/lectvar1.htm; accessed 8 June 2004.

_____. 2002. *Muslim women's survey*. Available online from http://www.infochangeindia.org/bookandreportsst22.jsp; accessed 7 June 2004.

_____. 2002. *Gender stats*. The World Bank Group. Available online http://devdata.worldbank.org/genderstats/home.asp; accessed 3 June 2004.

_____. 2003. *The world's women 2000: Trends and statistics*. United Nations. Available online http://unstats.un.org/unsd/demographic/ww2000/table1a.htm; accessed 18 May 2004.

_____. 2004. Matrimonials. *Times of India*, 30 May.

_____. 2004. *Women of South Asia*. Available from http://www.utc.edu/Faculty-/SarlaMurgai/wosa.html; accessed 18 May.

11

Christ in Their Midst:
Evangelism and Church Planting Among Southeast Asian Muslim Women

Mary Bennett

Mary Bennett's extensive ministry experience among a Southeast Asian Muslim people group has given her a clear and deep understanding of the worldview of these women. In this paper she clarifies many of the barriers that keep these women from faith and shares several bridges that have been effectively used to reach them, including some specific Qu'ran-based approaches.

This paper is written from my almost fourteen years of experience living among Southeast Asian (SEA) Muslim women of one people group in an urban village. This is a lower-class area in a large city with small houses built in close proximity and extended families living in a close-knit community. My contact with workers who live among other groups indicates that many of my observations are applicable throughout the region. Although the names have been changed, these true stories reveal the worldview of these women along with many of the barriers that keep them from faith. The paper also introduces several bridges to sharing Truth that have been effective among Southeast Asian Muslim women. May this paper inspire you to build deeper relationships based on love and friendship with Muslim women.

EXPLORING WORLDVIEW

Nina is a middle-aged mother of six children, five of whom are still living and healthy. She lives in an urban village. Her husband works as a driver, and she manages a little roadside stall, selling cigarettes, drinks, snacks, and a simple rice meal. She is an energetic and fun-loving woman, very "down to earth" and a little uncouth. She's not really worried about what most people think of her, so she was willing to befriend this foreigner who moved into her neighborhood.

When we first met, Nina was pregnant with her last child. One day as we chatted together at her house, I offered to take her to the midwife or hospital when she was ready to have her baby. Even if it was the middle of the night, I wanted her to wake us up, and my husband and I would be glad to help. She was very grateful and informed me that her husband was afraid of the *jinn* in the creek he would have to cross behind our houses in order to get to the midwife. She finally admitted that she, too, was afraid of the *jinn* in the water. I remembered another time I had visited. Her front door was wide open, and no one was in sight. I called to her, and finally she appeared, wet and wrapped in a towel. She had just bathed with her front door wide open, because she was afraid of the *jinn* that would come out of the water. She wanted them to go right out the front door and not stay to bother her!

The Lord prompted me to tell her about his power over evil spirits. "Nina, Nabi Isa (the prophet Jesus) has power over evil spirits. Do you know about him?" She didn't, and she wanted to hear. So I briefly told her about his miraculous birth and powerful life, his sacrificial death and glorious resurrection. "His resurrection is proof that He has defeated death, sin, and evil spirits!" Nina was amazed, and I believe she moved closer to the kingdom that day.

After that Nina often met with me and other neighborhood women to hear stories from the Holy Books and to pray and sing together. There seemed to be some growth in her life. But after two or three years, when she planned a celebration for the circumcision of her youngest son, she called a folk practitioner to her home to guide her to choose the right date and perform the proper rituals to ensure the family a safe and successful celebration. The shaman burned incense, chanted various mantras (in Arabic), and performed other ancient rituals, most of which pre-date the arrival of Islam in Indonesia. Even though Nina considered herself a Muslim and had begun to trust in the power of prayer through *Isa al Masih* (Jesus the Messiah), she still felt the need to be sure everything was done according to tradition so that the spirit world would not be disturbed.

Alin and Lina are sisters. They live in the same urban village as Nina but in a different area. My involvement with this family began when Alin's husband and daughter asked us to help take Alin to the doctor. Alin had breast cancer. She had found the lump many months before she went to the doctor. Her family had taken her to every shaman and "quack" that they had heard of from their extended circle of family and neighbors before they finally decided she should see a doctor. Sure enough, it was too late. Her cancer was already at fourth stage, they had no money, and even with the best of medical help, there was little hope. My colleague, a medical doctor and specialist in cancer, studied her lab reports and informed me that Alin needed lots of tender loving care. He suggested various pain medications to ease her through the last days of her life.

Knowing the imminence of this woman's death, I went to visit her in order to speak to her of her eternal destiny. Alin was laconic to say the least. Sometimes she didn't speak at all—she only nodded or shook her head. This discouraged me from visiting her, and yet the Spirit would not let me ignore her. Finally I realized that as the cancer progressed, Alin was alone for long periods of time. Though she had sisters, close neighbors, and a daughter around most of the time, she was often left alone. They took care of her but didn't stay long in the room. Alin's cancer smelled. Only with God's help was I able to visit with her for very long. But He did help, and He encouraged me to take advantage of the opportunity to share His story with her. Not long after she heard the story of Isa's (Jesus') resurrection, she passed away, and I have great hope that she is with him today. She had responded to the stories and to prayer. The day I told her the story of the resurrection, I asked her if she had trusted Isa to save her from her sin. She nodded her head affirmatively, and I hope that He had truly worked salvation in her hearing.

Several years later Lina became very ill with tuberculosis. She grew thinner and seemed to be wasting away. I began to visit her to pray with her. One day, her best friend was with her and urged me to pray for her to be healed. I assured her I would, but that I wanted to tell them a story first. I told the story of the woman with the issue of blood for twelve years and how Lina was like this woman—going to doctors and shamans and wasting all her money since she was not getting well. But this woman went to Isa (Jesus), touched his robe and was healed. "Isa is your only hope as well," I told her. Then we prayed together and God began to work. The next night she was so ill that her husband took her to the TB hospital where she finally received the care she needed. I visited her there to share more truth with her, and today she is healthy and has skin on her bones again. She recognized who healed her. Recently I challenged her to trust him in all areas of her life and offered to share more with her. Hopefully she will respond along with others in her family.

Hani is an older woman from our urban village. As a young teenager, Hani was married off to an older man, but she couldn't take it and returned home. Later she was married again. This marriage was a good one, but not without some work on Hani's part. Hani gave birth to several sons, and finally had a daughter. But because of difficulties in her marriage at that time, she asked her sister to care for the baby while she worked to help her husband stop gambling and learn to be a good husband and father. She succeeded, but it took longer than she thought. By the time she was ready for her daughter to return home, the baby was already attached to the sister and her sister to the baby.

Later Hani had twin girls, but one of them died. The one who lived, Sri, is over thirty years old now and has never married, which is usually considered shameful for the family. Sri's older siblings have taken her to shamans to try to get her a husband, but one time the glass with the "water" that she should drink in order to get a husband shattered before she could drink it. The other time she asked to take the "water" home to drink it there. She poured it out in the creek as she passed by on her way home. Hani has not insisted that Sri marry. She remembers her first disastrous marriage and supports Sri in her decision. Sri has come to know Isa (Jesus) as her Savior and is growing in grace and purpose in her life. He obviously protected her from the bondage of drinking the "water" and of a marriage that might have hindered her coming to faith. She shares truth with her family and is a wonderful blessing to all who know her. Though still relatively young and single, Sri is known for her pure life and her wisdom. She has maintained her identity as a member of the Muslim community, and many of the neighbors bring their difficult questions to her. Even her mother, Hani, has come close to understanding and accepting the truth about Isa al Masih (Jesus, the Messiah), the way to God.

Worldview Assumptions

The lives of these women reveal many worldview assumptions of the Southeast Asian (SEA) lower educated rural or urban-rural women. Their mindset assumes the nearness of the spirit world and the distance of God. Their communities are close-knit and yet often cover up discord and bad relationships. For a woman, it is considered shameful to remain unmarried. And their commitment to Islam is a commitment to their leaders and their community.

Many of these women are functionally illiterate. This doesn't mean they can't read, but they don't read. Yet there are exceptions. Hani can't read, but her daughter, Sri, is a voracious reader, even though she only has a sixth-grade education. This is one reason Sri came to believe—through reading the Bible and other evangelistic materials.

SEA women live in the "eternal now." They don't think about tomorrow. Today is what matters. If they have money today, they spend it, give it away, or lend it to the sister who needs it. There is a lovely generous spirit in their attitude towards money, and yet they don't plan for or even think about the future. This hinders them from thinking about eternity as well.

Another worldview element is belief that blessings and riches are limited. In other words, if my neighbor gets ahead materially, I probably won't, because there's only so much to go around. If she has a kind husband, no wonder I don't. Blessings like that are limited. This causes envy and fatalism. She got it, so I won't. I must keep her from getting it, so I can get it instead.

Appearances are very important. Dressing in the right way, providing appropriate hospitality, raising children who bring honor and not shame to their families, correctly following religious rituals and forms—all this is an integral part of the life of these women. Nina had begun to trust in Isa to protect her and help her. But even though she is not overly concerned about the opinion of her neighbors, she still wanted to be sure she did the "right" things for her son's circumcision party. This is partly to keep up appearances and partly to appease the spirit world.

BARRIERS TO FAITH

There are many barriers to these women coming to know the Way, the Truth, and the Life. Oddly, one of the major barriers is the established church in this particular country, which uses alien cultural forms and even a different spiritual vocabulary. I don't think that would be such a barrier if their witness was full of love and joy and grace toward the Muslim community, but too often the witness of church members is not.

Nur's husband worked faithfully and diligently for many years as a driver for a wealthy Chinese Christian man. This man appreciated Nur's husband so much that he bought a house for him in the lower-class urban village near this man's mansion. Nur's family understood that the house was to be theirs permanently. The Christian man was good to the husband until the husband began to get sick with high blood pressure. Without warning, the boss asked him to retire.

He offered him a good severance pay which would have been sufficient, except that he then pressured Nur's family to move. He wanted his new driver to live in that house. Nur's family had invested their own money into improving the house. Also, her daughter was going to school near their community, not to mention they had made close friends there after eight years. This was a difficult blow which was made even more difficult when the wealthy Christian boss didn't buy them another home. He only gave them the same amount of money that he had used to buy the first house close to his mansion. With inflation and with the amount of money that Nur and her husband had invested, they were definitely the losers. Nur and her husband used their severance pay to buy another home. They went from being fairly well off to now being almost destitute —all at the hands of their wealthy Christian employer.

Since then, Nur has tried to cook food and sell it out of their home. Her husband has looked for a job unsuccessfully since he is beyond the usual hiring age. One of Nur's sons helps out with his limited income as a motorcycle mechanic. They struggle to keep their daughter in school, especially since she has to pay more for transport costs from the new location. She sometimes skips school when she has no money. It is embarrassing for this daughter to be in such a position. When Nur and her husband talk about their problems, they are philosophical about it all. Life is hard. Chinese Christians are the way they are. They will find a way to make do.

Another barrier is the false teaching of Muslim leaders. Hagar is a serious Muslim woman who always wears the veil. She hears the teaching that the Bible has been falsified, that she shouldn't read it, and that all she needs is found in Islam. Hagar avoids contact with Christians. She keeps her children away from them too. She is representative of many women who simply believe what they are taught and don't seek for truth.

Some women, however, reject religious practice and have very little thought for God. Ita is a young divorcée, a materialist, and an extremely wounded young woman. She found out on her wedding day that she had been adopted—that the parents she had known all her life were not really her parents. Her husband didn't work often enough to meet her needs, so she found a job working at night selling lottery tickets which is not considered respectable employment. Finally they divorced in spite of the fact that they have a son. The son is a hurting little boy too. This woman lives for the here and now. Although she goes through the motions of Islam during the major Islamic celebrations, she has no concern for eternity. Her bondage to materialism is a common barrier to faith. Ita tries unsuccessfully to make her son happy by buying him things.

She is considered by the neighbors to be a bad woman and a bad mother. Ita would probably agree that they are right. She just tries to make the most of her situation. She believes her fate is fixed. She has taken a new husband who visits her house occasionally during the daytime when she is home. The neighbors gossip about the new husband and say that he has another wife. That may well be the truth. Her little boy bounces back and forth between families and neighbors and is increasingly becoming a discipline problem. Ita may be out of ideas, but the one solution she needs is the love and faithfulness of Jesus.

One of the major barriers of the worldview of SEA women is life cycle rituals. Everything revolves around them. Even before giving birth, women observe many rituals believed to assure a safe birth and healthy baby. From birth to circumcision to marriage to childbirth to death and the funeral, there are rites that families carefully observe. Many of these rituals have been mixed with Islam and so are considered religious, but most of them have little if anything to do with Islam. Understanding the importance of these rituals in their life cycle can help bridge the gap between truth and reality. Some of these rituals can be modified and given deep spiritual meaning and bring blessing into the lives of the community rather than bondage. Many of them have to be exposed as strongholds that bind them to evil spirits. As these women come to faith, they need to renounce them and seek deliverance through the power of Jesus' death and resurrection.

BRIDGES TO FAITH

Many bridges can and have been used to reach out to SEA women with the good news. Using the Qur'an is an excellent bridge to sharing the truth with the more religious Muslim women. One plan is even called The Qur'anic Bridge and uses the following verses:

- Al An'aam Q 6:34 Discuss: Can God's word be changed?
- Al Maa-idah Q 5:68 Discuss: Are the Torah and the gospel considered God's word?
- Al Ahqaaf Q 46:9 Discuss: Did Muhammad have clear understanding about eternal life?
- Ali 'Imran Q 3:45 Discuss: Who is the most exalted in this world and the next?
- Az Zukhruf Q 43:63-64 Discuss: What prophet is connected to the straight way?
- Read John 14:6 Discuss: Who is the way, the truth, and the life?

Another Qu'ranic bridge focuses on reading the third chapter of the Qur'an called Ali Imran, verses 42-55 and asking several questions to open Muslim minds up to the truth that Isa (Jesus) is divine. This method is sometimes called the Camel Training Method (Greeson 2004) after the Arab proverb that states that only the camel knows the 100th name of God:

- Read Q 3:42-44. Discuss: Who was chosen above other women?
- Read Q 3:45. Discuss: What was the announcement about Jesus? Do you know what the Messiah means? (promised one from God)
- Read Q 3:46-48. Discuss: What truth does Jesus bring from God?
- Read Q 3:49-50. Discuss: Who was given miraculous power of life over death?
- Read Q 3:51-53. Discuss: Who were called submitted ones or Muslims?
- Read Q 3:54-55. Discuss: What was God's plan? The word in Arabic for ending Jesus' life on earth is *wafat*. What does that mean? (dead) Where did Jesus go after God ended His life on earth? Do you think Jesus might have wisdom about God's 100th name? Do you think Jesus would know the way to heaven?

Yet another bridge using the Qu'ran to introduce the gospel is explained in a book by Fouad Accad entitled *Building Bridges* (Accad 1997). This book is available in the Indonesian/Malaysian language. The plan is called "Seven Principles," and uses the Taurat (the Pentetuch), Zabur (Psalms), Injil (New Testament), and the Qur'an to explain the plan of salvation.

One of the most effective bridges being used by many women is prayer. Whenever there is a need in the life of a Muslim woman, offer to pray for that woman. If she or a child or another family member is sick, pray with the woman for Isa (Jesus) to touch and heal the sick one. If there is a problem between two friends, pray for God to guide and resolve the problem. If there is a physical need, ask God to provide. If there is an inner need, ask God to come and reveal who He is to this woman and touch and heal her hurt and pain.

One colleague often uses prayer to lead Muslim women to faith and healing. She recognizes that in prayer she is introducing the women to Jesus and his love and healing power. In one experience, she was ministering to Della, a very needy Muslim woman who had just given birth to her fourth child. She'd been married and divorced twice, and this child was born out of wedlock. Della had not kept the other three and she admitted to having tried to abort this little girl in the fifth month of pregnancy. God has spoken to Della's cousin directing her to adopt the little baby girl, and also to take in the mother and care for her for the coming month.

My colleague invited Della to follow a prayer of repentance for her abortion attempt and her relationship with the baby's father. She then put her hand on the baby and blessed her, asked for the child to be freed of any result of her mother's sin and thanked God for her life. Placing the baby in her cousin's arms, Della then followed us in a prayer of release, handing the baby over to their authority and care and asking God to bless them. After an extended time of prayer in which Della experienced the presence and love of Isa (Jesus), my colleague led her to receive Him as her Savior.

Prayer is not just a bridge to share God's love and truth. It is our main strategy. We should not only be praying with others but constantly praying for the Lord to open women's hearts and minds to his truth and love. One colleague keeps a prayer journal for each of her Muslim friends. Each page has the name of a different Muslim woman. On that page she keeps track of what tract or verse or word of witness she has shared with her friend. She also writes the verse or verses that she is praying for each one. This not only helps her to remember what she shares with each woman, but this also helps her to stay faithful in prayer and reminds her of what God has done and is doing in each woman's life.

There was a time in my neighborhood when the younger teens seemed to be going wild—playing around with the opposite sex, using foul language all the time, even vandalizing by writing on the walls of houses. I began to pray more intentionally for these young people. I even went to two of their moms and expressed my concern for their teenage children. I offered to pray with them for their children, and they took me up on it. After we prayed together, I noticed they had tears in their eyes. I sensed they really knew my love for them and their children, not to mention the love of Isa (Jesus) for them. And God worked. That difficult period in the lives of the young teens has passed, and they all seem to be doing much better.

Incarnational lifestyle is extremely important to building bridges. We as foreigners are already outsiders. We should live more and more like the people we have been called to bless and serve. We should live in community with them, dress like them, eat as they eat, decorate our homes similarly to theirs, etc. Just as we would not feel comfortable visiting in a rich person's mansion, so they are not comfortable visiting in our homes when they are so different from theirs. If they see us live, dress, speak, and eat in ways that say "unholy" to them, how will we ever gain a hearing for the truth? Certainly these are only outward things, and God looks on the heart. But as we seek to bless others, we must understand their way of looking at what is right and good and holy and adapt ourselves to the highest of their standards. We also need to study the ways in which they communicate spiritual ideas and adapt our communication forms to theirs.

I must admit that it has taken me many years to figure out how to live more like SEA women. I'm still learning. I was given very little guidance in this area before I moved to SEA and had to learn by making mistakes. When my family first moved to our adopted country, we lived in a large American-style house with a large yard and carport. Our organization owned this home, and since it was empty, it was the house for us to use. After living in this house in an upper class neighborhood for three years, the Lord made it very clear to us that he wanted us to move and live among the people. We had tried to build relation-ships with our neighbors, but we found that not only were most of them not a part of our people group, most of them lived behind their locked gates and didn't want to be bothered. We realized that hundreds of families of the people group we wanted to love and bless lived in an urban village just behind the rich houses. At first, our leaders didn't want us to move into a lower-class neighborhood. We had three young daughters, and they were concerned for their safety. They also raised the question: "What will you tell them about moving into their neighborhood? They don't expect Americans to live like them."

Finally after much prayer, we had permission to move. When our new neigh-bors asked us why we wanted to move from the *gedung* (building) to their neighborhood, we answered, "We wanted to have closer relationships with our neighbors, but it was difficult to know them when we lived in the 'building'." Our neighbors totally understood, and they have warmly welcomed us as a part of their community. What we have learned by living more like them and in closer proximity cannot be measured. We have felt much safer living in community with these neighbors. In fact at times we have sensed they look after us to be sure no one bothers or takes advantage of us.

Is incarnational lifestyle really a priority for us as foreigners? Deep down inside it seems we think our way is the best way and that we shouldn't lower our standards. May the Lord have mercy on us and guide us to examine our hearts before Him and seek to live by his example of emptying Himself and becoming poor for our sake. We need to help one another with this issue and challenge one another to truly give up our way of life in order to become more like our Muslim neighbors in order to win them.

SUGGESTED MINISTRIES

Many workers are implementing strategies to build relationships with women and to communicate truth with them. One of the most effective ways is through children. As our children play with their children, we have a natural way of getting to know other women. If you have no children or your children are grown, you can still get to know and bless their children. You can offer to help them with their English or invite the children to come over for a play time and story time. Women love their children. When we bless and help their children their hearts open to us as well.

Women love to cook. Teaching them how to make a cake or cookies or a simple meal, even bread, gives you an opportunity to share who you are and to open your home to them. If you are out in a village, cooking over an open fire attracts many women. Perhaps as the cake bakes, you can naturally share a story from the Bible or a teaching from the prophets. You may also ask them to teach you how to cook their food. This shows your respect for them and your desire to eat what they eat. Eating together binds you together as friends.

Women are interested in better health. Gather them together with a health care worker, or do your own research and share about hygiene, diet or preventative medicine. I have found that my limited understanding of general health care is much greater than that of my neighbors. Often I can visit my sick neighbor and give wise advice in addition to prayer that helps them to get well soon. One example was when a neighbor's little girl wouldn't eat. She probably had strep throat and didn't want to eat, because it hurt. I called my pediatrician friend and asked his advice. She needed a simple antibiotic for the infection, and he suggested they tempt her to eat with anything she wanted, even ice cream. When I suggested this, they were shocked, because eating anything cold when you are sick is considered very bad. I took a popsicle to the little girl, and she wanted to eat it. The parents finally decided they could trust me. The little girl enjoyed the popsicle, and it was just the thing she needed to get her eating again. That, along with the antibiotic and prayer, quickly restored her to good health. This is one way of showing as well as sharing God's love with Muslims.

Cultural exchange is also a good way to share ideas and open your heart to theirs and theirs to yours. This could include ideas about how to have a good marriage or how to discipline and raise children, based on biblical principles. A good marriage is a wonderful bridge to sharing truth. If they see the way we relate in love and kindness to our husbands and vice versa, this is an attractive witness. We can teach biblical principles of love, marriage and child-raising and not only bless but perhaps attract Muslims to Jesus through His teachings on marriage. One way to share God's truth at a wedding is to print out a section from the teachings of Jesus about marriage and insert it in the envelope with your gift. In my country this gift would be an amount of money. I have been surprised at the positive response to this effort. This could also be effective when giving a gift to a new baby and inserting a section about rearing children. I haven't yet discovered verses that I thought would be accepted about circumcision, but maybe I ought to insert them anyway and hope His teaching will open up some hearts and minds.

Visiting from village to village is a way to discover women who are open to the truth. One brave colleague goes to the market and talks with the women there. She is careful to dress like a villager by wearing simple, loose, long clothing and no make-up. She has discovered that each village has distinct colors, usually dark. Shiny colors are for special occasions. She also goes house to house in the village, introducing herself, and offering to pray for the sick or needy. She is careful not to visit the same person each time to avoid appearing to be "owned" by a particular family. Some women say no to prayer, but most agree. When God's power is demonstrated through healing, people talk about it.

Some of the tried and true ways of communicating truth with Southeast Asian women are by telling the stories of the Bible chronologically, interceding for the sick, reading the holy books together, and living in close community so your life speaks and opens women's hearts to hear your words. Sri came to faith through both chronological story-telling and reading the Bible. Before I could even understand the language, I asked Sri to read the *Injil* (New Testament) with me and help me with correct pronunciation. It wasn't long until we could have simple discussions as I gained comprehension and vocabulary. Now we have long discussions about truth. We have had a weekly time to read a chapter together and pray for family and neighbors for many years. It's a great encouragement to my own spiritual life as well as her only true fellowship at this time.

One of my colleagues encouraged me with these words: "What most of us think we have to do to share truth is sometimes so complicated. Ask Jesus to guide you – to give you His heart for women. Jump in and do what He tells you to do and He'll teach you even more." The enemy tries to make us fear, but the opposite of fear is faith. We may not know what we're doing, but we must do what we can one step at a time. Learn from the Lord along the way. We can trust Him to lead us. You are light, and wherever you go, you dispel darkness.

REFERENCES

Accad, Fouad E. 1997. *Building Bridges: Christianity and Islam*. Colorado Springs, Co.: Navpress.

Greeson, Kevin. 2004. CAMEL training manual. Bangalore, India: Wigtake Resources.

12

The Unknown Sect of Islam: Reaching Wahhabi Women

R.A.

The experience of Muslim women varies depending upon their area's school of law. In this article, the author discusses the beliefs and practices of Wahhabism, one of the most conservative of all Muslim groups, and its impact upon women in Saudi Arabia. She suggests its potential influence on Muslim women world-wide through associations like al-Qaeda and how truth can be communicated to Wahhabi women.

During the weeks that followed the September 11 attacks and after Osama bin Laden and his al-Qaeda followers announced their responsibility for the destruction of the Twin Towers, the word "Wahhabism," sometimes called "Salafism," was used in media all over the world. In this paper I will discuss the origin and beliefs of Wahhabis, the Muslim people involved with the movement and how we as Christians in the twenty-first century can minister to these people.

DEFINING WAHHABISM

Wahhabism is a conservative and intolerant form of Islam practiced in Saudi Arabia that insists on a literal interpretation of the Qur'an. Strict Wahhabis believe that all those who do not practice their unique form of Islam are heathens and enemies of Islam. It calls for a simple, austere life and insists that any wealth one may have should be used for the good of the brethren rather than for plea-sureful living. The sect is driven by the belief that Muslims must return to the basic teachings of the Qur'an and the Hadith (sayings of Muhammad). They believe that all important issues of society are explicitly addressed in the Qur'an and Hadith and therefore Muslims ought to live according to those teachings. All practices outside of these two sources, therefore, are condemned; most Wahhabis will ban pictures, photographs, musical instruments, singing, video, suicide bombings, and celebrating the Prophet Muhammad's birthday among many other things (Wikipedia, 2004). Finally, Wahhabis are interested in estab-lishing a unified Muslim state based exclusively on Islamic law (Ahmed 1987, 305).

Islamic Society Prior to Wahhabism

Wahhabism originated out of a concern for spiritual decline. In the first half of the 1700s the Islamic world reached the nadir of its decline. Moral corruption was at its highest peak as people participated in adultery, theft, alcohol con-sumption and the use of opium. Spiritual decline was evident in the lack of worshippers and empty and abandoned mosques. Rather than following the principles of the Qur'an, leaders placed more value on philosophy than the Sunnah. They led people into superstition and mysticism. Because the people were ignorant, they followed blindly; making pilgrimages to saint's tombs and urging their leaders to intercede for them. Divesting Allah of His essential attributes and making incorrect interpretations of Qur'anic texts, Muslims believe the heart of Islam was pushed aside, leaving only meaning-less rituals and degrading superstitions.

The Man Behind Wahhabism

The person behind the movement was the son of a Muslim scholar and judge; Muhammad bin Abdul Wahhab. Born in Arabia in 1705, as a young man his appetite and yearning for knowledge took him to Medina in the Hijaz, the southwest region of Arabia. There he acquired Islamic knowledge from a num-ber of well known scholars such as Muhammad As-Sindi, moving eventually to northwest Arabia, present-day Iraq, where he studied Hadith, jurisprudence, and the Arabic language. His original intention was to travel to Damascus from Baghdad, but for some reason, he could not (Al Jumuah). Therefore, he traveled to Persia, present-day Iran, where he was introduced to Sufism or Islamic mysticism. As he learned more about the mysticism and superstitions

of the Sufi religion, he began to teach against it. It was during that time that he
wrote his book, *Kitab al Tawhid* (the Book of Monotheism) and Wahhabism
emerged as a doctrine. Rebelling against even the prevailing Sunnah schools
of religious thought, he established his own Wahhabi school ("Wahhabism,"
ahle-Sunnaht).

When bin Adbul Wahhab later returned to his village in Arabia and started
propagating his teaching, his philosophy was refuted by Arab leaders as well
as his family (Ibid). Despite these efforts, people from the surrounding villages
and towns came to Wahhab to hear him and to learn his philosophy on Islamic
teaching. Soon his teachings began yielding positive results, much to the dis-
pleasure of the ruling heads of the different tribes. The tribal leaders feared the
anger of authorities since his teachings called for the liberation of people from
the darkness of ignorance and from the excesses and oppressions of corrupted
and manipulative establishments.

Eventually, the tribal leaders evicted Wahhab from the region and he moved
to an area under the rule of Muhammad ibn Saud. In a turn of events, not only
did Ibn Saud accept Wahhab's teachings and embrace his principles, but he
also pledged him his support, calling for the application of the "authentic"
Shari'ah laws, and the propagation of the "pure" Islamic teachings. At Wahhab's
death in 1797, the entire region of the Hijaz and most of the Arab peninsula
had become unified under the banner of *tawhid* (Unity of God), the cornerstone
of Wahhab's teachings (Al Jumuah). He was ninety-two years old when he died.

Wahhabi Doctrine and Theology
Several doctrines emerged from Wahhabi teachings, the most important of
which is *Tawhid al-Ubudiya* (Hidaayah Islamic Foundation). *Tawhid* requires
an exclusive obedience to Allah and compliance with His commands. This is
a comprehensive term for doing everything that Allah loves, i.e., exhibiting the
words and deeds that please Him. The forms of worship, which are to be offered
to Allah alone, are many and include *salat* (performing the five daily prayers),
saum (fasting during Ramadan), *zakat* (giving the required alms), *sadaqah* (the
voluntary giving of alms), *udhiyah* (the ritual slaughtering of sacrificial animals),
tawaf (the ritual circumambulation of the Ka'bah) and *dhikr* or invocation (remembering God and invoking His Name). According to Sheikh Abdul Wahhab, anyone
who happens to direct any of these acts to anyone other than Allah becomes a
mushriq or idolater as it says in the Qur'an: "And whoever invokes (or worships)
besides Allah any other *ilah* (god) of whom he has no proof, then his reckon-

ing is only with his Lord. Surely *al-kafirun* (the disbelievers in the Oneness of Allah, polytheists, pagans, idolaters) will not be successful" (Q 23:117).

The second doctrine, *tawassul*, refers to making a fervent plea and is of two types: the permitted plea is by means of faith and one's own righteous deeds, and by the Glorious Names of Allah and his attributes. The prohibited plea is entreaty using the name of the Messenger, pious people, or saints. By means of this doctrine, Muslims were directed away from their superstitions including prayers to saints and ordered to invoke Allah and Allah alone: "O you who believe! Be mindful of your duty towards Allah and seek the means of approach and strive in His cause as much as you can so that you may be successful" (Q 5:35).

The third doctrine concerns journeying to mosques on pilgrimage. Muslims were directed not to make a pilgrimage to any mosque other than the three mosques given in an authentic hadith: "Do not undertake a journey but to the three mosques—the Sacred Mosque Mecca), my mosque (Medina), and the further Mosque (Al-Aqsa)."

In the fourth doctrine, the devout were not to construct buildings over graves or cover them with decoration; to do so was unlawful. They were also prohibited from burning candles over graves or from setting up stone inscriptions. It was even illegal to have custodians and caretakers at such shrines. Visiting shrines and undesignated mosques was considered equal to idol worship and could lead to other prohibited actions such as kissing the graves and circling around them. Numerous hadith were given to support these prohibitions including: "Should I not commission you with a duty with which the Messenger of Allah had commissioned me—to leave no statue but to crush it, and no grave raised above the surface of the ground but to level it down?" (Fiqh 4.66).

The fifth doctrine attested to the unity of the holy names and attributes of Allah. On this, the Sheikh Wahhab held the views of the Pious Predecessors and the four celebrated teachers of law, Hanafi, Maliki, Hanbali and Shafi'i; namely, affirming and recognizing the names and attributes of Allah without making His attributes equal to Him or questioning how He does something.

The sixth doctrine especially condemned innovations or *bid'ah* including celebrations and gatherings on Muhammad's birthday, the practice of *dhikr* (Sufi remembrance of God) and *salawath* (calling down blessings on Muhammad) before pronouncing the *adhan* (call to prayer); verbally pronouncing the intention, particularly before the two aspects of ritual prayer known as *takbir* ("God is greater") and *tahrim* (the prohibition), and reciting the hadith of Abu Huraira before the *khatib* (preacher) ascends the pulpit. The Sheikh also abhorred and condemned the innovated practices of Sufi orders *(tariqah)*, mysticism and other practices which he said have no authority or sanction from Muhammad or from his companions.

The theological principles of Wahhabism are similar in many ways to orthodox Muslim beliefs. Their belief in the absolute Oneness of God, for instance, is the core belief of all Muslims. They insist, however, that Muslims return to the original teachings of Islam as incorporated in the Qur'an and the Hadith, avoiding all the innovations or new practices unknown to Muhammad and outside the holy texts. Wahhabis also believe in the inseparability of faith and actions. In other words, if people pray, they must also give alms and follow the other laws of Islam. Wahhabis taught predestination, believed in an uncreated Qur'an, condemned all non-orthodox practices and stressed a literal belief in the Qur'an and Traditions.

The Growth of the Movement

With these beliefs in mind, Sheikh ibn Abdul Wahhab began contacting the tribal leaders, judges and imams of Najd in Central Arabia. Some responded positively to his call, while others rejected it. A few even wrote a treatise denouncing his teachings. Wahhab responded by refuting their objections. In addition, the army of his ally, Ibn Saud, was there to fight or scare those who threatened his safety or tried to limit the progress of his movement which they considered to be the revival of "true" Islam. After awhile the whole region of Najd and the neighboring Eastern regions of Arabia accepted his teachings and became part of this new revival movement (Al Jumuah).

By the eighteenth century Wahhabism had become the doctrinal foundation of Saudi Arabia. Thus, tomb visitation and other related practices so often observable in other Muslim countries are no longer practiced in much of the Arabian Peninsula (Gorden 2002, 89). Later, in the twentieth century, it grew as a result of its emergence in Al Haramayn, the Arabian Peninsula, a major geographical focus of the Muslim world. This heightened its visibility and lent an air of authority to its teachings.

Wahhabism has also grown in response to the massive oil wealth in Saudi Arabia, a portion of which has been used in attempts to propagate Wahhabism in the Muslim world and regions beyond (Algar 2002, 2). When Arabia officially became Saudi Arabia in the 1920s, Ibn Saud made an agreement with Wahhabi religious leaders that Saud tribe officials would run the political affairs of government and the Wahhabis would run the religious affairs, thus securing its influence in the country. Finally, Wahhabism's explosive growth in the 1970s occurred as Saudi and Wahhabi religious charities funded Wahhabi schools and mosques from Pakistan to California. Today Wahhabism claims eight million adherents. Its followers are spread throughout the world, but the largest populations of Wahhabis exist in Saudi Arabia.

Wahhabis encourage their followers to use ten ways of influencing people. They urge them 1) to select short messages and make pamphlets for distribution; 2) to record audio tapes and CDs for distribution; 3) to encourage competitive recitals of bin Abdul Wahhab's sayings and writings; 4) to build websites to disseminate his work and train his disciples; 5) to encourage the growth of Qur'anic radio stations which will reserve a special segment for his sermons and writings; 6) to encourage enthusiastic young men to reply online to seekers and critics; 7) to encourage pupils to read his writings in mosques, schools, and at all other religious activities; 8) to encourage media writers to distribute his writings in print, locally and internationally; 9) to print very high quality, attractive pamphlets; 10) and to expose the good image and contributions of Wahhabi evangelism by writing articles, collecting lessons and insights, and holding training seminars and lectures on its writings. The wide dissemination of their beliefs results in a significant if disproportionate influence on Muslims throughout the Muslim world.

Critique of the Movement

A brief critique of the movement may help us place Wahhabism in perspective. First, since Wahhabi doctrines and theology developed within a desert and tribal environment rather than in a metropolis its core values and perspectives were affected by that environment. Confined to tribal customs and practices in many areas, the views that developed were, in fact, not representative of many other Muslims. For example, the minority view that women must cover their faces is presented by Wahhabis as the only valid view despite centuries of scholarly writings from more liberal sects of Islam saying otherwise.

Second, because they have little exposure to non-Muslims or to a more vibrant and open society as can be found in the city, Wahhabi views are not favorable towards non-Muslims. This is ironic, given that they are the fastest growing Muslim sect in Western countries! Third, their limited background and exposure means that they are literalists in their Qur'anic interpretations and legalistic to the extreme. This means that they lack flexibility in adapting the Qur'an and Hadith to different cultural contexts. The insistence of Wahhabi adherents on a rigid, literal interpretation of the Qur'an has thus led them to misinterpret and distort Islam, in the feeling of many Muslims, giving rise to extremists such as Osama bin Laden and fundamentalist movements like the Taliban in Afghanistan.

In light of the preceding, it is clear that Wahhabism is a very conservative and intolerant form of Islam, and as such, holds very strict views on the conduct of women. Wahhabi perspectives on women are most readily available through their speeches. In a sermon from a very prominent Saudi Sheikh, Abdul Rahman Al-Sudeis, for instance, the woman is described as a "protected jewel" (Abdul-Rahman as-Sudais, 2001). A Muslim woman without the protection of Islam, in other words, is considered a mere plaything in the hands of the wrongdoers: "She is a mere object of amusement and merchandise of trade in the hands of human wolves who will destroy her chastity, her honor and her dignity, then throw her and disregard her as one does with a date fruit and its seed" (Ibid).

Thus, the Sheikh argues, a woman will never be able to reach the perfection that she desires, regain the lost glory of the past or achieve her highest rank and position unless she follows the teachings of Islam and unless she stops at the limits and boundaries of the Islamic laws. This will enable her to love others, appreciate good qualities and refrain from evil qualities.

The Sheikh also instructs a good woman to stay at home; by doing so she will please her household and create a happy home. She will also perfect herself in dress and chastity. In other words, when a woman abandons the teachings of Islam by neglecting the proper Islamic dress, being complacent about the *hijab* and wearing perfume, she exposes herself to men, her dignity and honor vanish and she becomes a source of temptation and trial for others. As the shaykh describes it, "evils" embrace her.

A good woman, in Wahhabi perspective will instead be aware of people with bad character and those who want to lower her from her esteemed position and dignity and remove her from her circle of happiness. She must avoid deception, the ruin of her chastity and liberalism.

As a result of these concerns, there are now repeated calls in the Islamic societies asking for the return of the woman to her protected home, to hold fast to the Qur'an and to follow the teachings of Islam and its tribal-inspired etiquette. Finally, the Sheikh reminds fathers and husbands of their duty to protect and maintain their women.

COMMUNICATING BIBLICAL TRUTH
TO WAHHABI WOMEN

Wahhabi women live a doubly restricted and conservative life. In addition to the strict religious and social rules demanded of everyone, a Wahhabi woman is constantly reminded of her restricted position. When a girl begins menstruation at the age of twelve, for instance, her family buys her the *hijab* dress or modest covering as a gift. For Wahhabi women this entails wearing a long thick black garment, black head veil, black gloves and black shoes. Thinking of wearing this kind of dress all year long, with very few personal contacts such as visiting family and sometimes friends or neighbors, can make life dark and depressing for a Wahhabi woman. They will marry during adolescence and bear children all their lives since birth control is not a permissible option.

If these women are to be reached, it will entail reaching the key person in the family and, more importantly, the gatekeeper in that society. Workers should bear in mind that the Wahhabi woman may be the least educated person in the family, or even illiterate. She is, however, capable, wise and manipulative in a constructive manner, for she takes pride in her vocation as mother, sister or wife and takes her role seriously, realizing that she reaps what she sows.

A family-oriented society means that everything revolves around the family hierarchy. On many occasions this will mean an extended family where the parents, older aunts or in-laws live with a young couple and their children. Keep in mind that reaching out to these women means reaching out to the family through the one who is at the center of all relationships. In light of these facts, programs of evangelism are vital, providing hope and salvation to those outside the fold, "That they might have life and have it more abundantly" (John 10:10).

Barriers and Bridges to Effective Communication

As we focus on the topic of communicating truth to Wahhabi women, I shall, by God's grace, address as completely as possible the differences between Wahhabi women and women from different Muslim sects by considering the major barriers and suitable bridges that might provide new insight on the root causes of her problems, and as a result, enable the design of relevant media programs to address these problems more effectively. In order to do this, I will draw on notes provided during the "Arab Woman Today Seminar" held on February 19, 2003.

To begin with, barriers may be divided into three areas: the physical, the cultural, and the religious. We shall look at each category separately and view the means to bridge that gap. It is important that we begin to understand the position of Wahhabi women in their households; while they are held in high regard on the one hand, they are overly protected on the other, to the extent that they are confined and excluded from public social life.

Physical Barriers to Communication

Physical barriers are restrictive environments where women are virtually kept apart in separate quarters and are barred from mixing with men. Wahhabi women are physically isolated, even in their social gatherings, such as feasts, weddings and funerals, which they observe separately from men. Members within the family, however, may eat and socialize together when the males are husbands, sons, brothers and immediate cousins. Women will not participate in any event where male strangers are present, hence separate quarters are necessary to safeguard the honor of women.

The physical barriers imposed on non-Wahhabi Muslim women are not as rigid. These women will, however, require the permission of their spouses to take part in social events where other men could be present. In extreme cases they would also have to ask permission to visit with their own families or with neighborhood women on the premise that the man is head of the household and as such must uphold the family discipline.

Of course, there are some countries where Muslim women are emancipated, enjoying the privilege of higher education, pursuing private careers and participating in decision-making at even governmental levels. However, under Islamic law, or *Shari'ah*, the woman is always subject to her father, brother or spouse. The father invariably has the last word on whom she marries, her brother has the right to safeguard her honor even if it means killing her to save face in the community, and her husband has the right to divorce her for no valid reason, whereupon she returns to her father's or brother's custody. As such, the Muslim woman lives in a perpetual state of insecurity, fearing that she will be separated from her children or will become second in line if her husband takes another wife.

In all these cases, it is obvious that the root cause for physical barriers lies in a male dominated society where men try to protect their women, who are considered delicate and physically vulnerable, from other men whose mindset is similarly rooted in deception, lust and infidelity, and thus keep them within the *Shari'ah* law.

Bridges to Physical Barriers

To begin with, bridges to isolated women must focus on the liberating message of Christ. This will provide women who have been isolated and deprived of their right to fulfillment and self-determination a sense of freedom. We must also introduce them to the love of God that passes all understanding and that can give joy and peace to all, as stated in 1 John. 4: 18-19:"There is no fear in love, but perfect love casts out fear, because fear involves torment. ... We love Him because He first loved us."

Second, our message should highlight the liberation of the soul, and a woman's inner freedom from the captivity of sin, guilt, fear, despair and despondency despite the physical restrictions that she might have to accept and live with.

Third, Wahhabi women need to be acknowledged, appreciated, and reminded of their uniqueness and equal status with men in the sight of God. The message, thus, for these women who have been separated from society on the premise that they are inferior to men, is that they are valuable in the eyes of God. Even though they are considered lowly and kept at lower intellectual and cultural levels by Wahhabi teachings, they should be taught to recognize their self-worth and the regard God has for them.

Fourth, effective bridges to physical barriers must also include breeching their isolation through physical contact, such as through a ministry of written corres-pondence, a telephone hot line, suitable publications, and radio or television broadcasts. Such programs should be prepared and presented by Christian women and definitely not by men, as women can be more sensitive and tactful in dealing with women's concerns. Media programs might include psychological counseling to help build up women's self-esteem and improve their self image. They should focus on teaching specific skills that will help women discover and develop their talents. They can also provide women with ideas to enhance their social communication skills such as how to start a conversation with their husbands and older children, how to manage their time wisely, and how to make their homes more attractive by utilizing flowers, plants, and other simple decorative tips that might draw appreciation from family members and boost their morale.

Cultural Barriers to Effective Communication

Cultural barriers among Wahhabi women are similar to the experience of women in other Muslim cultures across the Arab world. These are obvious in terms of dress codes, gender issues and, more seriously, in a collective suspicion of Western ideas and modes of behavior. In this respect, the main problem lies in the double standard which condones certain practices for men, but condemns similar behaviors among women.

Arab culture, which includes Wahhabis, is more conservative and reserved than Western cultures on issues pertaining to women's social liberation such as dating, sexual awareness, and choosing a mate. This becomes obvious in taboos that restrict women's freedom of choice and their self-determination in matters of dress codes, education, careers, and more seriously in the choice of a life partner. Generally speaking, Middle Easterners regard Westerners as liberal and disrespectful of older people. The Arab culture is more mindful of aging family members who are considered a blessing to the family unit, thus, they believe in home care rather than institutional care for the elderly. The culture is family centered with a religious respect for elders and peers, but this also implies that women bear the heavy load of caring for their own families as well as for their aging parents and in–laws. Women's roles, moreover, are many and diverse, imposing an extremely demanding schedule on the woman as wife, mother, sister, daughter and caretaker of the sick and elderly, whether in peace or war.

Bridges to Cultural Barriers

Bridges to cultural barriers, therefore, should be coupled with genuine concern and sincerity. Any consideration given to manner of dress or social attitudes should emerge from a deep sense of commitment and consecration to serve Christ, and should not in any way be considered as a personal sacrifice. In order to successfully bridge the culture gap the worker must be willing to respect the culture being addressed and adopt it as her own. In other words, the witness should be moved by compassion, which is the hallmark of Christ, so that the outreach may be powerful and significant. Helpful approaches may include cooking programs as well as development of the arts and foreign languages. We can also raise awareness of women's rights and dialogue on issues related to personal development and family care. These kinds of programs will draw people of different cultures together and reconcile gaps in cross-cultural understanding.

Religious Barriers to Effective Communication

Religious barriers, the third type of barrier, center around two major issues: a moral issue and a theological issue. The moral issue has to do with what Muslims consider Christian religious hypocrisy, in which adherents to the Christian faith preach about godliness, the holy life, and consecration, but do not match it in their daily lifestyle, or in their manner of dress and social behavior. Their words, in other words, do not reflect nor match their Christian testimony. The way we as Christians worship is considered too casual and the way we talk about God seems too informal and presumptuous for most Muslims. They sense a lack of reverence in our worship, and a lack of consistency in our daily behavior.

The greatest theological issues concern the authenticity of the Bible and the deity of Christ. When it comes to discussing theological matters, some Christians insist on using the Bible exclusively to make their point, while others have no reservation using parallels from the Qur'an to drive home their message. The equipped worker will want to consult the writings of the late Reverend Fouad Accad who served for many years in Bahrain, especially his book, *Building Bridges*, on how to live and serve among Muslims.

Bridges to Religious Barriers

Bridges to religious barriers should emphasize the similarities rather than the differences between Islam and Christianity. Here, we have Paul's example in 1 Corinthians 9:19-23, which is summarized in verse 22: "I have become all things to all men that I might by all means save some."This by no means implies compromise or denial of one's faith, rather the willingness to meet others on their own ground where they do not feel vulnerable. Most importantly, the worker should never ridicule or speak lightly of another's religion or reflect shock or rejection when they quote their own sacred book, especially regarding the deity and the holiness of God.

We find another very good example of bridging religious differences in Paul's attitude in Acts 17:16 & 22-31, with his reference to "The unknown God." This incident gives us a model of how to attract people's attention, first, by recognizing the way they worship, and respectfully using that as a springboard for further discussion and second, by always being sensitive and humble while seeking to further God's plan and purpose rather than our own. Thus, we read in 1 Peter 3:15-16, "But in your hearts set apart Christ as Lord. Always be prepared to give an answer to everyone who asks you to give the reason for the hope that you have. But do this with gentleness and respect, keeping a clear conscience, so that those who speak maliciously against your good behavior in Christ may be ashamed of their slander."

Television and radio ministries present a unique opportunity to gear programs with a suitable time schedule for the attention and interest of women. A sure way to enter every home is through issues that are controversial and sensitive. This is also a means of reaching the unreached who are alienated by virtue of their religious affiliation or social status. I speak from experience, since I am involved in the production of a weekly radio program. This kind of program generates feedback on a variety of religious and social issues that are answered by a follow-up correspondence ministry. The format for the program includes addressing a social issue for ten minutes and then linking it to the Bible in the last five minutes. Sample topics for this program and the web site include women's self-education; health and physical fitness; healthy marital relations; relations with in-laws; marriage counseling for youth; choosing the right mate; how to use your free time; responsible parenting; pregnancy and childcare; sexual awareness; developing an attractive personality; understanding and handling fear; witchcraft and sorcery; drug abuse and salvation through Jesus Christ.

Conclusion

To conclude, here are a few pointers that are worth highlighting. First, Wahhabi women may be rich in earthly treasures, but poor in spirit and without an experience of the true freedom in Christ. The Wahhabi woman needs to see that true freedom is not gained by our dress or our career or even living well, but by the salvation offered by Jesus Christ. Second, as workers we will need to be very sensitive in our appearance and behavior towards Muslim women. Third, we will need to show the clarity and systematic flow of biblical events, including prophecies and God's relationship with men and women in contrast with other religious books. Fourth, Wahhabi women will need to know how we pray, worship, and observe our times of fasting; not in order to receive a reward, but to truly fellowship with God and accomplish His will. This is in contrast to their religion where every act is meant to contribute to their major credit account in heaven. Fifth, these women need to know that Christianity offers freedom of worship with a much higher moral standard, prompted by a spiritual desire to please God, while the Wahhabi doctrine binds them with rules and regulations. Most importantly, we need to pray for Wahhabi women.

We must also recognize that the consequences for Wahhabi women who receive the truth are great. They face the risk of being shunned or punished by death for disgracing their families and elders: they face the risk of forsaking formal rituals for a modest, informal style of worship, which seems to have less weight or worth. They also risk being associated with political subversion through their contact with Western churches, especially regarding the Israeli-Arab conflict which challenges youth patriotism and regional loyalty.

There will undoubtedly be challenges to our ministry. By keeping our focus on God and promoting His agenda rather than our own we will see His power at work. As we advocate His plan of salvation through Christ, respecting and applying cultural patterns of worship, we will by His grace build bridges that will cross the barriers to effective witness among Wahhabi women.

REFERENCES

Accad, Fouad Elias. 1997. *Building bridges: Christianity and Islam.* Navpress.

Ahmed, K. J. 1987. *Hundred great Muslims.* Chicago: Library of Islam.

Algar, Hamid. 2002. *Wahhabism: A critical essay.* Islamic Publications International.

Al-Jumuah. n.d. Available online http://www.islamland.org/articles1/dawn.htm.

Anonymous. "Arab Woman Today" Seminar. 19 February, 2003.

Gorden, Matthew. 2002. *Islam.* Oxford University Press.

Khauli, Mona. 2002. The root concerns of the Arab woman. SAT-7 Annual Partnership Meeting, Nicosia, Cyprus, 25 October.

Oliver, James Haneef. 2003. *The 'Wahhabi' myth: Dispelling prevalent fallacies and the fictitious link.*

Sudais, Abdul-Rahman as-. n.d. A call from masjid al haram (Makkah) to the Muslim women of the world. *Wahhabism and women.* Available online http://tariqas@stderr.org; accessed 27 December, 2005.

Wahhabism. Sri Lanka: Hidaayah Islamic Foundation.

Wahhabism. Available online http://www.ahle-Sunnaht.org.uk/WAHHABI.html.

13

A Mystic Union: Reaching Sufi Women

Cynthia A. Strong

Sufism or Islamic mysticism was incorporated into orthodox Islam during the early Middle Ages. Sufi worldview and values, however, can often differ marked-ly from the faith of other Muslims. In this article Cynthia Strong explains Sufism's history and attraction and suggests a biblical response.

The rhythmic, mnemonic *dhikr* or chant of Sufi Muslims draws us into a world little known or understood by Westerners. It is a call that differs from the formal Muslim *salat*, or prayer; a call to a spiritual rather than family lineage; a search for salvation that ends in self-extinction rather than paradise. It is a way of self-discipline in the midst of emotion; a poetry that informs the heart rather than the mind; an ecstatic experience and, for many, a spiritual union that results in supernatural powers. For Sufi Muslims, the Five Pillars and the *Shari'ah* law can be dry and lifeless. Longing for a direct experience with God and a spiritual advisor who can guide them through the temptations of this world, Sufis belong to a community that brings unique spiritual dimensions to formal Islam. In its vitality, simplicity, aesthetics and worldwide links, Sufism poses a significant challenge to Christian mission. To address it, we must reflect not only on Sufi history and practice but also understand all we are and have in Christ Jesus. Reaching Sufis may urge us to recover some of the spiritual dynamic inherent in the gospel itself.

A SHORT HISTORY OF SUFISM

Sufism is often described as one of three sects within Islam along with Sunnis and Shiites. More accurately, Sufism is a mystical spiritual dynamic that can be found everywhere in the Muslim world. The word "Sufi" is thought to come from the Arab word *suf* or "wool," or *safa*, meaning "purity," reminiscent of the clothing and piety of early ascetics (Shah 1933:18). Like other religious movements there were several stages in its development.

Early Sufism had many similarities to Christian monasticism. Following the death of Muhammad, Sufi Muslims opposed the growing wealth and decadence of Abbasid rulers. They renounced material pleasures, practiced asceticism, and even wept out of fear of being rejected by God (Subhan 1938:11). Their simple trust in God for all things, Smith suggests, "very possibly," originated in the Christian gospel (1994: 62, 105).

As Islam expanded, Muslims came into contact with conquered cultures and different religious traditions. In the process, Sufism was loosed from its simple Semitic origins and became more philosophically complex, incorporating aspects of Neoplatonism from Greek philosophy as well as Hindu and Persian mysticism (Johns 1961:14). While this made Islam more attractive to Persians, Chinese and East Indians with their vast speculative religions it often violated *tawhid*, or strict Islamic monotheism.

Several changes in Sufi worldview resulted from this encounter. First, as in Hinduism, God became less distinct from His creation. Since "only Absolute Reality is absolutely real" (Glassé 1989:375) the physical world was often seen as God's emanation rather than an ex nihilo creation. The material world was therefore either a source of temptation to be avoided or an illusion without practical significance.

The way of salvation changed as well. The *tariqah*, or Sufi path, gradually incorporated East Asian ascetic practices into the Five Pillars, including spiritual guides and altered states of consciousness (Glassé 1989:374). The goal of Sufis became a Hindu-like *ma'rifa* or self-absorption in God rather than an eternity in paradise. Ascending from one altered state of consciousness to another, the Sufi worked to become the "Perfect Man" who realized the God within (Gibb 1953: 115). Through the work of philosophers like Ibn al 'Arabi (d. 1240) Sufism in the nineth through eleventh centuries shifted from moral self-control to a mystical knowledge that often rejected the need for *Shari'ah* law (1953:115). Because Sufis followed this Gnostic pantheistic theology, used music and delighted in ecstatic experience they were often considered heretical by orthodox Muslims.

In the twelfth century this changed. A successful Persian lawyer named Al-Ghazzali grew weary with the strict requirements of the religious law. Trying to find real knowledge or *'ilm*, by reason, he was surprised to discover it in mystical experience, "by a flash of light God sent into my soul" (Glassé 1989:138). Al-Ghazzali recognized that only someone totally devoted to God could fulfill the strict demands of the Qur'an. Thereafter, he replaced pantheistic Sufi teachings with teachings from the Qur'an and Hadith and brought Sufism into conformity with Islamic law. After al-Ghazzali (d.1111), the Sufi goal was no longer self-absorption in God, but a ethical union of God and human beings in love. Subhan argues that this synthesis brought Islamic Sufism "much closer to the Christian conception" and resulted in its widespread approval and appeal within Islam (1938:26- 28). Despite al-Ghazzali's work, tensions with heretical versions of Sufism have continued throughout Muslim history. Orthodox *shakyhs* and *pirs* will subordinate the non-Islamic elements in Sufism to the teachings of the Qur'an and *Sunnah*. Others, however, like the great Sufi poet Rumi, will follow its pantheistic streams of thought (Johns 1961:13).

In the eighteenth century Sufism was again threatened in a confrontation with Wahhabi legalists. Inspired by Ibn Taymiyyah and the conservative Hanbali school of law, Ibn 'Abdul Wahhab rejected Sufism as *bid'ah* or innovation. He rejected Sufi interpretations of the Qur'an for more literal readings, opposed the intercession of saints, destroyed shrines throughout Saudi Arabia, and condemned the celebration of the Prophet's birthday (Haj 2002). Even so, Sufism has survived. Denounced by fundamentalist groups like al-Qaeda today, Sufism is still viewed by many as the most vibrant and active expression of Muslim faith (Burckhardt 1990:3). In view of these successive waves of opposition, what are the elements that have enabled it to survive?

The Sufi Worldview

The popularity of Sufism can be traced to its promise to provide direct access to God. According to the Muslim doctrine of *tawhid*, the creator is a sovereign and transcendent ruler, holding sway over a cosmic hierarchy of stars and planets, minerals, plants, animals, angels and good *jinn* (Bahktiar 1996:73). To pray to other beings or seek their help is considered the gravest of sins, *shirk* (al Wahhab 1992:43). The very transcendence of God, however, works against knowing him and experiencing him personally. For many, an intercessor or link with God is needed. Sufis found permission for this link in the Qur'an. Although the Qur'an forbids worshipping other deities (Q 22:12) it appears to leave the possibility of intercession open—to the "one whom God would choose" (Q 20:109, cf. Q 43:86). Sufis believe that this intercessor, this point of contact with God, is the "great Master," Muhammad himself, whom they believe first taught esoteric Islam to his Companions (Glassé 1989:376).

Muhammad's superiority over other intercessors and right to intercede is drawn partly from the Hadith. In the *Mir'aj*, Muhammad's night journey to heaven, he is said to have traveled to Jerusalem and ascended through seven levels of heaven on a human-faced horse. Passing through 1,000 veils of light and darkness, he was reputedly greeted by all the prophets, entrusted with the secret of creation and empowered to understand all things (Kibbani 1995:87). Sufis believe, as a result, that Muhammad existed before the creation of the world and that God continues to reveal himself through him (Subhan 1938:58).

The primary metaphor for this concept in Sufism is light: "Allah is the light and Muhammad is his light" (Q 24.35). While Wahhabi Muslims may dispute Muhammad's right to intercede and oppose his celebration in stories and songs, his status among the majority of Muslims is unrivaled. This should help us understand the extent of Muslim devotion for Muhammad. In the Philippines when a Muslim patient read a devotional denouncing Muhammad at his hospital bedside all the community's anger was unleashed against the hospital and the missionaries who served there.

In the worldview of Sufis, Muhammad reveals God. But he also, through God, connects devotees with supernatural beings and powers in the universe. One of these powers is *barakah*, a spiritual blessing or influence that Muhammad received from God and thereafter transmitted to his disciples (Glassé 1989:176). The power of *barakah* is crucial in Islam, given the prominence of the evil eye, malevolent *jinn* and other dangers described in the Qur'an and hadith (cf. *Hadith of al-Muwatta* 50.1, 3, 4, 9, 10, 11). The souls of ordinary people are unable to transmit it, however, being impure and undeveloped. *Shaykhs* and *pirs* alone can disseminate this power and protect their followers from its adverse affects (Ewing 1983:255-256). According to Ewing, Sufis envision this power flowing from God through Muhammad to the Kaba in Mecca at the center of the world and from there to other areas of the dar al Islam or House of Islam (1983:254). *Shaykhs* and *pirs*, through their spiritual mastery and closeness to the Prophet, act as conduits of this grace as it flows from God through angelic beings to human beings (Kabbani 1995:20). Whether by uttering a verse of the Qur'an, writing out an amulet or conducting exorcisms that control the *jinn*, the *shaykh* or *pir* is believed to mediate God's grace on earth, channeling the

wisdom and blessing of Muhammad and dispensing God's *barakah* to devotees
(Ewing 1984:110-112). Finally, spiritual guides or *walis*, each a descendent of
Muhammad with his own specific territory, will pass it on to individual Sufis in
their respective groups (Ewing 1983:254). As the conveyor of knowledge about
God and the source of his *barakah*, Muhammad is unparalleled in Sufi thought.

Sufism also provides a way of knowing God through its philosophical assumptions. In Islam, human beings are born Muslim and pure. They believe Adam's
sin was not the beginning of original sin but simply a mistake forgiven by God.
The reason humans sin, they believe, is because they are ignorant of God's law
and refuse to submit to it. Recovery comes when a person says the *shahadah*
or creed. At that moment, Muslims believe, their sins are forgiven and they
recover their original *fitrah* or primordial purity (Bakhtiar 1996:18). Thereafter,
if they respond to their lower nature or *nafs* and are led away from rationality
and God, they sin. As long as they depend on their rational nature or *aqal*
Muslims believe they can know God's laws and discipline themselves to achieve
a good character. In short, a person's fleshly energies need to be controlled by a
balance of reason and knowledge. Knowledge is provided by the use of reason
in studying the Qur'an and the Hadith. Self-discipline comes through diligent
practice of the Five Pillars of Islam. The importance of striving against the lower
self in Muslim thought is evident in the concept of *jihad*: it is the lesser *jihad* in
Islam to fight against God's enemies; the greater *jihad* is to overcome the temptations of their fleshly self, the *nafs* (Subhan 1938:96).

Sufism, thus, provides a connection with God and offers a path of deliverance
from the *nafs*. Only through the guidance of *shaykhs* and *pirs*, however, can
Sufis find their way to "the Perfect Man." Spiritual leaders are tasked with guiding their devotees along a path of deliverance from the *nafs* by "remembering
God" (Q. 18:23). Whether in seclusion, group meditation or the practice of *dhikr*,
Sufis "remember God" by reciting the Ninety-Nine Names of God and using the
subha or rosary. They will also remember him in each act, reciting the *shahadah*
(there is no God but God), the *hamdalah* (Praise be to God) and the *tasbih*
(God be glorified) as a means of concentration. Even the obligatory daily prayers
or *salat* can strengthen self-control. As Siegel explains, "through the five prayers
humans can achieve dominance over the animal nature" (2000:115).

For many Sufis, rhythmic chanting also leads to a spiritual encounter. In the
dhikr, concentration on the names of God results in trance and "in the mature"
to a "union with God." Some Sufis report out-of-the-body experiences or "see
their soul sitting on the ceiling" (Baktiar 1996:88). One man, after a forty day

fast "was given two angels to always be with him and protect him like lions" (Baktiar 1996:89). When guided by a *pir*, Sufis believe their efforts toward self-discipline and the loss of self in trance can tame the "animal energies of lust and power." The devotee longs through *dhikr* to return to his or her original reason and a true love for God (Baktiar 1996:6-13).

Rabi'ah, one of the greatest of female Sufis, illustrates this progression. Born in 717 CE in Bosra, Rabi'ah was a slave who fasted in the daytime and served God through prayers and *dhikr* at night. Freed, she reputedly overcame her *nafs* through spiritual exercises and spent the rest of her life in continuous remembrance of Allah. Modest and humble, she arrived at the place "where she depended only on God" (Smith 1994:22-24).

Worldwide, women like Rabi'ah participate in Sufism in various ways. Among the Somali, women may belong to their own *tariqah*, or Sufi order. Like women in other Sufi orders, they trace their spiritual lineage and *barakah* back to Muhammad's daughter, Fatima. Women in Turkey may participate from the back of the room as the *shaykh* leads the *dhikr*. Still others will endow a Sufi order as a patron. Most women, however, participate by appealing to saints since the availability of shrines and festivals make large-scale participation possible (Lewis 1984:138). Shiite women will seek the help of departed *imams* while Sunni women will make vows at the shrines of Sunni *shaykhs*. The use of photo cards in place of shrines is also common. In one Middle Eastern country, a missionary woman was walking by a neighbor's house when she was asked if she was pregnant. When she said "no" the woman rushed to wave the photo of a Sufi saint across her abdomen believing this would give her the *barakah* she needed. In Pakistan women may ask the *pir* to help with fatigue, to produce an amulet for a sick child, or to give advice if the woman's husband is unfaithful (Ewing 1984:109). Central Asian women will depend on the saints' power to defend them from the evil eye. Increasingly, even North American women are turning to Sufism. Drawn by Eastern music and incense to meetings in strip malls, women participate in *dhikr* to rid themselves of selfishness and pride, overcome their dependence on alcoholism and return to their *fitrah* or pure, "primordial nature" (Bakhtiar 1996:18).

RESPONDING TO SUFI WOMEN

To reach Sufi women we must understand their worldview. John Subhan was a member of the Qadari order before he converted to Christ and wrote an assessment of their beliefs. To help them understand the Christian faith he suggests we first must know the difference between the Sufi concept of God and the Judeo-Christian understanding of God (Subhan 1938:320). In Neoplatonism, like Sufism, there is no sense of a holy God. There is also no trace of God's work to bridge the gulf between God and human beings through a holy sacrifice. The illusion that one can find union with Him through self-purification, thus, is easy to maintain.

Second, we must understand the true power behind the Sufi cult of saints. As we have seen, the doctrine of *tawhid* forbids dependence on anyone else but God (Subhan 1938:320). While Sufis try to circumvent this by tracing the powers of the *pir* back to Muhammad, the result is a naive dependence on human beings and the veiled demonic powers that give them power. We must demonstrate to women how they can trust God alone.

Third, we must show how Jesus is different from other saints. The Bible teaches that God is most fully revealed through His only begotten Son, Jesus Christ (John 1:1-17). Passages in John are difficult to teach, however, since Sufis see all mystical impulses as identical. They will separate Jesus from his biblical setting, for instance, and describe him as "the most perfect type of contemplative saint" rather than as our savior (Burkhardt 1990: 8). They will see his teaching on forgiveness and his command to turn our cheek as "true spiritual detachment" rather than the work of the Holy Spirit in the redeemed (Burkhardt 1990:8). These descriptions are in Sufi, not biblical, terms. To help them find the biblical understanding of Christ we will need to lay a new groundwork, correlating the life of Christ in the New Testament with its foundation in the Old Testament so it can be properly understood.

Fourth, we must know the stages of the Sufi path. Many of these sound familiar to Christians. Sufis also speak of "repentance," desire a "vision of God," long to "remember God" in every deed and follow a simple way of life. Their means of salvation, however, is through a loss of self in trance and the nature of their salvation is absorption in God. Since these are vastly different ideas from salvation in the gospel how are we to confront this message?

First, Sufis, like other Muslims, must be presented not with doctrines or beliefs but with a Christian worldview. That is, we must paint for them the picture of a holy, creator God searching for his loved ones in a fallen world. As we have seen, God is great in Islam but Muslims essentially achieve salvation through their own efforts, gaining self-discipline through the Five Pillars and relying on Muhammad's intercession and *barakah* (Subhan 1938:77). In Christian belief God is far greater—holy, exalted and unreachable by human efforts. The sinful person cannot understand the things of God or submit to his perfect law (Rom. 8:6-8). The Bible teaches that only God's Spirit can illuminate our minds and convict us of sin (Jn 14:26; 1 Cor 2:6-16).

Second, we must explain Christ's power to overcome sin. Rabi'ah recognized that sin harms the soul because it can separate it from the Beloved. She believed, however, that she could overcome her sin through self-discipline. Such over-confidence in the flesh diminishes the awful reality and power of sin. In the Bible, the point is not that envy, selfishness and pride must be overcome, but that a soul completely dead to God and enslaved in sin must be born again (Rom. 6:5-10, John 3:16). Only Christ's victory over death reconciles us with God (Ro 5:10, 2 Cor 5:18). Only by being born again of the Spirit can we have mastery over sin (Rom. 6:11-14). Through Christ, we are not resuscitated; we become a new creation (2 Cor. 5:17). The reality of God's presence in each believer also means that we are all, each one, a conduit of God's power and blessing; each believer, while benefiting from the spiritual gifts of others, has direct ties to God in Christ.

Third, we must understand the deception of supernatural powers. Power, as we have seen, is of central concern in Sufism. In the *dhikr*, the Sufi is surrounded by powers they believe are from God. Without biblical criteria to test these spirits, however, the danger of deception is real. When Rabi'ah asked God if he would allow a heart that loved him to burn in hell, an unseen voice answered, "We shall not do this. Do not think of us an evil thought" (Smith 1994:124). Sufis also believe that the final stages of the Sufi path are "beyond Shaitan's (Satan's) reach" (Friedlander 1993:13). The fact that London Sufis can hear "angels in the walls of the Sufi center" and "their father [the shaykh] talking to angels" (Baktiar 1996:84) is reason enough to suspect the involvement of demonic spirits.

The degree of demonic involvement in contemporary Sufism is, in fact, staggering. The book, *The Last Barrier* an American converts to Sufism and is mentored by a Turkish *pir*. At the close of the book, he is taken to Turkey and introduced to the "Perfect Man"—a human form only slightly visible, who emanated "a pure, white light." He was described as a "master"—one with no veil between himself and God (Field 1976:173). Receiving special powers from him, the convert was urged to enlist others in the cause in anticipation of "a new age, beyond all form, dogma and religious bigotry" (Field 1976:167). As is evident, the Sufi emphasis on a spiritual world, cosmic forces and spiritual guides in a non-theistic worldview has many similarities to the New Age. These forces, however, are not spiritually benign. *Shaykhs* and *pirs* in Islam, similar to spiritual guides in other religions, possess formidable psychic powers. Prayer is thus important to countering the deception of demonic spirits at the root of this movement (Wilson 1995).

Conclusion

The initial Sufi impulse in Islam was similar to the simple faith and asceticism of Christian monks. Its contact with Hellenistic and Indian philosophies, however, replaced it with a different worldview and a different path. Relying on esoteric philosophies and human effort, Sufism is unable to provide either a true knowledge of God or a sanctified spirituality. A "natural spirituality," is all it can provide—one accessible to all people everywhere in meditation, chanting, ecstatic dancing and altered states of consciousness. This will not lead to the truth of the Bible. As Miller states,

> Followers of the Narrow Way understand that man's natural state is fallen —he is not now as he was originally created to be. Thus the only spiritual realm that he can contact by natural means is likewise fallen— and extremely dangerous. To 'see the Kingdom of God' he needs a new nature; he 'must be born again,' supernaturally, by the regenerating work of God's Holy Spirit (John 3:3-8). (1986)

Since Islam rejects the work of the Holy Spirit and his glorification of Jesus Christ (John 16:14), Miller adds, it is incapable of delivering a truly sanctifying spiritual experience. Islamic spirituality can only put Muslims in touch with unholy spirits and pantheism, inherently incompatible with theism. The rise and popularity, not only of Sufi Islam, but of other mystical movements comes from a longing to surpass legalism. The tragedy is that Sufis can only aspire to a spirituality based on the flesh. In each case, Miller says, "the monotheism which originally upheld them degenerates into pantheism, and pantheism predictably opens the door to a wide range of pagan beliefs and activities" (Miller, 1986).

As we reflect on Sufis and their need for new birth, it is clear that we will not reach them without evidence of the pure spirituality available in the Holy Spirit. The challenge for the Christian is to live so free from sin that the forgeries of Satan will be exposed and to be so in love with God that his glory and truth will be revealed in all we do. Only when we embody a Christ-like spirit will the Sufi counterfeit be revealed for what it is.

REFERENCES

Bakhtiar, Laleh. 1996. *Sufi women of America. Angels in the making.* Chicago, IL:Institute of Traditional Psychoethics and Guidance.

Burckhardt, Titus. 1990. *Introduction to Sufi doctrine.* Transl. by D.M.Matheson Jakarta, Indonesia: Dar al-Ilm.

Ewing, Katherine. 1983.The politics of Sufism: redefining the saints of Pakistan.*Journal of Asian Studies* 42:2 (Feb):251-268.

_____. 1984.The Sufi as saint, curer, and exorcist in modern Pakistan. *Contributions to Asian Studies* 18:106-114 (orig.1979).

Field, Reshad. 1976. *The last barrier.* San Francisco: Harper and Row.

Friedlander, Shems. 1993. *Ninety-nine names of Allah.* San Francisco, CA: HarperSanFrancisco.

Glassé, Cyril. 1989. *The Concise Encyclopedia of Islam.* San Francisco, CA: Harper and Row.

Gibb, H.A.R. 1953. *Mohammedanism.* 2d ed. New York: Mentor.

Haj, Samira. 2002. Reordering Islamic orthodoxy: Muhammad ibn 'Abdul Wahhab,*The Muslim World* 92:3/4 (Fall):333. Proquest; accessed 9 April, 2004.

Johns, A.H. 1961. Sufism as a category in Indonesian literature and history, *Journal of Southeast Asian History* 2:2 (July):10-23.

Kibbani, Shaykh Muhammad Hisham. 1995. *Angels unveiled: A Sufi perspective.* Kazi Publications, Inc.

Miller, Elliot. 1986. Sufis:The Mystical Muslims, Forward Part III (Spring-/Summer):17-23. http://www.equip.org/free/DI200-3.htm; accessed 10 July, 2004.

Siegel, James. 2000. *The rope of God.* Ann Arbor:The University of Michigan Press.

Smith, Margaret, 1994. *Rabi'a.* Oxford: Oneworld.

Subhan, John A. 1938. *Sufism: Its saints and shrines.* Lucknow: Lucknow Publishing House.

Wahhab, Ibn 'Abd al-. 1992. *Kitab al Tawhid.* International Islamic Federation of Student Organizations.

Wilson, Gene. 1995. Reaching New Agers on their own turf. *Evangelical Missions Quarterly* 31:2. Available online http://bcg.gospelcom.net/emis/1995/-newagers.htm.; accessed 10 July, 2004.

14

A Quest for Identity:
Reaching Second and Third Generation Immigrant Women

Farida Saïdi

Muslim women face specific challenges as second and third generation migrants. In this article on God's unique work among French migrants, Farida Saidi describes how Christian ministries can be adapted to meet the physical, emotional and spiritual needs of Muslim women far from their family's country of origin.

Prior to the 1900s, Muslims could be found in traditional parts of the world, in areas where Islam had been at home for centuries. During the last century, however, more Muslims have come to the West than ever before, looking for job opportunities or better education. A significant number came because their countries were colonized or at war, others as refugees or for political reasons.

I grew up in France, where North Africans have come in large numbers through successive waves of immigration. The first wave occurred after the country was colonized; the second when North Africans served as soldiers during two world wars; the third wave when France needed workers for post-war reconstruction and the last and most important official immigration occurred in the '70s, when the French government authorized the reunion of families *regroupement familial*). During this time, hundreds of thousands of new immigrants were transplanted into France. From 10,000 Muslims in France in 1920, the number today has grown to approximately five or six million.

In 1979, I and a group of believers founded an organization called L'AMI that cared for the needs of the first, second and third generation of North Africans living in France. These women can be described broadly in terms of their date and place of origin. The first generation, for instance, is made up of the initial wave of immigrants to France or Europe who came for work opportunities and who now are sixty years of age or older. The second generation is made up of the children of these workers who came at a very young age, or were born in France or Europe who are currently between thirty and fifty years of age. The third generation, lastly, is made up of the children of the second generation who were born in France or Europe and are under thirty years of age today.

At the time we began our ministry very few Christian organizations were working among Muslims in France. Today, second and third generation Muslim women in great numbers are accepting the teachings of the Bible. This article draws from my interaction with North Africans in France but also with Muslims from other parts of the world. During my ministry I have traveled extensively in Asia, the United States, the Middle East and Africa and have seen similar needs in the lives of second and third generation of immigrant Muslim women elsewhere. In this article, I will discuss several important issues for Christians working with immigrant women and will offer suggestions as to how the church can respond to their needs.

FIRST GENERATION WOMEN

In order to understand the situation of second and third generation women, it is important to study the lives of those who had a major impact on their early years and the context in which they grew up. Thus, in this first section I will examine the first generation of Muslim women who directly impacted second and third generation women, particularly through the influence of their parents' and relatives' worldview. While I am aware that these second and third generations were also influenced by the broader context of their new culture, their first years, spent in the cradle of their family, were admittedly the most crucial for their development.

Major Transitions

First generation women go through major transitions when they migrate because their new context is often very different culturally and religiously from their homeland. It is crucial to understand this process of change if we are going to understand the identity of second-generation women raised in these circumstances. Women react to their new context in a variety of ways. Some will embrace it with joy and great expectation whereas others will refuse it and create their own world within the house where they live. Some women will have a high education and therefore experience less stress in their new context while others with less education and no family support will suffer greater disorientation. In this section, I will discuss the types of transitions that take place and how they can affect second generation Muslim women who are directly impacted by their relationship with their mothers.

Muslim women in the first generation were most often from rural settings. Migrating to large cities abroad where the social and family network was non-existent, they often fought harder for the preservation of their religious and cultural values than if they had remained at home. They frequently became more protective of their children, especially when the trends of the host society were against Muslim values.

As a result, second generation women often felt a greater gap between the values inside and outside their home. Inside the home they were Muslims while outside the home they interacted with friends at school who had different values. This often created a tension and ambivalence between the two worlds that seemed irreconcilable, especially if the mother had no direct contact with the new context.

Traditional Muslim families also commonly held to a patriarchal structure. While examples of matriarchal Muslim societies can be found in Asia and modernity is also shaping new trends toward less patriarchal communities in other contexts, women in traditional societies accepted patriarchy and would often base their identity predominately in motherhood. In their new nation, this role became even more emphasized because their husbands were often absent from home, at work or distant because they struggled with integration in the host society. Thus, the role of parenthood often fell on the shoulders of the mothers, especially those who stayed at home. Mothers therefore became a central and pivotal point in the family. Second generation women often tell how important their mothers are to them because of their sacrifices in raising them while the father was at work.

Another family transformation that took place when Muslims migrated was a change in family structure. The traditional extended family structure prevalent in most Muslim countries included grandparents, uncles and aunts along with parents and children. Following immigration, this changed to a nuclear structure with only parents and children. In this type of family, especially in a non-Muslim neighborhood, women felt often alone and without social support. This meant that mothers felt more dependent on their children and experienced a greater feeling of frustration because children became the only link with the host society. The strong bond that ordinarily exists between daughter and mother in the Muslim world was intensified by these circumstances. This explains why this bond is so strong between first and second generation women. Admittedly, the traditional family structure is undergoing similar changes today in big cities of the Muslim world. Families separate when members move away for jobs, cannot find large apartments for their extended families, or the wife and husband work and cannot take care of the extended family. One can never underestimate the relationship between daughter and parents, however, even if immigration also resulted in a number of specific generational conflicts that we will investigate later.

Women in Islam also play an important role in communicating religious values within the family. The first exposure of children to Islam is not through the Qur'an but through the words and the gestures of their mother. Leila Ahmed, professor at Yale, related that she learned her first lesson on Islam through her grandmother. During the night of Ramadan known as the "night of destiny," her grandmother used to take her to the roof to wait for heaven's gate to open up (Lieblich 1999). In the context of immigration, this religious role has new implications. Mothers are faced with the difficult task of wanting to raise their children with religious values that sometimes contradict the values of the host country. All cultural and social practices from the home country, therefore, will be interpreted as religious norms and communicated to the second generation as having religious value. This form of Islam will become religious truth for the children. First generation Muslim women thus acquire a significant religious power within their own family because they serve as the catalyst and the preserver of religious norms in a foreign context.

Another religious change in the first generation is a change in religious practices from communal to individual or familial. During the first wave of immigration, religious structures often did not exist in the host country and immigrants had to rely on their own efforts or the family practices to do their religious duties. This again changed the nature of Islam. Islam was silent politically, without much influence on the society but with a strong influence on the children, even if they questioned it when they were exposed to other religious or non-religious values outside home.

The links of first generation women with their home country, in retrospect, were very strong. Their relatives and friends were human ties with a society that was quite different from their host society. Women who came to the West because of their husband's work, therefore, often did not want to make the effort to take on the norms and values of the new country. They continued speaking their mother language and cultivating friendships with people from their own background. Even when they longed deep inside to adopt the new culture they often did not know how to connect their religious beliefs with the new context.

Sometimes the religious practices themselves made it difficult to interact with non-Muslims. How, for example, could they make friends with their neighbors when they could not share a meal with them because they did not serve *halāl* food? Many first generation women dreamed of returning to a Muslim land and being buried in the land of their birth. The screen writer Yamina Benguigui, for example, said there were always empty cardboard boxes piled in her parents' apartment in France because they lived with the dream of going back to North Africa after retirement. They wanted to be buried as Muslims in a Muslim land (1997). The habit of not "trashing boxes" helps us understand the difficulty of building roots in a new country and the inevitable tensions that exist between first and second generation Muslims.

Since the values outside the home were often so different from Muslim values inside the home, women created a safe haven in their house when they migrated. Home was not just the place where women felt happy or sad; it became the memory of Muslim lands, the model of Muslim family and even the religious community that did not exist outside home. Second generation women, as a result, will feel deeply connected emotionally with their home but at the same time disconnected with practices outside. This tension affects the way they shape their identity.

Implications for Ministry

It was important to study the first generation because the behaviors and attitudes of these women had a deep impact on second and third generation Muslim women. In particular, they can reveal hidden aspects of the daughters' and granddaughters' lives. Many times during my ministry when relating with Muslim women I realized I needed to take into account the areas of their life where they dealt with their mother's life story and experience. I could not neglect their relationship to their mother. When these women convert, they must

194 A WORLDVIEW APPROACH TO MINISTRY AMONG MUSLIM WOMEN

come to terms with their mother's legacy and will need to find biblical answers that relate to the values their mothers passed on, whether they accepted these values or not.

SECOND AND THIRD GENERATION WOMEN

Because the first generation did not return to its home country, the second generation began to take roots in the Western world. Evan Osnos (2004) writes: "For the first time in history, Muslims are building large and growing minorities across the secular Western world—nowhere more visibly than in Western Europe where their number has more than doubled in the past two decades." What is the identity of Muslim women of the second generation and what does it imply for Christian ministry?

As we have seen, the atmosphere at home had a great impact on the early years of second generation women. As they left to go to public school, however, these women discovered a world that is very different from their experience at home. Depending on how their parents value the outside world, the second-generation woman will either be in conflict with her family or not. If she is in conflict, she may reject her parents' training for a time, although this cultural heritage will have great impact on her later because of the importance of the socio-emotional development of the early years of life.

The same woman may feel free to criticize her parents' values at one time and yet vigorously defend these values at another time. It is not always easy to bring worlds with different values together. Thus, it is important for a cross-cultural worker to respect both sides of a woman's identity when interacting with her as an outsider.

It is also important to remember that women cannot discard their deepest socio-emotional memories. One woman who converted to Christianity faced a great deal of resistance at home. Believing her conversion to be part of a teenage crisis rather than a sincere belief, her parents opposed her. She left them at the age of fifteen and rejected her entire social network as well. Later she regretted those decisions. She wished that her Christian friends had encouraged her to stay at home with the support of her family and relatives. She also wished they had taught her to share her faith in a more appropriate manner, without such an extreme reaction. In retrospect, she felt that part of her behavior was due to her identity crisis as a second generation woman and had nothing to do with her conversion, but at that time, she had a hard time sorting things out.

Phases of Human Development

In 1980, a Christian worker told me that the second generation of Muslims in Europe would be very open to the gospel because it was open to new cultures. Although the number of conversions to Christianity is greater among second generation women than it is among the first generation women, I did not completely agree with this statement. On the one hand, as many studies have shown, Muslim conversion often occurs during the teenage years when individuals are open to new ideas. On the other hand, this may not be a complete picture. When looking at immigrants we have to understand that they have two sets of values. They may indeed relate to their new culture but they may also be attracted to their parents' or grandparents' teaching at some stage in their life especially when they become dissatisfied with their situation in the host culture. We can see that happening today. A number of second and third generation Muslims are returning to a conservative or, for some, a fundamentalist version of Islam even though their parents were nominal believers. It is not rare to meet young girls who are veiled, pray and fast because they find their identity in Islam. Thus, we need to take into account the different stages of development in human beings.

Sociologists and psychologists have defined several important phases of an immigrant's life. During the first phase, between birth to approximately age seven, individuals are greatly impacted by their family context, which in this case is Muslim. Later, interactions with people from other cultural contexts at school or at work change them and make open to other views and values. When they are beginning their own family and having children, individuals may change again, but often draw from both their childhood and the actual society for resources. Growing older, individuals tend to idealize what they experienced in their childhood.

Applying this to our current discussion, we can see that immigrants might swing back and forth between cultural contexts to find resources for values and identity in each culture. Furthermore, they may not necessarily have the same opinion about these cultures at every stage of their life. Are we ready to adapt our approach to these different stages of life, or will we use the same approach for each one?

Today a growing number of second generation women are turning to Christ. They often make this decision when they are younger, similar to those whom we have seen become more devoted to Islam as teenagers. Workers need to be aware of these stages and adapt their communication so that it is relevant to each phase in a person's life. I have seen a number of women, for instance, who converted when they were young return to Islam later. The message they heard in the church applied to them when they were young and in crisis. As they grew older, however, the message did not answer the questions they had as they married or raised their children with models from their mothers. I have also seen converts to Christianity struggle as they age because they felt so estranged from their community and lacked roots in both Christian and Muslim communities. They never learned, it seems, to integrate the legacy of their mother with their experience in Christianity.

Biculturalism

In the previous sections I have addressed the importance of being aware that second and third generation women will combine two cultures to make sense of their life. In a Muslim context, this affects women on a deeper level than men because the role of the former clashes more often with Western values especially if they come from a very traditional context. Second generation women cannot simply hide like their mothers in their home. They are required to interact with the new context. They go to school, work and interact with the society they live in. The majority embrace life in the West with no intention of returning parents' home where they often feel like foreigners themselves. As their interaction with society continues, however, their parents' values and the society's values often conflict. Areas where Western and Muslim values may differ include modesty, the relationship between men and women, the structure of postmodern family and the role of females in society. In the context of immigration, these cultural and religious issues are a source of frequent tensions. Benguigui, the writer of the movie "Migrant Memories" (*Mémoires d'émigrés*), says that "being exiled, uprooted, life in a country that is not your parent's country, creates a lot of damage: especially in a culture, where one does not use words" (1997).

How does this affect our ministry to Muslim women? First, since women cannot erase their history we may have to deal with several worldviews. We may need to find biblical examples of how migration affected the people of God. Severing roots with their past is not the answer. Jesus, we remember, was an immigrant who dealt with the influence of a variety of cultural contexts: his divine origin, his family context, his time in Egypt, the influence of the Roman Empire, to name a few. From him we learn that all facets of our lives need to be put under God's control. Numerous biblical stories, in fact, highlight the journeys of migrant women including Hagar, Ruth, and Rebecca. Hagar's story in particular shows how a woman who is away from her home and under severe pressure can meet God, recognize his action in her life and meet her deepest needs. Although this story might be more appropriate for first generation women it also speaks to the questions of second and third generation women who do not feel accepted by the host culture.

Migration and New Opportunities

As we have seen, migration opened up new opportunities and new models for the first generation of Muslim women. For many women, it was also their first access to education. Although women in the Muslim world may have greater access to university and high social positions today this was not the case for first generation migrant women to the West.

Second and third generation women are not aware of this change of pace. They grow up in a context where they have a different lifestyle than their mothers but they take it for granted because they grew up and went to school in Western cultures. They feel they are the same as their Western friends, although they differ because of the experience of their mothers. They are a new type of Muslim; following Islam yet having access to the same things as women in the West. As they make greater use of information through media and expand their worldview, it will change their social perception and the action they take. Thus, they will not have the same needs as rural Muslim women and should not be approached in the same way.

Second and third generations also make use of the latest technology. They communicate by internet, use cell phones and chat on the web. They feel that they are part of the global *ummah* in a new way. Talking about Islamists, Olivier Roy says, "The *ummah* they are addressing is a transnational one, or even a virtual one, through the Internet." This transnational *ummah* is a new phenomenon. Although what Roy said applied to Islamicism, it could also apply to second and third generation women who feel part of the global *ummah* through new methods of communication. Those who convert to Christ may need to find ways to connect to the global Christian community in new and creative ways. They will need to feel completely integrated in the body of Christ" (2005).

During my ministry I discovered there are five different models for being a second generation Muslim woman living in the West. In the first model, women will integrate their parent's faith into their own without adjustments. Women in this group will define themselves as Muslims and attempt to follow the spiritual and cultural values of their family by imitating their Muslim parents. In the second model, women will want to share their parents' values but also accept the norms of their host country. These women will integrate not only their parents' religious lifestyle but also the new values of their society, especially those things which do not contradict their parent's values.

Women in the third model will want to build a new Muslim identity in their host country. Instead of going back and forth between the values of their parents and the values of the host culture, they will define a new type of Islam: the Islam of immigration. In contrast, women in the fourth model will reject the norms of their parents and discard Islam as a whole. These women will not claim to be Muslims. Women in the fifth and final group will claim an Islamic heritage and totally integrate it into their lives but will also request the freedom to accept or reject a Muslim identity. As we interact with Muslim women, we must identify which model they embrace. Additionally, we must understand the model of Islam they embrace, whether modernist, conservative, fundamentalist, reformist, or postmodernist. The approaches to ministry we adopt will differ greatly depending on how closely connected the women feel to the Muslim community.

According to Olivier Roy, "Islam has now a permanent presence in the religious landscape of Western countries" (2005). Thus, immigrant Muslim women can now practice their religion differently than their mothers. How can we best describe this new form of Islam? Second generation women are not part of the silent Islam which was not practiced outside the home. Their practice of Islam is in the open, resulting in new expressions of allegiance. Second generation women, for instance, have greater access to the mosque as well as to Qur'anic teaching and religious knowledge. Some even become religious experts. They have greater freedom to practice their religion such participating in the fast during Ramadan. Many of these women are better educated in forms of Islam from the West. Non-Muslims, in addition, are more open to accept their commitment because of a longer exposure between the two groups. Most of the Muslim women that our ministry outreach teams encountered twenty-five years ago did not quote the Qur'an. Today, more and more know the Qur'an by heart or have access to Muslim theological education. I recently met several second and third generation Muslim women who are doing doctoral studies comparing Islam and Christianity. At a conference on Women's Issues in Islam held in Paris, the main speakers were all second and third generation women with Ph.D. degrees. To minister to them, we will need to understand their needs and often Islamic laws as well.

Islam, like the Old Testament, provides a great number of laws that codify life for the society. In Western lands these laws do not exist, or exist in only limited ways. Religious parents or family members of first generation women often take on the role of the *mufti* themselves, therefore become the guardians of the law. Marrying outside traditional norms, for example, can becoming a huge issue for women and their families, along with many other practices that differ from parental norms.

Because second generation women usually have citizenship in their host country, they will not expect to follow the same laws their parents followed in their home country. Rather, they will aspire to have a social context that allows them to practice their religion and creative ways to address the legal issues raised by Muslim laws. Sometimes they will be caught between pleasing their parents and following these new ways. One woman from our ministry who became a Christian in Paris, for example, refused to marry a French Christian because this would have upset her parents. Although she had many opportunities to marry a French person, she waited and prayed for a long time for a husband. It was more important for her to honor her parents and be also faithful to Christ in her choices than to marry quickly. Several church members who were not from a Muslim background had a hard time understanding her position.

Identity and Religion
Today, a growing number of second and third generation women are disappointed by the host country that their parents chose. In their quest for identity and because they have failed to bond with the country where they live, they look for other avenues of connection. Some find it in Islam. Desiring to reconnect with their Muslim religious heritage as well as its cultural and social expression, global Islam becomes their community. This search for identity can have many forms. If combined with a feeling of being estranged by the rest of the society it can lead to great frustration. I believe that Christians have many answers to these issues in the Bible and can show these women how Jesus and biblical prophets from the Old and New Testament addressed issues of injustice and showed how God defends the rights of the oppressed and the rejected ones.

Conclusion
How can these facts assist us as we develop ministries for second and third generation Muslim women? First, I believe we must understand that these are unique Muslim women whose needs differ greatly from the needs of others.

We must therefore study their culture and lifestyle to find out how they differ from the first generation and how we can develop new responses to their questions; they will not be satisfied with the answers that have been developed for other Muslim women in different parts of the world.

I am also convinced that second and third generation women are trying hard to make sense out of the encounter of these two worlds that have often clashed in the past. Even today, we have seen how the West may misunderstand Islam. These women live in a world that does not always embrace the presence of Islam and they struggle with their identity and heritage. When we share the gospel, we must be aware of that inner struggle and not add to their disconnection with the past. The gospel should meet every facet of these women's lives.

Immigration, on the other hand, may provide new opportunities to expose women to non-Islamic religious ideas. Second and third generation women may be attracted to Christianity precisely because they are in an environment that allows for multi-religious reflection. However, others, as we have seen, may become more rooted in Islam because it is a way to find identity and a sense of belonging. I have met second and third generation women who were more attracted by Islam than by Western secular ideas even though they were born and raised in the West.

Second and third generation women who come to Christ, additionally, will need to integrate the biblical message at every stage of their development. In France, we created fellowships for second and third generation women where they were allowed to express their crisis of identity and their deepest feelings as they searched for a new identity. These fellowships provided a sense of belonging. They could be French when they wanted or North African when they wanted, free to express their doubts and fears. They could also explore Christian beliefs without pressure, discovering how Christ is adequate to answer their every need.

The sophistication of these women means that modern tools are important for communicating the gospel. Second and third generation women, as we have seen, are adept with modern technology and media. They are high tech, using the internet and chat rooms and open to change. Recognizing that some so-called first generation women are also more educated than thirty years ago is important to our ministry. We cannot even generalize all that has been said here. While conflicts may exist between the various generations, which are often exacerbated by immigration, we must also acknowledge the ways that these generations can reconcile with each other.

Finally, we need to provide answers to the frustration of women in the second and third generation. Often they will feel a sense of injustice because they sense the rest of the world rejecting Muslims and Islam. The various current conflicts in the world demonstrate that younger generations of Muslims are deeply impacted by this conflict and often seek refuge in fundamentalism. On the other hand, we can acknowledge that a number of fundamentalist leaders have been immigrants in the West and have returned to their country disappointed and with a desire to take their future into their own hands.

When second and third generation women turn to Christ they will need to find godly models they can follow. They will need to interact with people who will help them find Christian practices that apply to their own context. They will certainly develop new forms of ministry that will be effective for women like them. Second generation women who convert, for example, want to know how the message of Christ is applicable to their daily walk in practical ways; as mothers, sisters, workers, and members of the church. The lack of appropriate ministry models that apply to their own context indicates there is a great need for developing tools and approaches that take their concerns into consideration. This work of sharing the gospel, however, is not our own work. For more than twenty-seven years, we saw God Himself touching people's lives. God has a plan and wants to use us as tools if we are ready to accept his role in our life first to become more effective.

I once heard someone say that if the second generation has no identity it will find it in Christ. I would express this differently. While this may be true theologically, on a sociological level human beings need to identify with a community and make connections with other humans. Therefore, I suggest that we allow second and third generation Muslims to grow in Christ and find their connections within the rich network they have with people from various cultural and religious backgrounds. This will enable them to be at ease with the Christian community as well as with their own relatives and friends within the Muslim community without losing their faith in Jesus Christ. The body of Christ as a church must be a place where second and third generation Muslim women encountering Christ can feel free to express who they are and find a sense of belonging. By his grace and through our godly lives, may we help this happen.

REFERENCES

Benguigui, Yamina. 1997. *Mémoires d'immigrés - l'héritage maghrébin.* (Memories of
    Immigrants: the Maghrebian Heritage.) Paris: Canal.

Haddad, Yvonne Yazbeck, and John L. Esposito, eds. 1998. *Muslims on the
    Americanization path.* Atlanta, GA: Scholars Press.

Hasma, Gull Hasan. 2000. *American Muslims: The new generation.* New York:
    Continuum.

Lemahieu, Thomas. 1998. Together: Interview of Yamina Benguigui. *Périphérie.*
    November.

Lieblich, Julia. 1999. Professor combats ignorance about Islam. *The Associated Press*, 12
    August, 1999. Available online at http://www.islamfortoday.com-/leilaahmed.htm

Osnos, Evan. 2004. Islam shaping a new Europe. *Chicago Tribune.* 19 December, 2004.

Roy, Olivier. 2005. Globalized Islam: interview with Olivier Roy. *Religioscope.* July.
    Available online at www.religion.info.

Part III

STRATEGIC ISSUES

Discipling Women in Muslim Contexts

15

Communicating Christ in Contexts of Persecution

Beth Stricker

Personal experience with persecution prompted Beth Stricker and her husband to do extensive research with persecuted Christians. She shares insights gleaned from more than 500 interviews and offers suggestions for more effective ministry among Muslim people groups where persecution is common.

"And we rejoice in the hope of the glory of God. Not only so, but we also rejoice in our sufferings, because we know that suffering produces perseverance; perseverance, character; and character, hope. And hope does not disappoint us, because God has poured out his love into our hearts by the Holy Spirit, whom he has given us" (Rom. 5:2b-5, NIV).

My husband and I began to experience the lostness of people in Islam in 1991. We saw hunger, devastation, hopelessness, and hatred firsthand. We witnessed the survival of the wealthy and powerful, and the blind eyes and closed hearts they showed to the people in despair around them. Christianity, in contrast, had a bad reputation in our new country. Christians were people who fornicated, drank, smoked, and ate pork. The citizens had no problem doing business with Christians—but Christians could never be their friends or brothers.

In 1994, three believers from our people group were killed in one day. Shortly afterward, fundamentalist Muslims released a list of 150 suspected believers (people sympathetic with Westerners), who were to be eliminated. The persecutors knew this number was exaggerated, but they calculated that eliminating these 150 would wipe out all traces of Christian influence and completely destroy the emerging church.

Persecution became personal and relevant. Questions filled our minds. How do we make Christ known in an environment that is hostile to anyone who is a believer or to those seeking Him? How can workers continue when Satan attacks the fruits of their ministry? How do workers cope with persecution personally and, even more importantly, learn to endure pain and guilt when others are persecuted because of their witness?

Our struggle for answers led us on a pilgrimage to more than fifty countries. We interviewed approximately 500 believers living in the midst of persecution. Our research continues today as the interviews are read, reread, and analyzed, and as other believers are interviewed. The security of those who suffer and are persecuted daily for their faith necessitates that only a few of the interviews be shared verbatim. What can be shared are the "findings," the similarities that have repeatedly risen to the surface. These common patterns can help us understand how to minister in the midst of persecution and suffering.

When I arrived in Africa for the very first time in 1984, I thought the Father had given me everything I needed to turn the world upside down. Twenty years later, alongside the experiences of the past seven years, the Father has taught me that I know very little. He has called me to sit at the feet of those who daily live out their faith on the edge of lostness where it costs a great deal—even their lives—to follow Christ.

When you learn to drive in some parts of Africa, the authorities require you to place a big red letter "L" on your car. This indicates that you are a "learner" and all other drivers must watch out for you. In much the same way, we are wearing big L's when it comes to persecution—we are learners. The Father has much to teach us through those who have paid such a high price for their faith.

Aisha (a pseudonym) and her family fled their country when her father's writings raised concern with the government. Aisha only lacked one year of studies to complete her university degree but had to start over again in her new country. In university she studied literature and was exposed to writers like Shakespeare and Dante. She even read some about Jesus but knew Him only as a prophet.

One day Aisha discovered a book called *The Good News* on her father's bookshelf. When she asked him about it, he explained that it was a Bible he sometimes used to quote Jesus in his articles. Aisha began to read the Book and was impressed with the life of this man. One evening she fell asleep with the Book across her chest. In a vision, she saw a door open across the room. A man entered, surrounded by a bright light. He walked across the room and touched her.

The dream scared Aisha. She sensed the Book she was reading had great power. As a result of her dream, she became a more devout Muslim, praying up to ten times a day while continuing to read the Bible.

For almost two years nothing else happened. Then she met some expatriate women who began to share their faith with her. The more they shared the more confused Aisha became, and the division in her life began to concern her. Finally she visited a theologically trained Muslim woman who told her to pray all night, and then the answer for her life would be revealed. Aisha purified herself and began this tedious ritual. About 4 a.m. she cried out to God, "I just want to worship You. I just want to know more about You. Is it Islam or Christianity? If You are Jesus Christ, show me so I can be sure." As she lay on the floor half awake and half asleep, she saw a vision of people worshiping. They looked at her and declared that they were worshiping Jesus.

When her mother came to wake her for morning prayers, Aisha announced that she could not participate because she was going to worship Jesus. Then her persecution began. Her brothers and uncles tried to win her back to Islam. She was not allowed to go out and her expatriate friends could not visit. Any visitors she had were closely scrutinized. Her family tore up her books. For days they would not give her anything to eat.

During this time, as she remained faithful to Christ, her family witnessed many miracles as a result of Aisha's prayers. Her mother was healed. Neighbors had visions. Slowly, the persecution relaxed.

As Aisha shared her experiences with us, we were inspired by the miracle of her story—the beautiful way the Bible was put in her hands, her dreams and visions, and the new friends God sent to her. There was the struggle, the oppression, and the agony, but there was an overpowering sense of peace that radically contradicted all the hurt and pain. Joy and victory radiated through Aisha.

Does this story sound familiar? Many expatriate workers could tell similar stories. Around the world accounts like this one are being repeated. Jesus is making Himself known. He is entering lives and bringing change. As the stories unfold, many describe horrible acts of persecution and deep loneliness. At the same time, they share about their deep love for Jesus and their yearning to be faithful. We are touched by their faith and challenged to live more like Jesus. They also challenge us to share boldly and awake in us a deep desire to help and partner with our sisters.

But many of us can tell stories of new believers or seekers who died or were not able to persevere. They began the journey but their lives were snuffed out. They disappeared behind walls. They were forced into marriages. They gave up. Their stories bring us to our knees crying out for help. Their faces haunt us in the night and call us to examine our ministry. Was it our fault? What did we do wrong? What should have been done better or differently?

What sustains believers in the midst of beatings, hatred, divorce, rejection, isolation, loneliness, poverty, fear, and even death? Why do some stay strong while others fold under pressure? What is the difference? What do expatriate workers need to know in order to effectively evangelize and disciple believers who are likely to be persecuted?

THE REALITIES OF PERSECUTION

Persecution exists. It is a common occurrence. When one young girl was asked how she felt about her father shutting her in her room, she looked puzzled and asked if that didn't happen to all new believers. Those who work among the persecuted hear daily about people who are kicked out of their homes, lose opportunities for education or work, are denied their inheritance, have their children taken from them, lose their husbands, or watch their families suffer.

Most workers from the West consider persecution to be abnormal. How often in the Western church is a sermon preached on persecution or a Bible study taught on the cost of bearing the cross? Christians from the West are so accustomed to the ease and comfort of their faith that they do not allow themselves to hear clearly Jesus' words: "No servant is greater than his master. If they persecuted me, they will persecute you also ..." (John 15:20, NIV). Or, "Blessed are those who are persecuted because of righteousness, for theirs is the kingdom of heaven" (Matt. 5:10, NIV).

When the persecuted are asked why they have not recorded their accounts of mistreatment so that others can learn from them, they ask in return, "When did you stop reading the Bible?" That is our textbook on persecution! One man, who endured years of torture in prison, was asked why he had never written his story. He replied, "How often do you get up in the morning, look at your three sons, take them to the window and show them the sun coming up in the East?" The interviewer replied, "I have never done that. Why would I point out something to the boys that happens every day?" "Exactly," said the man, "that is how persecution is. It is like the sun coming up in the East. It is normal. It happens every day."

What can we learn from the persecuted? That persecution is. Persecution for followers of Jesus is normal—then and now. Through modern persecution we share the sufferings of Jesus.

The number one cause of persecution is people coming to Christ. Therefore, if people come to faith there will be persecution. If expatriate workers are faithful witnesses they will "cause" persecution. The only way to stop persecution is to stop people coming to faith. When the three believers were killed in 1994, the shaken and grieving workers called their sending agency and talked to their mentor and friend. He reminded them of words he had spoken during their training: "If you are 'successful' and people do come to Christ, you will get someone hurt." The major goal of persecutors is to prevent the spread of the gospel. As long as new believers keep their faith to themselves, problems usually are minimal. The moment believers begin to multiply, persecution intensifies.

Persecution can come from several sources. Workers and believers should understand the causes of persecution in their own context. Is it the government? Is it the religious system? Is it the family? Or is it a combination of these? When governments persecute, the nonbelieving family often protects the believer. When persecution occurs in a clash between two religious systems, support and encouragement are usually available from fellow believers—and sometimes legal protection is available from the government. The most severe persecution occurs when governments, ideologies and families are partners in persecution.

Such is often the case in Islamic settings. Persecution comes not only from someone outside the family, it is present in the very heart of the home—sitting across the table from the believer, working in the kitchen with her, sharing her bed. Persecution that originates from within the family—from the ones who are supposed to protect and care for the Muslim daughter, sister, wife, or mother —is extremely difficult to bear. When it is supported and encouraged by religious and legal systems, the suffering of believers intensifies.

HOW GOD USES PERSECUTION

A clear pattern of the way God is working among Muslims was seen in the Muslim-background believers (MBB) interviewed. Surprisingly, 90% of the MBBs interviewed met an expatriate worker after they had come to faith in Jesus Christ—not before. For the most part, in contexts of high persecution,

God is not using expatriate workers to bring Muslims to Christ. What is He using?

First, God is using dreams and visions just as He did throughout the Bible when He spoke to people like Daniel, Joseph the carpenter, and Peter. People often encounter God in the way in which they have been culturally conditioned to experience the Divine. Dreams are part of Muslim culture and tradition. They have played a huge role in the Islamic faith from the time of its conception. It should not be surprising that God would use dreams and visions to draw Muslim peoples to Himself. For most of the interviewees, their dreams and visions sent them on a spiritual journey. Usually they left the mosque and Islamic forms of prayer and began searching for spiritual truth.

The second thing God is using is His Word. Approximately 95 percent of those interviewed had a miraculous interaction with the Word of God, turning to the Bible for answers to the spiritual questions raised by their dreams. Through this deep encounter with God's Word they met Jesus and learned that He was the truth they were seeking. An older man, for instance, had a vision of the Bible. Later, as he walked down the street of a Muslim city, a stranger walked up and handed him a package containing a Bible. A young girl had a dream and later found a Bible hidden under her brother's mattress. At work, a lady saw someone reading the Word and asked about it. A young girl got a job at a bookshop and, in the midst of the Qur'ans, found a New Testament. God makes His Word available to those who are searching for spiritual truth.

The third thing God uses is believers. Usually the seeker comes into contact with an in-culture or near-culture believer who helps them in the faith process. This three-step pattern is very similar to the way God worked in the Bible. Pharaoh had a dream, heard God's Word from Joseph, and obeyed God. Saul had a vision, Ananias bravely shared God's Word with him, and Paul became a missionary. A vision sent Philip to the Ethiopian to explain the Word he was reading. Soon he believed and was baptized. It sounds so easy—have a dream, find a Bible, meet a believer—but for Muslim women it is not so easy.

REACHING MUSLIM WOMEN

For many centuries and still today, most cultures in which Muslim women live consider a woman's testimony to be worth one-half or one-third of a man's. They are not allowed to vote or hold a public job; they are granted only one-half to one-third as much inheritance as their brothers receive; their husbands have the right to take up to four wives and Muslim women are provided few, if any, rights in the case of divorce. In almost every Islamic cultural setting their identity, as well as their religious and social relationships, are filtered through their father, husband, brother, or son. Their value comes primarily through being married and having children.

In Muslim societies women are also less likely than men to be educated. Most Muslim women are nonliterate, oral communicators. They have much less freedom—sometimes practically none either inside or outside the home. Men travel, have access to education, read, watch television, and listen to the radio; most women do not. Men have opportunities to be alone. Women are always in the company of someone—their children, if no one else.

In addition, the Islamic belief system does not encourage women to make decisions on their own. In many cases, they are not viewed as competent to stand before God without a male intermediary. Therefore, some Muslim women find it difficult to believe they can know religious truth or can stand before God on their own. They may have trouble relating to God as a loving Father because they have only related in fear to a demanding and distant father. The interviews suggest that only 20 percent of MBBs globally are women. This made it difficult to find subjects to interview so data is still tentative. However, the information gleaned from the 100 female MBBs interviewed revealed some disturbing facts.

First, the interviews indicate that the three-step pattern mentioned previously (dream/vision, encounter with God's Word, and interaction with a believer) is generally true in the conversion of MBB men but not MBB women. It became apparent that with married MBB women it was usually the husband who had come to faith in Jesus. After several months he would tell his wife that he was a believer. Then he would declare their home to be a "Christian home" and declare her to be a Christian, also.

In one country this method of pseudo-conversion became a deadly issue. MBB men were martyred and their "MBB" wives quickly returned to the mosque, taking with them the names of all the believers their husbands were discipling. Martyrdom dramatically increased because of the betrayal of other believers by these "MBB" women.

Muslim women must have the opportunity to know Jesus personally. Almost eight out of ten "MBB" women interviewed could not tell who Jesus was. Many times the husband was translating for the wife. In one instance, when the wife could not clearly share her faith in Christ, the husband looked at his wife and said, "I told you that. Why don't you remember?"

In addition, the interviews indicated that male MBBs usually witness to their fathers, brothers, and uncles. Seldom do they witness to their wives, sisters, mothers, or aunts. One interview in the Middle East was with a musically talented MBB. He had miraculously found Christ through a dream, by reading the Word, and by a friend introducing him to a group of believers. He now wanted to use his musical gifts to share his faith. He saw himself, and his gifts, as a key to the growth of Christianity in his country. When asked whether he had witnessed to his wife, he said she did not warrant a witness because, "She is just an illiterate village woman." Sadly, such a viewpoint is not uncommon.

Jesus came for all peoples—for both genders. Jesus changed the way women were viewed. He paused in a crowd to seek out the woman with the issue of blood who had touched His garment. He sat by a well to talk to an unclean woman. He spent time with Mary and Martha in their home. Our Lord is surely saddened that in many settings globally, Muslim women do not have opportunities to meet Him. Like Jesus, we must be radical. We must find ways to give Muslim women access to the good news.

The Role of Expatriate Workers
Expatriate workers can address this issue in several ways. Female workers must intentionally and consistently witness to Muslim women. When couples first go out as workers, they are enthusiastic and excited about their host culture. They jump wholeheartedly into language study and prepare themselves to effectively work cross-culturally. But often after and even during language study, the wife finds herself increasingly focused on raising and educating their children and providing for the needs of the family. Almost without notice, the wife's focus can shift to ministry in the home while the husband focuses his efforts outside the home. During these years, the vital task of touching Muslim women behind the walls of their homes or in natural ways within the community is often neglected.

Once the children are older, the wife may shift her focus to the Muslim women around her, but often her language skills have atrophied and she has difficulty getting involved at this point in her life. Also, at this stage in an expatriate family's life, some choose to return home for children's educational needs or for other reasons. This destructive non-witness cycle is repeated within many global environments.

Sending agencies and organizations should insist that workers' entire families be involved in witnessing to Muslim families. They must encourage and equip the wife to make contacts with Muslim women and encourage the whole family to follow up her witness. As the children make Muslim friends in their community, the family should be involved in visiting their homes. Even though men and women do not typically visit together in many Islamic cultures, strategies to access and impact Muslim families as a unit must be an important goal of our ministry. Witnessing as families will help these women know His story and allow it to take root and become their story. Befriending and sharing with the wives of new believers should be an intentional and important element of our strategy. Women workers must find ways to impact Muslim women.

The salvation of MBB men is miraculous—but changing their mindset and attitudes remain a challenge. They have lived for centuries under Islam and in a culture that does not value women. We must encourage and equip them to effectively witness to the women in their families. Discipleship of male MBBs needs to include specific teaching on the value of women and must stress their responsibility to share the good news with their wives and children. Of course, MBB women also must be equipped and encouraged to share their faith with other women as well as with their husbands, children, and other family members. All believers must understand that the gospel is for the whole family!

The interviews suggest that thousands of women may be having dreams and visions, but there also must be an encounter with the Word in order for faith to be born. The majority of Muslim women cannot interact with the Bible in a literate way. How will the believing world bridge the gap for millions of Muslim women (and men) who cannot read? More than half of the world's population are oral learners. It is estimated that nearly 80 percent of those who have never heard of Jesus cannot read or write—they must hear God's Word.

The Bible must be made accessible in oral forms and available in the heart language if Muslim women are to hear and believe. Chronological Bible storying, the distribution of Bible stories on audiocassettes, CDs, and DVDs, and media such as radio and television are some effective tools for telling the story. The Word in oral form rapidly crosses cultures while allowing the story to be communicated clearly. It is up to the believing world to find creative ways to achieve this.

The West continues faithfully translating the Word into literate forms in the languages of many peoples. Literacy, English as a Second Language and English as a Foreign Language are widely used, but millions are dying before learning to read. Literate people from the West more naturally reach other literate people. This exclusive pattern must be broken as believers seek to reach oral peoples with the gospel. Workers must have increasingly deep cultural and linguistic skills in order to take advantage of every opportunity to share God's story. Workers should model a witness that can move naturally and normally from woman to woman.

MBBs who can read are often persecuted when they are found with the Bible or other discipleship materials. When believers are placed in prison and their printed Bible is destroyed, it is the Bible committed to memory that remains. No one can remove the Word hidden in the heart. God's stories, as well as memorized passages of Scripture, can sustain God's people during persecution.

When MBBs were asked what they had learned from expatriate workers, many replied, "They teach us to be afraid." Workers fear being kicked out of the country. They are afraid their children will get sick or that they will lose their work permits. Sometimes, they are afraid of being killed. When they are tempted to be afraid, workers must claim the freedom that being a child of God provides. They should ask themselves what they are willing to risk for the kingdom of God. This includes the risks that involve their children. God does not call us to teach or model a spirit of fear to new believers.

In two very difficult places the MBBs interviewed reminded us that there are 366 verses in the Bible about fear and not being afraid. "God gave us 365 verses," they said, "one for each day of the year, and one extra for when we are having a very tough day."

We are not to teach fear, but what are we to do? How can we stand with confidence and obedience beside those who are being persecuted? Immediately we think of intercession. Our knee-jerk reaction is to pray for safety; however, when the persecuted were asked how we should pray for them, many requested that we pray—not that their persecution cease—but that they would be obedient through their persecution. "Consider it pure joy, my brothers, whenever you face trials of many kinds, because you know that the testing of your faith develops perseverance" (James 1:2-3, NIV).

If we are going to stand with our sisters being persecuted, we must develop spiritual toughness. We must learn, if God desires, to allow local believers to suffer. We must listen to the Spirit and ignore the accusations of Satan when he reminds us how easy it is to preach perseverance when all that might happen to us is deportation or the loss of a visa. Workers must be prepared for the potentially high cost of taking the gospel to unreached Muslim people groups. History indicates that responding to Jesus may cost the lives of many people.

Workers are tempted to extract persecuted believers to places where they can live and grow in peace. However, such "mercy" may harm the emerging church by removing current or potential leaders and teaching believers to look to man rather than to God in times of need. What would have happened in Egypt if a kindhearted friend had arranged to have Joseph removed from prison before he was called on to interpret Pharaoh's dream? Yes, potentially both Israel and Egypt would have died in the coming famine. When it is God's will for believers to suffer for a time, it is not the worker's place to rescue them. In the garden, Jesus stopped the disciples' efforts to save Him. Resurrection Sunday could only come after Friday's cross.

Acts Chapter 8 records how severe persecution scattered and multiplied the church as believers carried the Word into new places. Sometimes the church told Paul to stay among them. Other times Paul became the focus for opposition and local believers pleaded with him to leave because of the unnecessary attention he brought. Workers must be sensitive to the Lord and to the believers among whom they serve. When persecution arrives, it should be for Jesus and the cause of witness, not for secondary issues such as a relationship to an outsider or a job with a Westerner.

Workers need to consider the consequences of their difficult decisions. They must prepare for the emotional suffering that comes when, under the leadership of the Lord and for the sake of the church, they must refuse to help a believer leave the country—and the believer is persecuted, put in prison, or killed. These issues need to be discussed and prayed over in families, teams and within sending agencies before persecution begins.

Sending agencies and churches must help their workers gain a biblical understanding of persecution and suffering. They also must help their people develop wise approaches to sharing the gospel in ways that enable the rapid multiplication of believers while minimizing persecution.

Workers should be ready to stay the course and do whatever it takes for women to hear and for the gospel to take root in their hearts. After massive persecution and martyrdom occurred in one country, many of the workers evacuated. Believers there asked, "Why is it that local believers suffer, but those from the West escape persecution and death?"

In the midst of lostness and persecution isolated workers, families, or singles seldom survive. God made us for community. Workers can diligently strive to "bring the kingdom" to their people groups, but their efforts will be futile if spiritual vitality is not maintained. Jesus' model was to send out disciples in pairs. He knew that wolves preyed upon sheep that were separated from the fold.

Workers must find ways to care for each other. This is essential for their mental, emotional, and spiritual health. Family-based strategies and teams will not avoid persecution. However, the support they give one another not only enables teams to thrive, it enables the lost and believers to see what Christian families and communities look like.

After hearing of the tragic death of the children of Bethlehem after His birth, Jesus could have been discouraged from the task. Instead, He honored the deaths of those children by staying the course and continuing to obey the Father. As workers who minister in the world of persecution, we dare not desecrate the witness of persecuted and martyred believers by giving up. Instead, we must willingly share the sufferings of Christ, including the persecution of our children in the faith. Our life must be one of victory, not just survival. Our ministry must enable those we have brought to faith to be victorious in the midst of suffering. Jesus is worth it!

> "When he opened the fifth seal, I saw under the altar the souls of those who had been slain because of the word of God and the testimony they had maintained. They called out in a loud voice, 'How long, Sovereign Lord, holy and true, until you judge the inhabitants of the earth and avenge our blood?' Then each of them was given a white robe, and they were told to wait a little longer, until the number of their fellow servants and brothers who were to be killed as they had been was completed." (Revelation 6:9-11, NIV)

16

Using Qur'anic Themes for Apologetics and Witness

Yvette Wray

Using the Qur'an in witness is debated but many have found it helpful in forging a path of understanding with the Bible. In this article Yvette Wray presents several methods which have been effective in introducing Muslim women to the biblical Jesus and involving them in the study of the Old and New Testament.

A nineteen-year-old Pakistani girl, crippled at the age of six months, is directed to read about Jesus in the Qur'an. She begins to pray to Him for healing and is healed soon after (Esther 1984). A team of six Iranian surgeons prays to Jesus when a prominent government figure dies on the operating table. In fear of losing their own lives, they ask Him to raise the man from the dead; the man comes back to life (McCurry 2001, 191). In both cases, these Muslims left Islam, dedicated their lives to Jesus Christ, and were baptized. What caused these Muslims to pray to Jesus? How did they know He possessed such power? The Qur'an identifies Jesus as the One who has power to heal the blind and leprous, and even to raise the dead (Q 3:49)!

There are approximately 1.2 billion Muslims worldwide. Of the 6,798 Unreached/ Least Reached People Groups identified by Joshua Project, 3,177 or just under half are Muslim (Joshua Project 2004). Christians who have made an effort to witness to Muslims often end up frustrated. Others do not even try, thinking that Muslims are argumentative and too difficult to reach (Safa 1996, 106).

However, the task remains and must be completed, because Jesus commanded His disciples to "go … and make disciples of all the nations" (Matt. 28:19, NASB).

Traditional methods of evangelism include statements such as "Jesus is the Son of God," and "Jesus died on the cross for the sins of the world." These statements are true and must be accepted in order for one to become a Christian. When these statements are used as a starting point with Muslims, however, the conversation may quickly turn into an argument, or even worse—it may be over before the Muslim has a chance to hear the full gospel. In reference to Muslim work in one South Asian city, Joshua Pillai said, "The church has to come-up (sic) with appropriate strategies to reach the growing Muslim population which is around 900,000" (Pillai 2002, 48). Although Pillai's statement speaks about one specific city, the sentiment well expresses the situation worldwide.

Recently, evangelical Christians in different areas have chosen a strategy that begins in a place where Muslims feel comfortable using the Qur'an. The strategy of using the Qur'an as a bridge to the gospel is not without controversy. Because it is not the inspired Word of God, many people will not use it in Muslim evangelism. The significant point here is to remember that those who choose to use the Qur'an use it only as a bridge. Greeson says, "A bridge is designed to get us over barriers such as treacherous waterways or dangerous intersections. Once we cross a bridge, we no longer need it and can move forward" (Greeson 2004, preface ii).

In the New Testament, Jesus, and later the disciples, used bridges in sharing with unbelievers. Examples include Jesus sharing with the woman at the well (John 4), the apostles' use of the law and the writings of the prophets to share with Jews, and Paul's discourse to the people of Athens (Acts 17). Some argue that the inspired Word of God was used in those instances. In Athens, however, Paul specifically used the writings of Greek poets in his discourse, even though he knew they were not inspired by the Holy Spirit but were attributed to the sister goddesses named the Muses. "It is worth noting that the Spirit of God, who inspired the writer of the book of Acts, did not hesitate to include a statement from one of these Greek poets in the content of the Bible" (Accad 1997, 22-23). Accad stresses that using certain passages of literature to prove a point does not affirm the truth of the entire source. He states that references or quotations of Jewish and Greek non-biblical literature are used at least 133 times in the New Testament. Everything written by these writers was not considered true. Likewise, when Christians quote from other books and sources, including the Qur'an, they are not agreeing with everything in the books, nor are they considering the books to be divinely inspired (Ibid., 26). "Using Paul's method," Accad says, "we can introduce accurate verses about Christ from the Qur'an to Muslims, which will naturally arouse their respect for what Muhammad has brought them and at the same time open a door of curiosity about the full identity of Jesus Christ" (Ibid., 16).

That is the purpose of the CAMEL training method. It focuses on one specific passage from the Qur'an: Surah 3:42-55. The method itself grew out of a church-planting movement currently taking place in one South Asian country (for security reasons, SAM will be used to identify this country), which reported 250,000 baptized Muslims in more than 8,000 churches at the end of 2003 (Greeson 2004, 2). Current figures indicate more than 7,000 Muslims monthly are giving witness to their new life through baptism (Ibid., preface ii).

The goal of discussing Surah 3:42-55 with Muslims is to identify and draw out persons of peace—that is, men or women who already are being prepared by the Holy Spirit (Luke 10:3-12)—by elevating Jesus above other prophets in holiness, power, and position. Jesus supersedes all others in holiness because He was born of a virgin; He was not born with the sin of Adam like the rest of mankind. Jesus has more power than any other; He alone has power over sickness, and even death, our greatest enemy. Jesus also supersedes the other prophets in position since He came from God and is currently with God (Ibid., 51). Greeson states that once persons of peace are identified and become believers, they will be the ones to evangelize their communities (Greeson 2003).

There are many advantages of using the CAMEL method. Because only one passage of the Qur'an is required to reach the goal, one does not have to be a scholar of the Qur'an in order to use it. The CAMEL approach is much quicker and has proved to be more effective than friendship evangelism which requires time to establish a relationship. It also can be used anywhere, including in a mosque, to begin conversations with Muslims (Greeson 2004, preface i, 79). Kirk Vogel (a pseudnym) has traveled throughout Asia this past year, training and modeling the CAMEL method. He testified, "I never had a Muslim refuse to talk to me about Isa (Jesus) in the Qur'an" (Vogel 2004).

Greeson assures those he trains that he would not continue to use the Qur'an as a bridge if he saw Muslim-background believers (MBBs) hold on to their Qur'an as a holy book after coming to faith. On the contrary, he says that once new Muslim believers are given a Bible, they quickly discard the Qur'an as they hungrily read the true Word of God. Although new believers do not retain their

Qur'an as a tool for spiritual development, they do retain it as a tool for evangelism (Greeson 2004, 12). Steven Masood knew he could not forget about the Qur'an, because "I discovered Jesus Christ in the pages of that book … and I determined that I would give it a place in my testimony" (Masood 1984, 150-151).

I had the opportunity to travel to the country of SAM in 2003 and see firsthand how Muslim women responded to the CAMEL method. Initially, I interviewed a group of approximately thirty women MBBs who are a part of a group of 3,500 people in the city. This group has grown rapidly as the MBBs, mostly women, shared with their neighbors and relatives about Jesus from the Qur'an as they went about their daily chores. I asked the women how quickly they told fathers/husbands about their new faith after their decision to follow Christ. To my surprise, most of the women responded that they immediately went home and told them. They did this by pointing out the passage in Surah 3 to the men. When I questioned them about the persecution they faced because of their decision, some reported they had been divorced by their husbands, others that they had been beaten, but overall they said the persecution had been minimal and usually short-lived. Why? Because they had used the Qur'an to speak of Jesus (MBB women 2003).

I next visited three villages and spoke to groups of women in each. I was told that the women gathered in the first village already had been baptized. Not wanting to go back to the Qur'an, I only used stories from the Bible as I spoke with them. During this time, however, a much larger group gathered, mostly Muslims. One man became hostile, accusing me of coming to convert the people to Christianity. My interpreter stepped in and spoke on my behalf, but we quickly left before the situation grew worse. In the next two villages, I began by speaking about Jesus from Surah 3 and then went on to tell a story about Him from the Bible. Even though we were the first Christians to proclaim Jesus in the one village, we faced no opposition because we started with the Qur'an. A year later, I received a report that there is now a church of Muslim-background believers in that village.

I also use the passage from Surah 3 in my own area of ministry, both with my Muslim friends and with Muslims I have only just met. They always recognize Jesus as the One who is best able to show them the way to God; however, no one has chosen to follow Him.

Fouad Elias Accad, in his book *Building Bridges*, outlines a method he refers to as a "Scriptural means of telling Muslims who Christ actually is and why He occupies such a prominent place in their Qur'an—without alienating them

from their native culture" (Accad 1997, 8). While Greeson's method may be
used with friends or strangers, Accad outlines seven principles to use with
Muslims with whom you already have developed a friendship and trust. The
seven principles are:

- God has a purpose for our lives
- Sin separates us from God
- We can't save ourselves
- The cross is the bridge to life

- God's provision is a person
- Making Him ours
- What to expect when we accept
  God's gift.

These principles incorporate teachings from all of the Muslim's holy books—
"the Tawrah (the Qur'an's word for the whole Old Testament), the Zabur (the
Qur'an's word specifically for the Psalms), the Injil (the Qur'an's word for the
whole New Testament, not just the Gospels), and the Qur'an itself" (Accad
1997, 77). Accad suggests that one principle should be discussed every week
or two, requiring at least an hour each time. The principles are sequential and
build upon one another. The Muslim must agree with one principle before you
move on to the next (Accad 1997, 74). Accad claims, "More than 80% of
Muslims who finish studying these seven principles come to put their trust in
Christ—when the Christian who shares the principles does so in a way that is
personally and culturally sensitive" (Accad 1997, 71).

Accad and Greeson both provide information that can be used in apologetics.
Neither author advocates debating Muslims; but they do provide Qur'anic verses
that address topics to which Muslims often raise objections, such as whether
the Bible has been corrupted, and whether Jesus died on the cross. Ali Hadi
Al-Nouri's recent article "Should a Muslim View 'The Passion of the Christ'"?
provides excellent apologetic material on the topics of Christ's death and resurrection and the Bible's accuracy. He points to many Qur'anic verses in making
his presentation. Al-Nouri provides a word study of *tawaffa*, showing its use
twenty-six times in the Qur'an. Two times it is translated as "sleep" and twenty-
two times it is translated as "death." In the two places, however, where it is
used in reference to Jesus, it is translated altogether differently—being taken
into God's presence without death. He considers such a translation as avoiding
the obvious meaning and people who accept such a translation as being
against the Qur'an (Al-Nouri 2004, 4).

Testimonies of Muslim-background believers provide great support to the
Qur'anic Bridge method of evangelism. Some testimonies are documented in

books such as *The Torn Veil* (Esther and Sangster 1984), *On the Way of the Cross* (Hakkeem, 1984), *Captive of Christ* (Masood 1984), and the article "Why I Became a Christian (Paul)". The starting point in their search for God and truth was the Qur'an, which then led them to the Bible.

The effectiveness of using the Qur'an as a bridge, cited both by Accad and Greeson, should be sufficient to convince Christians of the validity of such a method. In addition to its effectiveness are the benefits that also have been documented: persecution is less severe, the MBB is able to remain within his or her community, and the Qur'an becomes a witnessing tool. These are significant benefits, as E-1 evangelism (sharing the gospel with someone from the same culture) is always most effective. Who is better able to witness to the Muslim world—an outsider or one of their own? Accad states,

> Conversion is seen by [the Muslim community] as becoming a traitor to family, clan, tribe, people, country, and race. ... If a Muslim could trust Christ without alienating his family and friends, he could become a means within his own community to testify to them about the extraordinary blessings they can obtain from knowing Christ better as the One who is so highly exalted by their own Qur'an. (Accad 1997, 8)

The apostle Paul said, "For though I am free from all men, I have made myself a slave to all, that I might win the more. . . . I have become all things to all men, that I may by all means save some. And I do all things for the sake of the gospel" (1 Cor. 9:19-23, NASB). Using the Qur'an as a bridge is by no means the only way to approach Muslims and win them to Christ. The Holy Spirit alone draws them. Using the Qur'an, however, is a valid approach that has seen hundreds of thousands of Muslims come to faith in Jesus Christ. We cannot continue to ignore the Muslim world. We also cannot continue to fail in our efforts to reach the Muslim world because we do not want to try something different that takes us out of our comfort zone. Too many souls are at stake. We must each be willing to do whatever it takes to bring salvation to Muslim people worldwide.

REFERENCES

Accad, Fouad Elias. 1997. *Building bridges: Christianity and Islam*. Colorado Springs, CO: Navpress.

Esther, Gulsahn, and Thelma Sangster. 1984. *The torn veil*. Madras, India: Evangelical Literature Service.

Greeson, Kevin. 2003. CAMEL training seminar, 24-25 June.

————. 2004. CAMEL training manual. Bangalore, India: Wigtake Resources.

Hakkeem, A. Abdul. 1984. *On the way of the cross*. Manjeri, India: Nur ul Alam Ministry.

Masood, Steven. 1984. *Captive of Christ*. Mumbai, India: GLS Printing.

MBB Women. 2003. Interview by Yvette Wray, 9 July.

McCurry, Don. 2001. *Healing the broken family of Abraham: New life for Muslims*. Colorado Springs, CO.: Ministries to Muslims.

Nouri, Ali Hadi al-. 2004. Should a Muslim view 'The Passion of the Christ'?

Paul, Sultan Muhammad. *Why I became a Christian*. Available online http://www.the-good-way.com/eng/article/a18.htm; accessed 26 July 2003.

Pillai, Joshua. 2002. *Karnataka mission challenge: Trumpet call to light up and transform Karnataka*. Chennai, India: DAWN Church and Missions Service.

Vogel, Kirk. 2004. Interview by Yvette Wray, 22 May.

Safa, Reza F. 1996. *Inside Islam: Exposing and reaching the world of Islam*. Orlando, Fla.: Creation House.

————. 1999. *Middle East evangelism training—training workbook*. Indianapolis, IN: Arab International Ministry.

————. 2004. Joshua Project interesting people group facts; available from http://www.joshuaproject.net/globalstatistics.php; accessed 18 June.

17

Signs and Symbols in the Land

Elizabeth Edwardson

God calls whole families to his work, not just individuals. He asks them to follow him, to share, to hurt, to look outward and to be signs and symbols in the land. In this article Elizabeth Edwardson explains how her family was of strategic value in pointing towards God and his redeeming message.

In our Asian city, my fourteen year old daughter is often likened to superstar Britney Spears. This would never happen if we lived in the States, since Mari has grey eyes instead of brown, dark hair instead of blond, clothes on her body in contrast to being half-naked, and is reticent, not an exhibitionist. But simply because Mari is western and pretty, new acquaintances often blurt out that she's another Britney. I usually don't have to fix the image, since our neighbors and friends are very quick to rebut with, "No! She's nothing like Britney. She's a good girl!" Then I hear them describe how our family is different from the generally-held assumptions of the American family. Since they're comparing us with TV re-runs of "Everybody Loves Raymond" and rental VCD copies of "Friends," our family is definitely different from their stereotypes. They've also been watching us live out our faith, and they're a bit curious to know what makes us tick.

Our family is different from the average Western family in still another way— our nuclear family is made up entirely of Third Culture Kids (TCKs). My husband and I each grew up in distant corners of Indonesia, met in boarding school in Malaysia, studied and married in the US, then moved back overseas. Our three children, now ages fourteen, twelve, and ten, have very little memory of our few years as a young family in Chicago. When we're "at home" in Asia it's obvious we're outsiders; when we're "at home" in the States, we feel like aliens.

Perhaps this constant state of "foreignness" contributes to my curiosity about families. Gazing at child-rearing across cultures and generations, I am fascinated to observe the many good ways there are to raise a family. A simple example: the goal of Indonesian parenting and American parenting is that children will grow to be responsible adults, but the two cultures use seemingly opposite approaches to achieve this goal. Indonesian families of twenty years ago maintained that babies can do no wrong and children shouldn't be denied anything they desired. The key balancing factor is that everyone must cater to the child or baby younger than they. And once there is a younger child present, the older sibling, cousin, or child must care for the younger. In rapidly multiplying extended families, any child has a very small window of opportunity to be spoiled rotten. Most children are babysitting their siblings and cousins by the time they're of elementary age, and taking part in household tasks is an obvious expectation. The family structure becomes more and more demanding as Indonesian children grow up. Traditional American families, on the other hand, begin with the assumption that you must teach babies and toddlers what they will need to know to survive in the world. They need structure, discipline, and education. As children grow, parents release them to increasing independence and freedom. The family structure is less and less demanding as American children grow up. And the resulting adults in both these cultures—we see responsible and productive citizens.

Is one of these approaches better? Which culture owns the right way to raise a family? Can anyone claim to have the ultimate formula for raising children? We all know that living and working overseas challenges us in many ways, both personally and professionally. We seek to be prepared in every way we can anticipate, and we consider how we can lessen the stress we experience daily. We're regularly quoted statistics that point to overseas workers as individuals who face some of the highest stress indicators there are.

One of the biggest stressors in our lives is the huge question of our family: how can we ensure that our family and children will thrive? How much do we adapt our family life to the local culture? How can we help our kids gain a sense of Western cultural identity while being immersed in the culture we've adopted? How do we maintain some sense of family identity in a culture that's often very different from our own? How should we educate our kids? The questions go on and on.

Our Western culture is one that demands answers to these questions. We're logic-driven and education-based, with bookstores full of best-selling how-to books for every topic imaginable. We feel that if we define the methods, appropriate results are sure to follow. So we attempt to build formulas for how to raise a family. But as I've talked with women from various organizations and family backgrounds, I realize again that there are many good ways to raise a family. There's not one schedule for feeding and naps that will work across the board. One schedule won't even work for the siblings in one family; no one set of disciplinary measures, no certain kind of educational system is best.

There is no one fool-proof formula for raising a family. This is true. But as I've talked with women who work cross-culturally, I hear one principle recurring consistently in every conversation about a family that thrives. That principle is this: God's call to us is a call to our family. As a wife, I am not left out of God's plan, nor does God forget about our kids when he asks us to live as kingdom people in a Muslim setting.

This truth is crystallized in the book of Isaiah, particularly the story of God's purpose for Isaiah's life, which is told in Isaiah 6-8. Isaiah's personal call to be a prophet of God (Isaiah 6) is a very familiar text. He realized that he was to take part in fulfilling God's purposes for the world when he said, "Here am I. Send me." Knowing that God has a specific purpose for us is an essential ingredient in our lives just as it was for Isaiah. God does not chain us to his desire for our husband's life, but has a purpose for each of us. He urges us to seek him out and to move forward in freedom, living as women of God in our marriage, our family and our adoptive culture.

But, we must not stop at the individual level. Isaiah continues with two more chapters that include his family and God's purposes for them together. Isaiah did not carry out his kingdom calling as if it were simply a job. Being a prophet was not a forty-hour-a-week profession that Isaiah worked at separate from his wife and children. Believing his wife was also called, he honored God's purposes for her life by writing about her as "the prophetess" (Isa. 8:3). Isaiah chose a wife who was part of the life God had called him to, and they naturally brought their children into that circle. They believed their family had a greater purpose in the world, and they acted accordingly.

Isaiah and his wife believed God had a larger purpose for their children than to simply be good "sons of Isaiah." They considered their sons to be kingdom people, sent by God. They named their first son "Shear-Jashub" (A-Remnant-Will-Return), and in Isaiah 7:3, Isaiah takes "A-Remnant-Will-Return" along with him when he goes to address the king. The story progresses as Isaiah and the prophetess come together to have another child (Isa. 8:1-4). They name him as God guides them to do. Only God's purposes would compel parents to name their child "Maher-Shalal-Hash-Baz" (Quick-to-the-Plunder).

Isaiah completes the word picture of his family with a bold statement, "Here am I, and the children the Lord has given me. We are signs and symbols in Israel from the Lord Almighty, who dwells on Mount Zion" (Isa. 8:18). "Signs and symbols," this was God's purpose for them together. God's call to Isaiah included his whole family.

My husband grew up in a family with this attitude. My mother-in-law tells us about the year when their family had returned to the States and Lincoln was in second grade. He came home from school one day quite distraught. The teacher had asked each student to tell the class what their dad's job was, and Lincoln hadn't been able to come up with an answer like his classmates—plumber, doctor, salesman. His mom said, "Well honey, didn't you tell them that dad's a missionary?" To which Lincoln responded in surprise, "That's not a job! That's a life."

What was the "life" that Isaiah and his wife believed God had for them? Reiterated strongly throughout the book of Isaiah is God's jealous passion for his name. "I am Yahweh. That is my name. I will not give my glory to another" (Isa. 42:8). Isaiah responds with, "Your name and renown, O Lord, are the desire of our hearts" (Isa. 26:8). Isaiah's family lived as people of God's kingdom, to declare the glory of God's name throughout the world. God yearns for our families to do the same: to live as kingdom people for his greater purpose—the glory of his name.

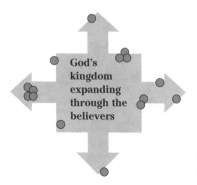

God's kingdom expanding through the believers

THE EXPANSION OF GOD'S KINGDOM

The kingdom, made up of families and individuals, is God's primary agent of change in the world. Our families are important aspects of the kingdom, living to declare the glory of his name. This principle of the family's place in the kingdom is shown in this diagram:

The family has its greatest impact when it sees beyond itself and takes its place in God's kingdom.

Implications:
- God calls entire families to his 'work'—not just individuals—to follow him, to share, to hurt, to look outward.
- Our job as parents is to empower our children to live as kingdom people in our neighborhoods and communities.
- Our children can thrive and can have a significant impact in the setting where God places our family.

This understanding of the family gives us great hope and freedom. For God, who knits us together in our mother's womb, knows just where and how we'll be born. He places us in families where he has a purpose for us. And the same is true for our children.

We will find ourselves struggling if we allow ourselves to think that God has a purpose for our husbands, but he isn't sure what part we'll have in the picture; that the wife and kids will have to figure out their place in it as they go along. This is a sure recipe for discontent and bitterness toward God and our husband. We'll also experience turmoil if we allow ourselves to think that God has a purpose for us and our husbands, but that he had no inkling of the children who would be born to us or what would happen with them. When God calls you or me, he does not do it oblivious to those intimately connected to us. In fact, he desires to talk directly to our children about how they fit in the picture. We are very shortsighted if we don't allow our kids to learn to hear God's voice. He calls our husbands and our children together with us, for the furthering of his kingdom in the world. And we can boldly declare: "Here we are, along with the children God has given us. We are signs and symbols in this land, called by the Lord Almighty."

This paradigm of family in ministry stands in contrast to several other paradigms I've heard espoused by friends and fellow workers. I'd like to spend some time exploring these before we talk about some of the challenges that are common to us all.

Paradigm 1: Nuclear family at the center
- The family is at the center of God's purposes and work on behalf of the world.
- This unit is to be the change-agent for a rotting world.

- Family is to be Truth center, haven and oasis, emotional stabilizer and recharging point for its members

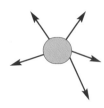

Implications:
- The biological family is God's most important institution on earth.
- I fulfill God's purpose for me by focusing on this subset of society, and from this place, I/we reach out to the world
- My family's well-being is my highest goal, for its thriving will reflect God's purposes

Presently there are many strong advocates of this view. I believe however, that with this view we see only a slice of the picture.

Weaknesses:
1. Viewing the nuclear family at the center can lead to an insulated, isolated family unit. The focus turns inward as we seek to build up the family.
2. Putting the nuclear family at the center means that singles, single parents, childless couples are side-lined from God's purposes through the family. It assumes these individuals can never be complete.
3. Placing the nuclear family at the center can lead to unrealistic expectations of family being a "safe haven" that's able to protect from all pain. It allows us to be influenced by North America's growing expectation that we can control our environment, freeing ourselves of unanticipated and unwanted pain or difficulty. Using everything from medicines and teeth whiteners to air conditioning, weather reports, education, and stomach stapling, we determine when and how we hurt; we decide when and how we sacrifice.
4. The primary weakness of putting the family at the center is that it puts the family first instead of listening to Jesus' call to put him first. Matthew, Mark, and Luke all dethrone the biological, nuclear family as they tell the same event in Jesus' life (Matt. 12:46-50, Mark 3:31-35, Luke 8:19-21). Mary and Jesus' siblings wanted to speak to him, but he rejected their familial rights to him outright. Was this necessary? Not only was it necessary, but it was critical to the disciples' understanding of Jesus' call and his view of the family. Jesus was demanding that Mary, so highly lauded by the angel,

would not hold tightly to her son. His was a bigger purpose. He was welcoming her to a new kind of family. We too, must put Jesus first. As we join Jesus' family, he rewrites our expectations.

My sister-in-law, Joyce, and her husband are foster parents for the state of Illinois. One day Joyce was at the beach with their first foster baby, Latoya, who'd been born to a cocaine addict. A little girl named Rochelle Kroger, who is an MK in Africa, walked up to her. Looking curiously at Joyce, seven-year-old Rochelle noted that Joyce's skin was white and Latoya's was black. She wanted to know how Joyce got Latoya. Joyce told her that she was watching Latoya because her mom was very sick and couldn't do it.

"Well," responded Rochelle, "we're the Krogers, and we help people. We'll help you take care of her. Where does her mommy live?" "She lives far away, and really, her problem is that she doesn't know Jesus. Her sickness won't go away until her heart is changed."

Undeterred, Rochelle said, "We can help. We're the Krogers, and we tell people about Jesus. We'll go talk to Latoya's mommy." Rochelle shares this knowledge with Joyce: families aren't meant to be an insulated haven of peace against a turbulent world. Rather, God's purpose for families is that they live beyond themselves, give to others, and love sacrificially.

Paradigm 2: Linear description of our personal responsibilities

This paradigm can be a continuation of the above set of assumptions, but can also be considered separately from the paradigm above.

- Individuals are at the center of God's purposes for the world
- The individual is the key to the family's thriving
- Personal responsibility is on the shoulders of individual family members to determine the needs of the other members

1. God   2. my spouse   3. my kids   4. ministry / the world

Implications:

- Balance and focus are achieved when we put our family in priority order
- Keeping these priorities will ensure that I, my spouse, my kids, and ministry thrive
- I'm personally able to control (at least to certain degree) the success of each element

It's quite likely this list of priorities grew out of frustration in families who experienced a "ministry-first" model of family. But rearranging the elements on a priority line doesn't resolve the problem of balance; it just gives a new order for our to-do list.

Weaknesses:

1. Lower elements of priority experience loss while I attend to the priority ahead of it. A clear example of this is that we often feel torn between family and ministry, since family is on a separate plane at a higher level of importance. All of us know from experience that our families will bring ever-present and constantly changing needs. If family is of primary importance, when will we be able to turn from it and attend to ministry?

   When our kids were little I remember coming home from teaching, having lunch and chatting with five-year-old Mari about how much I loved the three of them. "You guys are the most important thing to me!" I declared. When one hour later I needed to be at a faculty meeting, Mari burst out crying and said accusingly, "You said we're the most important thing to you. Wil needs you now, so how come you have to go to the meeting? Just tell them you're not coming!" She nailed me, but I went to the meeting anyway —miserable.

2. This prioritization assumes a clear-cut differentiation between the elements; I'll know where one starts and the other stops.

3. The spread of God's kingdom can be seen as a task to accomplish and God's call to ministry might be considered a job to tackle, rather than seeing the kingdom and ministry as an all-encompassing way of life

   I fall into this trap often. Priority lists are more easily defined. I determine that I'll be on "mom duty" at 4:00 every day when the kids get home from school. I'll be available to them until they head for bed. Then I receive notification that the neighborhood women's group is meeting tomorrow at 4:30. And Euis calls with a problem—can she come over and talk about the woman who's spreading rumors about her? This will mean hours this evening, and an hour and a half tomorrow. "Mom duty" will have to be put on hold. I can't turn my job on and off, nor can I work regular hours doing God's kingdom expansion.

4. Placing our family on a priority list assumes people are objects to be organized properly, in a timeline we can control. But God's kingdom is much messier than this—a constant juggling act.

A few years ago we welcomed a team of four women to our city for ten days, ending on the day our family was to leave for six weeks. Lincoln organized their schedule, including an overnight out in a village so they could experience immersion in the culture. I didn't see how I could get us packed up to head out the door, and go along on the village trip, so we asked the kids to go along with Lincoln and the women to even out the gender mix. (Much groaning from the kids was solved by our offering to pay them $5 each for the event.) By the end of the first day, two of the women were vomiting violently and running to the outhouse with emergency-level diarrhea. As soon as dawn arrived they asked Lincoln to take them back to the city, along with an escort of one healthy woman. Our three kids stayed out in the village as translators for the last healthy woman, and Lincoln raced the others back. Then out he went again to catch up with the adventure. I look back on that fabulous fiasco and wonder: Which elements on the priority list were served? And did we get them in the right order?

FAMILY GOALS AND VISION STATEMENTS

If our whole family is living for God's glory and the expansion of his kingdom, do we know what it will take to get there? What are the ways we hope to live out our kingdom membership? Drafting a family vision statement goes far in clarifying who we are. I asked some women whose families are thriving overseas if they had done this. One woman sent me the vision statement their family had written together a couple years ago. Another woman said, "We don't have family goals per se, but I believe we would all agree to the following vision statement. . . ." Depending on the age of your children and the personality mix, your family might draw up a family shield, write a family covenant, paint a mural for the family room wall. Work to be specific so that the concepts can be measured. Whatever the format, it is a very helpful exercise to think through where we're going as kingdom families.

Our family's goals, put simply, are these:
1. To love God and serve him freely (I Cor. 9:19)
2. To enjoy the people of our adoptive culture and identify with them
3. To live as witnesses, which means we will be exposed to sin, feel rejection, and need to understand our faith well enough to verbalize it
4. To receive all of life's experiences with open hands and NOT to avoid suffering
5. To be content in our identity as TCK's since our whole family experiences this
6. To be generous with all that we are and have

Challenges We Face

Again, God's call to the Muslim world is a call for our whole family. While this principle gives us confidence to obey God's voice, it doesn't negate the fact that difficulties will confront us along the way. One woman who I talked with said it this way, "There are difficulties in every life choice. I know that no matter where I am, our family will face them. Raising kids challenges us whether we're in the middle of Canada, or in the middle of our Muslim neighborhood. I'd rather be facing the challenges in an arena that advances the kingdom."

Meeting the Challenges

Among the numerous challenges our families face is, first of all, a difference in gender roles between U.S. and Muslim cultures. Submission to Christ is the key: if we are at peace with the cultural mores ourselves we will be better able to guide our children through the murky waters. Raising girls in a chauvinistic society where they are treated as sex objects is particularly challenging. It is assumed that they will take on serving roles and be demure in their behaviors. Raising boys is almost an equal challenge because they will grow up in a sexually charged atmosphere. All too often, girls will aggressively pursue Western boys without thinking of the moral cost. In one sense, it is almost like living between two worlds. Since the world of Muslim friendships is so different from Western friendships one of my wise friends has told her daughters that there are different rules for friendships with boys in their neighborhood than with the Western boys.

A second serious challenge our families face is sexual abuses. Abuse is very common and must be diligently guarded against. This is a particular problem if we ourselves have been abused. We must face our own fears so that we are not obsessive about the protection of our children. No matter how friendly and morally upright the people of our adoptive culture seem to be we must be alert to the underlying currents of sexual abuse that exist.

Third, we must be alert to spiritual attack. This involves being alert to the state of our own heart since our sin opens the door to the evil one. But it also means watching out for evil practices and territorial pitfalls. Since the enemy's desire is to thwart God's kingdom we must be alert to his attacks in our weak areas.

A fourth area of concern for families is in the area of education. Educational options often become the most significant factors in determining where we live. If we have not prioritized God's command to "go" we may simply live where we have the greatest degree of comfort. Searching our hearts for the basis of our choices is critical to accomplishing the task. We will also need to consider how, or if, our children will be socialized as "Westerners."

Many families face a fifth challenge in the area of perfection. Our children may feel they have to perform perfectly in all settings; that living as a witness means there will be "no messing up." Since a performance-driven mindset is common among Third Culture Kids (TCKs) we need to remind them that our friends and neighbors can see that faith is deeper than performance. Our desire is not that our children will be bound by false standards of perfection but that they will stay free to love God and serve him.

Sixth, our children may feel over time that the ministry is more important than the family. We need to listen to our children. Since many of us are worka-holics, we may also need to pay attention to what they are saying! Friends can help. Asking colleagues to tell us when we are failing in this area and seeking accountable friendships are important steps in avoiding this conflict. At the same time we want to teach our families to have "others-centered thinking." Talking through and praying about all our relationships and activities will keep us from the other trap of "prioritizing."

Finally, we face the challenge of transitioning back to North America. While it seems like it would be less of a problem than going overseas, returning home is a huge hurdle. We can help our children in the transition if we acknowledge the TCK struggle of never truly belonging. Even when we plan as much as pos-sible for support systems to be in place, we must also turn the transition over to God and assure our children that God has good plans for them.

GOD'S CALL IS FOR THE ENTIRE FAMILY

My friend Tina has a great husband, four children, and enough energy to keep their whole beachfront in order. Several years ago their family responded to God's leading and moved to this town on the coast with the desire to be a blessing and to share the love of Christ. Their home is now the central hub for everything they've got going, including two cottage industry handicrafts where supplies and current projects are all over the house, a weekly youth gathering, a weekly kids' club, team prayer, worship and shepherding, home schooling, and the mentoring of a new worker, who more often than not conveniently finds herself there at the time of the evening meal.

Tina says it gets really hectic at their home, to the place where their son Joshua, the third child, finds himself with no space and no place to move. Even their cubicle of an office is overrun with their new worker, Eti, continually coming and going. Joshua has felt increasingly suffocated, becoming angry about their "work" and uncharacteristically losing his temper. Tina told me that when he expressed his feelings regularly to her, she and her husband had to agree the chaos was overwhelming. They made extra effort to be sensitive, working to un-invite Eti from the evening meal and keeping the open spaces of the home more neat.

My heart groaned for them as I said, "Oh Tina, I'll pray hard that the property you've wanted to buy will become available, and that the purchase will go smoothly. You've got to get all those work projects out of your house." But Tina didn't want that. "Not to worry! It's not the top priority in Joshua's life."

She went on to describe that they regularly challenge Joshua to take his feelings to God; also to be alert to ways he can be part of the answer. As he takes time to be with God, his attitude changes. Now he extends grace to Tina in new ways—urging her to get out for her evening bike ride, offering to clean up, freely making space for Eti at the evening meal. Tina finished her story by rejoicing in what God is doing in their family. Joshua is learning a great deal about his place in the kingdom—and is doing well at living out the purpose God has for him. Together with Isaiah, we can say: "Here we are, along with the children God has given us. We are signs and symbols in this land, called by the Lord Almighty."

R E F E R E N C E S

Balswick, Jack O., and Judith K. n.d. The family: A Christian perspective on the contemporary home. Baker Book House, Grand Rapids, Michigan.

Clapp, Rodney. 1993. Families at the crossroads. InterVarsity Press.

Foyle, Marjory F. 2001. Honourably wounded: Stress among Christian workers. Monarch Books.

18

Networking:
Forming and Maintaining Strategic Partnerships

Janelle Metzger

This paper by Janelle Metzger examines some of the challenges, biblical princi-
ples and real-life examples involving cooperation. The end goal is to give mission-
aries practical tools to enable them and their organizations to examine their
approaches to ministry, make whatever personal changes are necessary and
thereby influence the culture of their organizations toward a more biblical model
of inter-agency cooperation.

It has been said that the gospel of Jesus Christ is the first casualty in a church dispute. Nowhere could this be more true than in seventh century Arabia. While there were many contributing factors to the inception and spread of Islam, one cannot ignore the fact that Muhammad's Arabian nation lived and died in the shadow of the Church. Both Constantinople and Rome, bent on acquiring the Church's seat of power, allowed Muslims to pass through this world and into a godless eternity virtually unnoticed. Today, 1400 years later, with Islam claiming one in five human beings on the face of the planet, we can no longer afford for the Church to engage in such turf wars.

As missionaries, we seek to bring glory to God and we do that best by cooperating with one another and offering our personal or agency kingdoms to Him to use as He will. This not only pleases and glorifies Jesus and the Father, but is perhaps the greatest gospel presentation we can give "…that all of them may be one, Father, just as you are in me and I am in you. May they also be in us so that the world may believe that you have sent me" (John 16:21). The purpose of this paper is to examine some of the challenges, biblical principles and real-life examples involving such cooperation. The end goal is to give missionaries practical tools to enable them and their organizations to examine their approaches to ministry, make whatever personal changes are necessary and thereby influence the culture of their organizations toward a more biblical model of inter-agency cooperation.

My own experiences in ministry have further underlined the value and importance of networking both in places where there is no church support and where the church is strong. My family and I had the privilege of joining a multi-agency team in the Arab world when we finished language school. This team had made commitments to one another and to the furtherance of the gospel that ran deeper than any other we had seen. Through them we saw a strength that came from putting aside agency politics and sharing resources that became a model for many other teams in that region. Because of the spirit of cooperation that existed, there were no turf wars in our country and we were able to benefit from top quality training in joint regional conferences.

Later, our family moved to the West and helped establish a ministry center to reach out to immigrant families. Because of the spirit of cooperation and networking in that city, we were able to establish a work quickly. In eighteen month's time, twenty churches or ministries became involved in supporting this outreach, offering people, felt needs, materials and financial support to the Lord's work. Had we tried to do all that has been done on our own, we would have failed miserably.

DEFINITIONS

Several definitions will help us in our exploration of networking. First, there is interdependence. Interdependence is the highest functional level that can be achieved in a relationship. In contrast to independence, interdependence is driven by the understanding that by working together all parties can achieve far more than by working separately. Note that the parties do not work together because they need one another as in co-dependence, rather it is a strategic choice for achieving the greatest common good. In the Christian realm this common good is always the glorification of God through making Him known in all the earth. Note also that interdependence can only occur between people.

Our relationship with God is always completely dependent. His relationship with us and with His entire creation, is absolutely independent. Although He chooses to maintain a sacrificial love relationship with us, He neither needs nor gains anything from it.

The second term is networking. Networking is the natural result of interdependence. It is communication among ministry partners (individuals, churches and organizations) for the purpose of sharing resources to make each one more effective in their individual tasks and callings. A network is a set of interdependent relationships deliberately formed among ministry partners as a result of networking activity. A network is often formed in a particular location but it can also be built around a common ministry calling, such as media.

OBSTACLES TO SUCCESSFUL NETWORKING

In order to become effective networkers both personally and organizationally within the larger body of Christ, we must deliberately cultivate a "networking culture." Such a culture will not develop on its own, for, in the vast majority of cases, we do not think like networkers. That is, when we plan our days, our personal ministries and our organizational strategies we do not naturally think about how we can collaborate with others to accomplish the task. Sadly, we become our own worst enemies by not doing this; we could accomplish so much more not only in our personal lives but also as a body of Christ if we would apply each others' skills and gifting to our tasks. I believe this resistance to networking comes about as a result of several factors or fallacies that we have adopted vis-a-vis our relationship to others in our line of work. I will address these fallacies first and in the conclusion offer some practical hints for getting started in networking.

The Fallacy of Personal Self-Reliance

The first fallacy is the fallacy of personal self-reliance. As those who minister among Muslims, we see ourselves as the "special forces" of the church—the self-reliant ones. We hear the call of the front lines. We make the tough decisions. We suffer everything from raised eyebrows to outright hostility from friends and family members concerned for our welfare, yet we remain unwavering in our commitment. We forsake all. We raise our support. We literally turn our back on everything familiar to go to the hard places, learn the languages, struggle with the cultures, pray over our sick children where medical care is unreliable. In the end, we have adapted, survived—even thrived—in a hostile environment. We've done it, we think, just us and God. We have become "seasoned," a family unit that can be trusted to serve faithfully in most any situation without causing a lot of headaches back at the home office, and we have done it independently of others.

On the field we come across other missionaries in all stages of this development process. Often they come from different organizations with different ways of doing things. We want to be friends with them. We may even try to cooperate with them and their organizations. We will plan joint meetings and even work out a joint conference or two. However, there is always a cost. Perhaps it was an irritating detail such as adjusting our schedule to theirs or adapting some of their procedures. Maybe it is a more serious conflict such as agreeing to a different doctrinal statement for a time or answering criticism from our home office. Our colleagues may criticize our mission's policies in a thinly-veiled boast about their own organization. Or they may want to try something risky and balk at our reticence as "lacking faith." In the end, we end up questioning whether it is all worth the effort. Couldn't we have done just as well investing that time and effort into our own outreach projects?

The fallacy of personal self-reliance is exposed when we realize God has called these other missionaries just as He has called us; that we are all a part of the body of Christ with all our spiritual gifts and that these gifts arrive in many different packages. In our pride, we may assume that our methods and ideas are best. But we also may put our own agenda above God's agenda in the process. We can reduce our involvement with others, reducing the corresponding problems and convincing ourselves that we are totally self-reliant. But we must admit that the task we can accomplish is likewise reduced.

The Fallacy of Agency Self-Reliance

The second fallacy is the fallacy of agency self-reliance. Agency self-reliance builds on the self-reliance of workers who have kept their independence in the field. As we continue to work in Muslim ministries we gain experience. In other words, we make lots of mistakes. In the end, though, we do learn. We adapt, we grow, we get to the place where we think we might know something. Our ideas are starting to impress leadership. Then we begin to lead other workers—first in our own country, then in other locations throughout the region. Eventually, we get the call from the home office and before we know it, we're packing up and moving to an agency leadership position. Now, we think, we are at the point where we can truly influence mission policy.

Then the subject of inter-agency cooperation is raised at a meeting. All we can remember is the grueling effort it took on the field and the paltry payoff at the end, so we put strict limits on the effort or squelch it entirely. Again, we feel we're better off just doing it ourselves; it's a lot cleaner and at least we are in control. Our impact will be reduced, we reason, but so will our cost and potential risk.

The fallacy of agency self-reliance is exposed when we recall that when Christians cooperate, Christ is glorified. When we serve only the interests of our own agency, we tend to glorify that agency. When we reach beyond we glorify Christ. The women's consultation on ministry to Muslim women is a perfect example of this concept. It is a group of agencies in cooperation with one another for kingdom purposes. At this and similar conferences, the emphasis is on Christ and His mission. The various agencies are simply the means He uses to get us there.

The Fallacy of Limited Resources

The third fallacy is the fallacy of limited resources. All too often we imagine that if we follow our own style of ministry or mission policy and avoid networking, we won't have to think about how to do it ourselves. The thinking part was done by others; we can get straight to the doing. Furthermore, we think we will not have to explain the "whys" of our style to anyone else. We won't have to share our already stretched budget or overworked office staff and we won't be spending enormous amounts of time in joint meetings ironing out procedures and working through differences. Most importantly, we can avoid having to share our precious mailing list. After all, our donors are already fatigued from the number of appeals we send out.

The fallacy of limited resources is exposed when we realize that God's work is not limited by our perception of resources. From Gideon to Elisha and the 5,000 Jesus fed, Scripture is replete with examples of God's provision where resources seem limited. We have a policy in our house to avoid two phrases: "We can't afford it," and "We don't have time to do that." That's not to say we're spendthrifts or in a continual state of busyness. Rather, we choose to look at the bigger picture and say: "We don't believe God has called us to own this," or "We don't believe God has called us to participate in that." Rather than a game of semantics, we truly try and view things from God's perspective. If God were indeed calling us to own an item or invest in something, is it unreasonable to think that He would be not also provide the money for it? The fear of limited resources should not keep us from networking with others.

The Fallacy of Protecting My Own Reputation

The fourth fallacy is a belief in my own reputation. By sticking with ourselves, we think, we won't have to explain our partnership to a wealthy donor who questions our decision. We won't risk a ministry partner suffering a moral failure and taking us down right along with them. The alleviation of those concerns requires more of that most precious commodity called "time" that we will have to expend investigating the organization prior to any partnership agreement.

Exposing this fallacy is more complicated, as the scripture says: "A good name is better than fine perfume..." (Eccles. 7:1) and "A good name is more desirable than great riches; to be esteemed is better than silver or gold" (Prov. 22:1). Surely with all of the corruption in organizations today we can't be too careful. Or can we? In another section of Proverbs it reads: "Fear of man will prove to be a snare but whoever trusts in the Lord is kept safe" (Prov. 29:25). Yes, we are to be mindful of our associations. At the same time, God's reputation is constantly maligned by evil men and Christians' behavior. In all this, He is not ashamed to call us "brothers." In the end, God is in charge of our reputation while we are called to obedience. My desire to protect my reputation should not be a greater goal than God's desire that I work in unity with others.

The Fallacy of the Poor Cost/Benefit Ratio

Finally, we face the fallacy of the poor cost/benefit ratio. Because of our independence and pride, we often find it hard to offset all the risks and costs of partnership with the promise of tangible benefits. We can't readily answer the question, "How will it grow my organization, enhance our reputation and accomplish our stated goals?" This fallacy, however, is based upon our absolute faith in our ability to accurately calculate the costs and benefits associated with ministry. To begin with, see Ecclesiastes 11:1-6. We will discuss this in the next section.

We served in the Middle East for seven years. Within a short time of our initial arrival we realized that there was no way to describe what our life was like and have our friends and family back in the United States understand. We began sending videos home. Eventually we felt it would be better to edit a short video for our supporters and churches to give a coherent picture of our life in story form. Watching people as they viewed our little production made us appreciate the power of the medium. As a result, my husband, Mike, began pursuing video production in a more serious way, even without education in this field. A year later, God brought us back to the U.S. for a one-year furlough.

During our furlough, Mike met with a man who wanted a promotional video for his potential supporters. His ministry was networking churches and Christian aid agencies together in our city. He wanted to move them from attendance and budget concerns to defining success in terms of the number of people helped and, ultimately, the number touched by the gospel.

Mike had begun to put together a script for the man. During the discussion, he asked him why he had wanted Mike to write and produce his video in light of the fact that Mike had never done this professionally. "Because you'll do it for free," the man replied. Mike had hoped for a more flattering response. Still, he felt it was a worthwhile cause and also a chance to get a little experience for when we returned to the Middle East.

Shooting the video was an exercise in networking itself. Mike and his client agreed the story would be most effective if it were largely testimonials about how this ministry had enabled their ministries to be more effective. This required many interviews with pastors, church leaders, NGO administrators and even a bank chairman. All of these individuals were part of the network Mike's client had established and they were impressed that Mike was a missionary volunteering his time to produce the video. Because of our imminent return to the Middle East, we didn't pay much attention to what would eventually happen with those relationships. The video took weeks and countless hours in the editing room. As Mike was not yet proficient with the equipment, much time was invested in the learning curve. The "cost/benefit" ratio went right through the roof!

Today, three years later, we are still in the United States where God has called us to a practical needs-based ministry to immigrant Muslims. Several of the agencies and churches Mike met through the video project have helped us in our ministry by providing clothing, food, medical services and even job training. Most recently, God has opened the door for us to do a weekly TV broadcast to reach our Muslim population that we would have been unable to contact otherwise. This is also going to involve lots of writing, camera operation, editing, and, most of all, finances. Our very first contributor to the project is the first pastor Mike interviewed while making that promotional video.

Evaluated on a cost/benefit basis alone, the project was a dismal failure. We did not have money to contribute, but we feel God blessed our willingness to give what we had. And He has multiplied and returned that initial gift in ways we could not have imagined.

WHY NETWORKING?

"You can't have a denominational strategy against a universal enemy" (Valdeviez, 2004). I might add to denominational, "organizational." We must learn to think outside our own organization or ministry if we want to overcome a universal foe. Satan surely does. As we learn to share resources and bless other parts of God's worldwide kingdom building, we present a stronger, united front against our enemy. "If one part suffers, every part suffers with it; if one part is honored, every part rejoices with it" (1 Cor. 12:26). Furthermore, networking models biblical community. I am delighted when I am able to portray the body of Christ in this way. Our Muslim friends who come to the ministry center often ask how we are able to do all that we do. When I explain to them how many churches and ministries cooperate to offer the services they are always amazed.

Beginning Steps

Here are some suggestions to get yourself involved in networking: First, have a good perspective—"Think Kingdom." The foreword to Max Lucado's book, *It's Not About Me*, begins like this:

> NBA championship teams have something in common: they play with one goal in mind. Each player contributes his own gifts and efforts so that the greater goal—winning—can be reached. But players who seek their own glory at the sacrifice of the team's glory drive the team away from success. So it is with life. The goal is not our own glory; in fact, trying to make life 'all about us' pushes happiness further out of reach. (2004:1)

It's easy to feel overwhelmed with all the needs of your own ministry or projects. I do all the time! The temptation is to hoard your time, talent and treasure so as not to dilute your own calling and ministry. I have found, however, that when I lend a hand to others God blesses me in unexpected ways. Often we see a need and have no financial resources to give, but there are other ways we can bless other ministries and churches. We can give our time, listen to a discouraged sister or use our skills to fill a need. Kingdom thinkers ask themselves, "How can I use the gifts God has given me to bless other ministries?"

Second, find out what networking is already happening in your area and join in. When we arrived in the United States we found a prayer group dedicated to praying for Muslims in our city. This was the nucleus that formed the ministry we are now directing. We also met a man who felt called to be a pastor to pastors. He arranged prayer summits for people in ministry as well as for business leaders. Our mayor arranged a once a month meeting for local pastors to come and pray for our city. A local rescue mission had a kingdom-minded director who benefited from my husband's video production skills and later gave us a much needed car.

Third, if nothing is happening, gather some pastors and/or ministry leaders and begin praying for one another regularly. It wasn't that long ago that we had little evidence of networking in our city. The vision of a few people changed all of that. It started by gathering Christian leaders and praying for them and blessing them.

Finally, be prepared to invest, be kingdom minded, and demonstrate sharing resources. "If you stay within your denominational [organizational, ministry] comfort zone, you will never access all that God has or achieve all that He wants you to achieve" (Valdeviez, 2004).

R E F E R E N C E S

Blackaby, Henry, and King, Claude V. 1994. *Experiencing God*. Nashville: Broadman and Holman.

Blackaby, Henry. 2003. *What the Spirit is saying to the churches*. Sisters, OR: Multnomah.

Love, Rick. 1995. *Peacemaking: A study guide*. Mesa, AZ: Frontiers.

Lucado, Max. 2004. *It's not about me*. Nashville: Integrity.

Schluter, M and D Lee. 1993. *The factor*. London: Hodder and Stoughton.

Valdeviez, Copi. 2004. Interview by Janelle Metzger, 4 June.

19

Discipling Muslim-Background Believers

Annette Hall

Effective discipling requires workers to intermesh their lives with Muslim-background believers (MBB) and to use teaching methods appropriate for the oral learning style of most Muslim women. In this article, Annette Hall urges that discipleship also must focus God's Word on the cultural and religious issues that can keep MBB women from experiencing victorious life in Christ.

*F*atma came to the Paris suburbs more than twenty years ago. Her neighborhood is filled with members of her people group. Some, like her, arrived years ago. Others came just weeks ago. Like most of the adults in her community, Fatma is nonliterate. She has never been to school, yet she speaks three languages —her heart language plus Arabic and French. Fatma's children have grown up in France and attend French schools. While all of them can read, they prefer oral learning to a literate learning style.

Six years ago, Fatma started attending a literacy class for women. The class uses chronological Bible storying (CBS) to teach immigrant women to speak French and how to read and write. After a few lessons Fatma decided she was not interested in literacy, but she loved the Bible stories told as part of the French lessons. As Fatma continued listening to the Bible stories, she came to understand that Jesus is God's Son who died for her, and that through Him she could be saved. Fatma accepted Christ and is now a Muslim-background believer (MBB).

The Content of Discipleship

Our team in Paris views conversion along a continuum. Fatma moved at times towards Christ and at times away from him. Today, however, she is fully committed to Christ. She is also a leader in her community. Most of the immigrant women know her and seek her advice. In the literacy class, Fatma translates stories into her heart language so the women who don't know French will be able to understand. Many of her friends have attended the class. While some continue to come, others have dropped out. Fatma remains friends with all of them. When Fatma visits her friends, she tells them Bible stories in her heart language. At home, Fatma shared the stories with her husband. He also has moved toward Christ and, while he has not reached Fatima's level of spiritual maturity, he is making progress.

Fatma came to Christ through chronological Bible storying. She heard stories that dealt with essential biblical truths as well as stories that worked against barriers keeping her from Christ. Now that Fatma is a believer, obstacles to living a Christian life are surfacing. She needs help overcoming these barriers so she can walk worthy of her calling in Christ.

Fatma, for instance, has practiced folk Islam all her life. She has always gossiped. She likes to tell off-color stories and jokes. biblical forgiveness doesn't exist in Islam (Saïd, 2004). How will Fatma learn to forgive? What does she need to know in order to build a Christian marriage and home? In her culture, lies and deceit between husbands and wives are normal. How should her faith in Christ impact her role as a mother? How will she raise her five children in the Lord? As a believer, what should she do about religious holidays like Ramadan and the feasts? Fatma's previous experience with prayer doesn't help her now that she is a believer. She needs to learn how to pray.

Fatma and her husband also need to meet with other believers to fellowship and to one day become a church. Most summers Fatma and her family return to their home village for vacation. Fatma needs to learn how to effectively share her stories with family and friends back in her home country. What will happen to Fatma when others learn that she is a Christian? She needs to understand Jesus' teachings about persecution. She also must learn about the end times and Jesus' second coming.

Methods of Discipleship

Since Fatma can't read, her discipleship and leadership training must be oral. Just as she came to Christ through hearing Bible stories, her discipleship will be through hearing more stories. Because Fatma and her husband are primarily oral communicators, their worship and Bible study at church also need to be oral. Fatma is not unusual; in fact, most Muslim women are oral communicators who have to hear the gospel and be discipled through oral methods.

When Muslim women like Fatma accept Christ, how can we help them grow into mature believers? We must follow Jesus' example. Jesus chose twelve people. Most of them were oral communicators who learned by observing as well as listening. They accompanied Jesus everywhere He went. They watched Him, listened to His public teaching, and had intimate dialogues with Him. They saw and heard everything that He did. For Jesus, discipling involved being with His disciples full time. Jesus not only taught the truth to His disciples, He lived the truth before them.

Jesus constantly observed whether the lessons were being applied correctly. He sent His disciples out to try things on their own. He gave them specific directions and equipped them for their journey. Afterward, Jesus talked about what happened and gave more full-time instruction.

According to the example of Jesus, discipleship is a matter of being. It involves making our whole lifestyle available to our students so they can learn from our example as well as our words. Too often, we want teaching to occur on a set schedule—once a week, for an hour, at a set time and place, using a specific guide to help us teach biblical principles. But, when we look at Jesus, we see that discipling involves being together all the time and allowing our students to absorb everything we say and do.

Jesus showed us how to make disciples. Then, at the end of His earthly ministry, He said, "Go therefore and make disciples of all the nations ... teaching them to observe all that I commanded you ..." (Matt. 28:19-20, NASB). After demonstrating how it was done for three years, Jesus passed the discipling task on to His disciples—including us.

Making disciples also involves intentional, planned teaching and implies that learning takes place. Learning can be defined as "a change in behavior." If the teacher has taught well, disciples or students will change their way of doing things, adopt a new way of life, and begin to act differently.

Teaching Oral Communicators

As stated earlier, Muslim women are oral communicators. Most of the disciples and people around Jesus were oral communicators as well. Jesus taught by telling them stories, by giving examples, and by modeling for them what to do.

The disciples learned in a group and not as individuals. Jesus was aware that oral communicators learn best when stories are told in group settings.

Jim Bowman, who teaches chronological Bible storying, says oral communicators learn by listening, by repeating, by example, from a holistic overview and through memorization. They use narrative, oratory, recitation, drama, and music. They are event-oriented and community-oriented. Most disciplers from the West prefer to teach by asking people to analyze, outline, summarize, divide into parts, compartmentalize, and study. We like to use exposition teaching and emphasize individuality. These two learning styles do not fit well together (Bowman, *Scriptures in Use Training Manual*). If we really want to make disciples, we must follow Jesus' example and use the preferred learning style of our disciples.

Paul wrote to his disciple Timothy saying: "The things which you have heard from me in the presence of many witnesses, entrust these to faithful men who will be able to teach others also" (2 Tim. 2:2, NASB). Acts 18 tells the story of Paul working with Priscilla and Aquila. Later Priscilla and Aquila meet Apollos and teach him. This story illustrates how 2 Tim. 2:2 works. Paul makes it very clear that there are two goals in our discipling: the continual personal transformation of our disciple into the image of Christ, and the transformation of our disciple into a fellow teacher. We need to keep both these goals in mind as we disciple MBB women. As we seek to apply 2 Timothy 2:2 in our discipleship, let's focus on the relationship between "Timothetta" and "Paulette."

Paulette selects several Bible stories to tell Timothetta and a group of her family and friends. Since Paulette wants Timothetta to hear and understand, she adapts her teaching to fit the learning style of oral communicators. Paulette will know that Timothetta has learned and understood the Bible stories when she observes a change in her behavior. Once Timothetta has understood, Paulette will commission her to tell these Bible stories to faithful women who will then go and tell others. If possible, Paulette should observe Timothetta telling the stories so she can confirm they are being told without error. When pressure or persecution comes, Timothetta will be part of a strong community that understands and is living out the gospel. Together, they will persevere.

Having determined her teaching style and goals, what will Paulette teach Timothetta? If Timothetta has heard the gospel through chronological Bible storying, she likely has a firm foundation of biblical truth on which to build. If Timothetta hasn't heard the stories in chronological format, Paulette will begin her discipleship by taking Timothetta through the entire evangelism storying track.

In Paris, a highly educated MBB was involved in a literate Bible study program of the book of Genesis. One day she exclaimed, "God always reacts in the same way. I didn't know that." This young woman did not have any Old Testament background when she became a believer. She needed to study the Old Testament stories in order to learn who God really is as He reveals Himself through those stories. With that knowledge, she has a better chance of growing to maturity.

Carol G. of Campus Crusade recently returned from a survey trip to Afghanistan. There she found believers who only knew the stories of Jesus. These women had never heard stories from the Old Testament. The women were non-literate and didn't have Scripture in their dialect. Carol told them the story of God's provision for His people as they wandered in the desert after leaving Egypt. The women loved the story, and they learned something new about the character of God. Carol came away with a new appreciation for Old Testament stories because they enable Christians to understand how God relates to His children (G. 2004).

Oral communicators need structure to help them organize and remember what they are learning. When Bible stories are given in chronological order, they can see how God reveals His truth. Things make sense and they can keep it straight in their minds. Once they have this chronological framework, oral communicators can add new Bible stories by putting them into their proper place in the chronological structure.

In the same way I tell you to open your Bible to Genesis 29, I tell the MBB oral communicator, "You know that Jacob is the son of Isaac and the father of Joseph. Today our Bible story tells us more about Jacob's family."

Discipling Muslim Background Believers

After telling or reviewing the basic chronological Bible storying evangelism set, Paulette will focus on discipleship stories. Just as she does a worldview study to determine the issues that kept Timothetta from accepting Christ, she will do a worldview study to determine the issues that impede Timothetta's growth as a believer. Then, she chooses Bible stories the Holy Spirit can use to help Timothetta deal with these issues. In addition, Paulette will share stories that help Timothetta learn what it means to be a cherished child of God. As an MBB woman, Timothetta has likely never felt unconditional love. How can she relate to God as her Father? What is her concept of a father, and does that image need to change so she can truly understand and relate to God as her Father?

One of Paulette's first tasks is helping Timothetta learn how to talk to her Heavenly Father, because MBB women don't usually pray in this way. Paulette will begin by modeling praise-filled, intimate conversations with God. She should take every opportunity to pray with and for Timothetta. She also will tell stories about people in the Bible who prayed, giving Timothetta many examples of different prayers and pointing out their results. In addition, she will share in story format the teachings of Jesus on prayer.

Paulette will emphasize Jesus throughout the discipleship process. She may go back through the chronological stories Timothetta has already heard, correcting any errors that have crept in and helping her see how Jesus was present in the Old Testament. Then she will teach her as many stories about Jesus as possible. The goal of every disciple is to be like Jesus! Each new story builds on the foundation already laid, strengthens new beliefs, and helps Muslim-background believers conform their lives to Christ's.

Confronting Folk Islam

In my work with North African immigrants, I've encountered many issues that could keep Timothetta from living as Christ wants her to live—folk Islam is one of the biggest. With thorough study, informed observation, and careful questioning, Paulette will be able to show Timothetta the evil spiritual reality of many practices she has considered normal all her life (Cate 2002, 171).

Paulette will share many stories to help Timothetta turn away from these practices. In addition to emphasizing the teachings of Jesus, there are multiple stories of kings and other individuals in the Old Testament who were involved in occult practices. These stories which explain what the kings did and how God reacted, should help Timothetta put aside her folk practices (cf. Joice Weibe's set of stories on spiritual warfare, available from Arab World Ministries).

I also found it helpful to create a story based on Ephesians 6:10-18. I got the idea from one of my MBB friends who was troubled by bad dreams and decided to "dress herself in armor" before going to bed. Stories demonstrating that Jesus is more powerful than any evil spirit—along with stories showing God's love for her and how He wants to be involved in her daily life—will help Timothetta overcome her fear and entrust her life into God's care.

Because folk Islam has been a life-long practice, it may take time and prayer for all aspects of it to be recognized and rooted out. The discipler's example of personal peace and faith in the midst of trials and difficulties, and her total depen-dence on God, can be crucial to the disciple's victory in this spiritual

battle. If the discipler is an MBB with similar cultural roots, her personal witness and example can be even more influential.

Another great need of MBB women is to learn how to have a godly family.
One way she will learn is by observing other Christian families. Families visiting
families will help her understand how they relate to one other within the family
setting. Most of my Muslim friends believe that they can never tell the truth to
their husbands. Lying about where they were and what they were doing is
the norm.

In addition, they teach their children to lie to their father. I have been present when mothers encouraged their children to keep things from their father or
to lie to him about what they were doing. It is the normal way of life and a very
strong pattern of behavior. Stories that show the consequences of such behavior
and what God expects of His children help with this issue.

Teaching Forgiveness and Reconciliation

Another major issue for Muslim women is forgiveness and reconciliation. They
believe that it is impossible to forgive. At a recent conference in Paris, the MBB
presenter said that the idea of forgiveness doesn't exist in Islam. Someone
might excuse another person but he would never forgive that individual. True
forgiveness would imply weakness. The idea of reconciliation is laughed away
(Säid 2004).

The story of Joseph has proven to be a strong illustration of forgiveness and
reconciliation. Parables of Jesus such as Luke's story of the prodigal son teach
this important lesson. The story of Jesus forgiving Peter and their reconciliation
after the crucifixion also is a powerful story that shows how Christ's followers
are to forgive. There are stories in the Bible of how forgiveness was extended to
someone who had physically harmed the "forgiver." There also are stories such
as the prodigal son that show forgiveness after an individual brings shame to
the family.

The most powerful lessons on forgiveness will be taught as the teacher consistently models forgiveness and reconciliation in her relationships. Jesus tells
us that we must forgive. MBB women need to understand why God demands
this—then they need to begin practicing the art of forgiveness. As "Paulettes,"
we all are called to help Timothetta recognize her lack of forgiveness when it
occurs. Stories and the discussions related to them provide an opportunity for
the Holy Spirit to bring conviction and transformation.

Sharing the Stories

Throughout the discipleship process, Paulette will encourage Timothetta to tell the stories she is hearing to her family and friends. Hopefully, Paulette will go with her as she tells her first stories to provide support. Paulette and Timothetta will discuss what happened after Timothetta told the stories to friends. Through modeling and assisting, Paulette can help Timothetta learn to share Bible stories with other oral communicators (Sargent 1999, 44).

While oral communicators learn best through stories, they also can incorporate God's Word into their lives through memorizing Scripture, especially when it is in the form of poetry or proverbs. The women's literacy class in Paris has memorized several psalms. As a part of her discipleship, Paulette can challenge Timothetta to memorize Scripture verses and proverbs.

An important issue in oral communication is the problem of keeping the stories accurate. Oral communicators rely on their memories—and their memories are good. However, without a source by which to verify the stories, error can eventually creep in. Each MBB woman deserves her own copy of Scripture in her heart language and in a format that she can understand and apply to her life. For most, that means the Bible should be in oral story format—so each woman needs to be given an oral story Bible on tape or CD. Of course, the stories should be as faithful to the Bible as possible.

This oral Bible will enable MBB women to hear, memorize, and tell the stories and will significantly decrease their dependence on missionaries or other literate believers. It also will encourage a more rapid spread of the gospel among the women and families of unreached Muslim people groups.

Recently, a colleague from North Africa shared her discipling experience: "When we tried to disciple couples, it became obvious that the women didn't understand the material. I took the women and formed a separate discipleship class using stories as the base. The women understood the concepts from the stories and grew in their faith. It didn't work to have the women with the men. They wouldn't talk, wouldn't ask questions, and the material didn't touch where they needed to grow" (P 2004). Through this experience she learned that women should be discipled apart from men.

Discipling women through stories can help MBB women mature spiritually and facilitate the rapid spread of the gospel. I have seen women who have heard and understood a story go out and share the story with friends that very day. Discipling MBB women in groups will help them persevere when persecution comes. Discipling them with stories, in groups, will enable churches to be planted. Our goal is to reach whole families and villages—not just individuals. MBB women can play a vital role in accomplishing this goal.

REFERENCES

Bowman, Jim. Communication bridges to oral cultures. *Training Manuals on CD*. Available from www.siuTraining.org.

Cate, Mary Ann, and Karol Downey, eds. 2002. *From fear to faith: Muslim and Christian women*. Pasadena: William Carey Library.

G. Carol. 2004. Interview by Annette Hall, 5 May, 2004.

Garrison, David. 1999. *Church planting movements*. Richmond, VA: International Mission Board.

Love, Fran, and Jeleta Eckheart, eds. 2000. *Ministry to Muslim women: Longing to call them sisters*. Pasadena: William Carey Library.

P., Elizabeth. 2004. Interview by Annette Hall, 27 January.

Saïd, O. 2004. Conference presentation. 29 March.

Sargent, Curtis. 1999. Model, assist, watch and leave. In *Church planting movements*. Ed. David Garrison. Richmond, VA: International Mission Board.

20

Leadership Development for MBB Women: Models and Resources

Mary Ann Cate

Throughout the Muslim world, women must minister to women. Agency support for women who are called to work among Muslim women in training, encouragement and logistics is therefore central to accomplishing the task. In this article a former administrator for Christar lays out the challenge for agency participation in women's ministries and describes three models for discipling and training new women believers.

GOD'S PASSION, OUR PASSION

As the prophet Abraham pleaded for God's recognition and acceptance of his son by Sarai's servant girl, so women of God today continue to plead with the Almighty for the souls of Muslim women. Often alone in cultural and emotional deserts, screened off from access to knowledge of a redemptive God, they stare into the blinding sun of ritual and folk practices which mask their thirst for love, acceptance and freedom from fear. Alone but surrounded by family and a culture which dominates their lives, they wait...

Standing by the counter at Starbucks, she waits. Soon a Muslim woman enters for a cup of coffee. Impacted from her youth by Muslim culture and a maid who chattered in short Arabic phrases, Amy prays again before she approaches the fashionably dressed woman to engage her in casual conversation. Prayed up and passionate for His reputation to be lifted up among all people groups (Psalm 96:3), Amy takes one more step on her path to reach the majority of least reached peoples—Muslim women and their children.

The Reality

Several years ago, Wendy Murray Zoba wrote in Christianity Today, "Women reaching women is the key to the future of missions" (2000, 40). From Morocco to Mindanao, Mosul to Mombasa, millions of women, almost one in four of the world's women, are Muslim. Often without access to education and health care, subjects of abuse, neglect and violence, they wait in alleys and apartments for someone who really cares to drop by. Locked out of the kingdom of God through religious ignorance, oppression and our indifference and dependent on holy books that offer little assurance that women will see paradise, many have never heard the name of Jesus. These women who are created to know and love God wait until women like Amy understand their desperate plight, hear their cries, learn their language and penetrate the veil of their hearts with the light of the gospel.

Young women like Amy come to our agencies with passion. Often wounded in life themselves by family and friends, they've learned mercy, compassion and survival instincts from their pain. Their enthusiasm for life outdistances their expertise but they are eager to learn, especially with the mentorship and encouragement of another woman. A nurturer by nature, Amy exemplifies the woman who is ready to extend grace to other women and children and to persevere in spite of fatigue and rejection. With a passion for God and the lost, consistent in a life of prayer, well-trained and with a good support network, Amy is equipped to walk into the life of a Muslim woman carrying water to quench her heart's thirst.

Care for Those Who Care for the Daughters of Ishmael

From my own experience as a missionary among Muslim women together with fifteen years caring for other missionary women, I am convinced that agencies must be ready to mobilize, support and train this new generation of women as they lift God's name up among Muslim women. At the Third Consultation on Ministry to Muslim Women held in Atlanta in July of 2002, a group of women agency leaders compiled recommendations for agencies preparing women to enter the unique world of Muslim women. Although some of these recommendations are not prerequisite for the new missionary, we feel they should be covered at some point in a woman's early career. Grouping them into categories of preparedness they include: 1) spiritual life, especially a conviction that God uses women who are transformed by Christ in the building up of His kingdom among Muslim women; 2) language and cross-cultural competency, including knowledge of the Muslim worldview and the importance of a learner's attitude; 3) personal skills such as the ability to deal with new sensations, challenges and stresses to her self-esteem, energy level and proficiencies as she is bombarded with new experiences; 4) theological understanding, such as awareness of the theological resources to live successfully, witness appropriately and navigate a culture where religion is integrated into every aspect of life; 5) missiological methods including preparation for church planting and an understanding of contextual issues and indigenous methods and 6) relationship issues such as being equipped for the variety of relationships and roles she will need to have including how to deal with gender issues, different kinds of authority, working in teams, and working with nationals.

Our agency is committed to the support, encouragement, and training of our women through our Women's Ministry program. To do this, we place godly, enthusiastic, and experienced missionary women on campuses and on the phone to answer questions and to meet women preparing for cross-cultural ministry. Women leaders are also placed at strategic levels of home and overseas administration to help shepherd our women and are included in our training programs where they are guided and equipped in woman-focused care. Missionary women are regularly debriefed on their overseas experiences and all our women prepare ministry descriptions and are accountable to their leadership on a monthly basis. To encourage them, a newsletter entitled "Heart to Heart" is available to them throughout the year, covering topics uniquely applicable to missionary women. As the need arises to reflect on and balance their roles, and access ideas for jump-starting their ministries, missionary women can turn to our manual, "A Woman's Touch." Recently, we have empowered women to serve alongside area, country, and team leaders as shepherds of women—caring for them and equipping them to be effective in their family and team ministries. All our women, equally with men, receive training in people and religious group issues throughout their careers, may pursue further study on home leave, and are encouraged to participate in consultations that focus on Muslim women in partnership with other agencies.

Believing strongly in the spiritual need of Muslim women, supported through prayer, finances, and a strong care system, our trained and gifted women settle into neighborhoods and model spiritual values out of their homes. As they visit Muslim women, they confront fear, fatalism, and the forbidden with the truth revealed in Jesus. A clinic can be a bridge from ministering to physical needs to meeting the pain of the heart while the organization of girls' clubs, aerobic, literacy and craft classes can meet the needs of women seeking relief from boredom. Wise counsel is offered using biblical principles coupled with female perception and insights. Singing gospel songs and applying spiritual principles to her every problem, the woman missionary can become a friend of her Muslim sister and open a way for the Spirit to penetrate her heart's veil. Praying and working over time, some will come to faith. As a shepherd, the missionary will then care for the new converts as they face family rejection, walking them through the valley of identification with Christ. Continuing to invest her life and her time, the missionary's goal is to see the daughters of Ishmael safely into the Kingdom of light and a taste of paradise.

Leadership Training Models

While our aim is to see Muslim women converts growing into spiritual maturity and planted into local, culturally appropriate fellowships, the reality historically and currently is that these women are not challenged to reach, keep and disciple others, much less to take leadership over women in the local fellowship. They are hindered by a lack of role models from within their own culture, a fear of criticism, and time restraints because of family responsibilities. Islamic teachings also give a higher priority to women teaching their children spiritual activities than leading other women in spiritual activities. While the role of female Qur'anic teachers among women is well established, the average woman could feel intimidated by being thrust into spiritual leadership as a new believer.

Despite the challenges, several models exist for discipling and training new believers. The following examples are drawn both from ministries currently effective in specific contexts as well as generic models that can be adapted to any setting.

Model A

The current model in use among North African Kabyle MBB women in France works well with women who are culturally more independent than other people groups and thus have more freedom to express their faith. Some in this group have even done theological studies and one is pastoring a French Reformed church.

The most effective way to train MBB women in this situation, according to the missionary working there, is through modeling leadership. After much prayer, she begins by identifying those women the Lord may be calling to leadership positions. She observes their ways of interacting with other women, the reactions of others to them and the response of the Christian and non-Christian community to their influence. She is concerned to identify those women who are considered good, respectable, trustworthy, reliable and a blessing to others. She is wary of women who may be bold in testimony but rebellious and disrespectful of their own culture.

As a missionary, she is careful to model Christ before these women, not the cultural liberation she may have as a Western woman; she is wary of unintentionally raising a North African-Western hybrid that would be considered a freak among her own people. Her goal, rather, is to train and equip effective MBB women leaders who can express their faith in culturally appropriate and powerful ways.

Once such a woman is identified, the missionary helps her recognize her spiritual gifts and talents as well as any personal interests that can be used for God's glory in leadership roles. The call to leadership, however, will come from the Lord Himself as the woman prays, studies the Bible, and ventures into ministry opportunities in tandem with the missionary. Together, as they affirm her identity in Christ, they will seek to balance the liberty and power inherent in leadership roles with teachings on humility, required of servant leaders through the study of Bible passages such as Philippians 2.

As the missionary models leadership roles alongside this MBB woman in her cultural community, she gives her helping roles that, while simple at first, gradually become more significant increasing responsibility as the training proceeds. Ongoing assessment of the MBB woman leader-in-training is important at this stage in terms of what is going well and what may need to change in order for her to be more effective. The missionary will then find ways to help her implement those changes.

Training materials are also critical to the new leader's growth and development. The missionary will make resources like commentaries, Bible study helps, storying materials, and teacher's guides available for her use (see below). The MBB leader must be taught to be sensitive to the group's needs and be able to adapt her methods to the group she is teaching. As the trainee works into the leadership role, the missionary diminishes her role as leader but continues in a supportive role as an equipper. She remains as long as is necessary while continuing to offer prayer and resources.

Model B

A second model was developed by women working in Suriname among lower and middle class women believers, some illiterate, in four cell fellowships (Cate and Eenigenburg 2001). These women were already discipled and attending cell worship and prayer meetings along with monthly meetings with women in other cells but since they were separated by distance and, in some cases, jealousies, missionary women sought to bring them together monthly through a ministry referred to as "Sister-Help." Their goals were to teach the Word and unite the women in bonds of love as they prayed for one another and spent time together. Since many of the women were poor, they also sought to teach the women life skills to raise their self-image and standard of living, including flower arranging, knitting, cooking, health, child raising, and positive women's roles in the home, church, and community.

Over the years, national women took leadership of the Sister-Help groups and indigenized them in at least three phases. During phase one, each believing woman was encouraged to join the monthly Sister-Help group in her neighborhood connected to a local cell. At this stage, the missionary woman did the planning for each meeting for the entire year, including Bible studies, outside speakers, and life skill training. To minimize jealousy, meetings were held in national homes each month where the hostesses were encouraged to serve simple foods. One or two missionary women would attend each Sister-Help meeting, providing transportation if necessary. By the second and third years, the national women collected very nominal dues to cover supplies and outings, with an elected treasurer responsible for the records. Once or twice a year all the Sister-Help cells would come together for a holiday celebration.

In the second phase of Sister-Help, missionary women worked with national women to plan the continuing programs of Bible studies, prayers, social events and skill development classes. By this time, however, the hostess was encouraged to lead the Bible devotional on her own even as the women found rides to cell meetings on their own. Occasionally the missionary woman would lead a study based on a common felt need in order to model good teaching methods and ensure a strong Bible program.

In the third phase of the ministry, missionary women were able to select a national woman for the leadership of the Sister-Help program based on widespread group approval and her natural abilities. A woman was considered to be ready for leadership when she evidenced spiritual growth, rapport with other women, and faithfulness to the cell group as well as counseling and leadership skills. As the lead woman planned the yearly schedule with the help of missionaries, she also was responsible to contact outside women as speakers, if needed. Transportation needs were minimized as husbands helped their wives get to the meetings and missionary women attended the meetings as advisors, not leaders. The national women leaders of each Sister-Help cell were available to the local cell at this point to serve as deaconesses.

This effect of this cell ministry was substantial. It fit into the total ministry of the local church by promoting unity among women in the cell, training women in leadership, providing deaconesses for the church and giving women an example of how they could work together. By providing a mentoring role, missionary women provided for future women leaders in the church.

Model C

A final model from Southeast Asia is contextualized for the persecuted church (Love and Eckheart 2003). Muslim women and men who come to Christ face enormous pressure and suffering from family and community. In the discipleship stage, both felt needs and systematic approaches were taken into consideration to enable the MBB's to continue the training of their own people. Chronological bible storying materials by J.O. Terry entitled "God and Woman" were found to be very effective. Because gender separation is practiced in the culture, women were trained to be leaders of other women and their children.

Teachability and faithfulness were key indicators of leadership potential for leaders in this group. Often the woman leader would be the wife of a church elder or another woman chosen according to her advanced age or status in the group. Pairing older and younger women in leadership roles allowed the stability and experience of the older woman to be combined with the giftedness of the younger woman. Major challenges for the missionary included helping believing women to trust each other, work together, and care for one another without fear of losing face. Also, in situations where men were trained for leadership roles in the church, women would often stop leading to give the responsibilities to the men, resulting in a diminished spiritual education for the women. The missionary should urge the women to continue shepherding and teaching women believers, especially in evangelism.

The missionary, for her part, was there to affirm, guide and love the believers as they taught scripture and its practical application. Again, the missionary woman's participation in role modeling and addressing women's fear of leadership was key to the program's success. The missionary, thus, worked one-on-

one through visitation in homes with women, modeling what she hoped would happen when women came together in the local church. This included prayer, worship, Bible study, and eating together. When women and men do come together in house churches finally, those women bring tremendous experience in caring, hospitality, and home management which can transfer easily to the local body of Christ. Training both husbands and wives for leadership meant that both gender groups in the church would have a culturally appropriate pastor geared to minister to their special needs.

In summary, the training process for this model revolved around role modeling: I do it, you watch me as I do it, you do it as I watch and finally you do it. The MBB woman must see the missionary model as trustworthy, loving, and wise. As the MBB woman begins to lead, she should be able to pray out loud, minister to children, develop indigenous music, and minister from a breadth of experience.

R E F E R E N C E S

Cate, Mary Ann, and Sue Eenigenburg. 2001. *A woman's touch: A guide for women in cross-cultural ministry*. Rev. ed. Reading, PA.: Christar.

Love, Fran, and Jeleta Eckeart, eds. 2003. *Ministry to Muslim women: Longing to call them sisters*. William Carey Library.

Terry, J.O. n.d. God and woman. Available online http://www.newway.org/articles/cases_a-g.htm.

Zoba, Wendy Murray. 2000. A woman's place. *Christianity Today Magazine*, August.

Part IV

CASE STUDIES

Worldview Transitions

21

From Newspaper Ads to Church:
A Case Study in Literature Evangelism

Not every country in the Muslim world has a free press, but some do. In one such country, a Christian ministry places advertisements in the most popular national newspapers. The advertisements usually say, "If you want to know more about the life of Jesus and receive a free New Testament, write us." The ministry responds immediately to every letter by sending an Injil (New Testament) and a small booklet with questions in the back (cf. "The Other Side of Religion," the first of a series of correspondence courses for Muslim seekers). The seeker is invited to answer the questions and return them to the ministry. Sometimes the newspaper ads focus on a specific subject, such as "overcoming fear," and a booklet on that subject is sent to respondents. Most communication is done via regular mail or by fax, but an increasing number of people are responding by e-mail. The ministry has an easy-to-find Web site where seekers may register and study online.

After reading the correspondent's responses, a "checker" decides which course to send next. The basic evangelistic series includes five courses that are usually sent in order. The last course teaches about the church and invites the reader to make a commitment to Christ. There also are some thirty discipleship courses available. Depending on the comments of the seeker, a checker may send other books or tracts, such as a tract dealing with Jesus as the Son of God. The *JESUS* film, a film of the life of Christ based on the Gospel of Luke, is often sent with the second or third course. Also, a video titled "God's Story: from Creation to Eternity" is sometimes sent (cf. www.jesusfilm.org or www.gods-story.org). There is no charge for any of the courses or materials sent.

Although the ministry was begun and is mostly run by foreigners, the checkers and those who create or translate the course material are national believers. When possible, local church members who live in the same area as the seeker follow-up with correspondents. There are seventy local churches doing follow-up around the country. Women check and do follow-up for women; men check and do follow-up for men. In 1998, there were seventy-five reported visits by follow-up personnel. In 2003, the total number of visits was 942. The work is a team effort with many ministries involved in the follow-up process.

In the last ten years, 84,738 students from all over the country have enrolled in the courses. Liberal urban areas with a more literate population have the most respondents. The majority of those who write in are between the ages of seventeen and thirty-three, and eighty-five percent of the respondents are men. An estimated one to three percent of the students—or at least 1,000 people—have become believers. In a country reporting 1,200 Christians five years ago, this growth is significant. Many of those who put their faith in Christ do so after completing just the first course. In this setting, other saturation evangelism projects with built-in mechanisms for precision harvesting such as radio broadcasts, mass literature distribution, and student events also are producing a growing number of new believers.

In contrast, workers doing friendship evangelism for years in the big cities have had almost no visible fruit from their efforts. Many of these workers are changing their focus and have requested lists of correspondence course participants living in their area. Some workers have relocated to cities where there are many respondents and few workers. Although the foreigners involved in follow-up all work as tentmakers, it appears that those who are willing to be more "high-profile" and gather the new believers together have seen more fruit. Sometimes new believers or mature seekers are invited to a seminar or an evangelistic weekend in order to meet each other. Small churches are forming all over the country through these newspaper ads. This is the story of one such church.

FROM EVANGELISM TO CHURCH PLANTING

A new national believer prayed for three years for another believer to come to his small city to help. Volunteer teams of short-term workers also prayed for his city—a city with no churches, not even a gathering of believers. In response, God sent a team of two families and one single man to the city. They worked as cultural researchers, spending their time learning the language, the culture, and meeting people. The men studied in the mornings and then spent much of the afternoon on the streets practicing language and making friends. They drank a lot of tea and learned to play the popular game of backgammon.

Since the wives needed to be home with the children, their community time was more limited. They focused more on opening their homes to the new friends their husbands were making. The women also visited their neighbors when possible.

The more the team learned about the culture, the more formidable the barriers to believing in Jesus appeared to be. The worldview of the local people was completely different from a biblical view. Everything had to be explained, starting with the truth that the Bible was God's Word. Most people believed the Bible had been changed from the original Word God gave to Moses, David, and Jesus, and was full of errors. They felt no need to study the Bible. These misunderstandings about the Bible were among the biggest barriers, but another key barrier was the fact that most of their friends were not really interested in reading.

The work did not really get off the ground until the team received a list of names from the correspondence course ministry. The ministry gave them the names and addresses of every contact from that city, regardless of whether the person had completed a course or not. The people on the list ranged from "mildly interested inquirer" to "believer." An interesting thing happened as the workers began contacting people on the list. Quickly they realized that when a national believer introduced them to seekers (or other believers) there was an immediate depth of trust that they would have required months if not years to develop on their own.

The first national believer with whom the foreign workers partnered was from a large city several hours away. He was in full-time ministry as a mentor to foreign church planters working throughout the country. In addition to helping establish trust relationships with seekers, he also modeled culturally sensitive ministry that touched the hearts of the local people. The national mentor's involvement became less as the team became more proficient in the language and more local people became believers.

Correspondence course contacts were called by phone, preferably by a national believer, to request an appointment. Initial meetings often took place in a public place, like a tea garden. Usually, two people—a foreigner and a national—would meet with the seeker. After explaining that they were given his or her name by the correspondence course ministry, the workers shared that the ministry had been unable to visit the person and had asked them, as believers, to establish contact with the seeker on their behalf. During the course of the conversation, the workers communicated their willingness to help anyone who wanted to learn more about the Bible.

When a seeker responded to the invitation to study the Bible, the workers would make arrangements to meet as often as the seeker desired, from once up to even five times a week. The workers also introduced interested seekers to other believers as soon as possible and encouraged them to participate in the community activities of believers so they could establish a support network. This action turned out to be essential. Not a single person who had contact only with foreign believers made a life-changing commitment to Christ.

Workers tried hard to respond to the particular needs of each seeker. They continued to maintain relationships as long as the person showed any interest. If a seeker continually made excuses for not studying the Bible together, the workers would invite him or her less and less. If a seeker showed minimum interest, workers would wait awhile before contacting the person again. Since friendship is highly valued in this culture, the workers never completely broke off communication with anyone, but some relationships were allowed to slide while others were nourished.

Generally, there was not a feeling of distrust among new believers as has been reported in some places in the Muslim world. It seemed that true national believers could spot the scant few newcomers who were insincere, most of whom did not join a group anyway. When new believers were introduced to each other, the common response was, "It's about time I met others like me."

As workers learned more of the language and met regularly with seekers and new believers, they began to figure out some of the biggest needs and issues. The nationals have a strong reverence for "God's Word," though they think that only the Qur'an is God's Word. It was helpful for the workers to show that the Qur'an also calls the Bible God's Word and says that God's Word can never change or be changed. They used several passages from the Qur'an to change the perceptions of potential seekers.

Speaking about the Old Testament, Surah 2:211 says, "Ask the children of Israel how many a clear message We have given them! And if one alters God's blessed message after it has reached him—verily, God is severe in retribution" (Asad 1984, 45). Surah 3:48 records, "And he (God) will impart unto thy son (Jesus) revelation, and wisdom, and the Torah (the Old Testament), and the Gospel" (Asad 1984, 74). The end of Surah 10:64 proclaims, "... nothing could ever alter God's promises, this, this is the triumph supreme" (Asad 1984, 301).

One worker reports, "If someone begins to explain to me that the Bible has been changed, I show him that his Qur'an says that is impossible. Then I ask him which he wants me to believe—his word or the Qur'an." Once the Bible was accepted as God's Word, people were open to studying it and enjoyed it.

There also was a positive response to Jesus as the Suffering Servant. The idea that God, who has all wealth and power, had humbled Himself to help truly poor and hurting people, appealed to the hearts of many. The workers developed a personalized Bible study for the group. They wrote it in the national language and then had a national believer proofread and correct it. The Bible study was an eight-lesson gospel presentation:

- The Bible has not changed
- God is love
- What is sin?
- Man's situation

- The sacrificial system
- Why did God have to come?
- Jesus' divinity
- Jesus' death and resurrection

As the seekers became believers, later lessons focused on teaching them to study the Bible for themselves.

The women workers identified the lack of language capability as the biggest hindrance to their involvement in evangelism and church planting, so they earnestly pursued language learning. As is true in other Islamic cultures, women had to be mentored by women, and this could not be done without knowing the local language. Early on the women workers learned to knit. Knitting together with national women was a comfortable way to spend the afternoon in the early stages of language learning when conversation was challenging. Knitting took away awkward moments of silence and gave the workers time to form their sentences in the new language.

The workers began to experience breakthroughs after their neighbors noticed that the everyday life struggles of the Westerners were very similar to their own. First impressions of the "rich" foreigners began to dissolve as the women saw mothers dealing with fussy kids and mountains of dirty dishes while struggling to learn a new language and culture. They related to their new friends' daily frustrations and became more willing to listen to them. In time, the national women became more open to reading the Bible together or watching the *JESUS* film.

Meeting national women and being in their homes was easy in this social culture. In every apartment building, there were women who stayed home every day. Many were lonely and craved social time. They loved to drink tea together and "hang out" while their husbands were at work. The custom was to meet in each other's apartments mid afternoon (kids in tow) to eat, drink, and chat.

The women workers learned to manage their time and money so they would have resources available to entertain. Deep relationships could not be formed without having an open home. One of the best places to share was in the kitchen —cooking and washing dishes together. One worker reported, "Out of all the books, classes, and seminars I have read or taken, the most useful thing here is just knowing the Bible well and knowing how to share my testimony."

The workers are encouraged that both believers and seekers are sharing what they are learning about the Bible with their families and friends. The gospel is traveling along friendship and family lines. There are a small number of "second-generation" believers who became believers solely through the witness of other nationals. The followers of Jesus see national holidays as a great way to share love with their neighbors. Most of the believers visit or call non-believing friends to wish them a happy holiday during the sacrifice holiday or at the end of Ramadan.

The new believers have experienced some persecution. One man had to stop meeting with the foreigners completely to save his marriage. Another believer was picked up by the police and beaten. One young man was almost not allowed to graduate from his university because he was a believer. There is family pressure not to become a believer, and at times believers are ostracized by their family.

The first Bible study has grown. People have come to faith through the correspondence course, by interacting with both local and foreign believers, and by watching the *JESUS* film. Some have had a dream or vision at some point in their spiritual journey. There is now more than one home group. They do not always meet in the same place (sometimes due to safety concerns or fear). Meetings usually begin with fellowship and food. Tea abounds. Sometimes singing and prayer are next. Usually a national leads these meetings. If a foreigner leads, he makes it very interactive, taking the role of a facilitator.

The workers never ask anyone to be baptized, but as new believers understand what Scripture teaches about salvation and baptism they are requesting to be baptized. By God's mighty hand, two short years after the church-planting team arrived in the small city, thirteen people were baptized in a private swimming pool. The police tried to follow the caravan to the "swimming hole" but gave up due to divine intervention. Two nationals—the mentor who people knew and a pastor from a large city—performed the baptisms. Each person gave his or her testimony before the baptism. One remarked amidst the praise and rejoicing, "It is like everyone's birthday party all at once!"

The group was about evenly divided between men and women. After the baptisms, the new believers participated in the Lord's Supper for the first time. As a result of the day's events, one family member of a new believer committed his life to Christ! At the time the case study was written, seven more people desired baptism. Some new believers were delaying due to family opposition.

The leaders are praying about the next step. They plan to teach the group what the Bible says about "church" with the goal of helping the nationals develop an awareness of themselves as a church. The goal is to establish a "four-self church" (self-theologizing, self-leading, self-supporting, and self-producing). Recently, a "house church" video was produced in the national language, which showed a small group of national families and singles meeting together for worship, Bible teaching, prayer, and communion in a home.

The workers do not want the body of believers to be dependent on foreigners for anything long term. The team discourages its members from loaning money to nationals and does not employ any local believers. The workers are trying to teach their new brothers and sisters that a church should not undertake something it does not have the means to do such as employ new converts and build buildings. The foreigners desire to move from the position of mentor (modeling for the new leaders) to trusted advisor—first from near, then from afar. In the future, all follow-up of local people who respond to the newspaper ads will be done by national believers.

This small group may not seem particularly noteworthy in its infant stage, except that it illustrates what God is birthing all around the country. Similar works are in progress in at least nine other cities that previously had no known Christian groups. One fast-growing fellowship began with just four correspondence course contacts.

Some common themes can be seen in the various works. Prayer brought harvesters to the harvest field and empowered their ministry. Friendship evangelism by foreigners did not produce significant results. Vast numbers of people were given opportunities to make themselves known as open seekers. Correspondence courses and careful follow-up were vital to the work. National believers and foreign workers have labored hand-in-hand at every stage, with several different ministries and agencies involved. Some sowed … some watered … and God brought forth fruit.

Resources

Asad, Muhammad. 1984. *The message of the Qur'an*. Melksham, Great Britain: Redwood Press Limited.

Discussion Questions

1. Why does the author in this case study find it so important that the "checkers" are national believers, and not foreign missionaries?

2. Why are so many discovering Christ through media–newspaper ministry, radio broadcasts, mass literature distribution, and other projects—while those doing friendship evangelism have seen almost no visible fruit?

3. The article says, "Not a single person who had contact with only foreign believers made a life-changing commitment to Christ." Why was it important for seekers to be in contact with another national believer prior to making a decision for Christ?

4. The author states, "Some relationships were allowed to slide while others were nourished." How would you determine which people to follow up and which to leave aside? Do you think this is a good strategy? What else could you suggest?

5. The author notes that in some Muslim countries new believers often harbor a feeling of distrust. Why would this be so? What would account for seekers or national believers in this country having "an immediate depth of trust"?

6. In discussing the authenticity of the Bible, the author uses passages from the Qur'an to show that the Bible is God's Word and cannot be changed. Do you think this is a good approach, or do you feel that this technique gives undue authority to the Qur'an?

7. In many Islamic countries, missionaries are bringing a message that brings persecution, ostracism, and death to many Muslims. How can a missionary justify the things she teaches her Muslim friend since they will likely bring persecution and even death?

8. The Christian workers in this country refrain from stressing the need for baptism until the new believer requests the baptism himself. Why would this be important? Do you agree with this decision?

22

Joining God Where He is at Work:
Facilitating a Church Planting Movement in Central Asia

*A*s part of a larger team involved with several organizations in prayer mobilization, Bible translation, and the broad dissemination of the Word, one
church-planting family was part of an amazing movement among an Unreached
People Group (UPG). Disciplined commitment to living among their people as
learners and a strict adherence to proven church-planting principles characterized the family's sometimes difficult but fruitful ministry.

Answering God's call, a young couple and their children relocated to live
among their UPG. The family's first two years in their new country were spent
like workers the world over—trying to learn language and adjust to their new
surroundings. They were pleased that one or two people became believers
during that time. The family then returned to the United States for a short visit
home. While there, a respected Christian anthropologist helped the family
evaluate their work. He then challenged and trained them to become learners.

The wife explained, "It became very clear to us that we had not approached
the work with our UPG as learners but as knowers. We were so full of ourselves
and our knowledge of God that we did not take time to understand their hearts,
their perspective, and their needs. Upon returning to the field, we committed
to try this new path of seeking to learn—not to be knowers but to be understanding. This was revolutionary for us. We saw that by engaging relationships
in a spirit of humility, the people began asking us for our opinions. As we were
earnestly seeking to know and understand the hearts of our people, they
began to show a desire to understand our hearts."

The husband asked the leader of the local mosque, "Would you teach me what you believe and what your people believe and practice as their religion?" For one year, the worker sat under the teaching of this mullah, learning not only how the local people practiced Islam but also developing language skills and learning how spiritual truths were communicated in that culture. The worker did not debate with the mullah, but he did answer direct questions as they arose.

The wife worked alongside the local women baking bread at the local oven, gathering water, and doing other chores together. She visited in their homes and received them as visitors. The family placed their children in local schools and became acquainted with their classmates and their families. They put away their American fashions in favor of local clothing. The mother dressed even more conservatively than some local women; the focus of her relationships was with fellow stay-at-home moms who wore a larger head covering and more protective clothing. She tried to pattern her lifestyle after that of the local women and through the "normalcy" of her life in the community built bridges with them.

The wife wrote about her work, "I feel women can be integral in the evangelism and church-planting process as they live out the gospel before their neighbors' eyes. The opportunities are so natural and found in everyday life as we share truth with our community. Of course this means we really have to become a part of the community, not just go to minister or have a house here. As I build relationships with the women, they can see our struggle for holiness, our struggle in living in tough places. These struggles open doors to share why, opportunities to pray for them, opportunities to cry and laugh with them."

The family attended weddings and funerals and other life rituals. They saw firsthand the many folk traditions that reflected a deep-seeded animistic belief, such as the use of eyeliner around a child's eyes to protect him or her from bad things. The goal of the workers was to be seen as followers of Jesus who also were part of the community. The family adapted their public worship to use forms that enabled the nationals to understand what they were doing, including forms for prayer, fasting, almsgiving, celebrations, and others. They also wanted the nationals to see and understand how they could embrace these forms and give them new meaning. They adjusted their lifestyle to be as close to that of the nationals as possible, even decorating their home as local people would. For instance, they did not hang pictures of people or animals on their walls since it would offend their neighbors.

Visiting the homes of friends and neighbors, they found, was the most natural way to develop relationships. They discovered that one of the best ways to enter a new relationship was through an introduction by a friend who was a family member or neighbor. This common friend was able to dispel any fears the new acquaintance might have.

After seven years of living side by side in community with their unreached people group (UPG), the family was forced to flee the country due to political upheaval. Many members of their UPG also were forced to leave. The family greatly grieved leaving their work, but they found God had even greater work in store for them, using the language and cultural knowledge they had acquired. Soon they were settled across the border in a neighborhood filled with refugees from their people group. They even found a school for their son using the language he already had learned. Though this new country had a few more freedoms, it still was staunchly Islamic.

An odd challenge in their new country was the presence of many workers who were reaching out to the local population. These workers loved to congregate together and sought to involve their new friends in activities. In order to guard their time and maintain their focus, the family determined that they would only see other Westerners once a week. When necessary, the family explained their decision gently but firmly. They met with two other Western families twice a month, which left two dates each month for social gatherings with other foreigners. Both the husband and the wife had Christian accountability partners with whom they talked at least once a week by telephone.

The husband began visiting various neighborhood shops and soon found a friendly proprietor who liked to play chess. The two soon began playing chess and drinking tea together. The shop owner had been a military commander in charge of hundreds of families in the workers' home country but was now reduced to selling secondhand goods in a foreign land. He was looking for hope and felt that neither Islam nor communism had given him answers.

Discussions at the shop ranged from weather to politics to religion. Because of the testimony some of their former neighbors had made after their escape, the workers found they were already respected in the community. In addition, they could effectively communicate with people in their heart language.

One day the commander asked his new friend for help finding work or economic aid for the refugees. He felt a great burden for the families who had been under his care. Since they were familiar with the culture, the workers understood why this man was seeking help for his people. However, they refused his request in appropriate cultural ways even as they sought to maintain his friendship. Explaining their decision, the worker wrote, "The first need our people see is the physical need. They come asking for money and jobs. By meeting this need, many do not come back with a longing to find more to their life. We often find we are short-circuiting a deeper faith in God when we try to dole out money instead of praying with them and seeking God in the matter." The workers tried to keep their relationships with seekers, believers, and churches free from ties to money.

Through the course of many conversations over the chessboard, it became clear to the commander that the foreigner was a sincere follower of Jesus Christ and knew a great deal about Islam. Even so, his new friend would not debate the differences between his faith and Islam. Even when someone made fun of his beliefs or directly challenged him, he would not defend himself or his beliefs. The commander found the worker to be very confident but not arrogant. The commander began to wonder if his new friend had some of the answers for which he had been searching.

Since the foreigner often shared what he was learning from the Bible and told stories from that Holy Book, the commander decided he wanted one. He asked his friend to give him a Bible. The worker politely declined but explained to the commander where he could buy one. By God's hand, a near-culture church located not far away had been impressed to reach out to this people group. The church had set up a bookstore that catered to the needs of their church but also contained resources that the UPG could understand.

The commander went to the bookstore to buy a Bible. He waited outside for a long time watching the store. When he finally went inside, the owner could not understand his language but finally was able to locate a Bible he could read. With a great deal of effort on both their parts, the owner communicated that a group of men was going to watch the *JESUS* film later that night. The commander returned that evening and saw several men he had known in the past. Two of the men told him that they had finally found the system they had all been seeking. After watching the film, the men gave the commander a book about what Christians believe. They invited him to come back to discuss what he was reading.

The commander knew it was against the law in his home country to convert from Islam to another religion, but he was curious about the books he was now reading and the changes he saw in his friends' lives. He brought his questions to his foreign friend, and together they sought the Bible for answers. The foreigner encouraged the commander to visit again with the men he met while watching the film.

God began a great change within the heart of the commander. Before, he had been known for his quick temper and harshness to his several wives and children; now he was more gentle. He began to share with others the hope that was growing within him. One night the commander met with nine other men with whom he had been discussing the books they were reading. He told them he believed Christianity was the truth. It could provide the hope for which their people had been searching, and they should all profess belief in Jesus as the true mediator between themselves and God. All nine men agreed.

This was the beginning of an incredible year. These ten men each gathered groups around themselves and taught them the things they were learning. They met and prayed together, worshiped together, sang together, studied together, and served each other. The commander asked to be baptized. He had read that this was the way to publicly proclaim his faith, and he felt all ten were ready. The worker asked a Christian pastor from a nearby country if he would baptize the men. The non-Western pastor was very hesitant at first because it was dangerous for him to baptize Muslim-background believers.

After spending two long days talking to the commander and the other leaders, the pastor baptized three of them. The next week the other seven leaders were baptized. These ten leaders decided to send three from among them back to their home country to see if their people were ready to receive Christ. The three reported that the fields were ripe, and they would be pleased to work the harvest. The group prayed for them and sent them back with their families to three different cities to start churches. At the request of these national church planters, hundreds of Bibles were carried into their home country.

In both the home country and the refugee country, cassette tapes also played an important role in evangelism and discipleship. Some of the tapes were recordings of radio programs in the Unreached People Group's language. This was key in showing seekers that there were others in their group who had become believers, which demonstrated it was possible to be part of their ethnic group and also be a follower of Jesus.

The commander took home a set of chronological Bible storying tapes the men had been sharing among themselves. This enabled his wives and children to hear and understand the gospel. The women listened to the cassettes at night and sometimes during the day while they worked. The cassettes told simple Bible stories about God creating the earth and relating to people; they told the stories of Jesus, His life, His miracles, His death, and His resurrection. Soon other family members began making commitments to follow Christ.

The *JESUS* film in the heart language of the UPG with a Muslim-sensitive introduction and summary also played a major role in drawing people to Christ. Luke was one of the first books of the Bible to be translated so that the *JESUS* film could be produced. Although there is not yet a completed Bible in the people group's language, there is a Bible in a related language and a complete New Testament in the trade language of the country. A book by William Miller entitled, What do Christians Believe? (also called "Beliefs and Practices of Christians" or "What is Christianity?"), has helped the more literate people understand Christianity (see "resources" below). A new radio series called "Church in the Home" has also been developed to facilitate house groups. The workers believe it will have a great impact if they can get tapes of the program into the hands of the groups already meeting.

The growth of the church among this Unreached People Group has been phenomenal. This case study has described one commander and his network of friends and family, but there were three other networks through which the gospel was spreading around the same time. Three things have characterized this true "people movement" toward Christ. Almost every believer testifies to meeting a believer and being confronted by the difference in his or her life. The testimonies of most of the early believers also included dreams. Another key element has been the clear communication of the gospel.

Group meetings in the refugee neighborhood are just for men. The men are expected to share with their wives and children. This is happening in some homes, but not all. In some areas, the lack of weekly opportunities for women to meet together is a major weakness of this work. The group meetings in one larger city include men and women who stay in separate places when they meet. Weekly meetings include drinking tea, sharing about recent struggles and victories, praying together, and reading and discussing the Word.

Discipleship is done locally. Most of the "teaching" part of the discipleship process comes from the male leaders. There are a few all-women groups led and taught by women. In the beginning, the commander brought questions to his foreign friend as situations arose in his life or within the group and they sought answers. The foreigner's goal was to always point new believers to Scripture and encourage them to read and meditate on it, asking the Holy Spirit to help them discern the answers to their questions. The workers would often pray with the new believers, asking God to reveal Himself and His provision for specific needs and to give knowledge. When the commander was not living up to the words he was teaching and there was a need for confrontation, the foreigner did so in love and in culturally appropriate ways.

Women have a role in the discipleship process though not usually as formal teachers. The interaction between women is more of a life-on-life teaching time —sharing needs, praying for one another, sharing what God is teaching them. When the foreign woman spent time with her unreached friends, they would invariably talk about needs in their lives or their families and the worker would lead them to pray together for those needs. The main role the foreigners had in the discipleship process was to point new believers to the Word as the authority.

Since the believing community itself has recognized leadership in its networks, the workers have simply blessed the leaders already in place rather than appointing new ones. Foreign support has mainly consisted of helping nationals understand scriptural principles for church leadership. Lay leaders are teaching current groups, There are no plans for a paid clergy. Training is on-the-job—learning by doing as opposed to learning in a classroom setting.

Due to the threat of persecution and the desire to have church be life-on-life, the nationals keep groups small. Some have been very intentional about dividing when they get too big; others have naturally spread out. When persecution grew too strong, the group laid hands on the person being persecuted and sent them away with the understanding they were to start a church wherever they went.

Baptism is a serious and significant step. New believers are considered outsiders and are not given leadership responsibilities until they take this step. After baptism, believers are expected to act on their faith—they can no longer just talk about it. Baptism is taught in the churches, it is modeled by the churches, and it is conducted by the churches. From the beginning, the foreigner workers were careful not to be involved in the baptism process. Some locals understood that; others pushed for their involvement and were even hurt by their lack of involvement. The workers felt it best not to allow themselves to compromise the security or independence of this important activity.

Because this church-planting movement is traveling along natural family and neighbor lines, the people are finding ways of grouping themselves. This eliminates most of the difficulties involved in introducing new believers to one another since they are within groupings. Trust with people from other groups is an issue since it is dangerous to change one's faith in that setting. Even so, new believers have been bold in sharing the good news with their community.

The foreign workers were careful not to tell others when someone had become a believer, but to allow the news to travel naturally. Once the foreign man sat in a room with five local men, aware they were all believers—and also aware that each one thought he was the only believer in the room. The new believers developed a "code" that enabled them to identify who was on the "Way" and who was not. A woman would ask a friend, "Have you seen the film?" If the friend said yes, then the woman knew it was safe to talk with her. If she asked, "What film?" it would indicate she was not yet on the "Way."

Terrorist activity targeting Westerners in the refugee country forced the workers to flee their second adopted home just as they had their first. God is faithful. He richly rewarded their faithful labor and their disciplined commitment to implement church-planting principles. Through their years of ministry they consistently led seekers and new believers to find their own answers in God's Word, encouraged believers to depend on God to supply their needs (both physical and spiritual), allowed the church to choose its own leaders, and encouraged and facilitated them as they discipled and trained members. The foreign husband and wife no longer work among this UPG, but they still maintain contact and even make rare visits.

At the time of this writing, the commander reported three house groups meeting weekly in his current town of residence. Another meeting provided a chance about once a month for seekers to watch the *JESUS* film and then discuss any questions they might have. A group in another city has grown too big and is dividing into three groups. Leadership is already in place for this change.

The work in another county, which to date is the most receptive area of any, also continues to grow. Another new city where the leaders recently sent a local church planter had many seekers and a few believing men who were growing as they shared their new faith with others. One area has become so saturated with believers that the mullahs are fearful of speaking out against it. The commander believes God is growing His church quickly so that within a few years the church can openly proclaim the truth and be able to withstand the certain persecution that will come with such an open declaration.

Resources
Miller, William. "What do Christians Believe?" also called "Beliefs and Practices of Christians" or "What is Christianity?" is available in many languages and can be viewed online at www.arabicbible.com/islam/christian_beliefs.htm.

Discussion Questions:
1. In this case study, the missionary studied under the teaching of the local mullah. Do you think this could be an effective way to share the gospel? In what ways could this strategy help or hinder the desire to share Christ

with the Muslim community?

2. The family in this article adapted their public worship to include local forms for prayer, fasting, almsgiving and celebrations. How do you feel about this level of contextualization? Would you adopt the Muslim form of prayer so Muslims would recognize that you were praying or do you feel this could lead to syncretism?

3. Many missionaries struggle with balancing their relationships. While it is important to have friendships with other missionaries and be mutually encouraged the main goal of the missionary life is to develop relationships with the local people and reach them with the gospel. How did the family in this story guard their relationships with nationals? How could you prioritize your relationships with the lost even now?

4. Missionaries are often very wealthy in comparison to the people they serve while the needs of the nationals are great. What struggles with money did the missionaries in this story face? What lessons can Christians in your setting learn from their example?

5. In the story, the missionary declined to give the commander a Bible when he asked for one. Why do you think he did this? In what situation would it be appropriate to give your friend a Bible?

6. After meeting together for worship and sharing, many of the converts in this story eventually became missionaries. What role did the Western missionaries play in their fellowship of new believers? Do you think they should have been more involved? Why or why not?

7. Were you concerned that the meetings in the refugee neighborhood were just for men? Why were their wives and children not also encouraged to meet together? In this situation, how would widows and orphans hear?

8. Persecution was a fact of life in this Central Asian church. When a believer encountered strong persecution, however, he or she was not comforted and protected but sent away and expected to start a new church. Why was this is their practice? In the same situation, what would you do?

23

Combining Local Witness and Non-Residential Church Planting:
A Case Study of Evangelism in Closed Countries

After seeing the nomadic Shep people (I will use pseudonyms for people groups and individuals in this article) listed as one of the top five unreached people groups on David Barrett's list in the *World Christian Encyclopedia*, Keith and Katy Rock felt God's call to minister to them. Because the Shep people live in a country that does not allow American residents, Keith and Katy prepared to be non-residential missionaries (NRM). They studied the book, *The Non-Residential Missionary* by David Garrison and also gained valuable training through the *Perspectives on the World Christian Movement* by Ralph Winter and Steve Hawthorne.

The Rocks began to diligently study the Shep culture. They searched the Internet but found little information. They read magazine and newspaper articles, history books, biographies, travelogues, and even the "Lonely Planet" travel guide about the country where the Sheps lived. Since the Sheps are Muslims, the Rocks also began to study Islam and its folk counterpart, reading Christian apologetics and the Qur'an.

The Rocks searched for a community of Sheps who might be immigrant or refugee people living outside their home country, but were unsuccessful. So Keith, Katy, and their two children moved to a country a short flight away from the Shep homeland. As there were no materials available to study the unwritten Shep language, they began to study a related trade language. Keith began networking with others who had an interest in the nearby closed country and its unreached peoples. He developed and distributed a "want ad" saying that he wanted to meet a Shep. Finally, someone in East Asia heard that a Shep college student there had come to faith and contacted Keith.

Keith flew to East Asia to meet this student and found that God had performed an incredible miracle. The young Shep man, Hussein, was indeed a believer— the first known Shep believer anywhere in the world. Furthermore, he was already actively sharing his faith! He had a heart for his Muslim brothers and sisters. When Hussein put his trust in Jesus, he already was well discipled in God's Word by a missionary who had faithfully shared with him every week for two years. Keith asked this missionary if Hussein could work with Keith in reaching out to the Shep people and his blessing was given.

Hussein had learned English in college, so he and Keith were able to communicate effectively. They quickly became friends and worked well together. Keith recorded Hussein's testimony in the Shep language. Hussein translated and recorded a concise 150-sentence from-Adam-to-Jesus story that Keith had written. The story which highlights God's relationship with the nomad Abraham can be viewed at the Web site, www.EveryTongue.com/story. In a darkened room, Keith filmed Hussein as he explained that he was the only Shep believer and asked Christians to pray for his people.

About this time, the closed country began approving limited travel visas for foreigners. Keith took a two-week trip with the required national travel guide to view the country. He visited the major city where the Sheps lived and was able to spend a night in the mountains with Shep nomads. Keith saw the needs of the people firsthand. He surveyed their accessibility to radio, television, and printed literature in the national language. He asked many questions and took mental notes on what language or languages the people were speaking, both on the streets and in the tents. Keith videotaped the Shep and later produced a home video combining the Shep footage with Hussein's request for prayer. He used this video to mobilize Western Christians to pray for and support the work.

After Hussein finished his schooling, he moved to the city where Keith and Katy lived. Together, they began to formulate a plan for reaching the Shep people. With Keith's encouragement, Hussein made his first visit back to his family in the closed country. He did not tell them he had become a Christian; he simply shared the Bible stories he had memorized. Hussein's mother, with whom he was very close, often cried when she heard these stories. Toward the end of his visit, she asked him, "I am wondering if you have become a follower of Jesus?" He just smiled.

Keith and Hussein continued working on evangelistic tools in the Shep language. They divided the "God's Story" script into fifteen segments and added an introduction and conclusion for radio use. Hussein worked with Wycliffe Bible translators, periodically checking their translation of the Gospel of Luke. Keith and Hussein together developed an evangelistic website for the Shep and put recordings of the gospel on the internet. Hussein's voice was disguised for these recordings.

Keith's financial help enabled Hussein to attend a school of Islamic studies that taught Christians to lovingly share the gospel with Muslims. At the school, Hussein met Sheila. Sheila was not a Shep, but she had a love for Muslim people like he did and already knew much of his language. God performed another miracle; after months of correspondence and visits, Hussein and Sheila married. Keith performed the wedding after he and Katy had provided marriage counseling. Soon, God called the couple to move back to Hussein's hometown. They obeyed with great anticipation and a little trepidation.

The first challenge Hussein and Sheila faced was finding a job. They wanted time to meet and interact with people and start a church, but they also needed and wanted a job. Foreign funds helped them move and find a home, but the church-planting couple did not want to depend on these funds. Neither did they relish explaining the source of their money to family members or, worse yet, the police. Also, the right job could provide access to the Shep. Keith worked with the couple on creating a job. After a few missteps, the job finally chosen was that of selling Shep handiwork—valuable, prized pieces already well-known in the world. With a financial grant from Keith, Hussein hired ten Shep families to produce the handiwork.

Keith and Katy struggled about the question of money for the ministry— whether to give, how much to give, and to whom. They strongly believe that national pastors should not be paid by foreigners. However, the Rocks felt that when a national was the first-known evangelist to a people group with no other known believers, then a limited amount of financial assistance might be necessary to begin the work. Hussein clearly understood from the beginning that the financial help was limited and temporary.

Keith and Katy visited a Christian handiwork salesman in America who agreed to showcase any goods delivered to his store. Keith also developed a website for marketing the handiwork. There were shipping problems, customs hassles, and international laws to consider, but all in all, this job provided money and a true and credible explanation of their income for family and friends. Best of all, the job put Hussein and Sheila in regular contact with Shep craftsmen and other Shep people involved in the production, transport, and marketing of the product.

Hussein continued to share faithfully with his family. Though Sheila was not a Shep, God granted her great favor in the eyes of Hussein's family. All who met her loved her. Though women often stayed in their homes, Sheila also was able to make new friends at exercise gyms and swimming pools during times reserved solely for women. Sheila began wearing makeup and jewelry similar to that worn by the women around her even though the style differed from her own. She also dressed modestly on the conservative end of the spectrum for that culture.

Sheila shared her faith, sometimes in stories and parables, but often through prayer. Soon, Sheila became known as a woman of prayer. Family members began to say, "Ask Sheila to pray for you. She knows how." Sheila found that meeting with women as a group for prayer was very non-threatening. When asked about Muhammad, Sheila answered, "I thank God that Muhammad spoke against the terrible things of his day. I thank God that Jesus came to pay for our sins." Sheila encouraged believers to share their weaknesses with non-believers as well as how God helps them deal with these issues. Her transparency allowed women to trust her and share their lives with her.

Hussein and Sheila ran into the same barriers to the gospel that have characterized Muslim beliefs for centuries. These included statements like, "The Bible has been changed; the Qur'an is the last book and is perfect; Muhammad is the last prophet, God cannot have a son; God cannot be born." In addition, there was a negative impression of Christianity because it was considered a Western idea. To overcome that prejudice, Hussein and Sheila used terms such as "student of Jesus" and "person who loves Jesus" instead of "Christian" because of the Western connotations attached to that word. In fact, those who have become believers still do not use the term "Christian" to describe themselves. Hussein and Sheila also found an additional barrier, particular to their part of the Muslim world, that most people are simply not interested in religion. Many people have become disillusioned with their Islamic government. They simply see Christianity as one more oppressive religion.

After hearing many Bible stories and seeing the change in her son's life, Hussein's mother could no longer resist the love of Jesus. She committed herself to Him. Other family members also believed. It began with immediate family, then extended family and friends. Hussein and Sheila realized that for many

Muslims, salvation was more of a process than a one-time (sinner's prayer) event. They saw people wavering between Islam and Christianity, saying, "I am a Muslim ... I am not a Muslim ... I am a Muslim," before making a final commitment to Christ. This church-planting couple found it valuable to continually disciple seekers, even before they were believers, just as Hussein experienced when he became a believer.

The new Shep believers began to meet at the home of Hussein's mother. At first, when the group was small, they did not meet on a particular day. But now the group meets every Friday afternoon since Friday is the cultural holy day. Everyone sits on the floor, even the teacher. There are pillows against the walls. The men in the group sit with men, the women with women. The church has no rules regarding headscarves; some of the women wear them and some of the younger women do not.

The group has communion once a month. Only believers are allowed to participate. If there are a lot of seekers on a day when communion is scheduled, it may be postponed. Believers check with the leader of the group before bringing new people. The leader then meets with the new people to assess their interest and any possible security risks before inviting them to attend the group. Hussein and Sheila instruct the believers not to criticize or degrade Islam.

Sheila and her mother-in-law joyfully serve tea and fruit each week, being careful to model hospitality that can be easily replicated. They originally considered serving a meal but decided it would be too burdensome as the house church grows and expands to other homes. They also believe the women need to be free from hospitality pressures to participate in the meeting. They need time to grow in faith and to learn to minister to each other. Also, the financial cost of providing a meal each week might be difficult for the host family.

All the women usually help with serving tea and clean up. Sheila encourages the women to pray for each other after the meeting. This may mean saying, "I am going to another room if anyone would like to pray." This allows the women to share more private needs with one another. Sheila models praying aloud and asks the women to pray aloud for her and each other.

Hussein is the main teacher of the house group, although everyone in the group talks and is able to share. Hussein and Sheila usually plan the meetings together, communicating freely about expectations. Sheila earnestly asks her husband, "How can I be of a help to the house church today?" They find the enemy often tries to attack their family before the worship meeting, so they are careful to stop and pray when disagreements arise between them.

Hussein has found that the people love to hear and see simple illustrations and stories. "If a cup of clean water has a tiny drop of mud in it, is it clean? No. No amount of good works can make us clean." Hussein notes who is in attendance; later he meets with absentees to go over the discipleship materials covered at the weekly meeting.

To encourage more members to be involved in leadership, a person, male or female, is asked to lead the music, prayer and sharing time each week. Hussein or Sheila asks the person in advance telling them the subject of the lesson. The person then chooses the worship songs, the Bible passages, and invites another member to share a testimony. Although Sheila has an electronic keyboard, she does not play for the meeting because it would not be easily reproducible in new groups.

Several new believers were reluctant to share what they had learned from the Bible because they were afraid they would say something wrong about such a Holy Book. Hussein and Sheila began asking individuals to read and report to the group on other Christian books in the trade language since there are no books in the Shep language. This increased the believer's confidence to share in a group and to share on a religious subject. The group leaves a tithe box by the front door similar to how an alms box is placed in a mosque. Two church members rather than Hussein or Sheila count the money together and keep a notebook in the box about the amounts collected. The group decides together how to spend the money. It has been used for such purchases as clothing for the poor and songbooks for the church.

Sheila has many roles in the church. The participation of children in the service can be a security risk since they do not understand the danger involved and may talk to nonbelieving friends about the attendees and their activities. For this reason, Sheila often plays with the children in a back room. When Sheila does attend the meeting, Hussein encourages her to check people's comprehension of the message and help elicit discussion. Sheila meets with individual women during the week to encourage and challenge them in their walk. She may say, "Try to talk to … about your love for God," or "Try to be more humble toward your husband." When Hussein is traveling among the nomads, Sheila meets with the women as a group, teaching on issues that pertain to them, such as, "should Christians wash after sex like Muslims do?" Hussein and Sheila are carefully discipling another couple to lead the next house church when the group is ready to divide. They believe a couple makes a powerful ministry team that is able to minister to both men and women.

Having learned a lot from their non-residential ministry to the Sheps, Keith and Katy expanded their ministry to other unreached minority groups in the closed country. Many things were easier the second time around. For example, producing the *God's Story* video took three years and many dollars to produce in the Shep language, but with the lessons learned, the video was produced in a different minority language in six months at one-fourth of the cost.

Keith also worked with two other agencies to produce the *JESUS* film in the language of another Unreached People Group in the closed country. Seventeen voices were needed to produce the script, but seventeen believers could not be found. Keith recruited one national believer who helped gather the necessary number of people and flew them to Keith's city where the script was recorded. The non-believing actor who spoke the lines of Jesus partied every night, but at the end of the recording, he professed a sincere interest in believing the words he had been speaking. This "Jesus" now meets with a house group every week back in his closed country.

Through God's provision, another evangelistic national couple was found. They were refugees living in the Rocks' city. The couple was being discipled by Keith and another worker and through the process became open to returning to their homeland. Although this couple was not from an ethnic minority, Keith encouraged them to reach out to an unreached people group where very little work was being done. The national couple was touched watching *Ee-taow! The Next Chapter*, a video, which shows an unreached people group hearing the gospel for the first time. They then share their new beliefs with another people group—all via storying. They moved back to their country to share the gospel with a second unreached ethnic minority group.

A single man who had come to faith while studying medicine outside the closed country showed great interest in yet a third people group. Keith began assisting him with medical supplies enabling him to travel to nomadic tents to heal bodies and to show the *JESUS* film and *God's Story* video that Keith had helped produce. The young man requested a movie projector so the movies could be shown to many people at once or could be shown outdoors. Keith gave him one. Dozens of unreached people have now heard the gospel from the ministry of this one man; he himself has baptized fifteen new believers.

What have Katy's roles as a non-residential missionary been throughout this process? In the beginning, her two children were preschoolers, and her time was limited. When their family moved to their Middle Eastern home, they chose their neighborhood very carefully asking: Is this a community where

people are interconnected or is this a neighborhood made up mostly of com-
muter couples with no moms at home during the day? Is there a butcher, a
green grocer, or a corner store where people shop and see each other? Is there
a playground nearby where nationals take their children. Before the move,
Katy walked around the neighborhood praying.

After their move, Katy prayed to meet friends her age with kids her kids' ages,
and within the first month three women matching this description befriended
her. Although these women were not Shep, they were Muslims who spoke a
related language, and they taught Katy a great deal about Islamic culture. Katy
began to study more about topics that were of concern to her new Muslim
friends.

Keith began to consult Katy about his questions on the Qur'an. Keith asked
Katy for advice on Bible translation issues, evangelistic tools, and Bible storying because she was in the trenches working with people and trying new
things. Intercession was a major ministry role. Katy kept a prayer journal for
the work, praying for Hussein and Sheila and others as they came to faith. She
prayed for the problems of the nascent church, and wrote down Scripture verses to pray for her husband and the expanding ministry.

The Rock family has seen many non-residential missionary families quit the
work because they failed to thrive where they lived—due in large part because
their ministry focus was on a people and culture in another country. Keith
encouraged Katy's neighborhood work and knew that what she was learning
also would bless the Shep people.

From time to time Hussein, Sheila, and the other national workers meet
together within the country for accountability purposes. They also visit Keith
and Katy every six months for a semi-annual training and spiritual refreshment
retreat. For a total of several weeks each year, Katy hosts the group in her home,
assisting them with their health needs and providing them a respite.

At the meeting, the church-planting partners receive encouragement for
their church-planting efforts and further Bible training. They also participate in
on-going leadership training, provide accountability for each other on moral
issues, and talk together about persecution and security problems they are facing in their closed country. They discuss details of the handiwork business and
the medical outreach. Since all of the national church planters have lived outside of their home country in the past, they are not tempted to permanently
stay out when they leave their country for training.

During these debriefings, Katy meets with the women to hear about their lives, to pray for them, to learn from them, and to offer suggestions from what she has discovered in her own neighborhood ministry to Muslim women. Katy finds that in her neighborhood many women gather and gossip at manicure salons, so she goes to have her nails done and tells a new Bible story each time to those around her. Sheila is now trying a similar strategy with her hairdresser.

Katy met every week for a year to do chronological Bible storying with a local Muslim-background believer who then went home and shared the stories with her five grown children. Katy shared these storying materials with the closed country workers and encouraged them to tell Bible stories. One of the new church planters plans to tell stories to her busy mother-in-law as they wash dishes together.

Katy and the women face many of the same questions and issues as they minister to Muslim women. Katy placed her children in a local public school and became close friends with classmates' mothers. She understands what it is like to have a believing child surrounded by Muslim children and teachers. The workers from the closed country also relate to Katy as her life is intertwined with her Muslim neighbors.

Katy encourages church planters, both male and female, to consider appropriate cultural norms and terminology for worship as many of them have already adopted Western forms—such as clasping hands together during prayer instead of holding out one's hands with palms facing up. There was some resistance at first because of the desire to reject all things Islamic. However, as the national workers (all Muslim-background believers) began to face some rejection due to the use of Western forms instead of the cross of Christ, they began to consider more carefully how to treat the Bible with respect, how to use the Qur'an as a bridge, and so on.

Both Keith and Katy are sometimes sad that due to their nationality they cannot be on the direct frontlines with the unreached people group they have grown to love so much. They want to be planting churches themselves, not just supporting others. They have had to humble themselves to accept God's role for them—serving national evangelists and church planters who do not need a special visa to live in their own country and who already know the language.

Keith and Katy and their kids were finally able to locate Shep-related nomads in the mountains about a twelve hour drive from their home. They have had the great privilege of sharing the gospel with them. The Rocks encourage the national church planters in the closed country to remember the people who have the least access to the gospel and ask them to visit nomads as often as possible. Baby churches are starting in the cities. Their vision is to reach their nomadic kin.

Resources

Barrett, David B., Gearge T. Kurian, and Todd M. Johnson. Eds. 2001. *World Christian encyclopedia: A comparative survey of churches and religions in the modern world* (2 Vols.) New York, NY: Oxford University Press.

Garrison, David. 1990. *The non-residential missionary: A new strategy and the people it serves.* Birmingham, Monrovia, CA: MARC.

Winter, Ralph, and Steve Hawthorne. 1981. *Perspectives on the world Christian movement: A reader.* Pasadena, CA: William Carey Library.

Zook, Mark, and Gloria Zook. 1989. *Ee-Taow! The Next Chapter.* Produced and directed by New Tribes Mission. 60 min. Videocassette.

Discussion Questions:

1. Many missionaries have a policy to not support locals financially out of concern it will lead to dependence and/or mistrust. In this case study, Keith and his family helped Hussein and Sheila return to their home-land and capitalized their handcraft business. What are the pros and cons of supporting Hussein in this story? If you were in Keith's situation, would you have supported him in the same way?

2. Sheila responded to a question about Muhammad by saying, "I thank God that Muhammad spoke against the terrible things of his day." Do you think this was a wise answer? Why or why not? How would you respond if a Muslim asked about your belief in Muhammad?

3. In the story, the new Shep believers were afraid to discuss the Bible out of fear that they would say something wrong about this Holy Book. How would you help new believers overcome this fear? Why would it be important? How could you encourage them to ask questions and discuss what they were learning?

4. The new believers in this country learned that rejecting some Islamic forms and traditions would quickly bring rejection. Considering what forms they could accept, they decided they should treat the Bible with respect and pray with their palms up. Do you feel that converts should be free from these traditions and forms of Islam, or should some be kept? What would you need to know about Islamic forms to make this decision?

5. Keith and Katy were not able to cross the border into Shep country. However, God allowed them to meet a Shep believer, who was able to take the message across the border. What are other ways non-residential missionaries, such as Keith and Katy might get the gospel message into a closed country?

24

Mobilizing Near-Culture Believers for Prayer, Evangelism and Church Planting:
A Case Study in Southeast Asia

*I*n our Southeast Asian country there are fourteen Muslim tribal groups that differ in their practice of Islam. Some are very strict in their adherence to traditional Islam, while others follow a form of folk Islam in which animism is practiced in daily life. All of the groups are influenced to some extent by local forms of animism. An ongoing war has characterized Muslim-Christian relationships in this country for more than 400 years. While some of the tribes are very militant and support and encourage rebel groups, others maintain peaceful relations with their non-Muslim neighbors.

Seven years ago my husband and I were called to reach out to the people in these fourteen groups. We had been in the country several years and were involved in a fruitful work with animistic tribal people when we began to receive death threats from an Islamic terrorist group in the area. As we prayed about what to do, God led us to shift our focus to these Muslim tribes. In the past there was a long, bloody history of attempted work among the tribes with little or no results. Missionaries have been kidnapped, pastors killed, radio stations bombed, and churches burned in the area. A hundred years of work had yielded only a handful of Muslim background believers (MBBs) and no churches. As a result, very few workers have been willing to minister in this environment.

God, however, has moved in remarkable ways among these people during the past seven years. His work looks different in each people group, but there are also many common threads. We have learned from both our failures and our successes during our ministry. We continue to adjust our methods as we encounter new obstacles and are given new insights. In this article I will present some of the key strategies and methods we have found successful.

The most important tool for our work is strategic prayer. Strategic prayer begins with "end visioning." We have learned to stop and ask God how He wants us to pray before we involve others in praying for our people. This is important because many times our idea of how God's church will look among a certain group is different than God's. End visioning—or seeking God's vision of the work—is essential to praying for the right things.

One of our initial prayers, for instance, involved asking God to send hundreds of laborers to go minister to these people groups. However, we learned this was not what God wanted; He wanted to raise up leaders from inside the groups. He began to give dreams and visions to the most hardened rebels. These rebel leaders then began to leave their groups and seek out believers who eventually led them to Christ. Then, they returned to their homes and became a light to their own people. Thus, our prayer strategy changed. We began asking people to pray that God would give dreams, visions, and miraculous healings to our people—supernatural revelations of Himself that would cause them to seek the truth.

Another early prayer was for peace in war-torn areas so national workers could share the message. This also was not part of God's plan. As we prayed, the war only escalated. However, the result was an increase in the responsiveness of people. Doors of opportunity were opened that we would never have ex-perienced otherwise as many people were displaced and moved into refugee camps. Often, traditional gatekeepers were not present to prevent these people from hearing the message and they eagerly received the Injil (New Testament) and other Scripture portions along with relief goods from aid workers. As a result, relationships were built and they began to see us as different from other "Christians." In fact, we stopped using the word "Christian" as we discovered the negative connotations that word carried. It did not describe to them who we were as believers. Although we want to see peace reign in our country, we are leaving that to God's timing. We now pray for opportunities in the midst of conflict and that God will use everything that happens to cause people to seek Him.

Persuading national believers to pray is a very big challenge. Most Christians know someone who has been killed or kidnapped in the ongoing conflict with Muslims. As we speak in churches near the Muslim areas we want to reach, we find it difficult to get anyone to commit to pray. Several things have helped change this, but the biggest factor is the "Condensed World Missions" course produced by Living Springs International. Churches attending this training begin to look at Muslims as a lost people and not as their enemies.

God also has used the testimony of one converted Muslim rebel. This man had been trained at the age of five to carry a gun and by age ten had killed his first victim. By the age of sixteen he was robbing banks to support the jihad (holy war). Then one day he began to have dreams about Jesus—powerful dreams. In search of answers, he disguised himself as a Christian and went to another town. There, he sat in the back of a Baptist church and heard about Jesus for the first time. The pastor led him to the Lord. This young man began going to churches and asking forgiveness for the sins Muslims had committed against Christians. Believers' hearts were softened by his testimony. Many repented of their hatred toward their Muslim brothers.

In our country, one Muslim group is feared by everyone. They are the warriors of Islam and are a very violent people. On their home island they constantly fight each other as well as outsiders. Other Muslims fear them and hold them in high regard. How could we reach this group? How could we pray down their spiritual strongholds? Another Muslim tribe wanders through the area of the militant group. They are very poor Sea Gypsies. They are considered beggars and despised by all the other Muslim groups. However, God is building His church among the Gypsies. There are many Gypsy believers who are committed followers of Isa (Jesus).

In answer to our questions, God opened our eyes to another very effective strategy. We trained thirty-six leaders from the Gypsy group in prayer walking and spiritual warfare then challenged them to go and pray among the violent tribes where no one else could go. They began a prayer boating ministry since some islands were too dangerous for even them to enter. This endeavor led to many miraculous events and opened doors for the message to enter this militant Muslim people group. It also was a blessing for the Gypsies; their faith grew when they saw God answering their prayers.

In the past seven years we have mobilized prayer for ten of the fourteen tribes. We began by mobilizing the national church. Then we mobilized prayer in the United States and in South Korea. In four of the groups we saw a breakthrough within two years after people began praying. God miraculously called out national believers to go, give, and pray. However, in two of the toughest, most resistant groups, it took four years of heavy prayer mobilization before we began to hear stories of Muslims having dreams and visions and their hearts opening to the truth. All of the fourteen tribes now have some form of engagement with the gospel.

One important aspect of our prayer strategy has been special days of prayer and fasting among the churches. We have all-night prayer meetings, for instance, on the Night of Power during Ramadan. Another organization in our country holds nationwide prayer and fasting events on September 11 called "Bless the Muslims." These events effectively mobilize prayer and increase awareness among CBBs (Christian Background Believers).

One hundred years of mission work by foreigners in our country was successful among every group except among these fourteen Muslim groups. White faces often created suspicion and caused persecution when workers tried to engage people in these Muslim groups. Many American missionaries received death threats, others were kidnapped, and some were even killed by Muslims. In the years leading up to 9/11 the violence escalated. Since 9/11 it has become almost impossible for foreigners to maintain a presence in Muslim areas and in some areas it is completely impossible.

This reality forced us to look for other kinds of workers—workers who could move freely and build relationships among these Muslim people groups. The people God is using are national workers with good cross-cultural training. They adapt easily and can gain access to Muslim cultures, though at times only on a limited basis. They have become highly effective messengers and are the key to reaching our people. Other Asian workers can also move through these areas more easily than Westerners but still not as freely as local believers. They can, however, play an important role if they are properly trained in cross-cultural and contextualization methods.

We have also had to adapt and adjust our methods. Traditional methods too often lead to severe persecution which silences any witness. Because of this, the crucial characteristics of effective national workers include a commitment to minister in accordance with the training they have received in cross-cultural adaptation, contextualized evangelism, and indigenous church planting.

Development projects have provided a new means of access. The war has left Muslim communities in extremely poor condition. Very little development has taken place over the years and the needs are great. If done well and in the right spirit, community development programs are a very effective way of entering Muslim communities. We begin development projects by identifying needy communities that are open to help. We determine this by first approaching religious and political leaders. We offer our assistance and ask them what kinds of help are needed in their community. If their response is positive, we formulate a community development plan. Then the entire community is gathered. The team always begins this general meeting by asking forgiveness for the sins Christians have committed against their community. Then we present a plan for community development that prioritizes the needs previously identified by their leaders. The plan for community development always includes values training in the form of Chronological Bible Storying.

After the presentation, members of the community decide whether they will accept the plan and which responsibilities they will shoulder in the endeavor. These responsibilities usually include housing the workers, providing for their safety, and providing a place for the training. Typically, community development plans may also include training in literacy, health care, sanitation, gardening, and livelihood skills.

In other places, God has raised up people from inside restricted-access areas to lead out in development projects and evangelization. These are often people who have had dreams and visions or a miraculous healing and are seeking more information. Frequently these people are already leaders in their communities. A key role we play in such insider movements is leadership training. These key leaders periodically leave their areas and meet in a neutral location for mentoring and training. Again, an "accepted" outsider does the training. Occasionally "accepted" outsiders visit Muslim communities to evaluate projects and determine needs or new directions, but the projects are fully run by the insider MBBs. They teach the skills and values training, lead worship, and baptize new believers. It is completely an insider movement. These projects tend to grow and multiply rapidly. The message soon travels through family lines into other communities and even neighboring tribes.

We have learned that Muslims love Isa (Jesus)—it is "Christians" who are the focus of their hatred. The *JESUS* film is well received by Muslims if it is not linked to Christians. We have found creative ways to distribute the film through small video rental places, so it is often considered to be an Islamic film, made in an Islamic country. In some areas we have teams showing the film publicly with little or no resistance.

Scripture distribution also has been successful when it is not linked to any

"Christian" source. There have been requests from imams for Arabic Scriptures, for instance, that can be distributed in the mosques. Workers in Muslim communities often give a gift of the Bible to community leaders at Christmas time. They take the Injil (New Testament), wrap it in a white cloth, and give it with a prayer mat to each of the religious leaders. These are so appreciated that, after receiving the gifts, leaders sometimes ask for Bible storytelling to be done in their homes.

Chronological Bible Storying is a work in progress for the teams. We are finding new ways to adapt methods of communication that are natural in each cultural setting. When an MBB tells the story in a contextualized manner, it is a powerful tool. We have heard of Muslims asking to be immediately baptized after hearing the story of redemption presented in this manner.

In the last seven years we have seen many changes in the work. More and more national organizations are springing up to reach out to Muslims. Many churches have an awareness of the lost and are finding ways to address the needs. The hatred and fear of Muslims among Christians is slowly turning into a love for the lost. The result is that more and more Muslims are coming to Christ!

Resources

Living Springs International. N.d. "Condensed World Mission Course." P. O. Box 149, #7 Roman St. Butuan City 8600, The Republic of the Philippines. Available from: lsinter@skyinet.net.

Discussion Questions:

1. Why do you suppose God is using dreams, visions, miraculous healings, and other supernatural revelations of Himself so frequently in the Muslim world? Why do you believe we don't see these types of revelations as often in the Western world?

2. In this case study, the missionaries stopped using the word "Christian." Discuss possible reasons why this might be necessary. Under what conditions would you stop using the term yourself?

3. The author states that many churches have begun to look at Muslims as a lost people, and not as their enemies. What do you think the general feeling toward Muslims is in our Western churches? How can our churches gain more compassion for Muslims around the world?

4. The missionaries in this country participate in development projects as a means of access. As part of the community development plan, they

include Chronological Bible Storying. Do you think this is a good mission strategy? Why/Why not?

5. The missionaries in this story said that the *JESUS* film is well received by Muslims if it is not linked to Christians. Why would Muslims have such hatred for Christians but still love Jesus? What do you think it would take for Muslims to change their mind about Christians?

25

Chronological Bible Storying in East Africa: A Case Study in Communicating Biblical Truth

*M*edina missed the lesson. On my way home, I visited her small but neatly kept hut. Her husband was there, and I surmised that he was the reason she did not attend. I could see she was burdened. She told me her sister had been sick for a long time, and people were saying she was cursed. Medina asked: "Can a curse make you so sick that you finally die?" "Yes," I said. "There are curses with great effect, but not every one who is sick has been cursed." "Why do we get sick all the time?" Medina asked. "Life would be so much easier without all this sickness." "You are right," I replied. "When God created us, He made us perfect and healthy. But then man disobeyed God. Since that time we get sick—and eventually we die."

Medina interrupted me to tell the story from Genesis 1-3 to her husband. She told it just as she had heard it in the storytelling session some weeks earlier. Suddenly she stopped and asked, "Didn't God promise to send a Savior to redeem us from the consequences and curse of sin? How can I be freed, forgiven and protected from any curse people might put on me?"

As I repeated the stories of Jesus, she was very attentive. Then her eyes changed from sparkling hope to doom. Outside, night was falling; I had to go. Medina accompanied me to the fence. "I know this is the truth," she said thoughtfully. "I want to follow Jesus. I need Him to protect my children and me! But what about my husband? I'm scared." I knew she had reason to be frightened. My heart was heavy. How can a woman like Medina ever fully accept the gospel and follow Christ?

Early one Saturday morning, two Muslim girls from my Bible study group appeared at my doorstep. Before they even entered the house, one burst out with her question. "Is it true that the Qur'an and your Bible both tell us that Jesus is in heaven right now?" Surprised, I nodded. She continued, "In our last session you told us that Jesus is busy preparing a place for us in heaven and is coming back to take us with Him to be with God. When I got home I remembered that Muhammad is still in his grave in Medina, which many Muslims visit every year!" She stopped, not knowing how to continue. I tried to help her. "Does this bother you? Is that why you came here today?"

Looking past me in deep thought, she continued, "Yes, I asked myself should we not follow the One who is alive, sitting next to God, coming to judge the world, rather than follow a dead prophet, who still waits for his own judgment to come?" As she continued, my heart nearly missed a beat. "Please help us. We want to follow the living One so that tonight, if we die, we will know we are going to heaven because we have been forgiven."

How were these ladies able to understand and apply scriptural truths in ways that so profoundly impacted their worldview, their religious view, indeed their very lives? These ladies and thousands more throughout Africa are hearing Scripture through Chronological Bible Storying (CBS).

The Bible is God's story to us and is best presented as a story rather than as a collection of teachings. It is a story with a beginning and an end, and should be told in sequence. Chronological Bible Storying communicates biblical truths in this way. The Bible stories are narrated in the order they happened. CBS is not primarily for children—it is for adult men and women.

Because the story form is the vehicle by which oral cultures collect, retain, and pass on information, CBS has been especially effective among oral communicators. CBS enables them to learn and gather information in the easiest and most memorable ways. They can become wonderful Bible teachers as they tell the stories to others.

Because CBS starts at the very beginning of the Bible and takes the student step by step in historical progression through the whole story of God's interaction with man, it is especially effective in communicating the good news to Unreached People Groups. These are groups of people who have never heard the truth and do not understand who God is or what He has done.

The Old Testament stories lay a firm foundation revealing who God is, who man is, and how God desires to relate to man. The stories lead the listener from the wonder of creation, the tragedy of sin, and the fall of man through the history of God's people and the prophecies and pictures of the promised Messiah. They prepare the listeners to understand the New Testament stories that reveal the climax of God's redemptive plan. God used thousands of years to prepare mankind for the coming for Christ. We often try to lead someone to entrust their lives to Christ during one single conversation or Bible study. Then we wonder how they could reject the good news of God's love. CBS does not im-mediately challenge Muslim beliefs or involve them in debates or apologetics. Instead, it allows God's Word and God's Spirit to speak truth into their lives. It enables them to understand and respond to God.

As people hear the stories that make up The Story, they identify and become part of them. The stories enable them to understand what God has done, as well as touch their hearts and open their spirits to the work of God's Spirit. An effective evangelistic set of CBS stories is designed not only to communicate the basic story of God's redemptive activity, it also allows listeners to interact with Bible stories in ways that challenge and transform their worldviews and religious views.

In order to choose the stories that will best enable a particular people group to understand and be transformed by the gospel, the worker must study the worldview of that people group. The goal of this study is to identity the barriers that presently keep them from faith as well as the bridges that God has provided in their culture to help them hear and understand the gospel. After these barriers and bridges have been identified, the worker chooses stories that confront and remove the barriers and/or affirm and strengthen the bridges. These stories are added to the basic evangelistic set.

The chart on the following page compares some Muslim religious beliefs with biblical truths. Understanding these differences can guide the worker in her choice of Bible stories.

Religious View of Muslims	Christian Doctrines Essential for Salvation
1. God is too great to be approached or known by men. He does not act in history, except to set the dates of one s birth and death.	1. God acts in history and communicates with man.
2. God is too great to be bound by His Word or by moral absolutes. He can abrogate and substitute His own word.	2. God is all powerful, but still faithful to His Word.
3. Holiness is not a moral attribute of God; therefore, sin does not have serious consequences.	3. God is holy and hates sin. He punishes sin by death.
4. Sin can be partially atoned for by works observing the five pillars, additional fasting, memorizing the Qur an, repeating the names of God.	4. Human beings are sinners and separated from God.
5. No Atonement by another person is necessary or possible. Each person will endure his own punishment on Judgment Day; there is no assurance of forgiveness.	5. God loves men and women and wants fellowship with them
6. Jesus did not die on the cross. God removed Him beforehand and substituted someone else there.	6. Man is answerable to God.
7. Jesus is just a prophet, not the Son of God. God cannot have a son.	7. Man can do nothing to save himself.
8. Muhammad is the last and greatest of the prophets. He is the seal of all prophets. He has universal status.	8. Jesus is the Son of God, the promised Messiah, who gave His life on the cross as a ransom for the sins of mankind.
9. The Qur an abrogates and supersedes the Bible as the last and final testament.	9. Man can approach God but can only have true fellowship with Him through the perfect Sacrifice. Fellowship requires faith and obedience to God.
10. The Bible has been corrupted by men and the original text is lost.	10. The Bible can be trusted. The main proof is in fulfillment of prophecies and the transformed lives of believers.

The Islamic religion does not emphasize chronology except for the fact that Muhammad is the last prophet. Stories in the Qur'an are recorded in fragmented form in different Surahs or chapters without reference to their setting in history. Islamic teaching jumps from one topic to another without encouraging the student to dig deeper or look for the truth in a logical way. The chronological approach of the Bible challenges the Muslim mindset. The Word recounts God's activity and character as demonstrated across thousands of years of history. It repeatedly illustrates through the lives of the men and women of the Bible how God wants to relate to mankind.

CBS is not just another rote learning process. During storying sessions, the storyteller asks questions carefully chosen to help listeners discover for themselves the truths in each story. CBS emphasizes the characteristics of God exhibited in each story. Then listeners can compare the biblical picture of God with the Islamic picture. Hearing and discussing these biblical truths over time enables listeners, with the help of the Holy Spirit, to examine and evaluate their beliefs and to change their views of God, themselves, and their world.

CBS not only answers the standard objections of Muslims, it takes the initiative to share the good news. It gives the worker a plan to follow that helps her stay on target instead of being sidetracked by irrelevant questions. The questions help the listeners understand and apply biblical truths in their daily lives.

The story sessions provide a context for building and developing relationships between the storyteller and the listeners. Women like to identify with other women—with their happenings, sorrows, pains, and joys. This is one of the main reasons women are drawn to storytelling groups. As women listen to Bible stories and discuss them with their friends, their worldviews and religious views can be transformed. Each story touches some aspect of their worldview barriers or bridges while communicating a new biblical truth. When the confrontational aspects of the life of Jesus are introduced, their established relationship with the leader and with each other helps women continue to listen to the stories and to process the new truths. This extended learning time is a key factor in helping women grow in their understanding and commitment.

The CBS evangelism story track emphasizes two important biblical truths about salvation: First, sin can only be forgiven by offering the blood of an unblemished sacrificial lamb. Second, throughout the Old Testament God promised to send a special person who would save His people and establish His kingdom. These two truths are fulfilled in Jesus Christ, who is both the perfect Sacrifice and the promised Savior. CBS permits Muslim women to understand the necessity of Christ's incarnation, His divinity, and His atoning death.

Chronological Bible Storying attracts listeners and keeps their attention.

It can be effectively used with groups in conjunction with educational programs like sewing, agricultural or occupational training, community health, literacy, or English-as-a-Second Language classes. It also can be used with students or teachers in school settings. People participating in such projects or classes already have a common interest or purpose and regularly meet. Sharing stories with such a naturally occurring group enables them to hear the same stories at the same time, talk about them, ask questions, and grow in their understanding together. This community-integrated approach can encourage an entire group to make a decision for Christ together as well as prevent ostracism or persecution of individuals as they become believers. CBS also can be used in sharing with one person, a family, or a small group of neighbors. Instead of just making small talk week after week, a worker can offer to tell stories at social gatherings.

Urbanization in East Africa typically clusters people on the outskirts of big cities, forcing them to live in very congested, impoverished slum areas. In one such area, Christians started a literacy class. Soon, they were overwhelmed by the number of Muslim women attending and asked me for help. I had just learned about the CBS method and saw this as a great opportunity to try it out.

We chose not to include the storytelling program as part of the official literacy program, but to meet separately on Saturday afternoons at a neutral place (a school) for an extra Bible lesson. We did not want to give the local Muslim leaders grounds to accuse us of deceptively sharing the gospel under the pretense of teaching literacy.

At that time the only CBS material I was aware of was the manual *God and Man* by Dell and Rachel Schultze (Schultze 1991). I generally followed it, but made modifications I felt would meet the needs of the Muslim women involved in the program. For example, I rewrote the lessons from Genesis 2-4 and the story of the offering of Isaac. I also added the story of Hagar and Ishmael. I emphasized the prophecies of Jesus in the Old Testament by making a picture chart. As we went through the New Testament stories, I used the chart to emphasize the exact fulfillment of the different Old Testament messianic prophecies. The Qur'an has no such fulfilled prophesies, and I found that this evidence of God's inspiration of the Word helped listeners trust the Bible.

In the beginning, approximately twenty-five to thirty ladies participated in the CBS sessions every Saturday. However, when the community leader responsible for bringing these ladies together died, the numbers dropped rapidly. After spending a whole year telling the stories, only one person accepted Christ.

I was very disappointed! When I asked the younger girls (who spoke English) why they didn't respond positively to the stories, they said: "These stories are all so new for us. We never heard them in this way. Please tell them again. We need more time!"

So the next round of story sessions began. This time I used J.O. Terry's story set *God and Woman* (Terry 1998). At the end, I included some stories from the book of Acts to illustrate how people responded to the gospel, how persecution began, and the price some had to pay to follow Christ. Two ladies made a commitment at the end of this set of classes, which lasted more than a year.

In the meantime the ladies requested that we start a sewing project. They reasoned that if they wanted to follow this teaching, they would have to earn money the "right way." Many of the women were widows or divorcees who were involved in prostitution. Others were involved in drug trafficking. The opportunity to learn a skill was a natural incentive through which a growing number of unbelievers could be exposed to the gospel through CBS.

In the third year of CBS, I included the Daniel story, which made a real impression. I also showed Old Testament films from time to time so that the women could picture the lives of Abraham, Joseph, Moses, and the other patriarchs. I ended the CBS classes by showing Campus Crusade's *JESUS* film in the women's own language. What excitement filled my lounge that day as twenty-five Muslim women watched the crucifixion. Some were crying. Some were sneezing. Some were laughing.

Instead of inviting the ladies to publicly respond to the film, I asked them to write me a note. If they couldn't write, I told them to ask a friend or neighbor to help them. A few days later, Medina came to me with her letter, determined to follow Christ whatever the cost. After her decision, she became very instrumental in encouraging others to believe. When I showed the *JESUS* film another time, the breakthrough came. Four ladies accepted Christ; slowly, others followed.

It was a long process and a challenging one. Fear of husbands and families kept some women from committing themselves even after they knew and accepted the truth of the stories. During this time, two things helped me not to give up: 1) I was following a plan I knew had worked in other places; 2) I had local co-workers who faithfully helped and encouraged me and shared feedback from the participants among whom they lived.

Through this experience I learned many things. For instance, it is best for CBS classes to meet in neutral places like schools rather than in church buildings. Also, the approval and support of a person of influence is very helpful—perhaps vital. It is best to keep the format as a class or storytelling time rather than structure the time like a church service since many Muslim women are shy about singing Christian songs in the beginning. Teenagers are more open, however, and you may be able to introduce culturally based praise music earlier in a group of young people.

I also learned that each group has a different concentration span. Some like short stories, others like to listen to two stories at a time. The storyteller must be sensitive to the group. As is abundantly clear from my experience, one round of CBS stories might not be enough to enable solid decisions and changed lives. I also learned not to lead a group alone—to involve a co-worker from the beginning. She will not only provide encouragement and support, she will learn from you and eventually be ready to start her own group. Finally, it is helpful for national co-workers to visit members of the CBS group in between sessions. This enables you to know what they think about the stories and helps you adapt the sessions to meet their needs and correct any misunderstandings.

When she moved to another area, the first believer in our group started her own storytelling group with the help of one of my co-workers. I have never been there. They have done it all by themselves. These same two women founded a school with more than 100 students—eighty-five percent of whom are Muslim. Three times a week they are telling a set of stories specifically adapted for children in the school. The parents of some of the students are participating in an afternoon adult literacy class. They use a collection of Bible stories titled *Sharing the Message* by LaNette Thompson (Thompson 2003). Other ladies have begun storying groups in their neighborhoods for women who do not participate in the literacy or sewing projects. We provide these groups with tapes of the stories and picture books as well as encouragement and prayer support.

After we had three believers, we began an extra discipleship class for them using a storying set specifically developed for that purpose.

God has used our storying session as a model and encouragement for others. From time to time, different missionaries have observed the CBS sessions be-fore starting a group of their own. One lady combined storying with a quilting class she held with educated Asian women. Others have included CBS lessons in a sports program for Somali refugee girls and women, and in women's sewing classes.

Irregularity of attendance is the biggest problem we encounter in the neighborhood storytelling sessions. Muslim women do not usually attend the mosque on a regular basis but are encouraged to pray at home. A storytelling program with many regular sessions is a challenge for a number of them. Weddings, funerals, sicknesses, and community celebrations also result in frequent interruptions. Another distraction for the women is the presence of children or too many outsiders. We find it best to have separate classes for children when possible and also to limit the number and frequency of outside guests/observers.

People are much more eager to participate in the sessions and more consistent in their attendance when the storytelling sessions are held in conjunction with some kind of project. The incentive of secular learning or training in a valued skill helps sustain interest.

When Muslim women become believers, most do not see the need to attend church. Many prefer to meet with their teachers for individual Bible study or discipleship training. Teaching that believers need to meet together regularly to strengthen and encourage one another should be a priority in the discipleship-storying track.

Another challenge is deciding what to do at the end of a cycle of stories. The group could easily dissolve itself after some have become Christians and the rest decline to do so. In that case, it would be best for the believers to continue as a discipleship group. However, people are usually involved in projects for a few years, so, it may not be easy to just dissolve a group. In such cases the challenge is teaching a mixed group of believers and nonbelievers whose needs are different.

It is important to adapt your teaching style to the needs of the group. In urban settings, especially among teenagers and young adults, you may need to be innovative. We found it helpful to integrate drama, pictures, films, and object lessons to make the stories more interesting and memorable. The use of indigenous music, which captures the major message of each story, also has been effective in a variety of cultural settings.

Whatever methods and teaching resources you use, the most important thing is to enjoy sharing God's Word through stories. Become a good storyteller and demonstrate your trust, joy, hope, and faith in His stories. Let your own convictions be contagious. Love always finds a way!

Resources

Schultze, Dell G., and Rachel Sue. 1991. *God and Man*. Bamako, Mali.

Terry, J.O. 1998. *God and Woman*. International Mission Board.

Thompson, LaNette. 2003. *Sharing the message through storying: A Bible teaching method for everyone*. Rev. Ed. Bamako, Mali. International Mission Board.

Discussion Questions

1. Medina asked, "Can a curse make you so sick that you finally die?" How would you respond to this question?

2. In this study, Medina is afraid of her husband. She believes that the gospel of Jesus Christ is true, but she has a justifiable fear of her safety, possibly her life, if she becomes a Christian. If you were her friend, how would you help Medina deal with this fear?

3. When the two girls from the Bible study came to the missionary's house, what was the thought that challenged the girls to follow Jesus?

4. Muslims believe that the Bible has been corrupted and changed over time, and is therefore not the reliable Word of God. How could you interest a Muslim in studying the Bible if this is his/her belief?

5. The author of this study said that irregularity of attendance is the biggest problem in storytelling sessions. What would be two or three ways to encourage the ladies to be more regular in their attendance?

6. Is Bible storying a method you could see yourself using if you were in a Muslim country? If you were to start a series of Bible stories, how would you initially get people interested in your meetings?

26

Ministry to Body, Soul and Spirit: Church Planting in a South Asian Village

*I*n 1963 two single women entered a Muslim village of approximately 15,000 people. They had been commissioned by their sponsoring body to open a dispensary for women and children in the village. God had assured them that He would build His church there. So, with confidence that "nothing was impossible with God" (Luke 1:37), they began their search for a home and ministry center. Exactly where to live and how to begin their ministry had been a constant focus of their prayers as they sailed to their new country. God's answer to those prayers was an abandoned fruit and vegetable market. It not only could be renovated into the kind of place they needed, it was available for a low rent.

A contract was signed and the entire first year's rent was paid in cash. The money was used to make needed alterations. A large inner courtyard was constructed as a waiting area for patients. A bathroom was added at the end of the courtyard. Windows and the door facing the road were bricked and plastered with cement and a new secure entrance was built. New doors leading from the rooms to the veranda were added and the veranda was screened. A kitchen and a store room were added.

During the month of renovation, the town's people mingled freely among the workers and talked about the new medical clinic. Yes, indeed, these two women were Christians who would live in the village without electricity and running water. They would operate a dispensary for women and children. No, it would not be free but it would provide medicines at reduced prices and there would be no charge for the women's services. Yes, they would teach the

Bible and have classes for children. Yes, they spoke the national language and wore the same clothing as local women except for the Islamic shawl covering. Advertisements were unnecessary as word of mouth rapidly spread the news about the new clinic. The crowd even urged the workers to finish the alterations quickly!

FOUR GUIDING PRINCIPLES

God gave the two women four basic principles that would guide their ministry. Prayer was to be their means of ministry. The Bible was to be their absolute authority. Their open hearts and open home were to be God's bright witness in the village. By meeting felt needs, they were to help people and develop relationships with the lost.

The Importance of Prayer

Prayer, lots of prayer, preceded their arrival and continued to inform and guide their decisions and actions. The workers had two set prayer times together daily in addition to their personal devotional times. They also had daily prayer partners in their sponsoring churches. A goal was set for each of them to daily write two of these partnering churches to inform the members about both prayer needs and prayer answers. A prayer coordinator was appointed in each church. This person would receive their letters and duplicate them for the other members of the church.

Seekers, visitors and, later, students were identified and given code names to enable their prayer partners to specifically lift up these key individuals in daily prayer. Later as God brought people in the village to Himself, their names/code names were also sent to individuals and churches thus enabling them to labor in prayer for these new brothers and sisters in the faith as they grew in the Lord in an environment of pressure and persecution from their family and community.

The women used every opportunity to pray with local people over the situations in their lives, including praising God for His blessings, requesting His intervention in the midst of crises, and thanking Him for answered prayer. They believed that prayer in the presence of their workers and with those who came to visit was essential. Praying publicly before work assignments—teaching, preaching, visiting, counseling—helped demonstrate from the beginning that the work was God's, not that of His servants. Wisdom, power, and discernment as well as boldness, kindness, and ability all come from God and so all praise must also go to Him alone. Public praise, petition, and thanksgiving taught the people to look to God in their time of need, not to the workers.

As God worked in their hearts and people in the village came to faith, daily prayer times were held with the new believers. By clearly and openly acknowledging through prayer their dependence on God alone in all things, they declared themselves as His willing, obedient servants and directed praise to the Lord and not to themselves or their success. This commitment was an important safeguard and a great help later for the developing church. By lifting up the true King, personal kingdom building and the idolatrous worship of workers was discouraged.

The Authority of the Bible

The Bible was their standard of operations. It guided every aspect of their ministry. As completely as possible they depended on God's Word rather than tradition, the Western church, local customs, or what seemed nice or looked good because they knew that God had promised to bless His Word, not the cleverness of His worker's or their wonderful illustrations. They systematically taught the Bible through both doctrinal studies and expositional book studies in small groups, in formal classes, and in the children's classes. The Word of God, not liturgy, format or music, was the central element in their church services. Sharing God's Word was also an important part of home visitation. They found that telling Bible stories was a good way to teach and reach others and that using good visual aids to illustrate Bible truths enabled the living Word to powerfully impact villagers.

In Bible classes, their goal was not only for Scripture to be understood and applied to daily life, but also that it be memorized. They found that even long passages could readily be learned when this was prioritized in the classes. Memorized Scripture gave the Holy Spirit a continuous opportunity to work in the lives of students as He brought to mind and applied God's Word in their life situations.

Open Hearts/Open Homes

Keeping their hearts open to the people in their village was absolutely necessary. They soon recognized that their love was not sufficient. It was essential that God's love flow through them. Believers simply do not have enough love of their own to get the job done, and if they love only with human love they will react humanly. Slights, false accusations, lies, the loss of precious possessions or the first false profession of faith, will cripple workers, and make them ineffective. God's people are dependent on God to give them hearts of wisdom, understanding and love.

The workers also quickly realized the need to remind themselves daily of the reason they came to their village. This was especially important in times of loss, danger, and illness because Satan would take advantage of those situations to pour fear and doubt into their hearts and the hearts of the believers. They learned that the only way to keep an open heart was to focus on Jesus and to be ever ready for His filling.

Maintaining an open home was a ministry basic. They began by dedicating the renovated market room by room to God's purpose, asking Him to cleanse it from all evil influence either past or present. They committed to share both their joys and their sorrows with their neighbors. The practice of inviting others to share such joys as a new job, an educational achievement, or the birth of a new baby as well as the sorrows of defeat, loss, illness or death helped them become a vital part of the community. These times also enabled them to demonstrate their trust in God especially when they didn't understand what was happening or the reasons they were suffering.

Privacy is a Western manufactured item. They quickly learned that anything lying out was available to be handled, picked up for closer examination, eaten, or perhaps taken back to the visitor's own home to share. With God's help, they learned to keep their attitude right—things are only things! They are temporal not eternal and these women had come to focus on eternal matters.

Meeting Felt Needs
Besides their primary ministry of meeting medical needs, the workers also met other felt needs by providing training. School tutorials, cooking lessons, or training in gardening provided a way for people to come to the center for teaching on a regular, perhaps even a daily basis. The students would simultaneously learn a skill or have a need met, develop a relationship with a believer, and study the Word of God, all in a way that was acceptable to their families and the community as a whole. The dispensary for women and children, the children's tutorial program, the sewing program for teenage girls, and the typing program for boys were used by God in the lives of many villagers. Participation in any skills training class also involved participation in a Bible class. Potential students had to bring a signed permission slip from their family before beginning study.

The workers discovered that children's Bible classes needed to be open to all

who desired to attend. Often the breakdown of ages common in children's programs in the West was impossible in their setting. The goal in every class was to
promote the work of the Holy Spirit in the hearts of students by emphasizing
the biblical accounts, teaching doctrine, and stressing personal application of
the truth. They were careful not to pressure children to make decisions. Scripture
memory work was an important element in the children's classes. They encouraged children to learn long passages, but only after they understood the meaning and the application of the passage in their lives. Prayer was also essential in
these classes not only because of the great needs of the children and the workers,
but partly because it enabled the children to witness our dependence on God
Himself and to experience His faithfulness and power through answered prayer.
The workers always explained the gospel and how to commit oneself to the
Savior for His cleansing in every Bible class for they never knew whether they
would see a child again.

A CHURCH IS PLANTED

As the workers followed these ministry principles, God planted a church in the
village. Grace Church now has its own pastor—a man who as a young boy was
crippled with tuberculosis and crawled on the ground when the workers first
arrived in the village. He now walks without a limp, lives locally and works in a
Bible correspondence school office in another city. He is a married with four
sons and a wife who serves God with him. Both are baptized and widely
known as Christians in the village. In the 1980's the church was organized with
two committees: men dealing with men and women with women. To this date,
fifty women and twenty men have believed and been baptized through this
church planting effort. Some have passed into the Lord's presence as a teaching
elder did this summer. Some have moved away. There are ten who have openly
denied the Savior after many years of living for Him. Most of the believers are
faithfully walking with the Lord.

The dispensary is closed and the workers have retired, but the church continues. Christmas, 1999, fifty people attended the service and took communion at
the church. The previous day, over 300 children attended a children's Christmas
celebration. In the spring of 2000 the JESUS video was offered to video rental
stores in the village. Sixty copies have been placed and are being rented. Home
visitation continues among both men and women. Prayer meetings are held
regularly. Children's classes are not, although there are at least ten women who
are able to teach and plenty of teaching materials on hand. The families of the

children object to not having a Westerner in the class to assure good moral standards for the protection of their women.

One of the women workers recently reflected on her experience, "In hindsight, I feel that we should have placed more emphasis on training villagers for jobs in the general work force. This would have helped families and also the church. The women are stronger believers and women's leadership in their area of responsibility in the church is also stronger. In my opinion, the general favoritism and pampering of the boys in a Muslim society has hindered the men from growing in their faith and excelling in their leadership. Despite twenty years of discipleship classes the boys and men have not yet overcome this cultural handicap. The decision against importing a pastor has proven to be a wise thing as was the decision to locally educate the pastor God raised up. The decision and years of effort put into becoming a part of the community in our village was a very important step." It is clear that "God has worked in power and to God is the glory and praise."

Discussion Questions

1. Why were these single women confident that God wanted them to work in a South Asian Muslim village?

2. What did they do to increase their personal security and insure the respectability of their ministry? How might their preparations be different in other regions of the Muslim world?

3. How did the workers facilitate faith in God through the medical care they offered?

4. Why was it important for them to realize that their love for the people was not sufficient? Is it important for supporters to realize their lack of love for Muslims, as well? How could you encourage your supporters to increase their love for Muslims?

5. What other kinds of training did the women provide? How did this training increase the credibility and spread of the gospel?

6. Muslim children learn the Qur'an by heart before they understand its meaning. How did the children's Bible memorization in this setting differ?

7. Why would it be important to train villagers for jobs in the local workforce as well as bring them the gospel? Why is leadership in Muslim societies often more difficult for men than for women?

27

Sowing in Tears: A Tale from Beirut

*I*t is a beautiful, sunny day in the southern suburbs of Beirut. It has been raining for days on end so the sun was a tremendous relief to the inhabitants of the shanty town where I work which houses over 30,000 people. They are mostly gypsies, native-born Lebanese without citizenship, and people from various Middle Eastern countries who looked for a better life by coming to Lebanon. When it rains, the roads in the shanty town become rivers and the mud and garbage flow freely through the streets. The houses, which are made of tin, cardboard, and wood, fill with water, soaking all the clothes and belongings inside. Sickness and disease are rampant under such conditions and the little two-room house that serves as a day clinic is over-burdened with patients all during the winter months.

On this particular day, I arrived early at the clinic to begin setting up for the day. The dead cockroach carcasses are being carried away by swarms of ants. Water runs down the walls and onto the linoleum-covered floor. Although by modern standards it would be considered primitive at best, this is a palace for the poor, forgotten, and unloved in the shanty town. Unrecognized by their own government, these women had found someone to consider their plight and put arms of love around them. Within minutes of my arrival, there are more than thirty faces crammed through the metal bars on the gate, begging for a place on the day's schedule. Only twenty patients will be seen and invariably a fight ensues between those unfortunate enough not to make it on the list and those who made it.

Among those waiting to be seen by the doctor, is a young woman who looks very sad and miserable. I noticed her because she stood to the side, quietly and timidly, while the others pushed and shoved to get a turn. Going to her, I asked her for her name. Fatime, I learned, was fifteen years old. Her two-year-old was at her side and her one-month-old was in her arms. I asked her why she had come and she said she was tired, her baby did not sleep at night, and she had no milk to nurse him. I could tell she was extremely depressed and needed someone to talk to. I invited Fatime in and made her a cup of tea. Her dress was soaking wet and when I asked her why, she told me that all the clothes in their house were wet from the rain. I took her in the back room and dressed her in clean, dry clothes and she thanked me with tears.

Fatime's story was heartbreaking. She told me how her in-laws who lived in the same house shouted at her because her baby cried during the night. One night when she slept through her baby's crying from sheer exhaustion she was dragged her off her mat and beaten by her husband. Tears ran down Fatime's cheeks as she described her life for me. How could she possibly have any milk to nurse her baby when all she had eaten for days was fried cauliflower and bread that her nephew had brought her from the garbage dump? I could not hold back tears myself as I realized how hopeless these women's lives were.

I sat in shock as she told me how a curse had been placed on her baby when a wicked woman had come to visit her and she failed to put a soiled diaper above the doorframe. Evidently this woman has "an evil eye" and it is believed that if she visits the home of a newborn baby and the proper "protection" is not present, the baby will be cursed. Fatime believed with all her heart that because she had not put the necessary dirty diaper above the door, this woman had cursed her baby and this was why he cried all the time. What could I say in response to such foolishness? I'd never heard anything so absurd in my life! I simply told Fatime that only God could protect us against evil and that she need only to call on Him and he would protect her. How could I possibly convey to her the message of a loving God who sees her pain and loves her deeply?

As I learned more about Fatime's life, I found out that she'd been married at the age of thirteen. Every night when her husband would approach her, she would scream and kick and run away to her mother's house for refuge. Angrily, her father would beat her and take her back to her husband, a man she detested in every way and could only speak about with disdain. Her husband had another wife who was much older and had who had born him several children. She was old enough to be Fatime's mother and took on that role, teaching her younger co-wife the ways of deception that all Muslim women must learn in order to survive. Since Fatime had never known the love of a man, how would she be able to comprehend the love of her heavenly father? I put my arms around her and held her tight as she wept.

Fatime came often to the clinic, not because she was necessarily sick but because she had found someone who truly loved her and was willing to listen to her tale of misery. There was little I could do to help her other than cry with her and physically put my arms around her, but this seemed to speak volumes to her. Although I never was able to tell her about God's love through His Son, Jesus, I pray that she sensed His love through me in a small way. I believe that the Holy Spirit can reveal Jesus to her in her dreams and I pray that when she sees Jesus, she will know that He is the only way to true peace and happiness.

WOMEN, ISLAMIC TEACHING AND SOCIAL REALITY

There are millions of women all over the Middle East like Fatime who are in bondage to a religion that considers them a man's possession, only valuable for the children she bears and the pleasure she gives. In 1915, Samuel Zwemer said of the Muslim girl,

> . . . she looks forward with fear and dread to marriage with a man whom she may never have seen; she is early trained in all those ways of deceit which are the protection of the weak and helpless against strength and authority, and jealousy is one of her ruling passions. Unwelcome at birth, always considered inferior to her brothers and father and husband, and surrounded by so much in this religion that means degradation and humiliation, who can blame her if she is not happy. (Zwemer 1915, 63)

In his book, *The Closed Circle*, David Pryce-Jones says, "Underage marriage, divorce by simple repudiation, appropriation and abuse of a woman's property by males in her family, even polygamy, are increasingly disregarded by authorities, in the correct belief that it is futile and unjust to pick on some man who is only doing what he believes is customary and sanctioned by Islam" (2002:136). In so many Muslim countries it doesn't matter what is written on paper; the social reality is what's important!

Working with uneducated Arabic-speaking women, I have observed that they try earnestly to follow the pillars of Islam, believing that if they can be good

Muslims in this life, they will at least have joy and peace in the next. They strive to pray five times a day. One woman told me she gets up and says her prayers in the early morning because God hears those prayers and answers them more than the others. In Muslim eyes, it is all about human efforts and what people do to please God rather than what God has done for them. Muslim women believe that the more difficult the act, such as waking up and splashing cold water on your face at 4 a.m., the more God will be pleased with you and answer you. The more people do here on earth, the more merit they believe will be stored up in heaven. Yet the conditions for offering pure, unadulterated prayer to God are so legalistic and impossible to perform consistently that I wonder how any Muslim could have certainty that all the requirements have been met. For a Christian who can come to God in prayer at any time of the day, in any condition, it is unthinkable that a woman would have to wash her private parts, for instance, or refrain from cutting her nails or removing her socks just in order to offer prayer to God! What do these things have to do with spirituality? What a dichotomy between law and grace! "And yet we find Muslims thanking Allah for revealing these directives that clearly define the will of God for even the smallest details of life."

The Problem of Pollution

Women are especially subject to scrutiny when it comes to offering prayer to Allah. They are obsessed with being ceremonially clean and it is often the main topic of conversation among them. "Did you take a bath after last night's sexual encounter?" "Are you having your period today?" Since a woman's main function in life is to have children, she is pregnant most of her child-bearing years and unclean for at least forty days after each birth. Being an OB/GYN nurse, I have had many women come to me desperate for some kind of cure for bleeding so that they can pray. A woman also cannot fast during Ramadan if she has her period or any kind of discharge. She can and must make up those fast days later in the year, however, or all the days she fasted prior to her bleeding will count for nothing. In Muslim perspective, God would not be pleased if an unclean woman offered prayer to him. He also would not accept the prayers of an unveiled woman. If a woman is uncovered and causes a man to sin, it is considered to be her fault and she must be punished. The majority of Muslim women will cover their bodies from head to foot, therefore, so as not to tempt any man who might otherwise lust after her and thus fall into sin. If a woman is uncovered and causes a man to sin, it is considered to be her fault and she must be punished. Can a Muslim woman understand the concept of a just God when all she has ever known is injustice?

Women and Folk Islam

Uneducated Muslim women seem particularly to be guided by the superstitious beliefs that have been passed on to them for generations. They turn their coffee cups over when they finish drinking, for instance, and determine their future in the coffee grounds. They believe the "eye" with its blue stone over the doorpost will protect all who enter the house and will pin all kinds of charms and trinkets with blue stones on a newborn's clothes to keep away the evil eye. Often they will put navy eyeliner on a newborn baby's eyes to ward off the evil spirits. This practice has been known to cause blindness and eye infections yet they continue to do it. How can we overcome these strong beliefs and their fear of the "spirit world" with God's message of peace and security?

Muslims also believe very strongly in dreams and often have them interpreted by a "professional." Thankfully, one of the ways that Muslims are coming to faith in Christ is through dreams. Nothing is more powerful than praying for the sick in Jesus' name and seeing them healed. A little five-year-old Muslim girl used to come to our neighborhood kids' club. She had an incurable kidney disease and carried her catheter bag around by her side. She was a beautiful little girl whose parents liked us a lot and who saw the joy and peace that we had. One day they brought little Zahara to the church and asked the pastor to pray for her. In faith, we all laid hands on her and prayed in Jesus' name that she would be healed. A week later when she went for her doctor's appointment, they removed the catheter bag because there was no more need for it! The little girl told everyone that she was healed at the church.

In an uneducated society, there is much reliance on supernatural understanding and the interpretation of dreams and visions. Muslims believe in a hierarchy of spirits and rely on more powerful spirits to intervene when the ordinary ones fail to work. A mother once recounted to me the story of her young daughter whose skin split open in several different places. They rushed her to the hospital where a surgeon sewed the skin shut. Within hours, the skin split open again in the exact same place. This happened several times. Finally, the family took the girl to a powerful *shaykh* in the camp who cast out her possessing spirits and she was relieved of this strange condition. There is a strong belief in the power of Satan and they understand perfectly the idea of casting him out, invoking the name of a higher spirit. We must learn to call upon the most powerful of all spirits, God Almighty himself, to show his power and might in situations where there is no hope.

No one should attempt to work among Muslims without the weapons of spiritual warfare. The war is raging on every front and will only be won as we claim the blood of Jesus over situations beyond our control or explanation and as we spend time in fasting and prayer.

Women and the Word

Without the benefit of God's word as a major tool of evangelism it is much more difficult to witness to uneducated, illiterate women. Thus, it is important to memorize key verses and rely heavily on memorization in the discipleship process. In one of our Bible studies we would have races and prizes for those who could memorize the scripture verses. The women were eager to learn and would quickly memorize these verses as well as the words to the songs we sang, singing right along with us. Literacy classes give women work skills that can help them become employable. They can also help their children with their schoolwork if they themselves learn to read. I have seen amazing changes in a woman's countenance when she learns to read. A whole new world is opened up to her.

MINISTRY ISSUES AMONG THE POOR AND UNEDUCATED

If we try to summarize the plight of the poor and uneducated Muslim woman, we will conclude that the complex issues in this ministry are much different than those with literate women and they must be reached with the gospel in a unique way. Boys, first of all, are always preferred over girls at birth because the family knows what a miserable life their daughter will face; even an uneducated boy can get a job and help support the family, but a girl is just a worry and a concern for them. Second, girls are married off at an early age, from twelve to fifteen years old in most families, because their poor parents cannot afford to feed them. Furthermore, if anyone receives an education in the family, it will be the boys; why would a girl need to go to school, they reason, just to have babies and tend to her husband? Third, although there are laws in many countries protecting women's rights, they are only laws on paper; society's rules are what count. Finally, women's lack of education breeds ignorance on every front, causing them to believe foolish myths and superstitions passed on from previous generations. Illiteracy prohibits women from knowing other opinions or ideas and binds them to what the men in their lives tell them is truth. Men want to keep it that way since they are threatened by the idea of an educated woman.

How can we overcome these barriers and allow for open dialogue and change to take place among women? How can we present a gospel of love, peace, joy, security, hope, and self-esteem when those qualities are only a far-off dream for most Muslim women? Where do we begin in our search for answers to their desperate cries?

I am convinced that the answers will not come through more book knowledge or study of the religion. There will not be a break-through into this society of Muslim women by simply praying for them or giving to their physical needs, although that is of utmost importance. I believe change will come when we are willing to go and live incarnationally among them; when we accept the challenge of walking in their shoes and listening to their story, of weeping with them and putting our arms around them.

We have too many "experts" on Islam living in their comfortable suburban America; it can be costly to live among Muslim women. It cost my friend and clinic co-worker, Bonnie Witherall, her very life. Had Jesus not been willing to leave heaven and come to this earth and live a holy life among us, he would not have been able to purchase our salvation. Loving these women through holistic ministries such as women's health clinics, literacy classes, pre- and post-natal classes is the primary way that they will see a different gospel. They'll see a gospel that is for THEM, a God who loves THEM and even died for THEM. By meeting their physical and emotional needs, we open the door for sharing the cure to their spiritual needs. The problem is that, in this age of quick fixes and instant everything, we are not willing to spend the years it will take to bring change to the Muslim women of the world.

Resources

Pryce-Jones, David. 2002. *The closed circle: An interpretation of the Arabs.* Chicago: Ivan R. Dee

Zwemer, Samuel Marinus. 1915. *Childhood in the Muslim World.*

Discussion Questions:

1. What is your opinion about the "wicked woman" who put a curse on the baby? Do you believe the woman really cursed the baby, or is there another reason why the baby wouldn't stop crying?

2. In the case study, the woman writing the account explained to Fatime

that only God could protect us against evil and that she need only to
call on Him, and He would protect her. Is there anything else you
would say to help the woman understand God's protection?

3. Every aspect of a Muslim's life must follow Allah's law, including when
they cut their fingernails, how they remove their socks, how they use the
restroom, how/and when they wash, how/and when they pray. Why do
you think many Muslims would thank Allah for giving them such a strict
law to follow?

4. In this article, the author says, "If a woman is uncovered and causes a
man to sin, it is considered to be her fault and she must be punished."
What is your reaction to this? Based on this worldview, how do you
think the Muslim world views the way Western women dress?

5. In the situation where the girl's skin split, she was taken to the hospital
and her skin was sewn shut, but after a few hours, it split again. After this
occurred several times, the family took the girl to a shaykh. He was able
to cast out the spirits that were causing this condition. What was the
authority by which the *shaykh* healed the girl in this example? Why do
you think this heakling worked?

6. Why do you think men are threatened by the idea of an educated
woman?

7. At the end of this article, the author states that there will not be a break-
through into the society of Muslim women by simply praying or meeting
physical needs. What does she say is the primary way to reach Muslim
women with the gospel?

1 Corinthians 13 for Muslim Workers

Though I speak classic and common Arabic
Smoothly and fluently
Enabling me to flawlessly recite all 114 *suras* of the Qur'an
But have not sacrificial God-given love,
I have only become a *tabafra* or clanging tambourine.

And though I can predict people's responses
And tell you all they try to hide
And have all knowledge
And perfect faith so much that Mt. Everest could be moved by it
And have not His love for Muslims,
I am nothing at all.

And though I triple *zakat* yearly to each poor person I meet
And join in the *Muhhran* beatings until I am a bloodied pulp
And have not His love,
It does me not a bit of good.

His love through me suffers long and is patient and kind:
His love is not jealous or covetous;
It is not the show-off, puffed-up type.

Nor does it humiliate or ridicule or broadcast its name
Over the mosque loudspeaker,
It is not quickly made angry, nor does it speak revenge or plan evil retribution.
It doesn't rejoice to see evil win, but rejoices as truth conquers.

His love in me
Stands up to all things
Believes all things
Hopes all things
Endures all things.

His love in me never fails.
But where there are forecastings, tea leaf, or coffee ground predictions, they will fail;
Where there is a babel of varied languages, they will end;
Knowledge, too, will vanish away quickly.

Right now we know only a little bit
And make up the remainder to suit our agenda.
But when that which is absolute perfection has come,
Then that which is in part will pass out of the picture.

Before I was accountable, I acted, thought, spoke as a child;
But when I was mature, I put away children's things,
Whether actions, words, motives, or worldly gain.

Now though face-to-face in a mirror
I can see somewhat
And know in some ways,
Then I shall have all knowledge
And be thoroughly known by all around me.

FAITH-HOPE-LOVE are reality forevermore.
Greatest of all is His love.

— Earlene Voss

APPENDIX I
Cultural Research Questions

Miriam Adeney

General

Briefly describe the people's physical environment, demographic statistics and political environment.

Family

1. What is the role of each member of the family?
2. How companionable is the husband-wife relationship? How much trust, respect and understanding is there? How much disrespect, deception, or tension?
3. How much freedom does the woman have? How much authority? Give examples. How much education has she had? What is her economic role?
4. How are the children taught? How are they disciplined? How important are other adults in socializing the child? How important is the child's peer group? How much does the father play with the child? How long do the parents control the child's choices? Is there a generation gap? How do people try to bridge it?
5. What do the old people do? How do other family members treat them?
6. How does the family make decisions? Who takes the lead? Are there discussions? How does the family settle quarrels? Describe some quarrels you have seen or been told about. Who are the most loyal family members? Who are the least loyal? Are there some marginal members?
7. How is the family related to other structures in society—to the neighborhood, to kin, and to community organizations?

Social Structure

8. Who are the community opinion leaders, including media and national or local figures?
9. What is the community decision-making unit and process?
10. How does the community settle quarrels?
11. What are the natural lines of affiliation? (these may tie individuals to several networks)

12. In their most common group what are the rights and obligations of members, their distinctive roles, special rituals or celebrations, myths or special group reputation, role models, villains, techniques of boundary maintenance and distinctions between formal and informal behaviors?

Communication

13. What are their topics of conversation, joys, achievements (from their point of view), failures, and heroes? What are they reading and listening to? Where are they traveling? What questions are they asking?
14. Do they have any in-group language, codes, or symbols?
15. Do they have any distinct kinds of humor?
16. What kinds of media do they prefer: books, magazines, newspapers, leaflets, comics, radio, TV, tapes, drama, music, demonstrations, posters?
17. What style of verbal arrangement do they prefer: nonfiction, narrative, poetry, myth, proverbs, comics, debates, frankness or subtlety, abstractions or references to tangible things, induction or deduction, lectures or case studies, memorization or problem-centered learning, enthusiasm or formal presentations?
18. What are the main themes of columnists in national newspapers and magazines?

Economy

19. What are the local natural resources?
20. What are the common local products made for home use or for sale?
21. What is the spread of occupations?
22. What percent of the population is rich, comfortable, subsistence level or destitute? Do these economic class lines coincide with other classifications (i.e., kin, caste) or do they cut across these divisions, tying people together?
23. What is the average daily diet?
24. Do they consider themselves impoverished, or not?
25. What kinds of expenditure do they delight in, such as clothes, parties, insurance policies, investments or labor-saving gadgets, etc.?
26. What kinds of expenditure do they consider extravagant?
27. What do economists think are the country's chief economic problems? Its assets? Its economic opportunities?

28. What do neighbors think the country's chief economic problems are? How do they experience these?

29. Is there a Marxist movement among university students? What are their specific complaints?

30. Is there economic tension between ethnic groups?

31. What percent own their own land and/or business?

32. What are some of the most powerful political and economic entities in the environment of these people? How do they feel about these?

33. In the main, what social class in the national system do these people occupy? What are the functions or potential functions of this class in the total system?

34. How are the large political and economic entities likely to affect these people over the next ten years? Hypothesize various alternative scenarios.

Religion

35. What do they turn to in a time of crisis?

36. What do they think is humankind's origin and destiny?

37. What do they think will provide a full and meaningful life?

38. Do they think there is any transcendent power in the universe? Do they think they can relate to it? If so, how?

39. What are their ideas of the supernatural, God, Christ, human beings, sin, and Christians?

40. What moral system do they actually try to live by?

41. Do they participate in more than one religion? If so, when, where and concerning what do they express these faiths?

Values

42. What are their distinct felt needs?

43. What are their distinct values? Economic problems, ethnic history, social tensions, marital or generational conflicts, problems in housing, schooling, medicine, legal justice, recreation, technology, childraising patterns, art, vocational aspirations, modernization or obsolescence, attitudinal emphases such as romantic love, loneliness, pleasure, family pride, friendliness, achievement, communal solidarity may contribute to values and or needs.

44. What do these people consider to be the significant events of the last thirty years or the last 500 years? How have they reacted?

APPENDIX II
Constructing a Worldview
A Cultural-Social-Religious Profile of a Target People
A Development Process and Instrument

This instrument is designed to be used during the ethnographic interviews among the target population as one gathers information in order to construct a people profile, a worldview of the culture. Adaptation of this instrument for use in varied settings is recommended. Answers to the questions should, if at all possible, be secured on-site, within the culture being studied. It is best that the research or survey be accomplished among those people who live in the ethno-graphic center of the culture. Avoid surveying only fringe people, or people who are no longer living within the boundaries of the culture being studied. Individuals being interviewed should be like the majority of the people within the culture.

1. Family Structure
   1.1 Is the family monogamous or polygamous? Describe the characteristics and conditions. Is the family matriarchal or patriarchal? Describe the "head of the house."
   1.2 What are the authority lines in the family? Who makes decisions—how, when and why?
   1.3 What are the expectations and rules for getting permission?
   1.4 What are the expectations and rules for getting forgiveness?
   1.5 What are the roles and consequent relationships between family members? Include husband, wife, children, relatives. What is the difference at different levels in the society and for the different ages? Who is responsible for whom, when and how?
   1.6 Identify kinship lines and patterns of the extended family.
   1.7 How do families support themselves in this culture? What are the traditional and non-traditional means of support?
   1.8 How does the family structure change as a result of death, marriage, separation, incapacity, incompetence, or other significant changes?
   1.9 How is a family's heritage passed from one generation to the next?
   1.10 Do families have totems? What are typical ones and how are they used?
   1.11 How is authentic news passed on within the family?

1.12 What are the rules of inheritance?

1.13 What are the sexual and mating roles and rules in the family? What are marriage rites and rules?

How are grievances settled within a family? What are the rules concerning mistreatment, separation, divorce, or a mistress?

1.14 What are the child-rearing practices and traditions?

1.15 How do children choose their life vocation, their role in the community?

1.16 What are the special days or events for families?

1.17 How is the family changing?

1.18 How does an individual defend himself or herself within the family?

2. Social Structure

2.1 How is the society of a community organized? What are the typical, the common homogenous and heterogeneous facets of society?

2.2 How do different families relate to each other? How do families meet other families in the community? What are the rules of meeting and making friends?

2.3 How is one's place in a village society or a community determined? Is there a caste system or other type of structure within the culture?

2.4 How does society relate to foreigners? Foreigners from another city, another race, another tribe, another country? What are the attitudes and rules of relating?

2.5 How is real estate handled? What are the rules of ownership, selling and buying?

2.6 How do individuals become an adult? Are there rules of recognition and rites of passage? At what age or ages do they occur? What are the circumstances of their occurrence?

2.7 What rights do individuals have within a community, within society? What right do families have? What rights do clans have within society? What rights do males have? What rights do females have?

2.8 How are leaders chosen? Who is eligible? When are they eligible? Under what conditions and by what rules are they chosen?

2.8.1. How are leaders recognized by society, by the community?

2.8.2. How are leaders changed?

2.8.3. What are the rights and responsibilities of leaders

2.8.4. How do leaders lose the right to lead?

2.8.5. How do individuals relate to their leaders?

2.8.6. How do leaders relate to other leaders in the culture?

  2.9 What are the basic values within society that give it cohesion and security?

2.10 What are the basic taboos within society?

2.11 What are common traditions within society?

2.12 What are the valued arts or art forms in society?

2.13 What are the learning preferences of the people? Are most of the people oral communicators or are they mostly literate communicators?

2.14 How is communication carried out? With whom? What are the rules?

2.15 What are the channels for news? Who can bear news? How? When and how is news recognized as official and authentic? Is there a certain place, time, or art form whereby truth or authentic and authoritative news is given to the community?

2.16 How are individuals "educated" concerning rules within the community, society, and the culture?

2.17 How are individuals educated? Is there a formal education system such as schools? Is it for everyone? Is it pervasive? Is it respected? Is it effective?

2.18 Describe the vocational respect ladder within society? What are the levels?

2.19 Describe how the society looks upon marriage? What are the rules in society concerning courtship, engagement, marriage and divorce?

2.20 What are the rules of dress within society?

2.21 Describe law and order within society? Structure? Processes?

2.22 Describe medical care within the society? Type? Structure? Practitioners?

3. Religious Structure

    3.1 Describe the predominant religious system or systems in society?

    3.2 Does the religion express belief in a god or gods? Name and describe them. If they have a pluralistic belief in gods, what are the relationships between the gods?

    3.3 Chart and describe the people's spirit world (beings, places and status).

    3.4 Where does the power and authority reside in the religion/s? What is the source of the authority and the power?

3.5 Do the people believe in miracles and magic? Are they superstitious?

3.6 What part do deceased ancestors play in the religion? Is there interaction between the living and the dead?

3.7 What are the primary documents of the religion?

3.8 What are the common religious rites and events?

3.9 What is their view about the Godhead and the position of God?

3.10 What are the characteristics of the God within their religion?

3.11 What are the basic beliefs? About God? About good and evil? About life? About the source of life & creation? About death? About mankind? About spirits? About wrong, sin, and guilt? About eternity? About salvation? About life after death? About sickness? About securing converts or adherents? About deviates from the religion? About women?

3.12 How does an individual relate to the religion? Is personal choice respected?

3.13 How does religion involve society? How does it relate to society? How does society relate to religion? What position does religion have within society?

3.14 How does religion involve family?

3.15 How does religion view foreigners?

3.16 How does religion view other religions?

3.17 Who are the religious leaders? How are they chosen? Under what conditions and by what rules? How are religious leaders recognized and sanctioned?

3.18 Does the religion teach and do the believers use charms, or amulets and enter into magical rites?

3.19 What is the relationship between the seen world and the unseen world?

3.20 Is/are the religion/s animistic or mixed with animism?

4. Economic Structure.

4.1 Is society's economic structure agrarian, industrial or mixed?

4.2 What are the primary drivers of the economy? Capitalism, socialism or others? Describe the economy.

4.3 What are the primary economic and vocational categories and divisions in the economy?

4.4 What are the structural patterns within society?

4.5 How are prices determined? What are the major influences on prices?

4.6 Who is in control of the flow of money?

4.7 Who is in control of the financial institutions? Are their private financial processes as strong or influential as the public institutions?

4.8 Describe the traditional classes in the economy? Lower/Middle/Upper

4.9 Is a barter culture in existence? Does it predominate? Is it significant? How does the economy relate to other countries?

4.10 How is social security provided? Within family, social, or governmental structure?

5. National Political Structure.

5.1 How does the national political structure differ from the local structure? This category varies so much in approach and sensitivity, that it is best for this to be constructed locally.

Prepared by: Dr. Jim Slack, IMB,SBC Global Evangelism and Church Growth Consultant. Used with permission.

APPENDIX III
Constructing a Worldview
A Cultural-Social-Religious Profile of a Target People
A Supplement Instrument for Chronological Bible Storying

This instrument is a supplement to the larger worldview instrument and is not a substitute for that document. The larger document is needed during the storying planning process in identifying the similarities and barriers to the gospel. The information coming from this documentation process is needed in determining story style and formats.

1. Literacy
   1.1. What is the literacy level of the population? Government's figure? Other authoritative figures?
   1.2. How is literacy defined by the government?
   1.3. What is the illiteracy level of the population?
   1.4. Functional illiteracy level of the population (percent of population that has not made it to or has not gone beyond the 6th grade level in school.)
   1.5. Percent of the total population classified as illiterate and functionally illiterate combined. Combine the percentage figures of 1.3. and 1.4. This figure, or percentage figure, is the oral communication percent of the population. A combined percentage of 50percent or more indicates that the target population is clearly an oral communication culture.

2. Heritage information.
   2.1 Do the people have a heritage that is passed on to successive generations?
   2.2 Is the people's heritage passed on by members of society to today's generation of children?
   2.3 What is the current status of the heritage information?
      2.3.1. Was it originally orally communicated?
      2.3.2. Has it been reduced to writing?
      2.3.3. Has it been recorded in audio or video format?
      2.3.4. Does the oral format also exist today?
      2.3.5. In what language or languages does this information reside?
      2.3.6. Is the heritage passed on privately or publicly?
      2.3.7. Is the heritage passed on through ritualistic rites?

2.4. How have the people traditionally passed on their heritage to the next generation?

2.5. In what way is the heritage information passed on today?

2.6. Is there a fairy tale/folklore collection that is distinct from the heritage collection?

2.7. Do the people have totems?

2.8. Are characteristics and values assigned to certain animals for use in stories?

2.9. Is there a primary, well known, and public heritage story of the people that has been produced in a textual format?

2.10. Do the people use storytelling as an artform to tell their heritage stories?

2.11. Do families perpetuate their heritage primarily by storytelling?

2.12. Is there a special time when the heritage stories are told?

2.13. Is there a specified place where heritage stories are told?

2.14. Are the heritage stories taught in the school system?

2.15. Are the heritage stories considered to be true, or are they understood to be mythological?

3. Storytelling.

3.1. Is storytelling common among the people?

3.2. Are there special words in the language for storytelling? Are there words that set apart storytelling from any heritage rituals that are told? Do they share the same terms?

3.3. Are stories told among the people that are distinctly different from the heritage stories?

3.4. Is there formal and informal storytelling?

3.5. Who tells stories? Do men and women tell stories to the same audience? Do young and old tell stories before the same audience?

3.6. Are individuals designated formally or known informally as storytellers?

3.7. Is storytelling an artform among the people? What are the primary artforms of the people?

3.8. What is/are the dominant artform/s? Narrative/Drama/Chanting/Singing/Drums/Mixture

3.9. Are the religion(s) of the people perpetuated by storytelling or variations of that methodology?

3.10. How carefully do storytellers stick to the story? Are changes or variations acceptable?

3.11. Does the audience participate in the story and interact with the story-teller?

3.12. In cases when songs are used in conjunction with stories, is the vocabulary of the songs the same as the stories?

3.13. Are stories told competitively?

3.14. What mnemonic conventions are used in telling the stories which aid memory and capture the hearer's attention?

3.15. How are stories introduced? What are the introductory words and phrases that are used by storytellers? Do some of the phrases denote that a story is mythological and other phrases that the story is true, an historical event?

3.16. How is repetition achieved within the story? Is there repetition, and how often does it occur within a given story?

3.17. Are imitation and mimicry common parts of the storytellers style?

3.18. Describe the use of tone by the storyteller.

3.19. Are the introductions and conclusions of the stories very similar? Are there stock phrases, or certain formulas that are common to the intro-ductions and conclusions of many of the stories?

3.20. How is the moral of the story revealed? Are individuals left to them-selves to discover the moral of each of the stories? Are there language markers that identify the moral of the story? Is the moral positioned in a certain place so as to be identified?

3.21. How much exposition, explaining of the story, is done by the story-teller?

3.22. Is there some kind of discussion or application of the story that takes place after a story is told?

3.23. How is the change of time, or a shift in movement, or focus within the story conveyed to the audience? Is this done verbally, by songs, or by other means?

Prepared by: Dr. Jim Slack, IMB, SBC. Used with permission

APPENDIX IV
Resources for Chronological Bible Storying

Chronological Bible Storying Web site: www.chronologicalbiblestorying.com

Condensed World Mission Course (CWMC) Living Springs International. P.O. Box 149, #7 Roman St. Butuan City 8600, THE PHILIPPINES, at lsinter@skyinet.net. Available through Living Springs International.

Hall, Annette. 1999. "Producing Mature Fruit." Makati City, Philippines: CMS Publishing

Schultze, Dell G. and Rachel Sue Schultze, 1991. God and Man. Bamako, Mali: [no publisher]; Bobo Dioulasso, Burkina Faso: [no publisher].

Stacey, Vivienne. 1994. Bible Studies for Enquirers and New Believers. Singapore: BAC Printers.

Terry, J.O. 1998. God and Woman. International Mission Board, SBC.

_____ 1999. Good News for Those With Stories of Grief. International Mission board, SBC.

_____ 2000. Heaven Is for Women. International Mission Board, SBC.

_____ 2000, rev 2003. The Water Stories. International Mission Board, SBC.

Thompson, LaNette. 2003. Sharing the Message Through Storying: A Bible Teaching Method for Everyone . Rev. ed. Bamako, Mali. L. Thompson with the International Mission Board

Wiebe, Joyce: 1999. Discipleship Bible Studies, Several story series on CD-ROM available from Arab World Ministries.

Willis, Avery, et. al. 2003. Following Jesus: Making Disciples of Primary Oral Learners. Set of CDs For information look to: http://fjseries.org or www.ProgressiveVision.org

GLOSSARY

adhan	the Muslim call to prayer performed by the muezzin from the minaret
adat	customary law, customs and culture
aqal	the human ability to reason in Islamic philosophy
Allah	the Muslim name for God
barakah	blessings from God giving special abilities and powers
bid'ah	innovation; a practice or belief not present in Islamic sacred texts
bilal	one who performs the call to prayer
bismillah	the invocation of God used prior to any activity
burqa	a garment that conceals the shape of the female body
dar al-Harb	the territory of war where Muslims are in a minority
dar al-Islam	the territory of peace where Islamic law prevails
dikhr	a rhythmic devotional practice among Sufi Muslims
du'a	a non-ritual prayer; written or verbal supplication in distinction to the formal *salat*
fatawa	a legal opinion given by an ayatollah or mufti (legal expert) in which the Shariah law is applied to a new problem or case.
fiqh	religious jurisprudence and application of the Shariah law
fitnah	civil strife, war, riots, chaos
fitrah	the "primordial nature"; a return to the pure human nature and harmony between God and human beings
Hadith	traditions or reports of the words, practices and interpretations attributed to Muhammad
hadji	a title given to one who has made the pilgrimage to Mecca

hajj	the pilgrimage to Mecca, one of the Five Pillars of Islam
halal	that which is lawful in Islam
hamdalah	"praise to God"; said at the end of meals, to mark the end of an activity and as an interjectory comment
haram	that which is unlawful in Islam
harim	the women's quarters in a Muslim home
hijab	"a veil" or "partition"; today it commonly refers to the veil that women must wear in order to adhere to the standards of modesty
hijrah	the emigration of the Prophet Muhammad to Yathrib/Medina and the starting date for the Islamic calendar
'ibadah	Islamic acts of ritual or worship
Iblis	the name of Satan in the Qur'an
ijma'	a consensus of the Muslim community on a question of law; used along with the Qur'an, Hadith and Sunnah as a basis for law.
ijtihad	"effort;" applied to questions not covered by the Qur'an or Sunnah, or through established precedent or direct analogy from known laws
'ilm	knowledge; especially religious knowledge
imam	one who stands in front; a religious leader in the community; among Shiites, one of the twelve legitimate successors to Muhammad
injil	the Gospel; the revelation or book given to Isā (Jesus)
Isa	the name of Jesus in the Qur'an
jaliyyah	the "age of ignorance" in pre-Islamic Arabia
jihad	striving; striving against the flesh internally and physical defense or fighting for Islam externally

jinn (sing.)	spirits made of smokeless fire; between angels and humans and often possessing exceptional powers
Ka'bah	the central structure in Mecca where pilgrimage is made and the object faced during Muslim prayers
kafir	a disbeliever or non-Muslim
kitab	a book
kufr	"disbelief"; unbelief in God, an infidel, blasphemy.
madrasa	an Islamic institution of higher learning
mahram	umarriageable kin; people to whom marriage would be incest
marabout	"attached;" being attached to God, especially in Sufism
ma'rifah	"knowledge"; in religious literature, gnosis, or mystical knowledge of God
maulid	the yearly celebration of Muhammad's birthday or a saint's birthday
mi'raj	the ascent of the Prophet Muhammad to heaven
mufti	a qualified Islamic leader who may issue a fatawa on a matter of law
mullah	"master"; the title given to religious scholars in Iran and Central Asia
nabi	a prophet who works within an existing religion
pir	a spiritual master or teacher; from Turkey to India a synonym for *shaykh*
purdah	in Afghanistan and India, the seclusion of women
qadi	an appointed judge of Muslim law based on superior knowledge
qarina	a *jinn* regarded as a spirit twin of each person

qiblah	the direction of the Ka'bah in Mecca; faced by Muslims when performing ritual prayers
qiyas	analogy; a means of discerning law when there is no precedent in the Qur'an or Hadith by means of analogy
Ramadan	the month of fasting in Islam
rasul	"messenger"; one who brings a new religion
sadaqah	voluntary almsgiving, in contrast to the obligatory zakat, to the poor
salat	"prayer," "worship"; ritual prayers said five times a day by Muslims; one of the Five Pillars of Islam
sawm	fasting, usually associated with Ramadan and one of the Five Pillars of Islam
shahada	the creed, one of the Five Pillars of Islam
Shariah	Islamic law based on the Qur'an and Sunnah
shaykh	a tribal leader, leading ulama or a spiritual Sufi master
Shiite	the followers of that brinach of Islam which accepts Ali as the successor to Muhammad
shirk	"association"; making anything equal to God or his associate
sihr	magic; often through sorcery, incantation, exorcism, and divination
subha	Islamic prayer beads, similar to a rosary, often used to recite the 99 Beautiful Names of God
Sufi	a follower of Islamic mysticism; one of three divisions in Islam along with Sunnis and Shiites
Sunnah	custom; the deeds and example of Muhammad
Sunni	"orthodox"; the largest branch in Islam
surah	a chapter in the Qur'an

tariqah	"road, way, path"; usually associated with orders in Sufism
tawaf	the ceremonial circumambulation around the Ka'bah in Mecca.
Tawhid	the doctrine of the Oneness of God
Tawrah	the Torah or books of Moses
'ulama	(pl.) learned persons; the recognized teachers and scholars of Islamic theology and law
ummah	the community of Muslims, Muslim believers
wali	guardian or helper; among Shiites, a title for the Imams; among Sufis, a saint, often used of eminent Sufis
wudu	ritual ablutions performed before prayer
Zabur	the Psalms of David
zakat	almsgiving; one of the Five Pillars of Islam
zena	fornication or adultery

INDEX